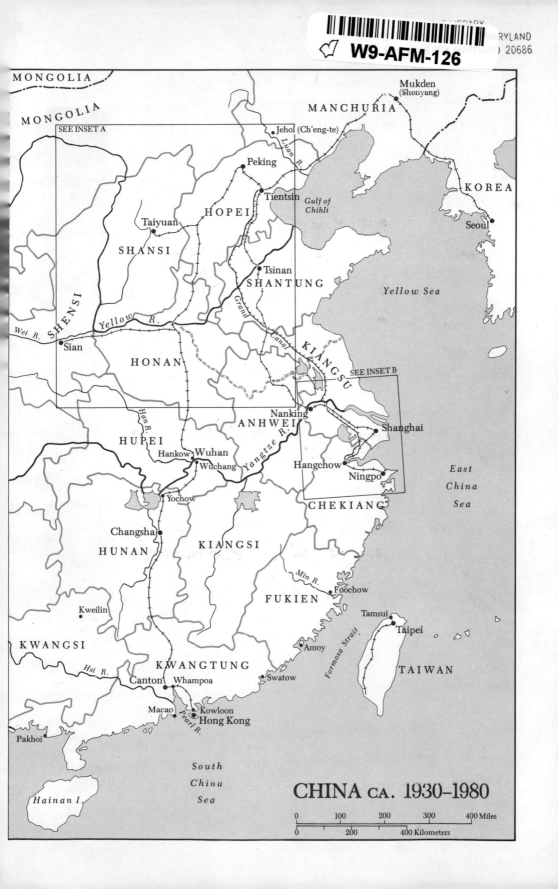

MONGOLIA

MONGOLIA

MANCHURIA

Mukden
(Shonyang)

SEE INSET A

Jehol (Ch'eng-te)

Lian R.

Peking

KOREA

Tientsin

Gulf of
Chihli

Taiyuan

HOPEI

Seoul

SHANSI

Tsinan

SHANTUNG

Yellow Sea

SHENSI

Wei R.

Yellow R.

Sian

HONAN

Grand Canal

KIANGSU

SEE INSET B

Han R.

HUPEI

Hankow   Wuhan
     Wuchang

Yangtze R.

ANHWEI

Nanking

Shanghai

Hangchow

Ningpo

East
China
Sea

Yochow

CHEKIANG

Changsha

KIANGSI

HUNAN

Min R.

Foochow

FUKIEN

Kweilin

Tamsui

Taipei

KWANGSI

Amoy

Formosa Strait

TAIWAN

Hsi R.

KWANGTUNG

Swatow

Canton   Whampoa

Macao   Kowloon
    Hong Kong

Pearl R.

Pakhoi

South
China
Sea

Hainan I.

CHINA CA. 1930–1980

0   100   200   300   400 Miles

0   200   400 Kilometers

CHINABOUND

Other books by John King Fairbank

The Cambridge History of China, general editor with D. Twitchett
> Vol. 10, *Late Ch'ing 1800–1911, Part 1,* ed. 1978
> Vol. 11, *Late Ch'ing 1800–1911, Part 2,* ed, with Kwang-Ching Liu, 1980
> Vol. 12, *Republican China 1912–1949, Part 1,* ed. 1982

The I.G. in Peking: Letters of Robert Hart, Chinese Maritime Customs 1868–1907, ed. with K. Bruner and E. M. Matheson, 2 vols., 1975

Japanese Studies of Modern China since 1953, comp. by Noriko Kamachi, ed. with C. Ichiko, 1975

Chinese-American Interactions: A Historical Summary, 1975

China Perceived: Images and Policies in Chinese-American Relations, 1974

Chinese Ways in Warfare, ed. and contrib. with F. A. Kierman, Jr., 1974

The Missionary Enterprise in China and America, ed. and introd., 1974

East Asia: Tradition and Transformation, with E. O. Reischauer and A. M. Craig, 1973

The Chinese World Order: Traditional China's Foreign Relations, ed. and contrib., 1968

China: The People's Middle Kingdom and the U.S.A., 1967

East Asia: The Modern Transformation, with E. O. Reischauer and A. M. Craig, 1965

Ch'ing Administration: Three Studies, with S. Y. Teng, 1960

East Asia: The Great Tradition, with E. O. Reischauer, 1960

Chinese Thought and Institutions, ed. and contrib., 1957

Japanese Studies of Modern China: A Bibliographical Guide to Historical and Social Science Research on the 19th and 20th Centuries, with M. Banno and S. Yamamoto, 1955

China's Response to the West: A Documentary Survey 1839–1923, with Ssu-yü Teng and others, 1954 (vol. 2, 1959).

Trade and Diplomacy on the China Coast: The Opening of the Treaty Ports 1842–1854, 2 vols., 1953

Ch'ing Documents: An Introductory Syllabus, 1952 (3rd rev. ed., 1970)

A Documentary History of Chinese Communism, with C. Brandt and B. I. Schwartz, 1952

Modern China: A Bibliographical Guide to Chinese Works 1898–1937, with Kwang-Ching Liu, 1950

The United States and China, 1948 (4th rev. ed., 1979)

CHINABOUND

A FIFTY-YEAR MEMOIR

JOHN KING FAIRBANK

A Cornelia & Michael Bessie Book

1817

HARPER & ROW, PUBLISHERS: New York
Cambridge, Philadelphia, San Francisco, London,
Mexico City, São Paulo, Sydney

FIRST EDITION

Designer: Sidney Feinberg

Maps drawn by George Colbert

Library of Congress Cataloging in Publication Data
Fairbank, John King, 1907–
  Chinabound : a fifty-year memoir.
  Includes index.
  1. Fairbank, John King, 1907–
2. Sinologists—United States—Biography.
3. United States—Relations (general) with China. 4. China—Relations (general) with the United States. I. Title.
DS734.9.F3A33   951'.04   81-47656
ISBN 0-06-039005-0   AACR2

82 83 84 85 86 10 9 8 7 6 5 4 3 2 1

For
WILMA

CONTENTS

Preface xiii

PART ONE
TOOLING UP: EDUCATION IN FIVE PLACES
1907–31

1 How I Became Oriented 3
2 Getting to China 19

PART TWO
OUR FIRST DISCOVERY OF CHINA
1932–35

3 Moving into Peking 35
4 Beginning to See the Land and People 51
5 Agnes Smedley's China 66
6 Harold Isaacs and the Terror 78
7 T. F. Tsiang and Modernization 85
8 Becoming a Specialist; Teaching at Tsing Hua 94
9 Chinese Friends 104
10 Seeing the Old Ports 114
11 Leaving China the First Time 125

PART THREE
LEARNING TO BE A PROFESSOR
1936–40

12 An Oxford D. Phil. 133
13 Starting In at Harvard 143
14 War and Policy Problems 162

PART FOUR
WASHINGTON, CHUNGKING, AND SHANGHAI
1941–46

15 Moving into Washington 173
16 Going to China in Wartime 185
17 Getting Set Up in Chungking 201
18 Mary Miles and OSS 215
19 Academic Centers and the American Interest 223
20 1943—CKS Begins to Lose the Mandate 241
21 Discovering the Left 265
22 With the Office of War Information in Washington 287
23 In Postwar China 298

PART FIVE
THE FALLOUT FROM WORLD WAR II
1946–52

24 China Policy and Area Study 315
25 Fighting McCarthyism 331

PART SIX
DEVELOPING THE CHINA FIELD
1953–71

26 Building a Research Center 355
27 Organizing the Field 366
28 Itinerating Around the World 376
29 Vietnam and American–East Asian Relations 390

PART SEVEN
TURNING SOME CORNERS
1972–81

30 New and Old in the People's Republic   407
31 Failure with the Soviets   425
32 Ups and Downs as a Friend of China   433
33 Epilogue   446

List of Abbreviations   460
Index   463

A section of photographs follows page 210.

MAPS

China ca. 1930–1980   x–xi
Peking in the Early 1930s   34

A

Kalgan (Chang-chia-k'ou)

Jehol (Ch'eng-te)

Great Wall

Ta-t'ung

Peking

Tientsin

HOPEI

Wu-t'ai Shan△

Tangku
Gulf of Chihli

Paoting

Ting-hsien

Taiyuan

Shih-chia-chuang

Tachai

SHANSI

Fenchow

Chieh-hsiu

Tsinan

Ling-shih

△T'ai Shan

Chao-ch'eng

SHANTUNG

Yenan

Anyang

Grand Canal

T'ai-hang Shan

Tsining

SHENSI

Yellow R.

Fen R.

Wei R.

Loyang

Chengchow

Kaifeng

Sian

HONAN

Course of Yellow River 1938-194_

0   50   100   150   200 Miles

0   100   200 Kilometers

B

KIANGSU

Yellow Sea

Nanking

Yangtze R.

Grand Canal

Woosung

Soochow

Wusung R. (Soochow Creek)

Shanghai

ANHWEI

Whangpoo R.

Hangchow Bay

Hangchow

Chen-hai

Yung R.

CHEKIANG

Ningpo

East China Sea

0   25   50   75   100 Miles

0   50   100 Kilometers

OUTER

INNER

Yellow R.

Lanchow

KANSU

SZECHWAN

Chengtu

Chialing R.

Chungking

Ipin (Suifu)

Li-chuang

Yangtze R.

KWEICHOU

Kunming

YUNNAN

Haiphong

FRENCH INDOCHINA

Gulf of Tonkin

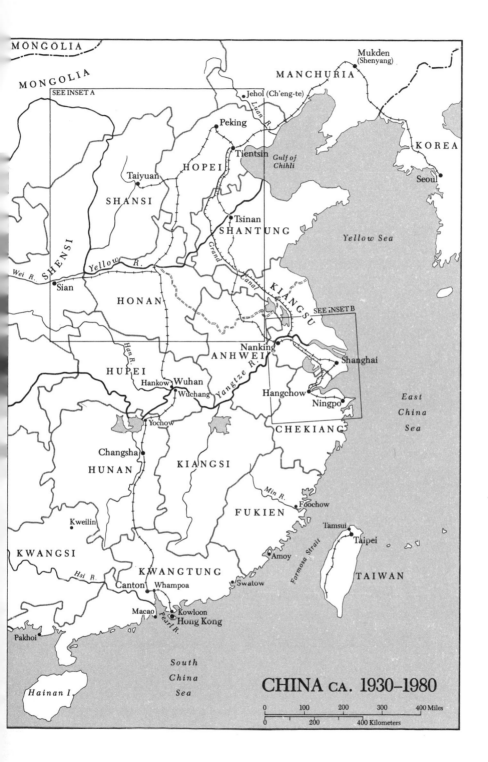

MONGOLIA

MONGOLIA

SEE INSET A

MANCHURIA

Mukden
(Shenyang)

Jehol (Ch'eng-te)

Liao R.

Peking

Tientsin

HOPEI

*Gulf of
Chihli*

KOREA

Taiyuan

Seoul

SHANSI

SHENSI

Tsinan

SHANTUNG

Yellow Sea

Wei R.

Yellow R.

Sian

HONAN

Grand Canal

KIANGSU

SEE INSET B

Han R.

Nanking

ANHWEI

Shanghai

HUPEI

Hankow Wuhan

Wuchang

Yangtze R.

Hangchow

Ningpo

*East
China
Sea*

Yochow

CHEKIANG

Changsha

HUNAN

KIANGSI

Min R.

Foochow

FUKIEN

Kweilin

Tamsui

Taipei

KWANGSI

KWANGTUNG

Amoy

Formosa Strait

TAIWAN

Hsi R.

Canton Whampoa

Swatow

Macao

Kowloon
Hong Kong

Pearl R.

Pakhoi

*South
China
Sea*

CHINA CA. 1930–1980

Hainan I.

0   100   200   300   400 Miles

0   200   400 Kilometers

PREFACE

THROUGH THE TELEPHONE on my desk I could speak to millions and millions of individuals in other countries whose speech would be unintelligible to me. Fortunately they don't call me nor I them. But the potentiality is there, as are the media and the missiles that now make the world a global village. This shrinkage of the globe we live on has made it more necessary to understand the other nations, and for the past fifty years I have been trying to understand China. The gradual enlargement of my circle of knowledge about China has of course also enlarged the circumference of my ignorance which surrounds it. Questions multiply faster than answers. But the effort to understand China better is now under way on a wide scale and is even seen to require that we understand ourselves better too. One cannot study China for long without becoming interested in, or amazed, annoyed, or appalled by, Chinese-American relations. In fact the student of China soon realizes he is functioning as part of the Sino-American relationship, just as any historian now recognizes that he inevitably contributes a good deal of himself to the history he writes. This line of thought justifies my writing about myself, which I wanted to do anyway.

Alas, when a historian starts his autobiography, the first thing he discovers is that he is still writing history. "The facts" still have to be carefully selected and then exemplified and organized in periods to represent general themes. It's as bad as writing a textbook. You have to summarize large masses of action, but not befuddle the reader.

The story I have to tell can be sketched quickly: I grew up in South Dakota when it was still a cultural frontier, so I came back East for education. From being a student in five places I learned how to make my way in a new environment according to its criteria. By chance I became interested in specializing on China and during four years there (1932–35) I absorbed some appreciation of Chinese motives and principles of conduct. Later, teaching history at Harvard (1936–41), I acquired an image of China's modern revolutionary process. Going to China again in wartime (1942–43, 1945–46), I got an impression of the Chinese revolution's spirit as well as its appeal and its methods. I became convinced not only that it was one of the great revolutions but that it would win out. Back at Harvard (1946–52) I felt research and education on China were a national necessity to help the American public accept the facts of life in China. I skated through the McCarthy era without much damage but was appalled at the size of the problem of Sino-American relations, so I joined in the development of training, research, and publication at Harvard and in the China field generally. The rapprochement with China since 1972 has left us facing many of the same old problems come round again.

I hope this personal record will offer some useful perspective. We are going to need all we can get.

Note: Passages indented are what I wrote at the time in letters, journals, or memoranda.

PART ONE

•

TOOLING UP:
EDUCATION IN FIVE PLACES
1907–31

1

HOW I BECAME ORIENTED

IT IS QUITE untrue that because I come from the plains of South Dakota I unconsciously want to fell the trees and level the hills of New Hampshire. On the contrary, the waves of mountains-behind-mountains that one confronts looking up the Pemigewasset Valley toward Mount Cardigan north of Franklin, New Hampshire, have an attraction that South Dakota never had. It is possible, however, that South Dakota helped me get into Chinese studies just by being so wide open and unlimited.

I was born in 1907 in Huron, near where Hubert Humphrey was born about the same time. One could stand in the corn on one side of town and see it waving in the fields on the other side. From the top of a rise under the big sky of the plains one could look farther over the quarter sections and farmsteads and see man more in control of nature than anywhere else in the world. Later on, when I was choosing a career, Chinese studies seemed like a limitless opportunity, stretching away to an unknown horizon, waiting to be explored and cultivated. In 1929 I did my senior thesis at Harvard on the outbreak of the Russian Revolution. In my imagination China seemed like only a further step. You can see how little I knew about it.

Setting my sights on China seems in retrospect to have fitted into my family history, though at the time I thought I was breaking out of it. My grandfather, John Barnard Fairbank, was from the long "J.B." line, mainly of Congregational ministers, which stemmed from the Fairbanks family that came to Massachusetts in 1633 and in 1636 built a house still standing in Dedham. He graduated from Illinois College, Jacksonville, in 1857 and from Union Theological Seminary, New York, in 1860. After settling at Waverly, Illinois, he served as pastor of Congregational churches in several small towns and some bigger ones, mainly in Illinois, Michigan, Indiana, and Minnesota. He was part farmer and carpenter as well as man of God, living off his own garden and in houses he helped build, but moving on every few years when the congregation began to know his sermons too well. Walter Mondale tells me his father was a Methodist preacher living mainly at Elmore, Minnesota, on the Iowa line, but he moved every few years to a different town with the same barrel of sermons.

My grandfather's notes for his sermons list the places and dates where he gave them between 1860 and 1906—towns like Waverly, Winona, Farmington, Spring Valley, Walnut Grove. On Romans 1:16 ("For I am not ashamed of the gospel of Christ; for it is the power of God unto salvation to everyone that believeth; to the Jew first, and also to the Greek") he preached twenty-six times between 1870 and 1906 in places as scattered, in the railroad era, as Fort Wayne, Elkhart, Michigan City, Winona, Peoria, Sleepy Eye, Ortonville, and Joy Prairie. His sermon on I Corinthians 3:9 ("For we are labourers together with God") he gave on forty-three occasions in almost as many places between 1862 and 1890, concluding, "But this we do indeed know, that we may heartily rejoice throughout the great future in the fruit of our earthly labors, if indeed we now give ourselves to labor consciously and faithfully for and with God."

A century later when I lectured on China in Peoria, Minneapolis, Brookings, Northfield, Grinnell, or Wichita, I felt I was in his footsteps, though my line—America's salvation through China studies— had become a bit more narrow and specialized. My lectures would note how our incomprehension of Chinese realities had led us into various disasters in China, Korea, and Vietnam and might do so again. My grandfather, speaking perhaps to some of my listeners' grandparents, had not been so worldly. He dealt with more absolute, less concrete matters. Nor did he run the China specialist's risk of having some more recent observer arise unexpectedly in the audience and say, "I took off from the international airport in Heaven twenty-four hours ago and conditions at that time were hardly as you describe."

Since I first talked about China to the Sioux Falls Rotary Club early in 1936, before I started teaching at Harvard, I suppose I have addressed as many audiences as my grandfather did, including some forty Harvard Clubs, although in the jet age they have been more widely scattered, among places like Peking, Singapore, Taipei, Seoul, San Diego, Milwaukee, Orlando, New York, and Paris.

At first glance you might say that I and John Barnard Fairbank, whom I never knew except to gurgle at, worked different sides of the street, but considered in the context of our times, I am not so sure this is true. He was part of a growth industry as churchgoing spread over the United States after the Civil War, just as area studies had their growth academically after World War II. Protestant missions had also spread abroad. My grandfather's brother had gone from Jacksonville to found a mission at Ahmadnagar, India. The missionary impulse indexed the health of the church, at a time before television when religion was a normal part of small-town life.

Obviously I had missionaries in my background but their influence was quite subconscious and made no connection with China. My upbringing was almost entirely irreligious. Today my acquired religion is Harvard and what it stands for in the secular world. That is, I put my faith in our ongoing institutions devoted to fostering the free working of the mind. Irrational faith appalls me.

For this freedom, as I conceive it, I am mainly indebted to my father, Arthur Boyce Fairbank (1873–1936), a minister's son who quietly broke free of organized religion. After reading the Bible through every year, my father concluded that he had got the Christian message and had received enough spiritual guidance to last for his lifetime.

He had been born in Fort Wayne, Indiana, and graduated from Illinois College at Jacksonville in 1896. Deciding to become a lawyer, he got his degree from Washington University, St. Louis, in 1901. Since he had grown up mostly in Illinois and Minnesota he naturally began his law practice in a less crowded area, farther west in South Dakota. After we moved from Huron to Sioux Falls in 1911, he became a leading citizen of the town in all its secular activities. He helped found the Rotary Club and the Minnehaha Country Club. Generally he loved, and was beloved by, his fellow men and women in the community and like his father was a gardener and a carpenter. He became a skilled trial lawyer and public speaker. In June he went fishing for bass and even pickerel in northern Minnesota. In the fall he hunted pheasants in the fields west of town and in November ducks in the swampy flyways near the Missouri River. When my mother campaigned for Votes for Women he drove her around in our 1911 Cadillac but did not speak for it himself, since he really doubted women's suffrage would make much difference. My father enjoyed life, home, and people. When he died of leukemia at sixty-three, a wide community missed him.

Lorena King Fairbank (1874–1979) had the greatest influence on me. I was her only child, and I have no doubt my attempting to study China resulted from two things she conveyed to me: self-confidence in responding to a challenge, and a sense of security in going off over the horizon. Indeed I was home only on visits and vacations from the time I went off to Exeter in 1923 at age sixteen. At one time I was out of sight for a stretch of four and a half years (September 1931 to January 1936), mostly living in Peking. My sense of guilt from this absence led to a lot of letter writing, but I kept on my course, always conscious of being unique and potentially superior—a feeling of self-approval which her devotion no doubt had inspired.

My mother was born in Hampton, Iowa, on July 4, 1874, one of four daughters of John Hereford and Permelia Andrews King, Quakers whose families had come west from Virginia. John H. King was a loving father, all the more so because his handsome wife grew ill and eventually suffered from minor seizures of petit mal and loss of memory. He was also an irrepressible optimist. He studied law with a judge and was admitted to the bar. He got himself elected as the youngest man in the Iowa legislature. But then with some friends he migrated west to found the town of Chamberlain on the Missouri River in Dakota Territory in 1881, years before North and South Dakota became states in 1889. In Chamberlain he served as postmaster, edited the paper *(The Dakota Register),* and went into real estate and insurance as well as practicing law. But the Milwaukee Railway took a long time to reach Chamberlain and supplant the steamboat connection on the Missouri. My grandfather was caught like everyone else in the panic of 1893 and practically had to start over.

My mother was a twin, and her twin sister Leona became very pretty and boy-conscious, which Lorena was not. Moreover, at age five a fever (polio) left her with one foot an inch shorter, not enough to prevent play and even dancing and yet a lifelong burden, requiring different-size shoes and special care for her footing. She became the studious one, but the depression after '93 delayed her education, though she taught school for a time, six grades in one room. Lorena was determined to rise above the crudity of the frontier and become an educated person. But not until she was twenty-one was she able to attend the academy at Yankton and complete high school. The frontispiece of a diary of that year is headed very simply, "Lorena King. 1895. It depends upon myself. Each one must work out his own salvation."

She entered the new University of Chicago in 1899 at age twenty-five. College remade her life. She found close friends, intellectual young women of a new age. She specialized in literature and speech, the new science of voice production so essential both for public life and for most entertainment in the pre-electronic era. In those days an inexperienced politician could lose his voice overnight, more disastrous than losing his mind. She studied voice cultivation and reading aloud as a performing art.

She became a professional in her self-discipline and mastery of an artistic technique. But her ego had been disciplined by adversity too. She had learned how to love others without dependence upon them, to share her enthusiasms and critical taste in literature and the arts as a self-rewarding way of life. No "career" was necessary. She found kindred spirits everywhere, especially among young people, and shared her interests generously throughout her life, which lasted till she was 105 and I was 72. My mother's interest in the culture that raw mid-America was avidly acquiring from Europe directed me outward and eastward.

When in 1911 my father became a partner of his cousin Jesse Boyce in Sioux Falls, they and their wives took a big house together in which I was the only child. Etta Estey Boyce was a New Englander fresh from the New England Conservatory of Music. She taught singing and among other things vigorously sponsored a concert series that brought the Flonzaley Quartet and other artists to our dinner table; except for this, I would never have known how some Europeans slurped their soup.

Aunt Etta and my mother and I, age five, spent the winter of 1911–12 in Paris *en pension* at 16 Avenue Mozart in Passy, near the

Bois de Boulogne. Of course such travel was a big deal, moving boy-high wardrobe trunks into staterooms on Cunard liners, importing an old family nurse, Erica, from Sweden to Paris to look after me. We were trailblazers when American tourism was still young. I ate roasted chestnuts in the upper story of Paris tram cars and ogled the shining breastplates and red plumes of the French cavalry. Also I learned to roll a hoop in the Bois but was not otherwise gallicized.

When I entered grade school on return to Sioux Falls my self-image of uniqueness was all the greater. The fact that certain boys chased me home from school as teacher's pet and a sissy, wearing knee socks, only confirmed this idea. I simply ran faster. However, I did not accept the self-image of being a sissy. In high school I startled my mother and the coaches by going out for football. The early-season squad was about seventy-five boys and I was on the seventh team. But by snow fly attendance fell into the thirties and so I was on the third team. I still remember scrimmaging the first team opposite an all-state guard, Red Steltzmiller, a policeman's son, who was very quick. I had been noticing that he wore a leather pad on his hand when suddenly the ball was snapped; I came to a moment later on the grass, my nose not broken though it felt so.

Later, after my junior year at Harvard, I again felt the need to balance my studiousness by red-blooded muscular work, so I took a summer job on an extra gang of the Canadian National Railways under an arrangement known as the Frontier College. The extra gang, mending track before the wheat haul across Saskatchewan, were Ukrainians, and I was to shovel and tamp with them by day and teach them English after supper. My tamping partner was Mike Tryhuk, a round-headed Slav from the village of Kobolowoki, who taught me to slow down to the steady pace of the all-day laborer. But all I could think about was the next meal. On an overcast day I would judge by stomach time that we must have reached the lunch hour, when in fact it would be only 8 A.M. One Sunday we were bathing in a river, when suddenly a man disappeared under water. None of his friends went after him because they had never learned to swim. I dove a few times, feeling like an Eagle Scout manqué, but to no avail. The drowning was accepted as just an unfortunate act of nature.

Though Mike at least made progress in English, I had few classes. Saskatchewan had daylight until 11 P.M., and overtime pay outlured the learning of English. I returned with new muscles but generally exhausted.

After three years of high school in Sioux Falls my preparation for study of another culture (though I didn't so conceive it at the time) was to lead me through four two-year stints in rather different academic settings east and west—Exeter, Wisconsin, Harvard, and Oxford.

I left Sioux Falls because the high school class work did not offer me much challenge. Several teachers were excellent but they could not set higher hurdles for me. My mother and I, rather in the dark, looked at prep school catalogues and sought the advice of our neighbors. My next-door playmate in Sioux Falls was Kenneth Pendar, whose father had come from Salem, Massachusetts and founded Salem, South Dakota. The Pendar family were expatriate New Englanders. First Oliver, then Kenneth, went off to St. Paul's School at Concord, New Hampshire. Oliver stroked his rowing club's eight. Ken visited friends on the Philadelphia Main Line. Their experiences left us tongue-tied. Both Culture and Education beckoned from Back East. With the Pendars' advice I chose Phillips Exeter Academy at Exeter, New Hampshire. What a sound, if fortuitous, decision that was! I got admitted to the third year at Exeter. And falling back a year in school helped me in the competition. I recommend it.

High school had been multipurpose—training girls to be wives or at least cooks through home economics, helping people enter business through double-entry bookkeeping, giving scope to the nascent enterpriser and the gladhanders and organizers. In contrast, Exeter centered on scholarship. The student body was more uniformly capable and the competition keen. The Fem Sem (Female Seminary was its actual name) went unnoticed. Sports in the afternoon, a class before dinner, indoors at eight, and lights out at ten provided an optimal environment for work.

At Exeter, by doing little else, I learned how to study. By this I mean not only how to master assignments but how to know when I had done so. For this, written records—notes, summaries, underlinings—were essential. Memory training was a good pastime too. And, since thinking, though it may be done partly in images and even in sounds, has to eventuate in words, sophistication in vocabulary and in syntax were both important. The best workout was on Cicero—the sequence of tenses, uses of the ablative, and all the other interlocking minutiae detailed for us in Latin grammar. Exeter rewarded me by confirming that I could achieve goals in the top competition, the big time. Saving time, keeping on the ball, was part of it. We all started equal in having twenty-four hours a day. What could I do in the time allowed? I was a slow eater and later became addicted to after-lunch naps. But fast walking substituted for more formal exercise. And I felt virtuous taking shortcuts. I learned to save time by buttoning only three buttons on my vest, though in retrospect I can only conclude that the style of wearing a vest at all must have lost me some seconds every day. To say that I was career-oriented would put it mildly.

In wanting to be efficient, to succeed, and to win approval, I was headed for the Establishment (business or the professions) like most of my Exeter classmates. But being an only child had made me self-sufficient. I could be my own group or even audience. I enjoyed being friendly with people, but only up to the point where it might interfere with my plans. This gave me an independent slant. I learned that excellence is the goal, but my line had to be my own invention. I didn't want to be a class leader or club president like all those others before me. I wanted to be unique. This would be my form of security. It removed the pressure to be gregarious.

In the four institutions where I spent two years apiece, the formula for academic success, as I plotted it out, was first to establish one's identity as a top scholar. That meant in the first year disregarding people and "activities," which invariably involved one with people and might even lead to time-consuming conversations with them! In the second year, however, one should branch out and know everybody.

Professor Cushwa, for whom I wrote themes, encouraged me by reading some in class. My other English teacher, Myron Williams, who years later turned out like most teachers to be much younger than I had realized, told me I had a sense of style. All this helped. So did the Lantern Club, where a shaggy man, Robert Frost, read poems to us; we also heard Exeter's own boy-Mencken, Dwight Mac-Donald, class of '24.

I wound up elected valedictorian. My friend Edmund Callis Berkeley had higher grades but by that time I was known as a debater who could undoubtedly make a speech, which I did. My valedictory to the assembled classmates and parents concluded with the unexceptionable punch line "May we be worthy of Exeter!"

Unfortunately, I paused for effect just before it, and our class leader, sitting just behind me with my text, concluded I had forgotten it, so we made the statement in unison. I guess the duet was effective, but I have never tried it again.

In 1925, during my senior year, I had won a prize essay competition among the New England prep schools with an essay on Anglo-American cooperation. A good New York lady had conceived this project as a way to help the situation and to celebrate an ancestor. My published essay concluded that Anglo-American cooperation, having made the modern world, could also save it. The prize was a trip to England that summer awarded at graduation by a florid promoter named Fanshaw, who bestowed upon me £ 100 plus a letter to the P.M., Stanley Baldwin. While I stood below the rostrum being publicized, our headmaster, Lewis Perry, gave me a broad wink. I took my mother on this windfall and in due time presented myself at 10 Downing Street as instructed, with a letter from the British Ambassador in Washington, to see the Prime Minister. A very nice young man just down from Cambridge explained to my relief that Mr. Baldwin was tied up but suggested we should visit Cambridge and see the Backs. We did so.

Spending some weeks in Scotland, London, and Paris in the summer of 1925 further focused my view of the world as many-centered. Sioux Falls already seemed a place I had come from. A picture of me, looking like any other unformed young man of eighteen, appeared in the *New York Times.* I felt sure I was going to get somewhere. So were most of my classmates, of course, but that was their business, not mine.

My congenial roommate at Exeter, Alan R. Sweezy, who had helped edit the *Exonian,* went on to Harvard, where he became editor of the *Crimson* and thus a leading figure among the student body. But I broke the cadence and entered Wisconsin instead of Harvard. This was partly because coeducation appealed to me. I knew how to study. What else was there to do?

I went to the University of Wisconsin at Madison also for family reasons, because it was La Follette country. My mother's elder sister had married Senator Bob La Follette's early law partner, Gilbert E. Roe, and their son Jack was my closest cousin. In 1925, Wisconsin progressivism, trying to regulate the vested interests and reform social evils, was at a high point. Senator La Follette, Sr., had just died but Bob, Jr., took his place, beginning two decades of skilled and devoted public service in the U.S. Senate, while the younger brother, Phil La Follette, became governor of Wisconsin at the age of thirty-two. Their family tradition gave me my first idea of politics as the cause of the common people against the interests of the few. Since Bob, Jr., and Phil were Betas, Jack Roe had pledged Beta Theta Pi, and so did I.

Fraternity life in the Big Ten in the gilded mid-twenties (1925–27), I found, was almost all "activities." Hertz had just invented rent-a-cars, others had devised roadhouses and various experimental drinks to defeat Prohibition, and fraternity brothers recommended sorority girls to date. Madison's fraternities and sororities were in fact a big socializing mill. Hertz's new model-A Fords moved the parlor sofa and the porch swing out into the country to sideroads of one's own choosing. Education proceeded apace. (One dean of women, trying to stem the tide, urged coeds to avoid pursing their lips at drinking fountains. It might be provocative. Happily this Queen Canute did not live to see Madison's women streakers of a later time.)

Since I was getting grades in the high nineties I was roomed in the Beta house with the pride of the Alpha Pi chapter, the great Rollie Barnum. Barnum was a nine-letter man who needed to keep eligible so he could continue to play fullback all fall, basketball guard all winter, and catcher in the baseball season. He was simply a natural athlete, mature, steady, undemanding, unflappable, and on the rare occasions when we met between his practices and trips away, I enjoyed his amiable company.

My best friends at Madison, however, turned out to be two Alpha Delts—Clyde Kluckhohn and Lauriston Sharp. Lauri's father was a professor of philosophy. When he invited me to dinner it was the first academic household I had been in. Sioux Falls style, I ate the hearts of my lamb chops and pushed the rest aside. Lauri's mother said to me in the kindest way, "John, in a professor's house we eat all of our chops. You will find out why if you become a professor."

Clyde was a charismatic leader and a romantic, who for reasons of health had lived among the Navajo and already written a travel book about it. He invented a secret society, called Begeotis by the initiates, which met in tuxedos by candlelight in a deep, cold cellar of a local family brewery and discussed highly intellectual topics. No doubt it was more like what the Greek-letter fraternities of the 1830s had originally been, before they became collectives engaged in sophisticating the small-town youth of the early twentieth century. I later founded Harvard, Oxford, and Paris chapters of Begeotis but they all died without delay.

Clyde was by all odds the most magnetic personality I met in college. He was a year ahead of me at Madison and then at Oxford, and we were later colleagues at Harvard and in the Office of War Information. He began the Russian Research Center at Harvard just as I was starting the Regional Studies–China M.A. program. When he died at fifty-six the faculty minute on his career was one of the few genuine panegyrics that have appeared in that judged-for-the-ages series.

I found the socializing side of college life easy to handle, up to a point. One made scads of acquaintances, people to speak to on meeting, but this might leave rather little time for genuine friendship. Fraternity life and activities trained one to meet and greet as if at a continuous cocktail party. But in those days we at least made meaningful introductions of people, unlike the "John, this is Mary" obfuscations in vogue in the 1970s.

In my sophomore year at Wisconsin I ran for election to the Union board. I got a manager from a minor fraternity to set up dates after lunch in the fraternity houses, where I would appear and explain why I was just what the Wisconsin Union needed to ensure its benefiting the community. Come election day we realized we had not reached the nonfraternity *barbaroi,* so I spent a hectic morning on the Hill in front of Bascom Hall telling people whom I didn't know: "Vote for Fairbank, he knows what to do for you." I got elected and was made secretary of the Union board, which practically ensured that I would be its shoo-in candidate for president the next year.

Confronted with the prospect of being a Big Man on Campus, which seemed like an alternative to getting an education, I decided to transfer to Harvard. I had a precedent for this move. In my third year in Sioux Falls High School, by addressing classmates by name on the stairs and in the hallways, I had become a strong candidate for senior class president, but I had left to go study at Exeter. Now it seemed time to go east again. Harvard had not yet reached out to cream off the talent of the whole country through Harvard Clubs and scholarships, and so it was full of Exonians. Transferring there was like rejoining my Exeter class after a vacation among coeds.

Harvard still had an upper social crust who joined clubs and might figure in Boston society. But most undergraduates were simply hard workers on their way up in the world. The large sprinkling of graduate students, who supplied the dormitory proctors and course section men, helped set a serious tone, rather more intense than the multipurpose atmosphere of a state university like Wisconsin. The president at Madison had been the smooth Glenn Frank, one of the early public-relations educators, who aspired, he said, "to make our house of education into a home of learning," and so on. A. Lawrence Lowell, by contrast, paid no court to a legislature but captained Harvard like a ship.

At Harvard (1927–29) I roomed with my Exeter friend Edmund Berkeley, who was into symbolic logic and ran his life like a clock, no trouble. We were next door to Alan Sweezy. Through his influence in 1928 I was elected to the Senior Council. I spent my first year getting straight A's in the three big courses: History 1, Gov. 1, and Ec. A, each one of which was its own universe. I also got an A in Greek, which I had begun at Madison. In the spring I branched out and helped revive the Harvard Debating Council.

In high school I had studied *Argumentation and Debating* by William Trufant Foster, a basic work of the cut-and-dried approach that made debating almost a branch of the law. The affirmative began and ended the proceedings. If three affirmative speakers and three negative each had twelve minutes for presentations and eight for rebuttals, two hours would elapse before the judges still awake could pick the winners. It was something for cold winter evenings before electricity brought us alternatives. But it taught us to state propositions, cite evidence if only the *Literary Digest,* "prove" a case and prepare rebuttals. On Philippine independence, for example, over which the Democrats were still thwacking the Republicans, we would develop a card file of quotations and arguments. As your honorable opponent set forth his case, you simply picked out the cards to refute his evidence and show up his faulty reasoning, and your rebuttal was all set. My mother gave me a course in the use of lips, tongue, and breath to make oneself heard distinctly, and I found it exciting to stand up, knees aquiver, and make my voice convey words that would undo the enemy. Though not many competed to be on the team, we still got audiences out of school loyalty.

At Exeter I had found a few kindred spirits and we revived the

Golden Branch and the G. L. Soule, two societies that once used to square off on winter evenings over "Resolved: that the pen is mightier than the sword" and the like. Desuetude had overcome them after the Ioka Theater in the town had installed its Friday-night movies for Exeter students. We wanted a single society that could debate other schools. I solved our problem by a constitutional provision that the G. L. Soule would consist henceforth of the elected officers of the Golden Branch, which could then represent the academy in debates with Andover, St. Paul's, Brown freshmen, and other outsiders. At Madison also I found debating moribund but revived it by getting Jack Roe and some others to join in. We traveled to Michigan, stayed at their new Union, and won a victory, though no record of the topic remains.

But at Harvard we few Midwestern disciples of William Trufant Foster ran into something new. Malcolm MacDonald, son of Ramsay, and an Oxford Union team had toured the East Coast and left disciples of the British parliamentary debating style. Harvard had a smart curly-headed young man named Fred Lorenzen who presented no case but a string of anecdotes and word pictures. Worse, he would get our small audiences laughing and win without benefit of proof or even logic. To try to outdo him by moral earnestness was a forlorn hope because he could talk about mothers and babies too.

Technology was also changing the nature of debating. Microphones soon moved us away from the old declamatory style by bringing us closer to the audience. And then the split-second timing of radio debating stripped away all the apparatus of propositions, cases, evidence, and proof. In the seconds allowed, you had to make your point in so many words, directly.

Obviously I was preparing to speak in public. But simultaneously I was becoming used to beginning languages. I had started Latin and French in Sioux Falls, begun them almost over again at Exeter, and added German and Greek in college. In each case I memorized vocabulary and laboriously learned to read. But language teachers had not yet caught on to the principles of constant repetition, total immersion, and speaking before reading that now make live language study so much more efficient. Working inefficiently, I became a professional language beginner. My French and German were as dead as my Latin and Greek, embryonic at best.

In 1929 I faced another transition: I had been given a Rhodes scholarship, at once a certificate of promise and an opportunity that I imagine my mother had long had in mind for me. International scholarships were still few in the 1920s, a Rhodes had a certain prestige, and for me it met the graduation problem of what to do next by keeping me within academia and out of the real world, where one had to make money to live on.

At a *Crimson* dance in 1928 Alan had asked me to take care of "the chaperone," a kindly old bushy-eyebrowed gentleman who asked me about education and seemed interested in my comparison of the four places where I had studied. Later I learned he was President Lowell. When I was interviewed by the Rhodes committee in Sioux Falls, one of them asked me, "Is President Lowell a relative of yours?" and showed me his letter to the committee. At the bottom he had written "This is a very unusually good candidate." Such accolades stick in memory.

But success in college can carry you only so far. The question comes up, what are you really going to do? This question was answered for me by a very concrete event that probably could have occurred only at a major center of learning. I met Charles Kingsley Webster, who had made himself a diplomatic historian with a keen interest in policy making and especially in the concert of Europe. For the British delegation at Versailles in 1919 he had put forward some lessons of the Congress of Vienna of 1815. One, for example, was to keep your wastebaskets under lock and key lest another Talleyrand learn your secrets from your trash. Charles's own massive work was a multi-archival study of Castlereagh's diplomacy as seen in all the European capitals. He had taken a chair in international history at the University of Wales, Aberystwyth, which allowed him half the year elsewhere, and so in the fall of 1928 he lectured at Harvard and often lunched at the Signet Society. In the days before President Lowell's House Plan, the Signet's selected membership of faculty and undergraduates made it one of the few places where the twain could meet.

One of Charles Webster's most engaging traits was his enthusiasm. He was a fountain of feelings, about his own work, about world organization, about opportunities for young men. Most of all, he was intellectually competitive, challenging, even combative—all in all, immensely stimulating. Some years later, after we had gone with the

Websters to their hideaway in Wales in 1936, I tried to describe this electric personality:

> We had a very lively time, C. K. making a large number of the indiscreet remarks about people of the sort that have as he says impeded his career but no doubt endeared him to a large number. When he thinks someone is a doddering old dodo, he says so in no uncertain fashion. His appearance is as fascinating as ever, tall with large bulk inclined to swell at the middle and brought to a climax in rather small eyes gleaming shrewdly behind extraordinarily heavy glasses, above a mouth of very odd shape, extremely mobile and somehow inclined to get mixed up, as I try to visualize it, with his chin. He is fervently emotional about England, and indeed cares a great deal about everything he is interested in—which is certainly a characteristic of greatness. . . . Nora is as lovely as ever, rather delicate and quite petite but with much strength as well as grace in the way she sets the stage for him. I suppose she would be an excellent Chinese wife of the sort who never appears in the world but is a full half of the combination in fact.

In 1928, finding how vague my future plans were—something about international law—Professor Webster told me the latest news, that China's secret diplomatic documents were being published in Peking. They would open up a whole new area of diplomatic history.

At that time, with the appearance of so many studies of the origins of the World War, diplomatic history had become a major magnet for talent, to work out when and why who said what to whom. It would be another seven years before William L. Langer's *Diplomacy of Imperialism* set the broader style stressing national interests and swings of public opinion (and another twenty-four years before his two volumes *The World Crisis and American Diplomacy* pretty well proved that it is no longer possible to trace the record in the comprehensive detail that so entranced us in Charles Webster's generation).

Charles Webster's suggestion to study China appealed to me at age twenty-two as something interesting that no one else seemed to be doing. I could be a pioneer and continue to be both academic and unique. It was an excitingly high challenge. Moreover, I was accustomed to pulling up stakes and moving into a new environment every two years. I knew no Chinese but a lot of people did, in China, so it must be feasible to study. And I sensed that Harvard and the United States needed to know about China—obviously an act of faith like that of my grand-uncle who had decided India, of all places, needed to know about Jesus.

Actually, the not-so-still or small voice I heard was that of Professor James Phinney Baxter III, who had chaired the Harvard examining committee that gave me my A.B. summa cum laude. He had asked me to keep in touch with him. I decided to do so with a view to returning to Harvard.

The state of China itself, about which I knew nothing, had little to do with my decision. Nationalist China in 1929 was newly unified at least superficially under the Nanking government headed by Chiang Kai-shek. It was just about to suffer Japan's aggression, which began in 1931 with the seizure of Manchuria (as we called it then, now China's Northeast). Japan's aggression in turn defied the League of Nations and soon led to its demise as an international organization for keeping the peace. Simultaneously came the rise of the fascist dictators Mussolini and Hitler, who eventually brought Japan into a Rome-Berlin-Tokyo alliance. The 1930s were thus to move inexorably toward World War II, which engulfed the United States in 1941–45.

The hectic 1930s were my period of apprenticeship as researcher and teacher. I was learning my trade, feeling my way. But I cannot claim that a prevision of events led me to study China as a major focus of revolutionary change. Like many undergraduates ambitious for a straight-A record, I was much more concerned about my own performance than about the state of the world and international relations. Studying China called for ingenuity, imagination, exploration, innovation, and, above all, initiative. Once started, I was fascinated. I had very little idea where it would lead me, either intellectually or in the world. But it was an enterprise, and what an exciting enterprise!

2

GETTING TO CHINA

WHEN I ARRIVED at Balliol College, Oxford, in the fall of 1929, I was no closer to China than I had been in Cambridge, Massachusetts. Indeed, Oxford was not at all the place to begin Chinese studies. It offered no instruction in Chinese language or history. I spent the next couple of years approaching China obliquely in a flanking attack. It took me several years more to make the graduate-student transition into being a China specialist.

I now think this untoward circumstance of being at Oxford was a blessing in disguise, or perhaps I should merely say that I was able to turn it to good account. It kept me out of any sinological rut and let me approach Modern China as the West had done in the nineteenth century, largely through British eyes. Living in England and acquiring some impression of the British imperial view were my first experiences on the way to China.

Oxford in 1929 was still more cosmopolitan than Harvard. (Perhaps it is even now.) Most of the past and most of the globe seemed to be represented there. One felt under the weight of all that had accumulated, as if absorbing even a part of it would be almost too exhausting. The individual scholar seemed smaller, set against Oxford's mass of learning and tradition, yet at the same time he was also less well equipped with library service to handle that learning. Widener Library dominated the Harvard Yard whereas the Bodleian was a tourist attraction that a student could use in winter only during the few hours of daylight. Widener ablaze at night was a beacon to all yardlings, but at Oxford one sought out books as though hunting for treasure. "I think you will find a copy of Mandeville at BNC [Brasenose College]," said one of my tutors, "but if not, then try All Souls." In short the equipment of scholarship—a union catalogue and interlibrary loans, for example—was still underdeveloped. I sensed less stimulus to innovation.

Perhaps this reflected Oxford's main function as trainer of a ruling elite. Since Balliol, though closely pressed by New College, still had the reputation of being the top college at Oxford, I felt myself near the heart of the British empire. Balliol dated from 1263 and its superiority, like Harvard's, began with its antiquity. Under Jowett as master (1870–93) it produced administrators of the empire—not only proconsuls like Curzon, Milner, and Elgin but at least one-sixth of the Indian Civil Service. Under Jowett's fourth successor A. D. Lindsay (1924–49), the tradition of hard work and social concern was at a new height. And in the Oxford University examinations of 1928, 42 percent of the Balliol examinees had won first-class honors.

My admission had been assisted by a letter from Lindsay's disciple Professor William Yandell Elliott of the Harvard Government Department. My own letter about myself, as the warden of Rhodes House remarked to a friend, made me sound like "a combination of Hercules and Jesus Christ." But this self-confidence did not solve my problem of how to break into Chinese studies in an institution where they didn't exist.

Charles Webster had told me to begin with H. B. Morse's *International Relations of the Chinese Empire.* I had ordered all three thick volumes from England and plowed through them crossing the Atlantic. I had a cut-rate stateroom over the propellers of the old *New Amsterdam* and spent most of the crossing reading in bed about the Opium War; the subject has made me feel a bit queasy ever since. Dr. Morse's summary of the British official record showed the British coercing the Ch'ing dynasty of the Manchus in China up to 1860, extracting their treaty privileges, and then supporting the dynasty thereafter.

After first signing up to do another B.A. in PPE (philosophy, politics, and economics), rather similar to the history, government, and economics I had just done at Harvard, I decided to begin a research degree on British policy in China, Anglo-Chinese relations.

This of course led me into the study of Britain's "informal empire," as some now call it, in nineteenth-century China, which was the major aspect of the Sino-Western confrontation.

Obviously I had to study Chinese, but first I had to begin research for a B. Litt. degree that would take a year, and then do a D. Phil. Unlike American degrees, these Oxford degrees required no preparation of fields, languages, or courses, simply the presentation of a thesis—plainly a bargain. But there were no seminars to get started in; in fact there was no historiographical or research instruction at all. I was on my own.

I noted that H. B. Morse, Harvard 1874, had spent thirty-five years as a Chinese employee in the Chinese Imperial Maritime Customs Service before becoming the historian of China's foreign relations. In his preface to *International Relations,* Morse said he had been planning to write the history of the Customs, using the journals of the inspector general, Sir Robert Hart, but that Hart's heirs had refused. For a beginner who would have to approach China through the British Foreign Office correspondence in London, I decided this peculiar Anglo-Chinese institution, the Customs, might be a starting point.

My B. Litt. thesis supervisor appointed by the university was a retired missionary, Dr. W. E. Soothill, reader in Chinese. Soothill was a kindly oldster, who explained that he was just proofreading his dictionary of Chinese Buddhist terms and would gladly see me at tea any time. But at least he agreed to write to H. B. Morse, who had retired outside London.

Dr. Morse was one of four classmates of Harvard '74 whom E. B. Drew, '64, one of Hart's early commissioners, had recruited for the Customs. In 1924 he had attended his fiftieth reunion at Harvard and received an honorary Ll.D. He was childless and his wife was anti-Chinese ("They will poison you," she told me), so that a young Harvard graduate interested in the Chinese Customs Service, an organization that inspired a devoted sense of mission in most of its commissioners, was a welcome addition to life in Camberley, outside London. He invited me to visit him.

I found a trim and alert old gentleman, who had just finished volume 5 of the *Chronicles of the East India Company Trading to China,* a masterly condensation of the East India Company record books that he had been allowed to work on at home, one at a time.

Morse kept his house cold—even for England—in order to combat his asthma. Two neighbor ladies put me up and took me about to see Camberley, and Dr. Morse took me to his vine-covered club, where a game of bowls was being sedately pursued by retired colonels and ex-administrators of India.

I felt I had found a spiritual father, or perhaps grandfather. He told me a multitude of things about the Customs and the China it worked for, more than I could absorb. He had served in Shanghai; Peking; Tientsin; Pakhoi, near Hainan; Tamsui, on Taiwan, during the 1894 Taiwan Republic; Lungchow, on the Annam border; Hankow; and Canton. On special assignments he had advised the China Merchants Steam Navigation Company in the late 1870s and opened Hunan at Yochow in 1899.

This was a complete world in itself, half the globe away. If Dr. Morse had not occupied himself as a historian, he would no doubt have withered and died as Sir Robert Hart did, after he returned in 1907 from fifty-five years of empire building in China to find himself an unneeded old man in the fancy chatter of his wife's London drawing room. Lady Hart had cut and run for home in 1882. Evidently the Customs, for all its satisfactions, offered wives little except fevers, boredom, dysentery (which can be very boring indeed), and the poisons that Mrs. Morse retained so definitely in mind.

From this invaluable initiation I drew the erroneous conclusion that I could best get a running start on the Customs by studying its origin in the Foreign Inspectorate that was set up at Shanghai in 1854. This overlooked the Iron Law of Retrogression that I have been able to warn students about ever since. History looks backward, seeking causes: if you want to understand events of 1980, start with 1980. You will be pulled back into the 1970s soon enough. If you start with 1970 supposedly en route to 1980, you will find yourself inexorably involved with 1960 and accelerating backward.

I would have done better to start with the Customs say in 1883, when Hart briefly accepted the post of British minister to China and then thought better of it. As it was, 1854 led me back at once to 1850 and my D. Phil. later began with 1842. I never got beyond 1858, which was actually where I had wanted to begin. How easily careers can go astray!

I began Chinese on my own when Dr. Soothill gave me the third edition, revised by H. A. Giles in 1923, of T. L. Bullock's *Progressive*

Exercises in the Chinese Written Language, a substantial do-it-your-self manual that took the novice into simple classical statements with a word-for-word (or word-for-character) translation. The translation was made to work, for example, by translating the classical possessive sign *chih* as "arrive." Thus *jen chih ch'u,* man's beginning, was "man arrive-at beginning." The classical sentences gave one a rather Chinesey, far-out feeling. *I chih wei shen* became "one arrive is very" meaning "once is the limit." I felt "Damn clever, these Chinese" might better be "Damn clever, these Englishmen." Bullock said nothing about tones but explained the radicals and listed all 214 of them. I began memorizing radicals and other characters purely by their shape and configuration, a new experience. The aesthetic form of the characters began to work its fascination.

For a specialist in beginning Indo-European languages, Chinese characters required a change of approach, like moving from walking to swimming. I soon found, of course, that most characters are combinations of simpler ones. Usually the left half was a radical of a generic sort like the signs for mouth, hand, water, earth, etc., while the right half suggested how the combination might sound. Dr. Soothill had in fact done a useful pocket dictionary of these "phonetics." By such means one learned one's way around in the maze of characters and could even find them in dictionaries. What they actually meant when put in a sequence was a further problem—quite a problem, too, because over the ages, while retaining the same shapes, characters had taken on successive layers of meaning as they were used for new purposes.

One could only conclude that the best way to study Chinese was from the age of five in China. But here I was in the typical foreigner's sweat, flipping character cards on the London underground and buses at age twenty-three. Fortunately I never asked a wise man if this was feasible. He could have proved it wasn't.

Later I heard a rumor that friends felt I must have gone into Chinese studies out of a nervous breakdown. This was not correct. But one new experience I had at Oxford was to find myself wide awake every night from 2 or 3 A.M. I had got a case of nervous exhaustion, and insomnia stayed with me the next several years. Doctors told me to rest, but what do you do while resting? In the cold, crepuscular Oxford winter, clad all in woolen goods, I went on a schedule of lying down before lunch, after lunch, and after tea and going to bed at nine, figuring that food, exercise, and bed rest would keep me going, sleep or no sleep. Fortunately no Oxford doctors seemed to know much about college boys above the neck and behind the face. I was spared the whipsawing of taking uppers in the morning and downers at night. From this time I retained a low-grade hypochondria as the best preservative of health. Perhaps it fluctuated according to the secure distinctness of my goals. I was in the graduate students' phase of adolescence, trying to find my scholarly identity.

Producing my B. Litt. involved learning to write, using words to convey meaning. I found this was complicated by learning to think, which required excavating actual meanings from set phrases. Like most graduate-student writing, my prose tended to progress by connecting one verbal noun to another. "Although the beginning of this development of revolutionary ardor was accompanied by several factors that were conducive to its acceleration, in the final analysis the proximate cause of this phenomenon was to be found in the fact that . . . "—and so on and on, saying nothing. One remedy, I found, was to begin with the key word and use only active verbs. "The revolution began when . . ."

In these doldrums I found friends. Gilbert Highet was one—a brilliantly sardonic Scotsman, who eventually became Anthon Professor of the Latin Language and Literature at Columbia and an entrepreneur in the Book of the Month business, conveying the classics, as in his *Poets in a Landscape* (1957), to an American audience who appreciated his taste and wit. At Balliol Gilbert lived up a winding staircase in the tower above the front gate. His extraordinary vitality as classicist, pianist, and critic generally was enhanced, I thought, by his origin in middle-class Glasgow. Like me he was an observer of the British. Also I found a lifelong friend in Anthony Lambert, a tall, impeccable Harrovian who wound up as a British ambassador in various parts of Europe. Gilbert and Tony read *The New Yorker,* quoted Damon Runyon, and welcomed an American. I enjoyed their company and learned many British things.

For instance, it is not necessary to talk. With a friend you can be completely silent for long periods. . . .

It is not necessary to make introductions. If A and B are walking along the Cher and meet a third party C, known only to A, B simply stands aside and thinks his own thoughts. An introduction is a serious, not casual, matter and might open an undesired contact.

Reticence, in general, is to be admired. Spilling the beans to a chance acquaintance, in the frontier fashion that presumably helped build America, seemed repugnant as either boasting or betraying secrets. To disclose too much to a friend was in a way to invade his privacy by destroying your own, like suddenly undressing. What one friend can expect from another, in short, is to be left alone.

Another thing to know was that "bloody" was too powerful a swear word to use before women, as potent as "fuck" would have been in Sioux Falls in those days.

Balliol, I found, harbored a Chinese student, Ken Cheang from Shanghai, an athletic though sometimes incomprehensible young man. He invited his friend Harold Lee from Pembroke (and Hong Kong) to play tennis with us. Tony Lambert and I found ourselves ten feet tall by comparison. We rushed the net menacingly. But each time Ken and Harold simply lobbed over us, so that we defeated ourselves making wild smashes. Ken later married Harold's sister but then went to the bad, while Harold Lee remained my good friend for fifty years. His father had sent him as a schoolboy to England and he became thoroughly bicultural, both English and Chinese. He also became a leading citizen of Hong Kong, where we met many times later.

Contact with tutors was less easy. Webster's friend B. Humphrey Sumner, whose rooms were next door to mine in my second year at Balliol, was a tutor of awesome erudition, spare and ethereal in looks but a bear trap concerning facts. He knew all about many things but lived the austere, shy life of a don, unmarried, and he published little.

The benign Dean Urquhart, a fellow from 1896 to 1934, "Sligger" to many generations of students, had rooms across a small courtyard from mine. Mornings we stood at our windows shaving at each other. He finally remarked that my straight-edge razor, which my father had given me, seemed like a lethal weapon. I said it did indeed, especially in a Pullman car washroom as the train swayed and other passengers kept their distance. It was of course a token of my uniqueness, and luckily I was never decapitated.

Most of all Balliol was an interlude of aesthetic enjoyment. We listened to music and argued the merits of Mozart and Beethoven. We took long walks through the perpetual cold mist that made every landscape a series of more and more shadowy distances. And I wrote letters to Cambridge, Massachusetts. I had fallen in love on St. Valentine's Day, 1929, with a blind date at a dance there.

Wilma Denio Cannon was the eldest of four sisters, then a junior at Radcliffe in Fine Arts, who lived in a big household at 2 Divinity Avenue, where the Harvard-Yenching Library now stands. At the dance she had worn a slim but curvaceous flame-colored dress that she had made herself. She was quick in repartee and amazingly in tune with the present, responding unselfconsciously to the scenes and the people of the moment. The fact that she was not goal-oriented like me and purposed only to enjoy and appreciate life here and now made me realize suddenly that I had been missing something I badly needed. Wilma's creative capacity for spontaneous play, thought, and action made her later an artist, explorer, bureaucrat, diplomat, research scholar, and writer in addition to being wife, mother, sister, daughter, and more recently aunt. This omni-talent derived, I found, from a whole family who were equally spontaneous. They revolved around Cornelia James Cannon, whom Wilma's sister Marian Schlesinger has portrayed in *Snatched from Oblivion: A Cambridge Memoir.*

Mrs. Cannon radiated energy like the core of an atomic pile, and her four daughters through both nurture and inheritance were similarly full of vitality. By their mother's example they were taught that a husband's work is sacred and he must be given his chance to accomplish it, but meanwhile a woman can do practically everything a man can do and a lot more that he can't. For a son-in-law, I would find, this formula combined security with stimulus.

In tracing my preparation for China studies, such as it was and was not, I should say about half of it was finding Wilma. I saw her again at Christmas, 1929, in Paris. Her father, Walter B. Cannon of the Harvard Medical School, one of the great physiologists, known to scientists all around the world, was lecturing in Paris, and the Cannon female hegira through Latin Europe was pausing there to study art. I then saw Wilma again in the spring in Seville and Granada and in the summer of 1930 at Oxford before she went back to finish Radcliffe. In 1931 she graduated magna cum laude with a thesis on "Nature in Painting: Recorded, Remembered, Inherited and Ignored."

Meanwhile my B. Litt. thesis effort involved an early-morning express from Oxford to Paddington, and the Bakerloo underground to Chancery Lane. In the Public Record Office rotunda a dim natural light filtered down upon the circle of sweater-clad, red-nosed women copyists and assorted mufflered researchers with their indelible pencils (ink was not allowed) and bound volumes of records. F.O. 17 was the series from the Superintendency of Trade and Legation in Hong Kong, whose numbered dispatches enclosed copies selected from the numbered series received by it from each treaty port in China. One could imagine the hours spent by consular assistants in making these fair copies: "Sir, With reference to my despatch no. 17 of the 27th ultimo concerning . . . I have the honor to report that . . ." on and on, with pen and ink on the durable rag paper, for miles and miles of tedium, doing the Queen's business. This was what built the empire, making records that preserved and developed institutional practices and eventually justified the movement of gunboats. No speech resounded in the PRO, but the devotees of documents occasionally went out to absorb tea, toast, and perhaps a giblet pie or raspberry tart at a Lyons eatery.

During Oxford's long vacations—a month in winter and a month in spring—I sometimes stayed in bed-and-breakfast digs in Torrington Square behind the British Museum, where the School of Oriental and African Studies now stands. Landladies charged five shillings a night. The bathroom, with a gas-heated geyser ("geezer") for hot water was often in the basement, and the house might reek of cabbage or Lysol depending on the day of the week. It was a rather solitary, morose existence.

In the Christmas vacation of 1929–30 I practiced French a few days in Paris and then went to join my friend from Wisconsin, Lauri Sharp, who was practicing German in Vienna as part of his training in anthropology. We had a good time high up at the opera and at sites like Schönbrunn, but I generally spoiled the occasion by continuing to write my B. Litt. thesis. Goal-oriented as I was, producing manuscript got me laboriously forward, whereas the German language did not seem necessary to my progress.

Back in London, I called on the Websters' great friend, Professor Eileen Power, who was just as beautiful and incisive as her legend claims. People around the London School of Economics seemed keenly aware of China as an academically underdeveloped area. As a medievalist, Eileen Power had worked on the European travelers to Cathay. She had attended the Kyoto conference of the Institute of Pacific Relations in 1929 and had visited Peking. Her colleague R. H. Tawney had just gone on a study trip to China. His classic *Land and Labour in China* appeared in 1932.

Eileen Power was very supportive, but I was still just a graduate student behind the eight ball, a self-proclaimed specialist without a product to show for it. Twenty years later at Harvard I was delighted to find that my graduate students' seminar papers were good enough to reproduce in an annual volume, *Papers on China,* which at once proved the authors' professional existence. Professor nurture has its needs the same as child nurture. We issued *Papers on China* for twenty-four years.

In 1925 I had got intelligent help from the English-Speaking Union, the pioneer Anglo-American friendship society, as one might call it today. I registered with it and was soon told that a Mrs. Young invited me to dine in Chelsea. There I found a cordial, sophisticated lady and her son Courtenay, age fifteen, who had been studying Chinese at London University with C. C. Shu. C. C. Shu, although I couldn't know it at the time, was Shu She-yu, a Manchu from Peking who was just becoming known as the preeminent novelist Lao She. Courtenay was still a schoolboy, a very bright one, and Mrs. Young saw that he and I might develop common interests in approaching China.

This began an interesting friendship across the Anglo-American cultural gap. Mrs. Young shortly became Lady Young when her husband's father, a baronet, died at ninety-three. By being invited for weekends I got a faint glimpse of the bind that was already clutching at the British aristocracy, suspended between upper-class social status and material insufficiency. The two daughters, Joan and Virginia, brunette and blonde, were very attractive, and the clever elder son, Gerry (for George), was headed for the diplomatic service. The old family place had been named Formosa Fishery by the original baronet, who had been a naval person in the Far East. Its garden sloped down to the Thames not far from Maidenhead. Such a family always had a lot going on, and I enjoyed being rescued from my molelike pursuits in the PRO. I realized too how foreigners abroad appreciate being taken into local family life.

Making one's way socially, however, was too much of a game, dependent on the front one put up. A letter of introduction to a certain Mrs. Evans Conway brought me before a dinner hostess whom I recorded as

> tall, dark, a beauty in her youth, retaining the idea and manner. Conversation is a series of leading questions as to what people I knew. I could have told her in two minutes. But then we'd have sucked soup silently. Stories about Mrs. Vandervere de Floop and self (did I know Mrs. Vandervere de Floop?) at Naragansett (had I been there?) where Mrs. Ogilsbie Obloid (did I know Mrs. O.O.?) entertained Carmaly Cuckle the soprano (sings beautifully, yes? no?) just as *Green Mansions* (read it?) reminds one of the Catskills near Boofus (been there?). I expected her to come out with, "Well, who the hell *do* you know?"

I concluded,

> Presenting letters is good practice: keep calm, give them your good points only when they are sure to go over, hold out generally as though acceptance were a matter of course. It never is.
> "South Dakota," with which I always lead off, since it must out anyway and I enjoy the consternation, usually leaves them up a tree. Conversely, "Harvard" begets "Oh, yes, *Harvard.*" Salaam. Selah. Come for a week. Silly? Put yourself in their place, under social pressure, fearful, knowing no other way to judge. A good man, on the other hand, pitches into a subject and watches your handling of it. Or asks for a biography outright.

In my father's Gladstone bag I carried both a black tie and dinner jacket and a white tie and tail coat. Dinner out in London in 1930 was presumed to be white tie if ladies would be present. One time, back in Sioux Falls when I had worn my tail coat, I backed into a candle and burned a hole in it; my cousins were uproariously delighted. They had already regaled me with that adage "You can always tell a Harvard man, but you can't tell him much." Oxford they associated with tea drinking. They knew South Dakota dentistry and house building were better than anything to the east. Travel and TV had not yet homogenized the English-speaking world.

Skating through English life with my Harvard-Balliol credentials gave me little sustained contact with the lower classes though they were all about. My successive Balliol scouts, Veary and Tuckey, who brought in the hot water at dawn and kindled the heatless little coal fire in my study, spoke cockney. Gilbert Highet and his beautiful Glasgow fiancée, Helen MacInnes, could lapse back into their dialect to demonstrate whence they had come. How strange it was to find two races left over from feudalism, the tall Lambertian aristocrats and the middle-sized workers!

Later in Shansi Wilma and I would stay with a CIM (China Inland Mission) missionary, Mr. Trickey, who seemed like a cousin of Veary and Tuckey. I realized that missions appealed in Britain to souls stymied by class, not simply by farm drudgery as in America. And the Americans replicated in China the schools and colleges they had built at home. But the British Christian colleges in China were few if any. British missionaries had not had them at home.

By the spring of 1931, I was more self-confident in my new persona as a China specialist. I persuaded Dr. Soothill to set me a written examination on Bullock's classical sentences and certify to the sincerity of my efforts. The Rhodes trustees had responded to the needs of scholars for research time in London or even Paris by allowing the third year of a fellowship to be used outside Oxford. I asked for Peking, about as far from Oxford as the antipodes and certainly not the kind of place the trustees had in mind. However, I could point to the fact that my D. Phil. research required the use of British consular records still at the ports in China, which I had permission to see *in situ,* while I also had a start in Chinese that could be best pursued in Peking. No doubt I was already developing the promotional knack which is so essential in seeking academic support for oneself, one's projects, and one's students. One must convey persuasively the ideas of high quality, public need, and practical feasibility, with a suggestion of inevitability (so why not now?) and opportunity (a chance to do something significant). As in all good salesmanship, the proposition was sound; there was nothing phony about it. I was much heartened when the trustees gave me permission, a precedent that another Rhodes scholar, James Bertram *(First Act in Sian),* followed a few years later.

In the spring vacation of 1931 my mother came over to England. I showed her Oxford and we visited the Morses, the Youngs, and the Lamberts. We saw Paris again and Italy for the first time. In the summer I went to see Wilma in Cambridge and in Franklin, New Hampshire, and she came to visit Sioux Falls. After this social windup, I completed Oxford residence for the D. Phil., and after Christmas 1931 took off with Courtenay Young in tow on the Nord Deutscher Lloyd freighter *Adler (Eagle)* from Genoa to Shanghai.

Ship travel gave time for acquaintance with fellow passengers on more than the one-sitting basis allowed by air travel today. We took six weeks to go through Suez and call at a series of famous ports— Colombo on Ceylon, Penang in Malaya, Medan in Sumatra, Singapore, and Hong Kong. While the *Adler* handled cargo, the six passengers saw sights at each stop.

In this way I arrived in China early in 1932 as an academic enterpriser, with the vague idea in the back of my mind that I might somehow make it back to Harvard in due time. I had succeeded there, up to a point, and so wanted to return. That seemed aspiration enough. I knew next to nothing of Chinese history, American China policy, or revolution and nationalism in East Asia. No one had taught me anything about them. My thesis work had been quite narrow. In short, I was in a pretty good position to learn something.

PART TWO

•

OUR FIRST DISCOVERY OF CHINA
1932–35

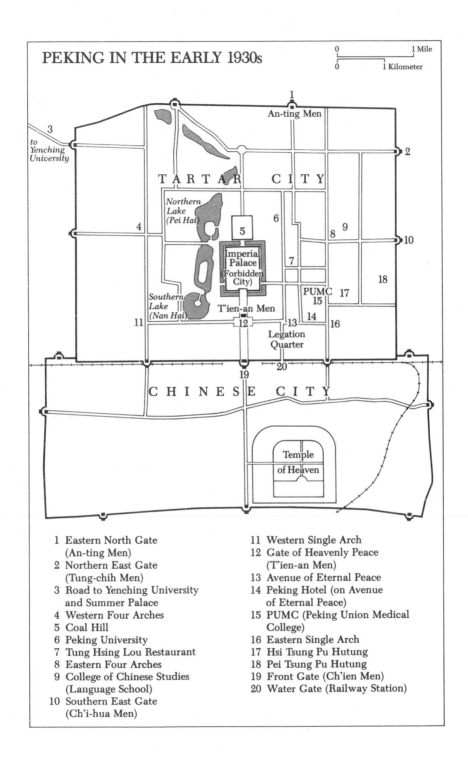

PEKING IN THE EARLY 1930s

0 — 1 Mile
0 — 1 Kilometer

1
An-ting Men

3
to Yenching University

2

T A R T A R   C I T Y

Northern Lake (Pei Hai)

6

4

5

8   9

Imperial Palace (Forbidden City)

7

10

18

Southern Lake (Nan Hai)

PUMC   17
15

11

T'ien-an Men

12   13   14   16

Legation Quarter

20

19

C H I N E S E   C I T Y

Temple of Heaven

1 Eastern North Gate
   (An-ting Men)
2 Northern East Gate
   (Tung-chih Men)
3 Road to Yenching University
   and Summer Palace
4 Western Four Arches
5 Coal Hill
6 Peking University
7 Tung Hsing Lou Restaurant
8 Eastern Four Arches
9 College of Chinese Studies
   (Language School)
10 Southern East Gate
   (Ch'i-hua Men)

11 Western Single Arch
12 Gate of Heavenly Peace
   (T'ien-an Men)
13 Avenue of Eternal Peace
14 Peking Hotel (on Avenue
   of Eternal Peace)
15 PUMC (Peking Union Medical
   College)
16 Eastern Single Arch
17 Hsi Tsung Pu Hutung
18 Pei Tsung Pu Hutung
19 Front Gate (Ch'ien Men)
20 Water Gate (Railway Station)

3

MOVING INTO PEKING

APPROACHING CHINA by sea, sighting fishing junks (or are they pirates biding their time?) among the jagged green islands off the mountainous coast, prepares one for action whether in trade, smuggling, travel, the wrath of war, or self-defense. It is quite unlike the approach by caravan or today by railroad from the continental side, which prepares one by degrees to seek accommodation and acceptance from something too big to be taken over. Western aggression has fitted into the landscape of its route of access.

Hong Kong harbor was dominated by the Peak, even though wintry mists half obscured it. We paused only a few hours, not going ashore, but were struck by the physical grandeur of scenery and the busyness of the harbor. Sampans (single-oared at the stern) and big junks with square lugsails mingled with liners, freighters, gunboats, and ferries as if on a page of the *Britannica* illustrating types of shipping.

After two days coming up the coast, rolling through the mist in the Formosa Strait, we reached the brown waters and saw the low-lying shore of the Yangtze estuary. Suddenly a flotilla of four destroyers of the Japanese Navy went past us—a fast column of lean, agile vessels with the red-sun-on-white flag flapping at each stern. The Japanese flag seemed to me by far the most potent national symbol. Looking like a bloodstained dressing, it said all at once, "Look, the sun has fully risen now, and moreover we will shed our blood for it."

Japan's undeclared war at Shanghai (January 28–March 4, 1932) was in mid-career, and as we came up behind them, the destroyers circled to take turns bombarding the Woosung forts which were still in Chinese hands at the entrance to the Whangpoo, twelve miles below the river port of Shanghai.

Japanese ships began the modern naval age in 1894 by keeping their stations in a column and circling the new Chinese fleet off the Yalu. The Chinese naval commander there, an old cavalry officer, had brought his fleet out line abreast, with the result that they could use only their forward turrets. Now here were the Japanese circling again, firing broadsides at Woosung.

Since the *Adler* carried munitions for Japan it prudently stayed outside. We went up to Shanghai on a white passenger packet. The warring Japanese and Chinese did not fire on it because it represented the unseen but not too remote hand of the treaty powers. How appropriate for a modern historian of China's foreign relations to reach Shanghai in the company of gunboats! Shanghai had grown up with gunboats, and in fact was still doing so.

The potency of the unequal treaties to control behavior was starkly plain at Shanghai. We landed on the bund of the International Settlement a few hundred yards beyond the Japanese cruiser *Idzumo* and other vessels that were bombarding Chapei, a Chinese part of Shanghai north of Soochow Creek, as foreigners called it (in Chinese, the Wusung River that led to Soochow). The 19th Route Army from Canton, dug in under the rubble of bombarded buildings, was being supplied at night across the creek, a hundred yards wide, and Japan's naval forces could not dislodge it. Japan was just completing the absorption of Manchuria and was not yet ready to take on the Anglo-Americans, so the heart of Shanghai, the International Settlement south of Soochow Creek, remained a neutral sanctuary as it had been during warlord battles.

Courtenay Young and I got rooms in the Burlington Hotel, a Victorian establishment right out of Bloomsbury, on Bubbling Well Road, the western extension of the main drag, Nanking Road. I got in touch with Professor Harley F. MacNair of St. John's University (later to be at Chicago). He had just finished condensing Dr. Morse's *International Relations* and expanding its scope to make a standard text, Morse and MacNair, *Far Eastern International Relations.* He was now very busy looking after refugees, and took us at night to an unfinished building downtown used by the refugee committee to accommodate thousands of sad Chinese from Chapei, family groups with small bundles containing all their possessions, huddled on straw in the damp chill. From the roof we watched the fires still burning north of the creek. Japan's aggression seemed to be just another disaster of nature, impossible to prevent. The Western role was to palliate China's misery, the same as in famine relief.

In the PRO I had been reading about the sudden growth of the nascent International Settlement in 1853 when the Taiping rebels' conquest of Nanking had roused a tidal influx of refugees, to whom the foreign land renters could sublet land they had just secured by perpetual lease from the local Chinese authorities. Their treaty privileges were real and still in place in 1932.

Dr. Morse had also given me an introduction to his successor as statistical secretary, Stanley F. Wright, a senior commissioner who in fact was just completing his masterly but little-known summary of the Customs archives, *Hart and the Chinese Customs.* Mr. Wright took me to lunch at the Shanghai Club and its "longest bar in the world" with other senior commissioners. I had the exciting discomfort of being the "griffin" or neophyte among bigshots, full of questions too jejune to ask, only half understanding the shop talk. Mr. Wright was cannily concerned lest I compete with his work in Customs history. When he heard I was going to Peking to begin Chinese, he relaxed visibly. He could rely on the language to sidetrack me indefinitely. Some people who went into it were never even heard of again.

In a few days we embarked for Tientsin in a coaster of the Indo-China Steam Navigation Co. (Jardine's line), untouched by the Japanese Navy. Here was another bit of the old China coast still alive. Plying China's inland and coastal waters under the Union Jack, our vessel had a steel-fortified boat deck complete with Sikh guards ready to use shotguns at the fire ports. The nondescript Chinese steerage passengers on the deck below looked innocent enough, in fact congealed by the cold, but cases of piracy were fresh in memory. The Sikhs were part of the service. I felt China's medievalism had been given modern garb without much change underneath.

We got over the Taku bar at dawn, disembarked at Tangku, the port for Tientsin, and with help from fellow passengers destined for the British legation soon entrained for Peking. (It was then Peiping, to be sure, and is now Beijing, but Peking remains enshrined in Western literature.)

In the flat North China countryside the most startling sight was the grave mounds that stood solemnly in nearly every field—filial reminders, of course, but also investments of land area that could ill be afforded. Though only a few feet high, these mounds were like memorial rooms set aside for the deceased in a city short of housing. I cannot say I asked myself, How long can this go on? I was too busy grasping the fact.

Approaching Peking by rail across the brown winter plain in 1932 still had the emotional impact it had had during the five hundred years since the city walls were built. For Peking until the 1960s was the world's most populous walled city. Granted Nanking had a bigger wall, but it lacked the setting on a plain. The crenelations, on top of the forty-foot façade, the regular row of bastions jutting out two bow shots apart, the sheer visual length of the walls, four miles on a side punctuated by corner towers and nine tall gates in the Northern ("Tartar") City, five miles by two-and-a-half with seven gates in the Southern ("Chinese") City—all this display of square, man-made strength rose clean from the plain, as yet hardly cluttered by suburbs. There was no other sight like it in the world.

The first glimpse was overwhelmingly awesome, as the builders had intended. Peking was last in the succession of North China's great square-walled capitals. Sian today retains the flavor for the tourist trade. But the Cultural Revolution of the late 1960s proved its validity as an updated peasant rebellion bent on blind destruction when Peking's walls and gates went down. Think what any novice in city planning could have done by using those walls and gates, cutting through and around them for traffic. For example, each of the imposing double gate towers could have been kept as the center of a traffic circle and focus of broad new avenues that Paris, Rome, London, Washington, and Moscow would envy in vain! But only the Front Gate (Ch'ien Men) was so preserved.

The brown brick buildings of the College of Chinese Studies with their plot of greensward between them might have been helicopt-ered into Peking holus-bolus from California. Like other schools, institutes, hotels, and hospitals that represented modernity in the old capital, this three-story complex sat rather arrogantly in the midst of the one-story gray brick housing around it. Within its compound was a tennis court, used without the aid of ball boys like those who aided the foreign player in the treaty ports. On this court we found a handsome young man named Martin Wilbur and his even more handsome wife Kay. (He became professor of Chinese history at Columbia and is now emeritus.)

The head of the college was W. B. Pettus, whose broad and rather hairless dome gave him a strongly cerebral and even sagelike appearance. As the autocrat in charge, he was struggling to adjust the institution to changing times. From the North China Union Language School (Hua-yü hsueh-hsiao, "School of Chinese Speech") he had recently rechristened it a college in English and in Chinese a place of cultivated learning (Hua-wen hsueh-hsiao, "School of Chinese Culture"). By affiliating it with a new stateside entity created for the purpose, California College in China, he had acquired the capacity to offer an M.A. degree for research. This academic potential Dr. Pettus hoped would make up for the sagging support of mission boards, whose trainees were growing fewer.

The language school was a halfway station, an air lock, in which one could get ready for a fuller immersion in the Chinese sea outside. It lessened our culture shock by leaving us with spring beds and showers in the hostel and a mixed cuisine at table. Suddenly confronting white bean sprouts, unseen before, I could think only of worms for the first several months. We were concerned about stomach upsets and Peking colds. It helped to live American with steam heat for a while.

China impinged upon us at first light, when a distant squealing and bugle blowing came through the dry cold air. The squealing was of pigs at a slaughterhouse. The bugles celebrated dawn in a local garrison. No connection.

On a still morning a week after our arrival we saw great cumulus clouds billowing high overhead. They were a strong yellow color. They brought dust from the Gobi (i.e., desert) far beyond the Wall to the northwest. Soon a yellow dust fell quietly as snow, covering everything. The high-up winter gale out of Mongolia was showing us how the loess had been deposited through geologic time. In some places in the Northwest this wind-born soil is 250 feet thick. The Yellow River has spread it over the North China plain. The yellow dust seeped into everything, even our textbooks.

Beginning spoken-language classes, I found that the direct

method, unlike Mr. Bullock, started with the four tones of the Peking dialect or national language *(kuo-yü),* formerly called Mandarin *(kuan hua,* official speech) plus the Wade-Giles romanizations geared to them by number. We recited *ma*^{1}, *ma*^{2}, *ma*^{3}, and *ma*^{4} like a class of schoolboys. Three British legation trainees were our classmates. The head teacher, nicknamed "Dearest," was a marvelous actor and for several weeks the direct method moved us along nicely.

When we reached abstraction, however, trouble arose. To convey *yu ching-shen,* "being spirited," Dearest would paw the ground and shake his mane. *"Ma*^{3}," *"ma*^{3}" ("horse, horse") we would say, to no avail. It was clear that researchers would need access to dictionaries, but Dr. Pettus urged us to follow the old Chinese example: learn sounds first, meanings later.

How to study Chinese has always been controversial among its students. Some refuse to believe the writing system can be the way it is and suspect a conspiracy. (Such it was, in fact, an open upper-class conspiracy to limit admission to membership.) Others, more escapist, invent their own romanization systems. In any case, it is hard to avoid deep emotional involvement. Logan Roots, the son of the Episcopal bishop of Hankow and a serious young Oxford Grouper, received in his quiet time one morning an unmistakable divine guidance to tell Dr. Pettus the shortcomings of the direct method. He did so after breakfast, but Dr. Pettus was so little amused that Logan found himself ejected from the college before lunch.

Most of the score or more of students in residence were missionaries, some of them scions of missionary families. One of the first I met was Guy Thelin, who came from a farm outside Sioux Falls and was teaching agronomy to Chinese boys for the Congregational Church in Foochow. My father knew his brother Art Thelin, whose mechanized agronomy just north of Sioux Falls was, however, a good deal more lucrative than anything muscle-powered in China. Nearly all the missionaries offered more than the evangelical message that had preoccupied earlier generations. They struck me as practical people engaged in helping their Chinese constituents. My lively and engaging friend Andrew Tod Roy, for example, ran a student YMCA in Nanking and read the current Chinese novels of rebellion against family tyranny.

Missionary educators, in short, were the foreigners most in touch with Chinese youth. I began to see that one could penetrate the

Chinese scene most readily through other foreigners already immersed in it. This applied even to language study, for the athletic Reverend John D. Hayes, a tall, broad-shouldered Rhodes scholar missionary who would marry Wilma and me in June, spoke a sparkling pure Pekinese learned from childhood. When I heard *him* use a phrase, it became part of me at once.

My first venture outside the language school was to go by ricksha on a rainy night to dine with Laurence C. S. Sickman. As instructed by the old-timers, I avoided sitting snugly back on the seat cushion lest I pick up a louse that might carry typhus. The ricksha puller's cloth-and-rubber-shod feet padded through the film of mud on top of the roadway, his big straw rain hat kept his head dry, and I was protected by the canvas of the vehicle's unfolded top and front curtain. Riding behind a human horse seemed already part of the drill. The pullers were eager to carry you. They needed the meager fares that their competition and lack of organization kept to a pittance. In short, for us foreign appendages of the better-off class, China's plethora of manpower was a public service, like taxis in the United States, except that the fare was a personal contract in advance, orally agreed upon.

Larry Sickman had studied with Langdon Warner at the Fogg Museum at Harvard and was already buying Chinese art objects for the Nelson Gallery in Kansas City. Using its funds when the depression had put other museums out of the market gave him a tremendous opportunity. He "had eyes" *(yu yen-ching)* as the Chinese put it and was already a master of style, provenance, and authenticity. Every day after lunch dealers brought in big bundles of paintings, jades, rubbings, lacquerware and the like for his examination. Larry saw everything, took his pick, and the outstanding Kansas City collection, from which he has just retired as director, attests the superb quality of his judgment.

My first impression, arriving on his doorstep in the rain, was one of transmigration—from the bare moral earnestness of missionary bean sprouts to a land of aesthetics where beauty was the criterion. His Chinese house, its polished furniture, paired scrolls, and paintings all revealed the taste of a connoisseur. His gowned servant was a professional. It was natural that artists and aesthetes from around the world retired to live in Peking if they could. They wanted to share in the refined existence that had been perfected by the Chinese upper class. Larry urged me to find a house before Wilma arrived.

The Sino-foreign social life of Peking was colored by its being a capital city. Everyone carried his own calling cards. Legation diplomats left them for one another as acts of courtesy to announce their arrivals and departures. "Ppc" on a card, *pour prendre congé,* meant one was going off in the constant flux of foreign service. Turning down the correct top corner of one's card had a special meaning I have forgotten. Cards were especially useful for Chinese names to establish their proper characters.

Letters of introduction went with this shifting scene. The problem was to present such a letter before one met the recipient through other channels. To say "I have a letter of introduction to you" implied the further thought "It has not seemed worth the trouble of presenting it to you."

Through a letter from Eileen Power I found R. D. Jameson in his Chinese house at 21 Hsi Tsung Pu Hutung. This was centrally located on the "West Lane of the Tsungli Yamen," the Grand Council committee that handled the Ch'ing dynasty's foreign relations from 1861 to 1901. It was not far from the green tile roofs of the Peking Union Medical College. Jim I described as "a man with a funny goatee and glasses, an enormous grin and charming manners," also an infectious laugh, and enthusiastic interests in Basic English, folklore, and English literature, which he taught at Tsing Hua University.

Inside its double red doors with shiny brass knockers on the *hutung,* or "side street," I found Jameson's house had a service courtyard for the staff quarters. Behind the brick spirit screen, really an anti-spirit baffle since evil influences (and the glances of the curious) can go only in straight lines, was the gateway into the main courtyard. There the flower beds could be totally changed from day to day simply by changing the pots of which they consisted. No need to wait for flowers to grow and bloom. They were always in bloom, or else. Behind the guest hall (living room) was another courtyard full of flowers. On the sides of both courts were studies, bedrooms, baths, and store rooms, counted as so many square sections *(chien)* marked out between the rafters under the gray tile roofs. The Jamesons were going on leave in 1932–33. I rented their house for the year, furnished as it stood. What a break!

My spoken Chinese was reaching that plateau where one can do the essential business of life with servants, shopkeepers, and guests, without remotely approaching those mountain ranges one must climb to understand the technical terms of a profession, to say nothing of the literary allusions and myriad metaphors of old-style discourse among scholars.

One noon I was bicycling up Hatamen Street, which ran from the Hatamen Gate north through the East Single Arch (Tung Tan P'ai-lou) toward the East Four Arches (Tung Ssu P'ai-lou) and the language school. (All these landmark arches, like the gates, are now gone, of course, except in name.) I was studiously avoiding the occasional "honey carts" that carried night soil out to the suburban fields, and also watching out for rickshas, other bicycles, trucks, and the street sprinklers who dextrously sprayed their scoopfuls of water on the dust.

Suddenly I was undone by the street-car track. My wheel caught in its groove and I overturned against an innocent pedestrian, who took one look at me and clutched his side in agony. Since the impact had seemed minimal, I proceeded to clutch my knee and lie in the dirt in my own counter agony. The crowd was thickening by the moment, not unfriendly but curious to see how much the wealthy foreigner might pay.

Just at this moment a double-width ricksha bore through the crowd—verily a *machina* bearing a *deus*—for out of it stepped Dr. Robert Gailey, a man of gigantic weight and proportions who had retired from a long career in the YMCA and lived at the language school. He had been known at Princeton, in the hard-knuckle days before the forward pass, as "Center Rush" Gailey, and in China had acquired a famous command of the Peking vernacular. The crowd were already laughing at his asides. By agreement my victim and I hobbled off with Dr. Gailey to the local police station, where John Hayes soon appeared; word had spread. I apologized for my unintended rudeness, and apologized also for being under the extraterritorial jurisdiction of the American consul. Gradually our injuries subsided. Neither of us could show blood (always a winner). I forced a gift of a dollar upon the man I had bumped into, and we all parted happily.

I had seen and heard two of the American masters of *pai-hua* (the vernacular) in action. It was, however, a great deal more than speech that they demonstrated. They identified themselves as fair-minded observers, they asserted incontrovertible general principles, they applied them to the injuries and interests of all parties, and sympathized with the police officer who was so onerously burdened with this problem. In so doing they saved me at least several hours and probably ten dollars.

In short, much of life's drama was to be found upon the street, and its content was usually interpersonal disharmony. The task of all concerned was to restore the shattered continuum of relationships according to the right principles that should underlie them. The appeal was to reason and common sense. For example, it made sense that I who precipitated the event should pay reparation. By the same progressive principle that undergirds the income tax, I might have paid more if my obvious capacity to feign injury had not been an offsetting factor. Legally speaking, my victim was either damaged by me, or he was not. But, in the reciprocity of life, possible damage to me made up for possible damage to him.

In Peking's kaleidoscopic foreign community the most interesting individual to me was Owen Lattimore. His father had taught in a government university in Tientsin and Owen had been sent to public school (i.e., a private school) in England but not to college. Instead he went to work for a wool firm and as their agent was sent to the railhead at Pao-t'ou in Inner Mongolia, where camel caravans came in from Central Asia. He decided to find out what was out there.

With a trusty servant he traveled by camel westward where few foreigners had recently gone. *The Desert Road to Turkestan* (1929) was a romantic adventure travelogue but also a good deal more, the record of a gifted observer who had spoken Chinese since boyhood and had begun to pick up Mongolian. Owen got a grant and did a year's study of social anthropology at Harvard. In 1932, while Japan's flagrant creation of Manchukuo was a white-hot issue, he published *Manchuria, Cradle of Conflict.* This layout of the area's modern international history linked it with earlier Chinese history and brilliantly adumbrated a theory of the ebb and flow of non-Chinese tribal power out of "reservoirs" on China's northern and northwestern frontiers. It qualified the author as a seminal thinker in "geo-politics," a term then being popularized in Europe by Haushofer and others concerned with "heartlands" and peripheries.

This book struck me as a fresh breeze in an area stale with the listing of treaty rights and interests, all from the European seaward side. The current authority on foreign rights and interests in China had put out three volumes on Manchuria, packed with legal minutiae that left the local populace and their earlier struggles quite out of the picture. Owen's main insights seemed to me self-evident, once stated. His big work of 1940, *Inner Asian Frontiers of China,* later gave me concepts I am still pursuing. As usual in the derivation of ideas, no doubt they were in the air and would have hit me from some other source, but how can one be sure? Owen's imagination fused his field observations with the known facts to build castles of historical theory. Sinologists, still making little bricks of knowledge, might scoff. But he was already a Mongolist, beyond their scope, and drawing on Russian sources too.

When I went to see the Lattimores I found a friendly but preoccupied man who wore a monocle and a big thumb ring and kept in his garden a mountain ram who might butt intruders. Having had a self-image of uniqueness myself, I could recognize someone who was more so. Owen's practical life was quietly managed by his wife, Eleanor Holgate Lattimore, daughter of a president of Northwestern University, a warm, lovely woman with a great and useful capacity for making friends all over the world.

Soon I met academic leaders. My future father-in-law, Dr. Cannon, wrote about me to physiologists he knew at the Peking Union Medical College. By this time I had realized that W. B. Cannon, ever since the publication of *Bodily Changes in Pain, Hunger, Fear and Rage* in 1915, was a venerated household word in medicine around the world. On May 10, 1932, his contacts responded by inviting me to meet some people I should know at the Tung Hsing Lou restaurant.

This famous old establishment, "The Pavilion Rising on the East," was near the main avenue that led to the Tung Hua Men, "The Eastern Flowery Gate" of the Palace. It was built up around a square central well, each balcony housing a number of private dining rooms. When a waiter sang out the name of a departing host, the attendants below shouted in reply. The size of the tip was subtly conveyed in the shouting as a form of encouragement.

I found half the luminaries of Chinese research awaiting me—Hu Shih (1891–1962), dean of Peita (Peking University); L. K. T'ao (1887–1960), head of the Institute of Social Research; and V. K. Ting (1887–1936) of the Chinese Geological Survey. They all seemed remarkably young and indeed were only in their forties. All spoke fluent English. Hu had been at Cornell and Columbia, T'ao at London, Ting at Glasgow, yet all had begun with a Chinese classical education. All played omnicompetent roles as scholars, administrators, and writers on current policy problems, inheritors of the tradition that the man of learning should advise the ruler.

As a dazzled greenhorn I was mercifully far from grasping the significance I can see in these men in retrospect. V. K. Ting, for example, whom I did not meet again, had spent seven years in Britain and returned to help found the Chinese Geological Survey and map China's resources (1916–21). He had then gone into the business of operating a coal mine, but he was so active in so many lines, constantly writing, that he had great influence. In 1926 he administered Greater Shanghai, trying to build up a Chinese municipality vis-à-vis the International Settlement. For twenty years he had been a public protagonist of science as essential for China's progress. After V. K. Ting's death in 1936 from charcoal fumes, Hu Shih wrote his biography. In 1970 Harvard published Charlotte Furth's *Ting Wen-chiang: Science and China's New Culture*.

As I wrote home, I was

> amazed to have Hu Shih, the modern Voltaire, at my elbow helping me to bamboo shoots and duck livers and everybody very friendly. I could not see exactly why this should be, but I had no objection and with the help of the usual Chinese wine felt expansive enough to tell them all about things. . . . How much work will it take to justify the honor?

This sudden contact with modern China's academic leaders surprised me and of course seemed quite undeserved except as I could be considered "promising." However, I was quite willing to be so considered. In fact I have seen myself as promising ever since, with the promise not all realized. In retrospect this cordiality to an American graduate student fits in with the idea that we were all part of a Sino-foreign liberal academic continuum. The first issue of *The Independent Critic (Tu-li p'ing-lun,* edited by Hu Shih, a journal of opinion like *The New Republic),* came out a fortnight later. I studied it as a text. Hu Shih's University of Chicago lectures on *The Chinese Renaissance,* which built up his image in America, were not published till two years later.

In 1932 I had barely heard of the patriotic May 4th incident of 1919, and little or nothing had been written about a May Fourth Movement in thought and culture. When Dr. Hu sent me his Chinese memoir, *Autobiography at Forty (Ssu-shih tzu-shu)*, I was surprised that anyone would write of himself at such an early age. I hardly knew or realized the significance of John Dewey's having lectured in China ten years before in 1919–21 for more than two years with Hu Shih translating for him. One can see now that Dewey's long visit may have been the high point of American liberalism in China. By 1932 party dictatorship was well established as China's new polity. The Peking liberals were in reality hanging powerless on the vine of politics. Yet their type of discussion was essential to China's eventual progress.

In June I visited Tientsin, back on the foreign side of things, to see the Deputy Commissioner of Customs, Everitt Groff-Smith. His father-in-law, Henry F. Merrill, Harvard 1874, whom I had met in Cambridge, had gone to China with H. B. Morse. Under Hart in the 1880s he had headed the Korean Customs Service, when Li Hung-chang's forward policy was to make Korea progress like China. Mr. Merrill had been Shanghai commissioner before he retired. His sole child, Helen, had married a rising Customs assistant. The two of them now welcomed me warmly in a big Tientsin residence with nine servants. Everitt showed me the working of his office.

Everitt's life was in British style, hard-working in hours and athletic out of hours. He played polo on one of his three ponies three times a week. Taken up also in the Tientsin Club's many activities, he had little time to pursue things Chinese. He was culture-bound, in short, like most of his friends in the treaty port culture, where he stood for the integrity and effectiveness of China's administration of foreign trade according to the treaties.

Low moral standards, Everitt felt, were gnawing at the Customs Service. He blamed the current I.G. (Sir Frederick Maze) for "a lax and conciliatory policy." Where his predecessors had been aggressive in protecting China's credit with her foreign bondholders (i.e., maintaining payments), Maze had to bend to the demands of the new Nationalist government. Tariff autonomy was claimed, recruiting of foreigners was stopped, and some Chinese were made commissioners at the top level of the service for the first time.

Again, the old order of nineteenth-century Western imperialism was slipping, but so slowly! Japan's aggression after 1931 now preserved it as a counter to the new enemy. Foreign nationals as Customs commissioners, like foreign missionaries in colleges and hospitals, still had their uses in China's behalf against the Japanese invader throughout the 1930s.

One close friend we learned a lot from was Ida Pruitt, head of hospital social service in PUMC. This was the commonly used name for the Peking Union Medical College, also sometimes identified as the Rockefeller hospital because the Rockefeller Foundation invested some $34 million in it between 1915 and 1947. Ida Pruitt had come into the world in a small town near P'eng-lai in Shantung. Her fascinating memoir, *A China Childhood,* makes it plain that under the care of her Chinese nurse, speaking Chinese from infancy, she grew up peculiarly aware of the strange, non-Chinese ways of her missionary parents. Culturally she was half Chinese. She was like her contemporary Pearl Buck, who has described how she also "grew up in a double world, the small white clean Presbyterian American world of my parents and the big loving merry not-too-clean Chinese world, and there was no communication between them" *(My Several Worlds, A Personal Record).*

Ida Pruitt went to school in Georgia and studied at Teachers College, Columbia. Then she went into social work in Philadelphia and eventually at Massachusetts General Hospital in Boston, where she worked with Wilma's aunt, Ida M. Cannon, a pioneer in this new field. Her fifteen years' experience of the social problems of PUMC patients gave her insights no ordinary foreigner could have.* Ida was heart and soul with the Chinese common people, all the more so because she knew the statistics of what modern life was doing to them.

In late June, when I moved into Jameson's house, Ida was about to go on leave and she let me have her cook, Yang. This at once guaranteed our household's stability, for Yang's seven years with her had made him wise about the care of foreigners, and moreover he would answer to her for our welfare. I invited Ida to occupy one side

---

*She was also putting her command of Chinese to good use. She had translated a local magistrate's memoir of 1900, *The Flight of an Empress* (published by Yale in 1936), and was preparing to take down the life story of a peasant grandmother from P'eng-lai. (This became *A Daughter of Han: The Autobiography of a Chinese Working Woman,* Yale, 1945.)

of the front courtyard, opposite Courtenay, pending Wilma's arrival and her own departure.

At the end of May 1932, Wilma entrained for China by way of Sioux Falls and the Rockies, whose grandeur she spent a day looking at from an open observation car. She then embarked on the Canadian Pacific line's *Empress of Japan.* This progression halfway round the globe, visiting family friends in Vancouver, Honolulu, Yokohama-Tokyo, and Kobe, was an experience of travel in contact with land, sea, and local people, long continued like reading a novel. In contrast, today's air jumps are as casual as the constantly shifting TV images. It is hard to leave home, nowadays, no matter how the scenery rushes by. One's attention is only briefly engaged.

Since Wilma was due at Tangku on the *Chojo Maru* June 27, I went a day ahead to Tientsin to stay with the Groff-Smiths and take a 4:30 A.M. train to Tangku. There at 9 A.M.

the *Chojo Maru* came steaming in across the fields on time. Wilma and I "exchanged glances" from the boat and dock, and when there were at last only a few feet left out of the distance around the earth, I stepped to the edge and articulated distinctly, "Hello, have you got a raincoat?" "Yes," murmured Wilma.

We caught a four o'clock to Peking to find Courtenay, fan in hand, on the platform at 7:30 and Gin the ricksha boy looking very neat outside the Water Gate through which one leaves the station. . . . I brought Wilma home by way of the Imperial Palace. We rode under and through its entrance gates for a quarter of a mile, collecting local color, and reached our own *hutung* at dusk. So I lifted Wilma over the big red wooden door beam and had her walk sightless till she stood at the inner gate from the servants' court into the front quad full of flowers with the living room dimly lit through Chinese windows and its big double door, behind it.

In this courtyard we were later married by John Hayes,

who had previously brought flowers and planned the setting in which he was to officiate with the same serious and decorous care with which he inspects famine relief works.

The American consul stood by as witness in his polo garb en route to a match.

Thus we began a three-and-a-half year adventure in China with maximum opportunity and minimal risk. Friendly American doctors were just down the street at PUMC. We were already a small Harvard outpost in an exotic scene where special privileges gave us security. We had hardly left home. The challenge was whether we could.

4

BEGINNING TO SEE THE LAND
AND PEOPLE

Two-year stints in four different academic environments—Exeter, Wisconsin, Harvard, and Oxford—as I have suggested, no doubt prepared me to keep my sense of direction even in the exoticism of Peking. Specializing preserved my identity in each case. I aimed at specific goals and avoided distractions. But I couldn't live in Peking in 1932 and say to China: "Don't call me; I'll call you." The Chinese environment surrounded me and had an influence. Wilma remarked soon after her arrival that I seemed to understand Chinese situations.

I recognize that the treaty-port cemeteries are filled with foreigners who understood China well enough to live and die there. Partly this "understanding" was a result of temperament, partly perhaps it also came from sharing the Confucian awareness that each person is a moral animal playing multiple social roles. Sensing others' circumstances and motives is no doubt a Chinese specialty. At Oxford, I had picked up some appreciation of the gentleman's code. China had an equivalent worth equal appreciation—the scholar's rational impartiality, a capacity to objectify one's situation. (Actually I am not sure how to phrase this. "Culture" is elusive because it is lived, not defined, least of all in polysyllables.)

Because Wilma was a painter attuned to sense impressions, she found the sights, sounds, smells, and feel of Peking life endlessly stimulating. Her steady progression into closer contact with the local scene carried me along happily in her train. During our first year in Peking, living on savings and studying language, we savored the amenities of foreign life in China. Only gradually did we become aware of the prospects of Japanese invasion and social revolution that were all too soon to burst over the land.

In the summer months of 1932 in our Peking courtyards, we were served by cook, houseboy, amah (cook's wife), and ricksha boy. Wilma was soon using her beginner's Chinese to superintend their household tasks. Of course she could have done it by sign language or by mumbling and grunting, since the servants knew the drill better than she did. But it gave her self-confidence in speaking.

High cumulus clouds sometimes brought showers, followed by sun again before sunset. Flocks of pigeons with whistles tied to them veered overhead, making bars of organ music. Street cries, really salesmen's advertisements, echoed over the compound wall as peddlers patrolled the *hutung* with their specialties. The flower man kept changing the flowers, just as the cook provided a varied diet. We learned not to ask for more of yesterday's entrée. It was probably on another foreigner's table, for the cooks cooperated. You might come upon your own tableware helping out at a friend's party, but never fear, it would be home again before you were.

We were in fact the beneficiaries of an ancient tradition of service to foreigners. China's "northern capital" (*Pei-ching*, Peking) had been dominated by non-Chinese conquerors during most of its history. Founded in 947 as a capital of the Khitan Mongols' Liao dynasty, it had been taken over from them by the Tungusic Chin dynasty (1122–1234), then by the Mongols' Yuan dynasty (1234–1368) and finally by the Manchus' Ch'ing dynasty (1644–1912). The Western embassies that came in after 1860 were only the most recent non-Chinese-speaking bigshots to be accommodated. Over the centuries all the skills of foreign household management, special entertainments and goods made to order, catering and procurement, banqueting and picnicking had been harmoniously developed among the serving class and tradesmen. We were in good hands.

As the summer went on, we explored the city, whose monuments were all available to us. One could take a picnic lunch on top of Coal Hill, the man-made eminence protecting the north gate of the palace, which overlooked the city. One could dine on a sampan in the South Lake (Nan hai) west of the palace, which had been still closed to the public when the young Kuang-hsu Emperor spent his last years there (1898–1908), and would be closed again when Liu Shao-ch'i, Mao Tse-tung, and others lived there in the 1950s and '60s. Our simplest expedition was a picnic supper on top the east city wall at the end of our *hutung*. Chinese never climbed the ramp; adventurous foreigners could have the run of the place.

As Wilma wrote,

> The slightly crumbling stones are covered with weeds growing up in the cracks between them and the whole stretch of wall from high gate tower to gate tower is a beautiful lonely neglected promenade made just for us. Besides a full moon in the east that night, there was a thunderstorm far across the plain to the north with constant vivid flashes of lightning and in the west the hills stretched out beyond the city making a dark dramatic horizon.
>
> Viewed from the city wall, Peiping itself is thrilling at night, for its dark streets and walls are illuminated only at intervals by dim points of light giving the whole city an appearance of lantern-lit festivity, the mysterious and romantic sort. These warm summer nights every courtyard holds a solitary flute player or a group of silent listeners with their attention centered on a singer. There is no trace of self-consciousness to the arts as these people practice them.

The terrain broadened in the fall when a British legation friend, my language-school classmate, gave Wilma a black horse. Night-time (Yeh-li), as she named it, had gone lame for polo but was ideal for riding in the park around the Temple of Heaven or in the countryside outside the city gates. Stable upkeep including the *ma-fu's* (groom's) wage was $8 Chinese a month. For another few dollars I could hire a horse too. All through the winter on sunny days grooms and horses could meet us at the easterly north gate, An-ting Men, or the northerly east gate, Tung-chih Men, or the middle east gate, Ch'i-hua Men. Once beyond the gate's suburb we could follow cart tracks or a sunken road across the plain, or when the ground was frozen gallop over the fields toward an ancestral temple or a prince's tomb sighted on the horizon. North of Peking beyond the Yellow Temple stood the still massive earth mound left from the Mongol city wall, Khubilai Khan's "great capital" (Daidu, also called in Turkish

Khanbaligh, Marco Polo's Cambaluc, the "city of the Khan"). Wilma made a painting of it.

The plain in winter was bare and windswept, its farms dilapidated. The tree cover of today was missing as well as the irrigation water and rich crops that now impress the visitor. We were enjoying our privileged existence at a time of downturn in the ever-precarious fortunes of the North China peasantry. Yet the code of courtesy seldom failed. If you addressed the old farmer in the proper fashion and became his guest, he would respond as the host, perhaps even offer a cup of hot water.

A farm wife would seldom meet strangers, even though she might be stumping about on a threshing floor doing farmyard chores. In the 1930s bound feet were still to be expected in rural women over thirty. Footbinding was so perverse and yet so pervasive that modern patriots have wanted to forget the whole thing. Yet it would be almost impossible to find a Chinese woman of today whose great grandmothers did not have bound feet.

Footbinding had begun, it is said, at court in the tenth century and spread among the upper class in imitation. It is amazing that it then spread widely among the peasantry in the Ming and Ch'ing periods (1368–1912). The process was ingenious: binding cloths, say ten feet long and two inches wide, wrapped a girl's foot from the ages of five, six, or seven so as to press the small toes under while pressing the big toe back toward the heel, both narrowing and shortening the foot. In the process the arch was broken and the instep became a crevice between the heel and big toe. Ida Pruitt's old peasant woman in *Daughter of Han* testified:

> They did not begin to bind my feet until I was seven because I loved so much to run and play. Then I became very ill and they had to take the bindings off my feet. . . . When I was nine they started to bind my feet again and they had to draw the bindings tighter than usual. My feet hurt so much that for two years I had to crawl on my hands and knees. Sometimes at night they hurt so much I could not sleep. I stuck my feet under my mother and she lay on them so they hurt less and I could sleep. But by the time I was eleven my feet did not hurt and by the time I was thirteen they were finished. The toes were turned under so that I could see them on the

inner and under side of the foot. They had come up around. Two fingers could be inserted in the cleft between the front of the foot and the heel. My feet were very small indeed.

A girl's beauty and desirability were counted more by the size of her feet than by the beauty of her face. Matchmakers were not asked 'Is she beautiful?' but 'How small are her feet?' A plain face is given by heaven but poorly bound feet are a sign of laziness.

Only Manchu and other nomadic peoples, low-class boatwomen, the so-called Hakka immigrants from north to south China, and some others escaped the hold of the custom. The end of footbinding began among Chinese reformers and under missionary prompting in the 1890s. But judging by cases still visible in the 1970s, it lasted well into the twentieth century.

Footbinding was obviously a hyper-civilized triumph of man over woman. How can we begin to understand it? The females fixed themselves, mother teaching daughter, so that they were weaker than men, unable to run away (a man could catch them at a walk), and resigned to being housebound.

Motivation? To be in proper shape for the marriage market, essentially a family affair, not a girl's choice. Indeed, a bride was ideally supposed to be bloodily deflowered on her marriage night by a bridegroom she had never seen before. Rape today may be an easier experience.

Old poems and essays make it plain the three-inch golden lily was a fetish. What an achievement! Bound-feet women had two extra private parts for men to toy with. Constantly covered in winsome, fancy shoes; seen and touched only by wife and husband in the bedchamber; fully supplied with sensitive nerve endings otherwise neglected by modern man—golden lilies were lifelong symbols of eroticism, a sexual invention that makes Western deviants, sadists, and assorted kooks seem like pikers. The voluptuous mouthing of deformed little feet may not rouse males of today but it evidently worked in its time. Thus a sexual fetish, self-perpetuating, reinforced the ancient male domination. In the 1930s we accepted it as part of the landscape, a quaint custom. This showed our lack of imagination. It has taken me forty years of *arrière pensée* to get exercised about it.

In venturing outside Peking we soon went further afield, over-night or for several days to temples in the Western Hills. We had a honeymoon in Dr. Gailey's compound in the Temple of the Sleeping Buddha, Wo Fo Ssu. (It was still there in 1979 though no foreigners were honeymooning in it.) If we went by car or bicycle, Yang the cook and his boy might follow by donkey. With Larry Sickman we went by train overnight to the Lung-men rock-cut temples outside Loyang and to the cave temples at Yun-kang near Ta-t'ung.

On such safaris one carried a bedding roll, water canteen, flash-light, tin cup, camera, towel, and emergency food supplies as self-sufficiently as possible, but never camped out. Instead, we made camp in a room of an inn or a temple. We never achieved the true sophistication of putting the four legs of a bed in saucers of kerosene to keep bedbugs from climbing up to join us.

It was essential to have a "boy" along, whatever his age, to scout for food, lodging, or transport and to be an intermediary, announcing our provenance and intentions in a way that we could not. As foreign-ers we were rare birds worth looking at, all hairy legs and red faces, but we were in channels accustomed to minor officials and urban Chinese, not unique. In fact we could eat noodles at a roadside stand like normal human beings and even converse. Speech made us friends for the moment.

For visits to monumental sites like the rock-cut Buddhist statuary and bas reliefs at Lung-men or Yun-kang, we needed proper intro-ductions, letters from some recognized authority who would vouch for us. The aim was to create a chain of personal responsibility to the bottom of which we could hang on. A letter from the patriarch of Peking's American community, Dr. John C. Ferguson, might start the sequence.

Dr. Ferguson was a big man with impressive white hair and mus-tache. He had functioned in China under the empire, having come as a Christian educator and soon been asked to head the new indus-trial college set up about 1898 under the Nanking governor-general. He had later founded and made a success of a Shanghai newspaper and in Peking had been an advisor to some of the warlord govern-ments. He was now on the commission to oversee the Palace Mu-seum and try to keep its documents and paintings from disappearing.

Dr. Ferguson had a big Chinese house full of servants, with sev-eral courtyards and a library plus a curator-teacher. He published on fine arts, knew the local politics, and befriended all the half-dozen American students in Peking. On Thanksgiving he brought us all together, an imposing figure living in both cultures. His daughter Mary was the devoted secretary of PUMC and has written its very interesting administrative history.

Launched with a letter from Dr. Ferguson, we could arrive at a site with a letter to the local curator from his Peking superior. We politely informed the Loyang or Ta-t'ung police of our presence, without giving them an opportunity to ban it. Their responsibility was not accompanied by any control over us. They had to calculate the risk of our getting into trouble against the risk of our complaining if they stopped us. At Loyang they gave us an escort of a couple of soldiers, thus warning the bandit-minded: "Note—foreigners. Not worth the possible trouble." Our transport donkeys or rickshas were similarly contracted for at a responsible hostel. With our American passports we traveled in a cocoon of relative untouchability. We were top-level untouchables, not bottomlevel like those in India. But our untouchability was neither as rapidly mobile nor as hermetically sealed and supervised as today's more expensive China Travel Service kind of quarantine in cocoonlike buses between hotels, sites, and Friendship Stores. We picked up appropriate contacts as we went along, and of course spent a lot of time on the food supply and the sleeping arrangements. Eating and sleeping have only to be in jeopardy to claim one's priority solicitude.

On the P'ing-Han (Peiping-Hankow) line we found we could sleep both on and underneath the fixed table between our facing seats. In the railroad junction town of Chengchow in March 1933 Larry Sickman and Wilma and I found that the only hotel had a room with a board bed but no bedding. We spent a cold night fully dressed and in overcoats under our bedding rolls. On the P'ing-Sui (Peiping-Suiyuan) line to Ta-t'ung we found our ultimate and best resting place was overhead lying in the sturdy baggage racks. The train attendant was not amused, but what could he do? We bought him off.

When we reached the Lung-men caves, where Larry had been before, he was horrified to find that the lovely frieze of a donor with ladies had been hacked out of the rock and carted off for sale, just as might have happened in warlord days when some local officials would sell anything. Larry set to work and traced bits and pieces of the frieze scattered in the hands of Chinese dealers in Peking and other cities. By 1939 he was able to start reassembling it, with some gaps, in the Nelson Gallery in Kansas City.

On the same trip in 1933, when we got to Kaifeng, the ancient Sung capital of the eleventh century, we found the Episcopal bishop of Honan, Dr. William C. White, serving both God and art. He seemed to be fully occupied not only in the religious business of his Trinity Cathedral but also in the collecting business. At his back door he took his pick of the bronzes, tomb figurines, and other *tung-hsi* (things) dug up by enterprising Chinese grave robbers. After Bishop White retired in 1935, he became curator of the magnificent Chinese collection he had largely made himself at the Royal Ontario Museum in Toronto. In Honan he was succeeded as diocesan bishop by one of the great Chinese Anglicans, Lindel Tsen. God did not lose out.

When the People's Republic forty years later sent to Europe and America its exhibit of "Cultural Treasures Unearthed During the Cultural Revolution," one of its great merits for art historians was that all the bronzes, jades, ceramics, and figurines were of known provenance marked on a map with dates of excavation. In the imperialist era when foreign collectors tried to preserve/purloin Chinese art by buying it for museums abroad, they seldom knew exactly where their collaborators, the Chinese vandals and tomb excavators, had got their stuff. Jan Fontein of the Boston Museum of Fine Arts in 1973 mounted a fascinating exhibit by pairing well-known pieces of unknown origin in Western collections with very similar items of known origin in the PRC exhibit.

In the uncontrolled archaeological scramble of the 1930s Bishop White was able to contribute more than most foreigners. A year or more after our visit, we found out what the bishop had been up to —a work of salvage and scientific archaeology achieved by very diplomatic dealings with local Chinese who sought to profit from China's past.

William Charles White, "sometime Bishop of Honan, Associate Professor of Archaeology (Chinese), University of Toronto, Keeper of the East Asiatic Collection of the Royal Ontario Museum," published in 1934 *Tombs of Old Loyang: A Record of the Construction and Contents of a Group of Royal Tombs at Chin-ts'un, Honan, Probably Dating 550 BC* (Shanghai: Kelly and Walsh) with 187 plates and a foreword by John C. Ferguson. Wilma did the line drawing for the cover. The book was a careful study of objects that had been excavated by Chinese parties unnamed with whom Bishop White was able to develop contact and a chance for observation. These people were excavating a set of eight tombs. They found chariot and horse trappings, horse skeletons, tomb furniture, implements and weapons, ritual objects, jades and stones, glass, bells and stone chimes. Some bore inscriptions that established dates. Only one of the eight tombs was completely excavated, "the labour entailed being so great. The others were entered by vertical shafts being sunk to the doorways. . . . This meant that many of the larger pieces of tomb furniture, such as massive bronze tripods, could not be removed from the tombs very readily, and in some cases these were ruthlessly broken, in order to bring out parts of them" (p. 20).

Plainly this was no fly-by-night or surreptitious thievery but a long-term operation which must have been given protection by local men of substance. The Nanking government had no rice-roots power in Honan. Academia Sinica was just getting well started on the Anyang excavations, one of the first done by trained archaeologists. Even at Anyang the original tomb excavation when thoroughly studied was filled in again. (When we asked to see it in 1972, we were shown a wheatfield.) Land for crops was too valuable, and the excavated Chin-ts'un tomb was filled in.

Bishop White remarks laconically, "After the objects had been numbered and the list made, a group of some eighty pieces of bronze came to light, which the promoter of the excavation had cached in his home when the tombs were first opened" (p. 59).

Dr. Ferguson's foreword holds it "most fortunate" that Bishop White was nearby and "through trusty agents was able to follow every stage of the operations and secure so many specimens from the contents of the graves. . . . One with less tact and knowledge of local conditions would have been baffled . . . but in this instance the man best suited for the work has been on the spot at the time when he was needed."

Modern archaeology, in short, took hold in China by degrees, often through the medium of foreigners who began studies in which modern Chinese later became the experts. The building of art collections outside China was part of this process, a transitory phase like the foreign administration of Shanghai for a hundred years. In the case of the Chin-ts'un tombs, the bishop achieved what he could, even though it was a bit like medieval surgery, when doctors had to operate on a lady by feely-feely under a sheet.

Both Kaifeng and Loyang had impressive missionary establishments, with compounds and buildings more imposing than the vestiges of ancient temples and palaces and more useful than local government installations. At the Augustana Synod Mission in Loyang, founded in 1911, we met the Lindbecks from Minnesota. Their ten-year-old son, John Matthew Henry Lindbeck, seemed studious and shy. Twenty-seven years later, with a Yale Ph.D. in political science, he became my deputy director of the East Asian Research Center at Harvard and later director of the center at Columbia.

Our most spectacular trip was the simplest. En route to Shanghai in October 1932 we simply got off the dusty train at the brown square-walled town of Taianfu, presented a letter at the gray brick Methodist mission, and received cots, blankets, and food for the trip up the 7,000 stone steps that bring pilgrims to the top of Shantung's sacred mountain, T'ai Shan. The peak is 4,600 feet high and the route of ascent about 10 miles. Our chair bearers and porters expressed this very sensibly as 45 *li* up and 15 *li* down, since the *li* (nominally about one-third of a mile) is a calculation of distance plus time and trouble —precisely the combined figure you need to know for your planning and payments.

> After jouncing half a mile in the swinging chairs, we gave that up and walked almost the entire distance. . . . Cypresses shaded the road on the lower slopes and twisted Chinese pines covered the rocky cliffs up near the peak. . . . Little temples and shrines lined the path at enlivening intervals . . . the sun gradually sinking made every moment varied until we came through the big red gate at the top of the steepest climb and saw the last glow of the sunset in the cold twilight.
>
> T'ai Shan towers, very barren and rugged, above a chain of dwarfed hills on the north and a vast plain on the south, a patchwork of tiny brown fields as far as the eye can see. . . . The steps go straight up to God and the plain below goes on to infinity, and it has all been there forever.

We camped in the Temple of the Jade Emperor on the topmost crag, supping by lamplight that made our shadows vie with the gilt emperor on his throne and his four fierce warrior guardians nearby.

The two monks living at the top gave us hot water for tea. After a cold night we rose in the chilly half dark to greet the dawn and watch the sun come back over the earth. Just beyond us was the stone set up by the First Emperor, Ch'in Shih Huang-ti, in the late third century B.C.

> Below was the temple of Confucius, who looked at the world below and felt himself small. On one edge the Cliff of the Love of Life, meaning the opposite: pilgrims throw themselves off ecstatically.

We stayed all day painting, and a second night.

Thus in the 1930s we were exposed to the adventures of the open road, like Chaucerian pilgrims. This is the chief thing denied the modern tourist. China was far more interesting than the rather "Chinesey" sumptuousness and entertainments of the legations. Participation in Chinese life, in short, was not denied us. No patriot was as yet in overall charge intent on doing so. We could listen to storytellers in the market or watch the jugglers and tumblers at the Bridge of Heaven (T'ien-ch'iao) outside the Front Gate (Ch'ien Men) in Peking. We could also watch the incredible acrobatics and fastidiously differentiated makeup of heroes, villains, generals, beautiful women, comics, and others in the old Peking opera. Its bare-stage conventions—stepping over thresholds, mounting and dismounting horses, the undulations of a boat on the waves, long journeys through mountains—all registered so neatly with a sophisticated audience of cognoscenti, many of them common people.

We could also haggle with shopkeepers over furniture, objets d'art, or household supplies. Prices, being unfixed as yet, would naturally be higher for a foreigner wealthy enough to be there. The game was to work out a compromise, all things considered. If we had been to the shop before, we came again as "old friends." If the man said $10, we said $5. We explained how little we needed the object. He reminded us how rare it was. But, he said, for us it could be $9. We greatly regretted we could only offer $6. We started to move away. "One last word," he said. In view of our friendship he would take a loss at $8. This sincerity moved us to $7 and the sale was agreed upon, naturally, at $7.50. Everyone enjoyed it.

After a studious, carefree summer of 1932, we presented all our Peking letters of introduction in September and for two weeks saw half a dozen people a day, sometimes attending three teas in an afternoon. From this pulse taking among foreigners in touch with the situation I recorded

> that the Chinese will never be able to manage themselves, that there will shortly be a revolt against the Westernization now proceeding so rapidly, that Westernization, however, is not proceeding rapidly and is indeed barely scratching the surface, that communism will engulf the place and us too in the end, but that the Chinese will never be susceptible to the appeal of Communist ideas, that Christianity has a great chance to give an ideal to this people, but has never made any progress worth mentioning . . . and that the mandate of the Kuomintang and their god Sun Yat-sen, who was to replace Confucius, has finally run out. The last is definite.

> Dr. Gailey, who arrived about 1908, felt that China in the next few decades inevitably will be divided into a much smaller area through having further chunks bitten out by Japan and presumably by Russia. Far from being upset by this outlook, his reaction is that it will be the saving of the country, reducing it to a negotiable size and consolidating the warring factions against a common foe. . . . Japan will probably take Hopei and Shantung provinces to give it the security of a large section of mainland along the sea. Already she seems to be on the point of taking Jehol. . . . That leaves Mongolia for Russia, I suppose.

This conventional wisdom from an old resident was shared by many foreigners. Few could foresee the peasant nationalism that would be aroused by the Japanese invasion after 1937. The future was more accurately forecast by our friend Lucy Knox. She returned from a trip to Japan as a stenographer with the Lytton Commission of the League of Nations, taking down the testimony of Japan's civil and military leaders concerning their rape of Manchuria in 1931. She reported the Japanese military rulers were "in a state of feverish unrest, fired with a mission to spread Japanese culture to the rest of the world by conquest. Their conclusion is that they have in sixty years assimilated Western culture and developed beyond it so that the blind and outstripped rest of the world must now be enlightened. Of course this is the attitude of the military class now in power and of the farmers whom they have propagandized. The more conservative intelligentsia are now voiceless."

Our year of reconnaissance included a six-week trip to Shanghai with Hangchow, Soochow, and Nanking on the side. In my cautious fashion I ushered Wilma into Shanghai life at the Burlington Hotel, where Courtenay and I had stayed in February. Its long white corridors and dining room with a double row of old ladies facing each other at their single tables impressed Wilma as highly dispensable. In her usual adventurous fashion next morning she cased fifteen places advertised and within twenty-four hours had us in a rented room on the main street of the French Concession in the slapdash household of an ex-Marine named Kinnard and his Shanghai-Russian wife whose old father, an ex-Tsarist officer, liked to wear his medals. The bed springs, of the early chain-mail type, practically dragged us on the floor until we folded up the floor rugs and put them under the mattress.

Presenting letters, we found foreigners in Shanghai reciprocated the feeling of foreigners in Peking—they enjoyed visiting the other place but they wouldn't want to live there.

We found Shanghai upper-class homes were behind walls, like London's. Sir Frederick Maze, the Inspector General of Customs, behind his big house had "a small place the size of two football stadia, all green grass." He invited us to dinner and movies, and on three Sundays we joined the Customs staff paying court there. The last time Sir F. took me into his study tête-à-tête to be sure that History would understand his actions: he had lowered the flag of foreign supremacy only to be sure that his uncle's great institution would survive in the new age. We talked about "what a grand man Robert Hart was and how the present I.G. is much like him."

Maze was so obviously politically motivated that, without really knowing anything, I had vague suspicions about him, probably unjustified. The Customs after all had been a chief bone of contention during the Nationalist revolution of the mid-twenties. In 1923 Aglen as I.G. had refused to let Sun Yat-sen's revolutionary regime have the surplus revenue at Canton, and the diplomats at Peking had backed him up with fifteen gunboats in the Pearl River.

As a newcomer innocent of strong feelings, I was touching casually on old scars and current strains. Foreign true believers in the unequal treaties that preserved foreign-run Shanghai were like the

Chinese Kuomintang stalwarts who thirty years later would support the claim of the Republic of China on Taiwan to be the only China —both had well-established vested interests in a system that had worked at least for them. The Shanghai mind and the later ROC mind had something in common. For example, on Taiwan the KMT party dictatorship and martial law have corresponded to the imperialists' extraterritoriality of an earlier day—abolish these props to vested interests and the heavens would tumble down, for some people. The Barry Goldwaters of 1932 Shanghai were always ready to "get the gunboats in a circle," as we had seen the Japanese do at Woosung.

Stanley Wright had us twice to dinner and was very kind as usual. He did not stress the fact that the early Customs records were being brought in from the ports to form the Customs Library under the Inspectorate General in Shanghai. Fortunately for our relations, I had already knocked myself out of competition with him. The chronological retrogression of my thesis topic left me unconcerned with details after 1858. This removed me from Mr. Wright's turf.

In Shanghai I also found my Balliol friend, Ken Cheang, living in opulence with many brothers and cousins in a castlelike stone mansion equipped with a swimming pool, tennis courts, one Daimler, two Isotta-Fraschinis and sundry smaller cars. His grandfather and granduncles had gone overseas as laborers from the same place that Sun Yat-sen had come from near Macao. Some perished abroad but some came back from California, the Philippines, or Peru with wealth that Ken's father's generation had invested in Shanghai. Ken's older brothers went to Cambridge and were now high up in the management of the big Nanyang Brothers Tobacco Company, the chief competitor of the Duke family combine, the British American Tobacco Company. As *nouveaux riches* industrialists, they had gone into real estate and now owned two theaters. Ken was no longer a solitary, rather shy student in the damp chill of Oxford but part of a bustling crowd who enjoyed their worldly goods.

On our later visit to Shanghai in November 1934 Ken took us in his Isotta-Fraschini out to the Municipal Civic Center, six miles east toward Woosung, where the Chinese municipality of Greater Shanghai had put up a grand "Chinese-modified-temple-style administration building and meeting hall," as bait to draw new urban growth. As I noted, "The idea is that the bankers who previously bought up the land there, as well as the Municipal Government, the chief land-owner, will clean up through the rise in land values." So far it hadn't happened.

Through a friend in the National Economic Council we inspected the big Nanyang Brothers cigarette factory. We found 3,000 women and 39 toilets, modern machinery, a 10-hour day, and rather bad air, but saw no great evils. In contrast the YWCA took us to

> a silk filature where children aged nine to twelve stand for fourteen hours a day, with half an hour for lunch, vigorously stirring [dethreading] cocoons in a pan of live steam and water which eats the skin off their hands, and so get ten cents a day.

In the biggest cotton mill

> hollow-eyed girls, perhaps sixteen, stand or run about, twelve hours a day, tending spindles and weaving looms in a roar and vibration that shakes your fillings loose. Remembering my twelve-hour days on the railroad gang, I could not imagine staying in this forest of machines that long, even lying on a rubber mattress.

What a contrast! Gleaming machines in serried ranks, the acme of efficiency, and among them "here and there a few score worn down and grimy girls, dressed like alley cats"—no one of them worth a spindle. Pay? Forty cents a twelve-hour day, to be divided with contractor, foreman, subforeman, *et al.*, leaving twenty cents to take home.

Here, in short, we were seeing the profuse evils of early industrialization, which we knew could be matched in Hankow, Tientsin, and other cities. Here in Shanghai we had also met scions of the new Chinese capitalist class and behind them the foreign treaty-port establishment that administered the Customs and the concession areas. This was a social scene with potentialities for revolution, vastly more somber and dynamic than the aesthetic joys of our upper-class life in Peking. We gained more insight through particular individuals.

5

AGNES SMEDLEY'S CHINA

MY CHIEF OCCUPATION in Shanghai was to read the *North China Herald* for 1850–54 but my thesis seemed remarkably superficial to Chinese life. The Shanghai Municipal Council's sanitation trucks still picked up dead baby girls from the streets every morning because female infanticide was a seemingly unavoidable necessity for many of the poor, and in the city they had to rely on the municipal services. Meanwhile, ricksha men plied their precarious trade in the fumes of the car traffic. The Chinese people's poverty was the biggest fact in China, even though their numbers were less than half what they are today. The size of the problem left one numb and helpless—unless one organized with others. This was the Communist message, which we got first from Agnes Smedley.

In her autobiography, *Daughter of Earth,* Agnes Smedley refers to a "Mr. Lion" who got her out of the Tombs in New York during World War I after her arrest on an inadequate charge of helping Indian rebels against Britain. "Mr. Lion" was actually my uncle, Gilbert E. Roe, whom she had named rather well. When my aunt, his widow, wrote Agnes Smedley about my coming to China, she replied to the effect that a Harvard-Oxford academic toff was about the last thing needed in Shanghai but she would see me if she had time. When I met her with the help of Randall Gould, editor of the Shanghai *Evening Post and Mercury,* she tested me out by dropping a few four-letter words into the conversation (an event, in those days). But it was soon evident that I really was an underdone liberal—well meaning and quite ignorant of the revolution. We liked each other's sense of humor.

Agnes was one of the great American battlers for social justice. Stockily built and square-jawed, she looked more powerful in 1932 than her ailing stomach allowed her to be. She had grown up on the bottom level of Colorado mining towns, where the American dream turned nightmare. Her father died of drink, her mother of overwork, her aunt became a prostitute. Agnes survived by sheer force of intellect and personality. Instead of getting a husband and babies, she managed to educate herself and become a journalist. The cause of Indian freedom and her Indian lover taught her a lot. A nervous breakdown in Germany and writing her autobiography (now a classic) eventually had brought her to China as correspondent for the prestigious *Frankfurter Zeitung.*

She arrived after the 1927 split in the first united front when the Chinese Communist Party was barely surviving under the KMT's white terror in the cities and was turning to Mao's rural Kiangsi base as its only hope. Her reporting put her on the KMT black list and in Shanghai she was regularly tailed and felt hunted. Our chief first impressions of Agnes were of her broad human warmth, an often earthy sense of humor, and an outspoken rebelliousness against political tyranny—also of her living in a conspiratorial world of real danger.

Of course her extraterritorial untouchability made her useful to the CCP underdogs in the current political struggle, and foreign friends like us could be very useful to her in turn. Foreigners had often figured in Chinese politics, especially when they were Mongol khans with hordes at their backs. But now extraterritoriality, which stuck to Westerners like their skins, impossible to shed, made each one a potential pawn in the domestic power struggle. For example, Agnes could not be seized and searched, and so she was an ideal letter carrier for the CCP underground.

MacArthur's G-2, General Willoughby, in his book on the Soviet's Sorge spy ring, *Shanghai Conspiracy,* reports that Agnes Smedley served as a letter drop for Sorge in Shanghai. When we met her in late 1932 she spoke repeatedly of "Lusin" (Lu Hsun), now venerated as the greatest revolutionary writer. He had moved left but stopped short of becoming a CCP member. Agnes scorned the CPUSA but was enthusiastic about the CCP. That she was an organized agent of the Comintern or any other part of the CP apparatus has always seemed to me doubtful. The main fact about her was that she was a self-starter, consumed with the injustices visible in China on every side, quite ready to help the communist cause of her own accord, and no doubt willing also to accept guidance uncritically.

Her conversation was full of the struggle and its horrors—for example, the KMT in 1931 taking five young writers and burying them alive out near the Lung-hua Pagoda (a fact). The KMT were very ingenious and could pump a mixture of kerosene and feces up your nose so that you didn't drown but swallowed a lot and your body would stink for a long time afterward. We got a new view of Shanghai, which was only heightened when we were invited to the races (in what is now the People's Park) by the American consul general, Mr. Cunningham. I recall Mrs. Cunningham wore purple furs.

Our friendship with Agnes in the winter of 1932–33 was a classic example, I suppose, of the limitations both of liberalism and of communist subversive and united-front tactics. Six weeks after we returned to our house in Peking in early November, we got an urgent query from Agnes asking if she could stay with us, so we put her in the front guest room opposite Courtenay Young. Wilma wrote on December 30:

> Just now Agnes Smedley is staying in it. She has fled incognito from Shanghai for a few weeks' rest here. Our conversations at meals all hinge on communism now with Court's "But it is not Good Form" attitude as an antidote to Agnes's withering scorn of all capitalist, imperialist and antirevolutionary phases of every subject.

Wilma reported further on January 6,

> Agnes Smedley is a very stimulating member of the household. We have long discussions and arguments on communism, the missionary movement (for which she has no use and which, lacking a social program and expending its funds and energies on fostering Good Will and other moral abstractions in the minds of a few, seems ill-adapted to coping with the elemental needs of the people of China), Soviet Russia, the situation in Germany, American strikes, and a great many

other things we don't know anything about. But we are learning something about them from the Communist-sympathizer's point of view. We listen with equal outward sympathy to communists, socialists, Legation diehards, missionaries, everybody. This satisfies John with his somewhat detached analytical point of view seeking like the true historian for a broad unbiased picture of the present China. But I am not of these and am apt to burst out into violent partisanship at any moment.

Agnes and Court, whom she baited as "the son of a lord," got on well enough. January 13 we all four went outside the Front Gate (Ch'ien Men) for a superb Chinese dinner, and then in below-zero temperature and the bright light of the full moon

> walked back on the city wall from Hatamen to the east wall nearest us, all alone in the vast moonlight. . . . So we all had some port, A's gift, and ran the Victrola and locked the servants out so we could clog dance, quite the wildest and most unrestrained orgy since we entered the house. But we got tired and went to bed at twelve.

Agnes Smedley's mission in Peking—various men came to call on her—seemed to be the setting-up of a Peking branch of the China League for Civil Rights. She got Hu Shih and the Harvard-trained anthropologist Li Chi to head it and we and a number of our Chinese academic friends later joined up.

After she went back to Shanghai we got a succession of conspiratorial messages. Her farewell note asked me to keep for her anything left for her by a Chinese friend who had come to see her.

"I wonder what you think about joining the League for Civil Rights. If you wish to do so please drop a note of application to Dr. Hu Shih or Dr. Li Chi and ask to join. But in case you do this I wish you would simultaneously get in touch with my professor friends, through my Korean friend, and carry out a common program in the League with them. Without this, the League will become utterly useless. I wish you would join. But I do not know how you feel about it."

February 1 she sent me a letter for her friend Mr. Kim. ("Write me please what your attitude is on this procedure of mine. If you do not wish it, I shall stop.") "One of them, and one alone, can have my address, the confidential one I gave you . . . give it to Mr. Kim and say that it shall not be opened until they up there decide which one of their group shall have it for correspondence with me . . . one and one alone shall have it, for I must have some means of control in case it gets out. . . . Mr. Kim shall take the envelope and discuss with his friends who shall have it. They shall decide among themselves."

This hope that I would work with a secret faction, *if* I should join the league, was then stated more explicitly: "I see by a press report that 4 Americans have joined the League up there. I . . . wonder if two come from your household. If so, I am glad. But I would suggest the procedure mentioned in my last note to you—that you carry out a common program with them. This means to hold your own group meetings to decide on the line of action to be adopted in general meetings, and to carry through the line courteously and without indication that you have reached a common decision outside. We do that here."

But then came a letter dated February 1: "Dear John, I wrote you a longer letter today and enclosed something for a friend. I asked you to give my address to others. But now I must request you not to do so. Inform them that it seems best not, as things are not so very good with my mail. . . . If you ever write me, write me directly to my home, but cut off your own address before you do so. Do not fail to do this. Sign only your first initial. I will know. Then, also, type only; do not use your handwriting to write. . . . Sincerely and with love to you both, Agnes."

In the half century since 1933 many thousand books have described secret operations. Allen Dulles, 007, Helen MacInnes, John Le Carré, various KGB and CIA defectors, even Solzhenitzin have told us how to hide our identities, send untraceable messages, and maintain secret contacts. Such knowledge has been forced upon us by Stalin, Hitler, World War II, and the Cold War. But, even allowing for this surge of sophistication since the 1930s, any spy-story reader will surely have to agree that Agnes's performance above noted was that of an amateur, and hardly a gifted one, either.

In particular, to recruit someone to work, for reasons as yet unknown, in a party-type secret faction even before he had joined the front organization itself, seems essentially romantic—a projection of tactics for their own sake, before any strategic goals were in view, pursuing form without substance. Use of the imperative "shall" is no more certain to ensure compliance at a distance than an incantation would be. Truly, with Agnes on your team you could self-destruct with no need of enemies.

Equal inefficacy dogged the liberal performance in this episode. Hu Shih and Yang Chien (Yang Ch'üan), the League for Civil Rights secretary general, demanded a look at conditions in Peking's political prisons. We had met Yang through Agnes in Shanghai. He now "came to see us with his little boy—an active and enthusiastic man."

This was in a context where human conditions in general were not very good in North China. A representative of the Society for the Prevention of Cruelty to Animals, we were told, had had a hard time concentrating on the donkeys and disregarding the men pulling beside them. Dr. Macintosh of the PUMC told us how he had been asked to visit the infirmary at the Summer Palace barracks for the Young Marshal Chang Hsueh-liang's troops. He found

> two rather small rooms with a continuous *kang* shelf-bed along opposite sides onto which were packed two hundred sick soldiers tightly wedged together. Of these about a third were suffering, among other things, softening of the eyeballs from malnutrition. Money being low they are fed almost entirely on millet, while according to Dr. Mac one egg apiece a week could save their eyesight. A large proportion of them were deathly sick with typhus and other louse-borne diseases . . . there was no attempt at delousing . . . all the rest would catch whatever diseases were present . . . no doctors or nurses were in evidence, the place being simply a concentration point for those unfit to do the camp routine. This provided a place to lie down, and it was up to them to die or recover.

How do you define and assert civil rights among cart pullers on the street and sick soldiers in barracks? The China League was a pressure group on behalf of political prisoners, who would be primarily of the student class or intelligentsia. The implicit claim was that these vestiges of the old scholar ruling class should be treated better than criminals, coolies, and soldiers. Sound enough in traditional terms.

Dr. Hu and Dr. Yang had never been prison inspectors. The conditions they saw were not too bad and they so reported. The only record I have of the dénouement is a family letter by Wilma dated February 14, 1933:

We have had only one meeting of the big group, about thirty. J. was sick but I went and sat through interminable speeches by Hu Shih and Yang Chien all in Chinese very rapidly spoken so that I had to get them translated for me for the most part by my neighbors. The following day Hu Shih and Yang Chien went to visit several prisons to see political prisoners and investigate the conditions in which they were living. The following day they published a brief report of their findings . . . that the prisoners were allowed to read and study but that the food was bad and that they resented the shackles on their feet and wished to have them removed. The prison authorities explained their use by saying that without them the expense of keeping ample guards to prevent escapes would be beyond their means. A day or two later a letter was smuggled out to Hu Shih from one of the men with whom he had talked, and signed by him, repeating these complaints and adding a few of a like nature. All this investigation gave a verifiable workable basis from which the League could proceed to try through its influence and publicity to effect reforms in treatment of political prisoners. Then a few days later a minor disaster struck us.

Agnes and the group in Shanghai issued to papers all over the country a copy of an *unsigned* letter supposedly smuggled out of one of the military prisons here and describing in detail the refinements of torture, filth, starvation etc. which make up the lives of the political prisoners there. The morning that it appeared we went to call on Hu Shih. He was very much exasperated at the whole business. The prison from which it ostensibly came was one of those he had visited and the conditions reported were entirely untrue as far as he had been able to find out through looking about him, talking to the prisoners, and through the uncensored letter which had been smuggled out to him by the wife of one of the prisoners. But since the sensational publication was authorized by the Shanghai branch of the League (calling itself the national headquarters) and was accompanied by the wild demand for unconditional release of all political prisoners all over the country, its inevitable effect was to put Hu Shih in hot water and hamper any intelligent functioning of the League in the situation here. Hu Shih's explanation of the letter was that it had been written by some of Agnes's Communist friends here as a means of working up anti-Kuomintang feeling and then handed to her, trusting her well-known ferocity at hearing of any social injustice to find publicity for it. In other words unwittingly she was being used as a tool by the Communist machine here. J. and I were inclined to believe this true. She received the letter from some of her friends while she was staying with us and brought it in a state of great excitement to John to translate for her. The running script was beyond him, but she later had it translated in Shanghai and evidently hastened to have it published before the somewhat conservative Yang Chien should return from the North and give his measured picture of the situation.

As often before, Hu Shih as liberal citizen number one in Peking was obliged to back off. In February I sent Agnes our complaint that she had disregarded the Peking branch of the league and used us for ulterior ends. My files contain only her reply: "The prison authorities, according to Yang, prepared the prison and prisoners for the investigating committee—cleaned everything and had them all sitting around in clean clothes. Nor could they speak to the prisoners without military officers hearing every word." In sum, the whole thing was staged.

The China League for Civil Rights deserves study as an attempt by liberals as individuals to counter the increasingly authoritarian efforts of the KMT government at Nanking. It was trying to destroy its opposition by repressing dissent and stifling freedom of expression. The vain effort to protect individual rights was led by the liberal residue among the supporters of the deceased Sun Yat-sen, beginning with his widow, Soong Ch'ing-ling, and the top educator in KMT ranks, Ts'ai Yuan-p'ei.

Agnes Smedley wrote me about February 14, 1933, "George Bernard Shaw arrives here Friday. Well, since we have nothing better to do, the Executive Committee of the League will talk with him for an hour at Mrs. Sun's home. I myself expect nothing from him except a few poor jokes." A photograph credited to Eastfoto shows five people in Shanghai in 1933: Agnes Smedley, George Bernard Shaw, Soong Ch'ing-ling, Ts'ai Yuan-p'ei, and Lu Hsun: in other words, an American leftist correspondent for a German paper; a Fabian socialist; Sun Yat-sen's widow, educated in Macon, Georgia; the head of Academia Sinica, trained in Chinese classics and German philosophy, who had presided over Peita in the May 4 era; and the great satirist, who had originally studied medicine in Japan. "Holy smoke!" I said when I first saw this photo a few years ago. "What a collection of people!" The two foreigners had civil liberties because of extraterritoriality. The three Chinese were protected only by their fame.*

The spark plug of the league, Dr. Yang Chien (Yang Ch'üan, Yang Hsing-fo, 1893–1933), had been briefly a pupil of Hu Shih in Shanghai about 1908. He had joined the T'ung-meng hui (Revolutionary Alliance), participated in the 1911 Revolution and been a secretary of Sun Yat-sen when he was temporarily President. In 1913 he went on a government scholarship to Cornell and then took an M.A. in business administration at Harvard in 1918. In China he was secretary of the new Science Society, 1919–22, taught at Southeastern University, joined Dr. Sun at Canton, went north with him as his secretary, and after his death in March 1925 had charge of his funeral. He then served in the KMT organization in Shanghai but in 1927 became chief assistant to Ts'ai Yuan-p'ei. When Academia Sinica was set up in 1928 as China's central research organization directly under the Nationalist government, Ts'ai was its first president and Yang Chien its secretary general.

In 1932, under the impact of Japan's seizure of the industrial base in Manchuria, there was an unavailing effort on the part of several Westernized supporters of the KMT to damp down the bitter all-or-nothing struggle between the two Leninist parties (KMT and CCP) created during the Nationalist Revolution of the 1920s. These people

*Since writing the above I have found this photo indeed suffered from holy smoke. As originally taken by Yang Chien in Mme. Sun's house it showed two other luncheon guests on right and left of the hostess, namely Harold Isaacs and the writer Lin Yu-t'ang, both also members of the executive committee of the league. They appear in the original now hanging in the Lu Hsun museum in Shanghai. But the airbrushed version is more widely known. See for example, Fairbank, Reischauer, Craig, *East Asia: Tradition and Transformation*, p. 794; most recently, *China Pictorial*, No. 11 (1980), p. 40. Harold Isaacs is writing his own account of why he was made into a nonperson.

expressed the widespread view that all Chinese should unite against the invader. During the five-week undeclared Shanghai war of January-March 1932 (when I arrived there) Yang Chien had worked with Soong Ch'ing-ling to set up a hospital for the wounded. In October 1932 Yang Chien, Ts'ai Yuan-p'ei, Lin Yu-t'ang and others protested against the arrest of Ch'en Tu-hsiu, who had been dean of letters at Peita before he headed the infant CCP in 1921–27 and after his expulsion became a Trotskyite.

Many Chinese tried to foster political unity in the crisis of the early 1930s, but the KMT-CCP split set the tone. Liberals were pulverized in between. Agnes Smedley wrote me in early February 1933 from Shanghai:

"I am glad that you met this friend Yang of mine from here. He is one of the most amiable and active persons in China; and he is one of the most cunning. He has been a friend of mine since I came to China, but I could no more make it a real friendship than I could with a fox. I decided this once after I left my room and returned to find him searching my desk, and then smilingly turning the subject and talking merrily. Wherever he goes he tries to ferret out every person I know, and why. I work with him, but treat him as I would a porcupine, as I said. That is, I keep at good distance from him. I smile and he smiles. So that is that."

In mid-February she wrote, "The detectives have been taken off my house and they have been put on Dr. Tsai Yuan-p'ei and Yang Chien! I laugh myself sick at the thought of it. Dr. Tsai having a detective following after him!"

In May the talented writer Ting Ling was abducted by the KMT. She was given the kerosene-and-feces treatment but lived to report it and indeed be victimized again in the Cultural Revolution. Yang Chien tried in vain to get her released. Anonymous letters warned him to stop impeding the anti-CCP campaign.

About 8:45 A.M. on Sunday, June 18, 1933, Yang Chien and his elder son got in their car in front of an Academia Sinica office in Shanghai. Four or five gunmen opened fire and killed Yang instantly. The report was that "policemen near the scene of the murder gave chase and brought down one of the assassins, Kuo Te-tsung, who then committed suicide."* One is reminded of how Lee Harvey Oswald

---

*H. L. Boorman and R. C. Howard, *Biographical Dictionary of Republican China,* vol. 4, p. 6.

had suicide committed for him. Obviously the police had been in on the job. The League for Civil Rights blamed Yang's murder on the government but had no way to prove it.

Looking back on these events I had largely forgotten, including Agnes Smedley's letters, I am struck with the impenetrability of Chinese politics, which were quite beyond my ken or even attention at the time. But there is one striking motif in China's modern history: the demonstration effect of putting away the leader of a potentially troublesome opposition movement. It might be called the political mode of teaching by negative example. Thus when young Sung Chiao-jen originally put together the KMT and won the parliamentary elections of 1913, the president (Yuan Shih-k'ai) had him assassinated. When the ex-KMT politician Lei Chen, editor of *Free China*, tried to organize an opposition party in Taiwan in 1960, he was ostentatiously railroaded into ten years in jail. When Wei Jing-sheng advocated freedom of expression at Democracy Wall in Peking in 1979, a court solemnly gave him fifteen years. The formula: wait for a recognized leader to emerge, then knock him off—this fits Yang Chien's assassination. His mentor Ts'ai Yuan-p'ei soon retired from public life. The event represented Chiang Kai-shek's decision, just as the sudden cashiering of the head of the Library of Congress or the Smithsonian would require a presidential decision in Washington.

The explanation of Yang Chien's assassination put about in Peking was that he had been involved with a woman. This invoked the ancient syndrome: morality supersedes legality; the law should not protect immorality; immoral conduct should be punished; therefore (by the no-smoke-without-fire rule) punishment indicates prior immoral conduct. After Lei Chen was railroaded in 1960, an esteemed Chinese academic said to me, "But you know, he was not a good man. He made love with the wife of the librarian." How fortunate it is, for American politicians and the wives of American librarians too, to live under law, not morality!

Agnes Smedley wrote Wilma from Leningrad March 20, 1934, "You say China needs an enlightened dictatorship like this country. This is an iron Communist dictatorship, and I think the only ones who could give such to China would be the Communists. Anything else would be Fascist, which would only fight for things that are, prolonging the agony of the people. What China needs is not peace, as you say, for that is the peace of death for the masses. It needs war—war to the finish. Until the last shred of slavery and subjection is wiped out. Peace today would benefit no human being except the handful of exploiters at the top, and the foreigners.

"There are many kinds of mistakes and undesirable things in this world, and the greatest of them all is the system that rules most of the world today. And, also, all the writers who accept the outlook of that system, defend it, tolerate it, fight for it."

Her commitment to rebellion blazed high as usual, but added to it was belief in the evil of one system and faith in the salvation to be found in the other. She had given us a copy of Bukharin's *Historical Materialism: A System of Sociology* (translated from the third Russian edition, International Publishers, 1925), "with the hope that this book will help you improve your minds, if any." It would be another four years before Bukharin would be executed by Stalin as an Old Bolshevik who had gone astray.

In Shanghai in November 1934 Agnes came to see us, back from Moscow but worn down by living in a constant state of anxiety. Her second book, *China's Red Army Marches* (1934) tried to give the Western public a picture of the CCP's revolutionary cause in rural China, just as Edgar Snow's *Red Star over China* (1938) would later do to a larger audience. But Agnes was distinctly more propagandist than journalist, while Ed seemed to me the other way round.

I saw Agnes Smedley again in the late forties but she died in England in 1950. Her several books on the Chinese revolution are still of value.

6

HAROLD ISAACS AND THE TERROR

IF WE LEARNED about dedicated fellow travelers from Agnes Smedley, we learned something quite different from Harold Isaacs. Where she was willing to be used in what she considered a common righteous cause, Harold was a journalist who tried to report the factual events of the KMT terror against the CCP.

Since Harold Isaacs is alive and well and living in Newton, Massachusetts—also eloquent as usual and a professor emeritus at MIT—let me not try to encapsulate him. Wilma and I learned a lot about the Chinese Revolution from him at second hand, after he had learned about it in Shanghai at first hand.

Harold's China experience began at age twenty when he left his solid middle-class family in New York to see the world. He became a reporter or editor for two Shanghai newspapers, the American-owned *Evening Post* and the Chinese-owned *China Press*. After his first brush with Shanghai realities, he and a friend, a South African Marxist, Frank Glass, took a trip up the Yangtze into Szechwan.

The year 1931 saw the great Yangtze flood. As the dikes were topped or washed out, the flood spread a few inches of water over enormous areas of farmland, threatening the starvation of many millions. An international effort was mounted to help China, whose disaster was made more tangible to American newspaper readers when Charles and Anne Morrow Lindbergh came to fly over and survey it.

It has always been my conviction that Harold Isaacs, despite his bourgeois origins, comes in fact from a long line of minor prophets. His experience of 1931 gave him a sort of enlightenment, a perception of China's plight and of a possible way of salvation, a condition that lasted about three years in his Shanghai contact with the Chinese Communists. The basic fact is, as I was to discover twelve years later, that one cannot understand a revolutionary situation unless one gets at least a whiff of the heady faith of the revolutionaries. As Harold said in 1974, "The effects of all these exposures, the shocks, the encounters, the learning of that year came together for me not long thereafter when Communist friends and friends of Communists I met in Shanghai suggested the possibility of my starting up a paper of my own. I took them up with alacrity and the result was the *China Forum.*"*

When Agnes introduced us to Harold in Shanghai in November 1932 we met his very pretty wife Viola as "Miss Robinson" and discovered only later that far from living in sin they had been college sweethearts and were duly married on her arrival.

The *China Forum* was one man's achievement in recording a somber slice of history. The *China Weekly Review* and other Shanghai organs covered the general news of the day and so did the *Forum*. But it specialized in publishing translations of leftist short stories and reporting the facts of the disappearances, extraditions, imprisonments, and executions that Shanghai's KMT and Green Gang underground were visiting upon the remnants of the CCP. The young Communist leaders were mainly intellectuals and their best troops, after Chiang Kai-shek's smashing of the CCP labor unions, were young writers seeking to create a literature of the revolution.

Harold published thirty-nine issues of the *China Forum* during about two years, in circumstances that only he can adequately describe. The facts came from many sources; some were funneled to him, and he had the journalist's task of trying to verify details before publishing them. The *China Forum* for readers outside Shanghai had to be smuggled across the boundary or through the Chinese post office in plain wrappers and in other forms. Inside foreign-run Shanghai, the International Settlement and the French Concession, Harold

---

*Harold R. Isaacs, ed., *Straw Sandals: Chinese Short Stories 1918–1933*, introduction, p. xxviii.

was protected by his American extraterritoriality even though the consul general regarded him as a dangerous red. The Shanghai Municipal Council saw its bread buttered on the KMT side and in two years extradited more than three hundred Chinese accused as Communists into the hands of the KMT executioners. Printing shops that helped produce the *China Forum* were scared off. Harold worked with CCP helpers whose identities he seldom knew. He was an isolated and marked man but he accomplished his purpose, to give voice to the oppressed, up to the inevitable moment when he refused to distort the facts as he saw them and the whole operation collapsed.

In April 1934 Harold and Viola moved to Peking and became for more than a year our close neighbors in a house Wilma found for them at No. 1 Ta Yang Yi Pin Hutung. (We were at No. 10.) They brought with them Harold's translator-assistant and a thousand pages of rare documentation, from which emerged a classic, *The Tragedy of the Chinese Revolution*, published in London in 1938 with a foreword by Leon Trotsky. This study of the tortuous course of the KMT-CCP united front of the 1920s was a tour de force in contemporary history, which established a major interpretation of the CCP disaster in 1927 as due to Stalin's cynical readiness to sacrifice the Chinese Revolution for his own political needs in combatting Trotsky. It is the if-only story of a might-have-been. By it a whole wing of the young Chinese movement tried to explain the débacle to their hopes which historians now generally see as having been pretty hard to avoid in any case: the CCP and China were simply not meant for each other in the 1920s. Several things—a rural base, an army, a bigger organization—would have been necessary for success against the city-based Nationalist movement of those years, no matter what strategies the nascent CCP might have adopted. The might-have-beens, however, are still in dispute.

The final disillusion that emerged from the record was the probability that the five martyred young writers of 1931 (see p. 68) had actually been part of a larger group, along with nineteen others who were the outgoing CCP leadership. The incoming CCP leadership group newly arrived from Moscow apparently tipped off the KMT, betrayed their rival comrades, and so got rid of them and acquired martyrs to agitate about, both at once.

Harold was a great admirer of Trotsky and went to see him in Norway. But you couldn't call him a Trotskyite. He remained always

an Isaacs, slightly scornful in a friendly way of my academic pursuits
in history remote from the vital issues of the moment. His confrontation with the foibles of humanity kept on expanding as he cast a fresh
eye on one problem after another. In World War II he went back to
China as a war correspondent for *Newsweek*. Later *Scratches on Our
Minds: American Images of India and China* was a fruitful pioneering study of national stereotypes. He wrote other studies, of black
Americans *(The New World of Negro Americans)*, of ethnic minorities *(Idols of the Tribe)*, and the like, as a staff member of the MIT
Center for International Studies. Inevitably he became a Ph.D.-less
professor at MIT, still rather arrogantly anti-academic and an inspiration to a lot of students.

In June 1934 we and the Isaacs, two couples, all wearing shorts
(knee-length), made a trip from Peking to Ch'eng-te, capital of Jehol
province, which the Japanese army had seized a few months before.
Wilma negotiated with the Japanese legation, who said visas could
come only from the government of Manchukuo. But in the end she
got a letter from the Japanese military attaché. Loaded with a few
blankets, cameras, and nonperishable food supplies, we boarded a
Japanese-run open Dodge truck at 6 A.M. and rode on top of our
luggage all day in the blazing sun. By nightfall we formed a jellyfish-
like mass lying unabashedly all over each other. At Kupeikou ("the
old north pass"), north and a bit east of Peking at the Great Wall, we
ran into the Japanese military border post. Wilma was deputed to act
while the rest of us feigned no knowledge of anything but English.
"I was thus favored," she wrote, "because of my ability to be stupid
and insistent." The border officials said we must stay overnight,
"shunting me off finally to their superior officer who was at the end
of a long dusty uphill walk at the other side of town with dugouts and
armed guards along the way." Finally we all clambered up another
side of the town to see another general and get our passes.

From there on, Jehol proved to be all sharp, jagged mountains,
range after range, "like a stormy sea," except for some high flat
valleys making an occasional saucer surrounded by peaks. We found
Ch'eng-te's main street lined with shops, lights all ablaze at 9 P.M.,
an army town, with officers' limousines threading their way among
the trucks. Japanese girls had been imported to maintain the officers'
standard of living in the brothels.

At the Catholic mission Père Canard welcomed us warmly,

though he had not expected us; he accepted our gift of brandy and offered us his own wine, bread, and cheese. His gray beard flowing down over his Chinese gown, he spoke an eloquent mixture of English, French, and Chinese. During his first thirty years in the mission he said he had spoken only Dutch to his superior, but now all his languages were getting confused together. What a witty, urbane individual he was! with a broad understanding of men and affairs that we had not found in many Protestant missionaries.

Having become briefly a correspondent for the London *Daily Express,* Harold picked up many insights into the Japanese occupation. Their installing of roads, railways, public utilities, and hospitals was giving work to many people, their police kept order, and there was a bustle of progress. At the same time they continued the old warlord policy of taxing farmland so heavily that only by growing poppies could farmers meet the taxes. We saw whole vistas of white opium poppies and discussed with the cultivators their technique for slitting the seed pod in the heart of each flower and for several days collecting the few drops that daily emerged. Their opium supply helped the Japanese program of narcotizing North China. Japan sought not only revenue, as the British raj had done in selling Indian opium to China until 1917, or as Chiang Kai-shek was currently doing with Szechwan opium brought down the Yangtze to Shanghai. We felt the Japanese also had a political purpose.

After we had seen the local sights for three days, Wilma found a white-toothed smiling boatman named Hao who would take us down the Luan River. Our five days in his seven-by-twenty-foot boat were an adventure.

The crew consisted of Hao, his cousin named Hao, and a mangy boy-of-all-work, in his teens but unmarried because as Hao explained, "he didn't have any money so nobody would give him a wife." They worked the boat fore and aft in the sometimes strong current, seldom using the sail, while we four centered on the flat bottom, watching the spectacular mountain scenery slip by. The Luan River sometimes churns through gorges like a small Yangtze, and all day we passed teams of naked boat trackers laboriously plodding along the shore path, hauling boats like ours and many bigger ones back up the stream. The crew cooked their millet twice a day in a big iron wok over a charcoal brazier, and we used the same equipment for our own messes of mixed rice, eggs, bacon, and raisins, washed down with tea and cocoa.

Every day we found a clear tributary stream where Wilma and Viola managed to bathe out of sight. At night we simply tied up on shore and made hip holes for sleeping on the sand. Sometimes we awoke to find a silent assembly of peasants sitting or standing at a respectful distance to have a look at us. As *mao-tzu* ("hairy people," foreigners) Harold and I were already showing signs of that migration of hair which soon would leave us uncovered on top, where civilized Chinese hair belongs, and more fully insulated on the chest, legs, and arms—not as fully of course as dogs, horses, cows, or goats but certainly tending in their direction. From the local point of view we were far more remarkable than Jo-jo the Dog-faced Boy that I remember gawking at in the Sioux Falls carnival. If unshaved, hair would even take over our faces.

Wilma and Viola on the other hand were obviously shaped like Chinese wet nurses yet denied having any children. Their hair was not black and seemed to curl of itself. They looked overprepared for dealing with babies, had enormous feet, and acted like men, quite without inhibitions. What a peculiar combination of qualities!

Hao had many questions for us. "How many wives do you have in your country? Only one? But how can she get all the work done?" "How many wives do your officials have?" "What does it cost to get married?" One night, seeking folklore, we asked him about the bright firmament of stars. "Yes," he replied, "I have already seen them." Our toothbrushing interested him. Why didn't he do it? "I don't have much spare time," he said.

One stop was at his native village. Everyone was named Hao, the wives having been secured from other villages. His own house was spotless and held seventeen people, who slept on the flue-heated brick beds *(k'ang)* in four rooms. "No wonder," I noted, "that they marry off the children at the earliest possible age."

We left Mr. Hao's boat at Luan-chou, entrained to Peitaiho, the foreigners' coastal summer resort, and found at East Cliff Mrs. John D. Hayes, who alleviated our undernourishment with two loaves of bread and strawberry jam. Japanese guards had searched our luggage as we came through the Great Wall onto the North China plain. But, considering the recent Sino-Japanese hostilities, our trip was still another triumph for our old friend and protector, extraterritoriality. One of the civil liberties of foreigners under the unequal treaties was the right to travel.

In March 1935 Harold's year-long collaborator "Liu" with his wife and two small children left to entrain for the South but were arrested at Peking station when a baggage search found CCP pamphlet materials. Liu had been overconfident. Harold was distraught. After several days he succeeded in getting the wife and children released through representations via Ida Pruitt from the Chinese administrator of PUMC. But Liu's fate remained a mystery. He had no extraterritoriality. Later it appeared that he was released from prison in the Japanese war that began in 1937. We were reminded again how our foreigners' privileged status let us observe close at hand the agonies of Chinese who lacked our good fortune.

7

T. F. TSIANG AND MODERNIZATION

WHEN I MET T. F. Tsiang through Charles Webster's introduction, I had no idea of his career up to that point, or of the pioneer he was in Chinese historical studies. I was intent on reading the Chinese diplomatic documents whose publication he had superintended. I can see now how my own self-absorbed and limited pioneering fitted quite naturally into his broader situation.

To call on T. F. Tsiang I caught the bus at the YMCA on Hatamen Street and rode for an hour across the city through the West Single Arch and Western Four Arches to the northern gate on the west side, Hsi Chih Men. Thence a paved road led out five miles toward the Summer Palace. The Western Hills were visible beyond by the time we reached the campus wall of Yenching University and turned east a mile to reach Tsing Hua University. We passed the ruins of Yuan Ming Yuan, the old summer palace destroyed in the Anglo-French invasion of 1860.

Tsing Hua, set up after 1908, was some fifteen years older than Yenching. Its site had been a princely estate. Its buildings were a mixture of Chinese and foreign and could not rival the fresh symmetry and neo-palace style that the Yale architect Henry Killam Murphy had devised out of modern cement and traditional tile roofs for Yenching. He had even put the Yenching water tower inside a cement pagoda! (The old Yenching campus forms about one-quarter of the big Peking University of today.)

Yenching under President J. Leighton Stuart was the bellwether of the dozen Christian colleges while Tsing Hua was a national government university that already rivaled Peking University (Peita) within the city. After the rendition of some American Boxer indemnity funds in 1908, Tsing Hua had started sending students to the United States in 1909. The thousand or so who had been thus trained were scattered through Nationalist China's universities and government agencies. But American students coming in a reverse flow for training in China were very few.

Professor Tsiang was no doubt flattered when Charles Webster sent me to him, but a grownup student who could speak and read only like a child was something of a problem, rather like having a fully grown but unhousebroken St. Bernard pup on your hands. What do you do with him? All I could offer was promises, but I arranged to buy a set of the documents photolithographed by the Palace Museum, *A Complete Account of the Management of Barbarian Affairs (Ch'ou-pan i-wu shih-mo).* Twenty years later I would still be working on them while teaching my seminar students how to do it.

T. F. Tsiang (Chiang T'ing-fu, 1895–1965) when I met him was thirty-six and already the leader in study of China's modern history. He was of medium height, the round-faced type of Chinese, handsome because of his quick intelligence. His dynamic wife had gone to both Vassar and Bryn Mawr. He told me he owed his start to an American Presbyterian woman teacher in Hunan who helped him to study English as a teen-ager in 1906–11 and then to seek higher education in the United States. Since he left some memoirs for the Columbia Oral History Project, I can understand T. F. Tsiang in retrospect more fully than I could in 1932.

As a talented child he had come under heavy family pressure to become a scholar and win gentry status. He dutifully tried but in the process became Americanized. His teacher (Mrs. Jean Lingle) became almost an adoptive mother, and he became a sincere Christian, very strongly oriented toward the West. He reached San Francisco all alone, age seventeen, but Mrs. Lingle had arranged for him to enter a small self-help school, Park College in Parkville, Missouri. He completed his college preparation there while also learning to do manual work on the farm, mow the grass, and wash clothes, to pay his way like the American students. Then he went to Oberlin

1914–18 and in 1919 spent a year as a YMCA secretary with the Chinese labor corps in France.

Returning to enter graduate school at Columbia, he became a very active student leader, editing *Christian China,* writing on current issues and discussing how "social Christianity" could be "Chinaized" to meet his country's needs. Here two patterns overlapped— the Chinese scholar speaking out, the American liberal sounding off. When the Versailles peacemakers left Japan in possession of Shantung province in 1919, T. F. Tsiang's equivalent of Peking's May 4 patriotic demonstration was to go on a speaking tour in the United States. He was caught up in the surge of nationalism.

In the face of the anti-imperialist movement in April 1922, alas, the Protestant missions in China set an all-time record for obtuse nonsalesmanship by publishing a book entitled not *Christian Help to China* but *The Christian Occupation of China!* It was full of militant maps and statistics and was so utterly foreign-minded it was a real giveaway. It must have made a lot of Chinese Christians feel they had been had. From this time, T. F. Tsiang, like others, became less concerned about Christianity for China, more concerned about national rights.

He began his Columbia Ph.D. in political science. But the abstractness of political theory turned him off and he shifted to Modern European History under Carlton J. H. Hayes. He wanted a "knowledge of politics as it was actually played."*

After eleven formative years abroad T. F. Tsiang returned in 1923 to teach at Nankai University, the remarkable institution built up by Chang Po-ling at Tientsin. As has only recently been revealed, he was invited partly through the operation of CCH (Ch'eng-chih hui, an association for the "realization of one's ambitions"). This was the most effective of several secret brotherhoods organized by Chinese students abroad. Chang Po-ling and several other Nankai professors were members. During their student years abroad they gathered in summer retreats and gave one another moral as well as practical support. Maybe American liberals have something to learn: young

---

*T. F. Tsiang's *Memoirs,* p. 3 in chapter 9, quoted in Charles Lilley, "Tsiang T'ing-fu Between Two Worlds, 1895–1935," University of Maryland Ph.D. dissertation, 1979, p. 130, also p. 251.

men going back to remake warlord China in the 1920s needed all the mutual help they could get. Once in action, they found they could teach what they had learned about the West, but about China they had little knowledge, few sources to use, no textbooks in Chinese, hardly any reference materials, and not much chance for research.

With his usual realism T. F. Tsiang spotted very soon the great gap between American education and China's problems. The returned students were trained to be progressive-minded American reformers, believers in Deweyan pragmatism. But, he said, "we are ignorant about the things that affect our daily lives, and we neither know their causes nor the conditions surrounding the causes." Chinese professors of local government "know about the governments of New York and Paris, but they are almost entirely ignorant of the governments of Peiping, Hankow and Chengtu."

In 1929 T. F. Tsiang moved to Tsing Hua University as head of the History Department. Under the Nationalist government Tsing Hua was being reorganized and built up. It had the enormous advantage of an assured regular income of about $400,000 from the remitted Boxer indemnity funds. T. F. created a course structure to provide instruction on major areas of Asia and include graduate seminar training. Like Charles Webster he saw historical knowledge as the handmaiden of diplomacy and peace among nations. He was eager to build up the Chinese side of the record, to get beyond Dr. Morse's "bluebook history," based mainly on British sources as the only ones available. T. F. was appalled to find how ignorant the Manchu court had been in 1842 about who the British were and what they wanted. They had hardly known what they were doing. T. F. already had several young men in training to specialize in different sectors of China's foreign relations. He contributed articles to British and American journals demonstrating what the new Chinese documents could offer.

This vigorous development of Chinese research, like so many achievements of others in his generation, was menaced by Japan's aggressive seizure of Manchuria in September 1931. The issue thenceforth was not how to progress but how to survive. When the British medievalist R. H. Tawney *(Religion and the Rise of Capitalism)* visited China in 1931 to write his classic *Land and Labour in China,* he advocated a program of modernization to create a Chinese state capable of preserving itself. Coming a decade after John Dewey, Tawney gave fresh support to the American-returned scholars like T. F. Tsiang, who believed in change by gradualism, not cataclysm. Tawney urged the piecemeal buildup of a modern state emanating from the core area of the Lower Yangtze. This meant through the Nanking government of the KMT, which had begun as a Cantonese regional regime and had never been very potent or popular in North China. The Nanking-Shanghai area must play the role of Prussia in Germany and Piedmont in Italy, and the implied leader was Chiang Kai-shek. Tawney was in China also as a League of Nations adviser on education, and his report laid out a panoply of weaknesses and suggested remedies. Between his two writings on the economy and on education he set forth the full agenda of what from this time began to be called "modernization" *(chin-tai hua)*. Tawney's prescriptions of 1931 are very close, poignantly close, to China's Four Modernizations of fifty years later.

Thus inspired, T. F. Tsiang's prescriptions began with genuine land reform and wound up with the remaking of the Chinese personality. To him, the problem lay not in seeing what to do but in getting it done. He came out for strong, even dictatorial leadership, such as only Chiang Kai-shek could supply. In 1934 Chiang asked T. F. on his leave in Europe to go to Moscow and sound out the Soviets on possible help against Japan. T. F. Tsiang spent his 1934–35 leave partly in Moscow and partly in London. Charles Webster wrote me (November 2, 1935): "We enjoyed his visit very much. He made a deep impression here and taught many more about the real background of Chinese politics than they had ever known before. We are looking forward to printing his excellent lecture in *Politica.* You will have seen his address at Chatham House."

In this address* T. F. Tsiang sketched the ideological collapse in China since the turn of the century. "Confucianism torn apart from monarchy is like a flying buttress without the cathedral walls to make it functionally useful." He saw how China's modern-educated scholars had brought together a potpourri of political ideas from foreign and Chinese sources, ancient and modern, and achieved no consensus. Western liberalism had been adopted by many like himself just

---

*"The present situation in China," *International Affairs* (July 14, 1935).

when it was losing its paramount position in the West. Marxism, fascism, and old Chinese ideas contributed to ideological disunity. Moreover, the returned students' ideas seldom took account of Chinese realities. "We have sinned in living apart from the people. . . . We read foreign books and are engrossed in things in which the people have no interest. . . . [We can be] eloquent in the class room, in the Press in Shanghai and Peiping, even come to Chatham House and make you think we are intelligent, and yet we cannot make ourselves understood to a village crowd in China, far less make ourselves accepted as leaders of the peasants." Even so, T. F. Tsiang concluded, "history has made the intellectual class the leaders of the Chinese people and we have no intention of abdicating."

This basic belief was made urgent by the persistent Japanese encroachment on China: in 1931 seizing Manchuria, in 1932 setting up the state of Manchukuo, in 1933 taking Jehol province, in 1934 infiltrating the Tientsin-Peking area, in 1935 trying to detach all North China. It was a time for action.

In December 1935 Chiang invited T. F. into the government. He never got back to academic life. Dr. Tsiang wrote me on December 21, 1935, from the Political Affairs Office of the Executive Yuan in Nanking: "You probably were surprised by my change of work. I had no idea of a change when I left Peiping for Nanking. But when I found that the position offered me was one of importance, through which much can be done, I accepted. It is what the French would call chef de cabinet politique, with seat in cabinet meetings. The work is very miscellaneous, some routine while others extremely critical. Dr. Wong [Weng Wen-hao], the geologist, who holds the position of Secretary-General, and I are the two political watch-dogs for the General in his capacity as Head of Executive Yuan.

"As life I much prefer being professor. When I recall the leisure, the books, and the writings connected with teaching, my tears sometimes drop. Here is rush from morning to evening. Many inconsiderate people waste my time by refusing to speak to the point. Job-hunters simply drive me mad. One morning, one fellow rushed into my room at 7 and shouted, 'Here you are. I haven't seen you for 20 years.' He turned out to be a classmate of elementary school. Fellow-provincials, schoolmates in China and U.S.A., students from Nankai, Tsing Hua, and Peita all think I owe them jobs. But my office is already over-crowded by clerks. I can do better work by dropping half of them. Then my boss is against indiscriminate discharge of public servants. He wishes to give security of tenure to all public servants who are doing well. In this respect, he is even more modern than American presidents.

"I am much afraid I shall not see you and Mrs. F. before your departure for U.S.A. But don't let our geographical and professional separation interrupt our relations. Somehow I hope we will always remain intimate friends."

In 1933 after Wilma and I had spent a year in Peking but run out of funds, T. F. gave me my first teaching job, instructing at Tsing Hua. When I returned to Peking in 1972 at Chou En-lai's invitation, I was invited one morning to address ninety men and women who I believe were mainly from the Foreign Office. I opened by saying that I could not proceed without acknowledging my debt as a student to my teacher, T. F. Tsiang, who before his recent twenty-year defiance of the People's Republic as the Nationalist Chinese ambassador on the Security Council of the UN had once been professor of history at Tsing Hua. This was a cheeky opening, on the top floor of the Peking Hotel in 1972. But I figured my audience were Chinese first, Communists second, and I think I was correct.

Modernization to strengthen China against Japan's aggression was the cause in which T. F. Tsiang and others supported the KMT government at Nanking. This cause, as it turned out, could not stop short of remaking peasant life upon the land. In late 1934, en route to Shanghai, Wilma and I saw some of the modernizing efforts under way in the countryside around Nanking, where we stayed in early November with Andy and Margaret Roy at the American Presbyterian mission.

With his usual enthusiasm Andy took us on bicycles into the countryside to see Frank Price's rural project that sent students of the Presbyterian Theological Seminary into fifty villages. Their urgent aim, I noted, was

> to get acquainted with the farmers, improve their agriculture, and on the rebound win them for Christ. Like all such things it must start slowly: the Berkshire boar in the back yard of the station is so tremendous that no non-Christian farmers have yet had enough faith to let their little lady pigs be put into the same pen with it.

Before we found Frank Price we came upon two symbols of what he was up against—two stone lions of the Liang dynasty (A.D. 502–557)

> standing up to their knees in a rice field as natural as life. We went over and got acquainted with their wings, bulbous eyes, gaping mouths, kangaroo-like tails and general point of view —really admirable creatures, and ancient as you could ask, older than France and Germany at any rate.

They suggested the fifty villages, where the agronomically-untrained theological students were now active, had some continuity behind them.

We also got a glimpse of the Nanking government's effort to modernize administration. George Taylor, who had come to Harvard from England on a Commonwealth fellowship and then to Yenching with Harvard-Yenching support, was now teaching at Chiang Kai-shek's Central Political Institute for training administrators. He showed us through the Spartan spick-and-span barracks, eight men in a room in double-deck bunks. The regimen filled each day with training for discipline. A similar school trained army officers. The Officers' Moral Endeavor Association tried to inspire the officer corps. Chiang's New Life Movement tried to spread this Confucian-fascist amalgam of discipline and loyalty to the urban masses. In areas of Kiangsi recovered from the Communists, missionaries were being asked to help, though they found rural poverty there so great that little morality could be implanted.

At dinner at Bill Fenn's (then head of the English Department at Nanking University) along with Frank Price, Andy Roy asked

> a question I had asked of Andy—whether helping the Nanking government to rehabilitate rural China by cooperatives, bet-ter cropping, irrigation, and education would not be more or less useless so long as the Nanking government remained the representative [as we then thought it was] of Shanghai bankers and big landlords, and a growing middle class which would never give up but rather tend to increase their share of the country's wealth.
>
> Frank Price held out for doing what can be done under the only government that now holds any promise of remaining

strong—in power, able to control local despots and build the machinery of government, with the roads and education necessary to any sort of progress.

While we were talking, though we didn't know it, 100,000 troops and followers of the hard-pressed CCP were battling their way out of Kiangsi province on the beginning of their Long March to the Northwest. They had their own ideas about China's modernization.

8

BECOMING A SPECIALIST;
TEACHING AT TSING HUA

HOW DO YOU get started in a field that doesn't yet exist? The answer is, of course, that the field is there all the time; you have only to recognize and proclaim its existence. As our neighbor in New Hampshire used to say, "There are wells in all these hills, if you just dig for them." Part of my task was to dig out the Chinese record in order to create a more adequate view of modern Chinese history.

For this purpose I had no teacher. Despite my cordial personal relations with T. F. Tsiang, I never was his student formally or received his instruction in a lecture course or seminar. My Chinese was then inadequate, and I had trouble understanding his Hunan accent. I saw him occasionally, lunched at his house, and got his help in a number of ways, but they were not pedagogical. This was part of a larger pattern.

If I had been properly trained, I could never have put together the combination of approaches I made to China. Language training would have taken all my time. So would thesis research in a well-developed field. I would never have had time for first-hand "area" experience through casual travel. My combination of approaches was possible only because I was entirely on my own, not under anyone's direction.

The Oxford D. Phil. degree had no language requirement because any young gentleman would of himself "get up" the languages he needed. The two-year program of the College of Chinese Studies, which Courtenay Young and I with our headstarts completed in a year or so, was mainly for speech, certainly not for research. So we tapped the reservoir of experienced teachers known to our legation friends and had lessons also at home: two teachers, each for an hour, in the morning and a third in the late afternoon. With them we wasted no time and used dictionaries.

In 1931 the China Inland Mission put out Mathew's *Chinese-English Dictionary,* still widely used, which updated others, including H. A. Giles's big second edition of his *Chinese-English Dictionary* of 1912. I found Giles of most use for nineteenth-century Ch'ing documents because as a consular officer he had included many late Ch'ing documentary terms. I bought a copy from my long-term legation friend, Lieutenant Haydon Boatner (later a major general and famous in Burma and Korea). Giles was the size of a family Bible and served me as one.

The memorials and edicts by which the Ch'ing government did its business were far more efficient than Western diplomatic documents. Surname first and given names second, which we resort to in our own phone books and bibliographies, where order really counts, are the normal Chinese order. No need to change Joseph E. Simpleton to Simpleton, Joseph E. So too a memorial begins with the memorialist's name. No need to turn to the end of the document to see who is "your obedient servant." His degree of obedience is expressed in the character following his name, which indicates the type of document he is transmitting as from a subordinate, an equal, or a superior. Chinese documents were for official action, even if it was only inaction. Every character counted. Dating, quotation, and manner of transmission were meticulously indicated, and when someone wanted to be vague, he could do it in spades.

As I hardly realized at the time, I was getting in on the ground floor of a new historical industry. Of forty-three published collections of Ch'ing documents that I eventually listed for my students (in *Ch'ing Documents: An Introductory Syllabus,* 3rd edition, 1970), thirty-nine were published in 1930 or later. Photolithography made possible facsimile reproduction. I happened to turn up at the opportune moment when this flood of thousands of pages was just beginning. Today it is still accelerating from both Taipei and Peking.

The result of having no teacher was that I never really graduated. The continual publication of more documents kept on expanding the subject matter awaiting attention. It was a constantly new world.

In my third year in Peking I engaged as teacher Mr. Kuo Yu-hsiu, a thin scholar-gentleman of the old school who had served in some of the many offices of the Peking government and was willing in hard times, for a price, to consort with a foreign student. We took him for the summer of 1934 to live in a mill on a mill stream in the mission-ary-haunted valley of the Yü-tao ho. This stream was near Fenchow on the north side of the plain beyond Taiyuan in Shansi province. The mill had been leased by Dr. A. W. Hummel, director of the Orientalia Division of the Library of Congress, who kindly lent it to us. Mr. Kuo manfully arose at dawn to read documents with me and later made me vocabulary cards enshrining Giles's Victorian phraseology. He found the local Shansi peasant dialect incredible. His eyes would enlarge behind his glasses as he repeated things he had heard, "like the twittering of birds." But he was at heart a raconteur. Over wine after dinner he would wax eloquent about the Empress Dowager, her extravagant tastes and vicious ways. He stopped short of the eschatology purveyed by that talented trickster Sir Edmund Backhouse (uncovered by Hugh Trevor-Roper in *Hermit of Peking*), who was a still-living legend hidden away in the West City. But short of getting our palace lore from Sir Edmund, we were supplied very well by Mr. Kuo. His later stories about us must have been truly marvelous to hear.

Documents were the most elementary materials for China's modern history, easy to read because so procedural and full of stereotypes, usually concerned with incidents and action. Those of the mid-nineteenth century gave a fascinating Chinese view of the British invaders, their red hair, blue eyes, beak noses, and barbaric customs. Yet, if I had been undergoing a proper classical training, it would have been years before I got onto this bonanza.

In 1932 as I approached the end of support from the Rhodes trust, I began to discern the structure of American academic studies of China. I discovered a curious bifurcation between Harvard and the rest of the United States, a source of strength and also of problems. I found that the Harvard-Yenching Institute in Cambridge had been set up in 1928 by a concordat between two great academic entrepreneurs: President J. Leighton Stuart of the new Yenching University in Peking and Dean Wallace B. Donham of the relatively new Harvard School of Business Administration. The basic fact was that the inventor of aluminum, or at least of the Aluminum Company of America, Mr. Charles Hall, had left an estate of some $8 million (big money in the 1920s) to promote "Christian higher education in Asia." The genius of Messrs. Donham and Stuart was to give this idea concrete form by conceiving that Harvard (even though godless) could provide scholarly guidance to help Yenching, which was undoubtedly at work in Asia, in a modern development of Chinese studies, in effect, sinology. A tripartite Harvard-Yenching board of trustees represented the interests of (1) Christian mission boards, (2) Harvard, and (3) the general public. The statesmanlike concept was that a department and a library at Harvard could monitor and help raise the standards of the sinological work at Yenching and other Christian colleges in China.

The key to success would lie in establishing the highest quality of scholarship at Harvard. To direct the effort the Harvard-Yenching trustees appealed to Professor Paul Pelliot of the Collège de France. He was the acknowledged master of European sinology, which was then engaged in getting a modern grip on the sources and facts of China's multifaceted history and culture. Its aim was to do for China's civilization what European scholarship of the nineteenth century had done for the classical civilizations of Greece and Rome. It was recognized that Japanese studies of China would be a necessary help.

Pelliot refused Harvard's offer but recommended a junior colleague, Serge Elisseeff, who as a scion of the leading food-merchant family in Moscow had attended Tokyo University as a youth, become highly proficient in Japanese and other languages, and after the revolution acquired French citizenship. His scholarly work had been chiefly in Japanese literature. Pelliot said in effect that no Frenchman could be lured out of Paris into the Harvard boondocks, but Elisseeff, having already come out of Russia, might be available. So he was, but he retained his French citizenship and academic status during thirty years at Harvard and went back to Paris when he retired. His erudition, linguistic grasp, and critical standards all suggested he could guide the Harvard effort to success, and he did so—as a teacher of great vitality and an administrator who gradually learned how to deal with both Americans and Chinese, though he was always more at home with Japanese and Frenchmen.

Part of Harvard-Yenching's success lay also in the work of Professor William Hung and others, who at Yenching turned out, for example, a Sinological Index Series that provided textual control over the great corpus of Chinese classics and biographical compendia. Another success attended the long career of Alfred K'ai-ming Ch'iu as librarian at Harvard; he began in 1928 to bring together a copious and remarkable research collection, with all the advantages of being first among American universities to have adequate funds.

Just as these ambitious efforts were getting under way in 1932, I applied for support from Harvard-Yenching. There was nothing in my proposal to ensure that I would be able to develop as a sinologist. I was working in Anglo-Chinese diplomatic relations while getting some spoken Chinese at a missionary training center. I did not propose to study Chinese classic texts under a scholar like William Hung, or even at the major centers in Paris or Leyden. European sinology was wedded to the ideal that a Western scholar of China must be able to handle Chinese texts, using the vast paraphernalia of Chinese reference works, all by himself. It decried the China coast sinology of missionaries and consuls who, when the going got tough, always had their faithful teacher available to refer to in a back room, just as I seemed to be doing. My application was turned down, quite rightly, I should say.

This had not deterred Wilma's and my getting married and continuing our exploration of China. My Aunt Etta Boyce had left me a bequest of $1,500. This we converted at the 1932 exchange rate of about 5 to 1. It gave us $7,500 Chinese to live and travel on for the year 1932–33.

As that year came to an end I applied again to Harvard-Yenching. Nothing much had changed, except that I had realized the need to study Japanese as well as Chinese. I proposed to continue writing my D. Phil. dissertation for Oxford in Peking, but to take a trip through the original five treaty ports (Shanghai, Ningpo, Foochow, Amoy, and Canton) to see the local consular archives *in situ*. This was hardly what Harvard-Yenching was all about, and I was again turned down.

In 1933 I found moral support from a non-Harvard quarter in the person of Mortimer Graves, executive secretary of the American Council of Learned Societies in Washington, D.C. ACLS had been set up in 1919 to function in the International Union of Academies. It represented a dozen learned societies such as the American Historical Association, the American Anthropological Association, the Modern Languages Association, the American Political Science Association, and so on. The list ran to a score of organizations in the 1930s, and totals forty-three today. While Waldo G. Leland handled the foreign (European) relations, Graves promoted the growth of new fields such as Chinese studies. I wrote him and received a warm response.

I discovered that there were two camps in American China studies: Harvard-Yenching, which had funds to use and frankly followed European models, and a more native American camp, rather scattered and generally unfunded. The native Americans were led largely by people from missionary backgrounds. Dr. Arthur Hummel of the Library of Congress had been a missionary educator. He was just embarking on a massive biographical dictionary, which, given the great prominence of official biographies in the Chinese historical record, was eminently sound strategy.

The two camps were partly a matter of style. Dr. Hummel after retiring from China had done a doctorate at Leyden. His Orientalia Division of the Library of Congress had more Chinese books than Dr. Ch'iu's collection at Harvard-Yenching. The difference was that the Americans studying China operated inclusively in committees, getting everyone together. (The only place with more committees than an American college faculty was a Protestant missionary gathering.)

When Mortimer Graves got Dr. Hummel's biographical project started at LC his idea was that it would be a training center for Americans who were developing their language skills. Their joint circular of March 1936 inviting further participation went to 180 persons worldwide, a very mixed bag of savants, beginners, and amateurs. As it turned out, the contributions of the fifty or so of us outsiders and of the trainee fellows financed by the Rockefeller Foundation were far outshadowed by those of Dr. Hummel's two highly qualified staff assistants, a husband and wife, Fang Chao-ying and Tu Lien-che. Training and definitive work are water and oil. The Fangs really pulled it off, and with Dr. Hummel's editorial management produced the single most important foreign work on modern China: *Eminent Chinese of the Ch'ing Period 1644–1912* (published by the U.S. Government Printing Office in 1943–44, 2 vols.). This was both a Sino-foreign product and a triumph for American sinology. Perhaps more important, it showed what Sino-foreign collaboration could do.

European sinologists, in contrast, did not operate in committees, groups, or teams. Fields were entrusted to major professors, whose chairs, as in Japan, became individual, almost feudal citadels, usually with an entourage of lesser beings helping the work. Coming from Paris, answering only to his board of trustees, Professor Elisseeff wasted no time in nationwide committees but trained his staff to meet his standards and fill out his faculty plan. The question in his mind was whether a scholar could actually discover what the Chinese and Japanese writing meant. For this he found that many felt called but few were worth choosing. American critics, not for the first time, were jealous of Harvard's money and in this case a bit xenophobic.

When the ACLS Committee on Far Eastern Studies, after promoting the field through summer seminars and conferences, finally sparked the organization of the Far Eastern Association as a learned society in 1948, a slate of a dozen names including Professor Elisseeff's was proposed for election as a first board of directors. Someone moved that in order to represent Canada, Dr. James Menzies, a pioneer in the study of Chinese archaeology, should be added to the list of candidates. This made a slate of thirteen for twelve positions. Sure enough, Professor Elisseeff was the man left out. He had no American constituency, so to speak, until he had trained a number of the leaders in the coming generation.

After my second failure to get a Harvard-Yenching fellowship in 1933, T. F. Tsiang came to my rescue and offered me a job lecturing at Tsing Hua, while the Customs College in Peking invited me to give a course on Customs history. When I received a Harvard Graduate School grant of $800, followed by $600 from ACLS, on condition I spend full time pursuing my studies, I had already arranged to teach full time at Tsing Hua and the Customs College. What a fortunate break! I was ejected from preparation into action, catapulted into being a teacher, not anyone's assistant, but a producer of lectures of my own devising—a real challenge. Like every graduate student I had reached the point where I needed to hear myself enunciating to a captive audience the great truths that my studies had disclosed. Lecturing, I might hear myself having an idea.

Perhaps more important, being shoved off the gravy train, Wilma and I needed to make a living in the local Peking community. This led us into far more contact with Chinese life than our language teachers could have provided. We responded to the stimulus of poverty by living by our wits. Wilma began a painting class in February 1933 and in April exhibited twenty-one of her own watercolors (and sold a few) at the Peiping Institute of Fine Arts. She wrote a report on local army hospital care of Chinese casualties resisting the Japanese in Jehol province north of the Wall, and got it published in the Boston *Herald.* In April she began a new industry, the "restoration" of Chinese rubbings by inking in the places damaged on the stones, thus recapturing the original appearance. In September she exhibited her products, sold some, and took orders for more. Meanwhile she began editing the English of medical research papers produced at PUMC, especially in parasitology, which was rather long on tapeworms and liver flukes. PUMC corridors were lined with glass jars of truly remarkable organisms removed from patients—food for nightmares. Wilma also designed rugs for the Fetté Rug Company, a leading North China manufacturer run by an astute and public-spirited American woman, Ruth Fetté. I meanwhile tutored young Russell Fetté for the College Entrance Board examination in English —my first student. He got a grade of 37. When I saw him next he was a naval officer in World War II.

I completed my first research article using Chinese as well as British documents on "The Legalization of the Opium Trade before the Treaties of 1858," and lectured on the subject at the Chinese Social and Political Science Association. T. F. Tsiang, editor of the association's *Review,* published the article in July 1934. Having not yet decided to refer to a Chinese source with a triple sequence of romanization, characters, and translation, I inserted footnotes in Chinese only. This made them impressively unintelligible to Professors Webster, Baxter, and other recipients. The point of the article was that by 1858, when opium importation was permitted by treaty, it had already carved out its channels and was being informally taxed because it couldn't be stopped.

I also talked to the Sino-foreign shop club presided over by Carl Whiting Bishop (an archaeologist from the Freer Gallery in Washington), to the Tsing Hua Economics Society, the Rotary Club, the YMCA, and the whole Customs College.

The Customs College, I found, was not under the foreign Inspectorate General but had been set up by the Chinese government's Department of Customs Affairs, which from 1906 superintended the Inspectorate General (formerly directly under the Foreign Office).

This Chinese direction of the college in Peking made it a training school for bureaucrats. Foreigners in the service told me they favored holding open examinations, which would pick up Chinese talent trained abroad and bring in men of a caliber to be commissioners. But instead the college kept on producing clerks for the lower echelon as before. I found little intellectual vitality among my students and spent little time with them.

Tsing Hua was far different. The coeducational student body was a collection of talent from all over China, as was the faculty. The atmosphere was quiet but intensely serious. Ch'iao Kuan-hua, later PRC foreign minister, was a student there, though I met him only ten years later.

Once the term began in September 1933 I arose adventurously three mornings a week pre-dawn to catch the silver-and-blue bus for Tsing Hua. Immediately I could observe one of the great Chinese problems—featherbedding, overstaffing.

> The bus crew are worthy of Captain Hook. Sometimes they outnumber the passengers. There are assorted drivers with large round unshaven faces, the little man who collects the money and gives out the tickets, the big man who receives the money, and has the ticket supply, the accessory individual who is no doubt the bus starter or a nephew of the president.

> Together we all rumble down Hatamen Street . . . and turn west at Tung Tan P'ai-lou. Thence we proceed on the broad and magnificent paved avenue in front of the Palace, honking and buzzing madly at zigzagging rickshas and deaf pedestrians and going through the series of gates that stretch across the avenue, like an express train through shadows.

> The road to Tsing Hua is the main road in North China, that from Peking to the Summer Palace. It approaches the Western Hills, on which the early-morning light makes a constantly varying pattern of color and shade—sometimes with snow on the peaks like the Himalayas themselves and sometimes seeming very intimate. . . . We pass two sides of a vast plain nearly a mile across, on the far sides of which are the barracks at the Summer Palace. . . . On this plain in the early morning are drilling soldiers looking like a panorama of the

Battle of Waterloo . . . dark rectangular masses marching and countermarching in the distance.

At the university I lectured at nine, ten, and eleven. For my course on Economic History I found the Tsing Hua library well stocked with books, including Rostovtseff on Rome, Pirenne on medieval Europe, J. H. Hexter on mercantilism, and Mantoux on the industrial revolution in Europe, as well as Tawney on China. My students were given a lot of map work and lists of books and readings but mainly a printed syllabus that outlined the lectures, and listed special names and terms touched on in the course. I lectured slowly, enunciating distinctly, repeating the syllabus, saying everything twice. Students flocked to it because my teaching in 1933–34 was actually not what it seemed. My Chinese students for the most part regarded my courses quite sensibly as an opportunity to listen to spoken English. I could equally well have summarized Shakespeare or the morning news. It was I who learned the history. Both sides were satisfied.

For the Renaissance and Reformation I fortunately found a copy of Preserved Smith, a compendium from which we all learned probably more than we wanted to know. My third course was a History of the Chinese Maritime Customs Service, i.e., my thesis, which I also gave two hours a week at the Customs College in the city.

When I had office hours to see students, the boys came bouncing in to promote their individual causes but not many girls came to see me. The first one, when I closed the door, became quite agitated. Someone tipped me off. A man and woman alone in a room always leave the door ajar, or else. A closed door in such a situation implied the worst—not necessarily a fate worse than death for the unfortunate female, but some kind of relationship not for the public scrutiny that accompanied all the rest of one's crowded daily existence, even including latrine trips.

In this way, under T. F. Tsiang's aegis, after some floundering I became a teacher and published a research article. I was launched on the academic scene.

9

CHINESE FRIENDS

OUR CLOSEST FRIENDS in China (or elsewhere, for that matter) were Liang Ssu-ch'eng and his wife Lin Whei-yin, two people who combined the Chinese and the Anglo-Saxon cultural traditions. It is not easy to write of very close friends objectively. But the Liangs filled a role in our experience of China that made a great difference to us, and an account of Wilma and me as cultural intermediaries must include them as well as their close friend and neighbor Professor Y. L. Chin (Chin Yueh-lin).

Several things shaped their lives and also formed bonds between us. First, they were a neighboring household on Pei Tsung Pu Hutung at the end of our street near the east wall of the city, very accessible. Their household included Mrs. Liang's mother, a small daughter called Pao-pao (Precious Thing) and a baby boy, and the Liang house connected with Professor Chin's through his garden. They were a family.

The most formative influence upon them was probably their parentage. Liang Ssu-ch'eng was the eldest son of the famous writer-reformer-academic-political-leader Liang Ch'i-ch'ao, whose place in early twentieth-century China corresponded roughly to the combined roles of say Elihu Root, Hemingway, John Dewey, and Walter Lippmann in the United States. As a *Wunderkind* from Canton, he had worked closely with his teacher K'ang Yu-wei in sparking the young Emperor's reform movement of 1898. When that fizzled,

Liang Ch'i-ch'ao fled to Japan. Until 1911 his brilliant writings fed the mind of Young China on all the fruits of Western thought, as only an erudite Chinese classicist could do it. After the 1911 revolution Liang formed the Progressive party and served in various cabinets in Peking. Being his son was like being a Roosevelt or a Kennedy except that filial obligation was so much greater in China.

Lin Whei-yin's father, Lin Ch'ang-min from Fukien, had been a close political associate of Liang Ch'i-ch'ao, in government with him and also an observer at the Paris peace conference in 1919. The son and daughter of these revered fathers had married partly to please them. Both slight of build, like southerners, they had known each other since childhood. They had both studied architecture at the University of Pennsylvania and taken on the patriotic task of rediscovering the national monuments of Chinese architecture by scientific field work.

As part of her bicultural upbringing in Chinese and English, Lin Whei-yin had been given the Christian name of Phyllis, though she found there was nothing for her in Christianity with its ugly crucifixes and non-Chinese righteousness. She was creatively gifted as a writer, a poet, a woman of great aesthetic sensitivity and broad intellectual interests, and socially charming. The household, or any scene she was in, tended to revolve around her.

Y. L. Chin was a philosopher trained at Columbia, Harvard, London, and elsewhere, and China's leading logician. Twelve years abroad had perfected his grasp of the finest nuances of English. One of his trainees in symbolic logic, Wang Hao, has had a brilliant career in the United States. We knew Y. L. Chin, the professor, by the familiar and affectionate name of Lao Chin ("Old Chin"), a common sobriquet. When I wrote him from Shansi about the Wang sisters, who were the women's tennis champions of China, that "each was more beautiful than the other," he cherished the (il)logic.

Any contact with such friends was a delight in itself. In addition we could be windows for each other. We relished the "simple fare" *(pien fan)* of Chinese dishes that formed their daily cuisine, and the gossip that analyzed the numerous idiosyncrasies of mutual acquaintances among the local faculties at Peita, Tsing Hua, and Yenching. Being so centrally connected with the Chinese grapevine, they of course knew everything about everybody. They could all recite Chinese poetry the way it should be recited, with a strong but shifting beat, and they could contrast it with Keats, Tennyson, or Vachel Lindsay. They knew their Sung painters and calligraphers and of course all the landmarks of Peking.

Through their eyes we began to sense the Chinese problem of cultural integration—the necessity to winnow the past and discriminate among things foreign, what to preserve and what to borrow. It was a kind of double cultural frontier that few human beings have ever been on so pervasively and so consciously. It took intelligence, stamina, and courage to live actively in two cultures. Come the revolution after 1949, the strain proved too great for the aged Mao Tse-tung's crowd of nouveaux in power. The purist xenophobia of the ironically-named Cultural Revolution of the late 1960s would destroy a good deal of what the Liangs' generation had built up. Tearing down is so much easier than putting together—hence the satisfactions of wars and rebellions.

For them we offered of course a renewal of Western contact—casual talk of Harvard Square, of New York artists and exhibits, Frank Lloyd Wright, the Backs at Cambridge, Plato and Thomas Aquinas, the New Poetry. In addition, however, Wilma, with her usual creative inadvertence, moved into the Liangs' field. This happened so spontaneously that it makes an exciting story.

As Wilma pursued the hobby of "restoring" rubbings by inking in areas where the stone originals had become faulty, she was especially attracted to the stout Han dynasty horses, roofed chariots, battle and banquet scenes depicted on a set of variously shaped stones known as from the "Offering Shrine of Wu Liang" (Wu Liang Tz'u), dated early in the second century A.D., at a remote site in Shantung province. In April–May 1934 she and her friend Marie Peake made an expedition third class down the Tientsin-P'u-k'ou railway to Shantung. (Cyrus Peake, who came from Fargo, North Dakota, taught modern Chinese history at Columbia and was in Peking for a year to study Chinese law.)

In Tsinan they saw Dr. James Menzies, the Canadian missionary and pioneer archaeologist, whose "Oracle Bones from the Waste of Yin" in the 1920s alerted Western scholars to the discovery of these relics of the then prehistoric Shang dynasty. With introductions from Dr. Ferguson, these two lady-archaeologists saw the collections in Tsinan. They even went off on their own into the mountains with chair bearers as guides to see some Sui cave sites. Farther south at

Tsining they found their "delightful" missionary host, Mr. Eames, was from Jacksonville, Illinois, and had known Arthur Fairbank in college.

Finally, after getting to Chia-hsiang by bus, they found the famous stones, from which rubbings had been circulated in Chinese publications for a hundred years, cemented unprotected into the wall of an actively used schoolroom. Rubbings in the triangular shape of gable ends came from slabs of that shape. Wilma had the idea of reconstructing the architecture of the original shrine, something no one had ever thought about.

Back at Harvard two years later she photographed a complete set of Wu Liang Tz'u rubbings, and set about arranging them as they must have been originally to form the shrine's interior walls. Iconography helped. Thus the gable showing the Queen Mother of the West could be properly placed on the west. She also found, as has since been confirmed in newly excavated sites, that the shrine had had a recess in the north wall.

When this article was published in 1938 in the *Harvard Journal of Asiatic Studies* it showed what the asking of a new question could lead to in the very midst of traditionally famous artifacts. It remains a gem of scholarship. Wilma was promptly made a foreign honorary member of Ssu-ch'eng's Society for Research in Chinese Architecture and went on to do other archaeological reconstructions in other ways, which Harvard-Yenching, through the assistant director Glen Baxter, collected and published in 1972 as *Adventures in Retrieval.*

This and much more were in the future in the summer of 1934 when the Liangs joined us at Dr. Hummel's mill in the narrow valley of the Yü-tao ho in Shansi. There we were living coolly in spacious rooms right above the stream in a community of a dozen missionary families dispersed in other mills up and down the valley. We had arrived with my teacher Mr. Kuo, coming from the narrow-gauge railhead at the provincial capital, Taiyuan, by bus across the hot plain to Fenchow and thence out to the foot of the mountains. But we came without a cook or household equipment. The latter we borrowed from kind missionary neighbors, the Reynolds, from Berea, Kentucky.

Getting a cook was more difficult. Our first try produced a man who soon proved not only unable to cook but afflicted with a loathsome disease. When he took our money to get medical attention, spent it otherwise, vociferously demanded more, and refused to leave the premises, I found myself with an excellent moral sanction for using violence. I grabbed him from his bed, hauled him by one leg across the cobblestone courtyard, and threw him bodily out the front door with his belongings. Since I was in the right, this worked. He meekly went away. The community applauded.

In his stead we acquired a quick learner named T'ing-fang, like the esteemed diplomat Wu T'ing-fang, except that in local dialect it became "T'i-fa." He was far more willing than bright, a congenital optimist, believing, for instance, that more supplies would turn up even if we were all out and had placed no order with the man who daily went to the city to shop.

Early in August the Liangs arrived for a vacation before a field trip, Phyllis very natty in white trousers and a blue shirt, contrasting with Ssu-ch'eng's khaki. Lao Chin did not come but wrote from the heat of Peking: "The weather has been rather negligent of our feelings, it teases us, irritates us, and puts us into that terrible state in which we are way below our sense of humour and just slightly above our level of consciousness. I for one am far from civilized. I was going to say that I am far more like the animals than they are like me, but upon reflection there seems to be something wrong with the statement.

"According to your description of the weather, you ought to be wearing a couple of fur coats each. How can you play tennis? How can the Wang sisters play tennis? Perhaps, besides being more beautiful, each is also hardier than the other."

The Liangs' field trip south down the Fen River valley was prepared like all their trips by library research in the gazetteers (local records) of the towns in the area. If a temple was founded in the T'ang or Sung period but not listed as destroyed or repaired in the Yuan, Ming, or Ch'ing periods, perhaps it was still standing as the original building.

Once arrived at a temple, Ssu-ch'eng with his Leica would photograph every aspect while Phyllis with our help took measurements for scale drawings. All this might take a day, punctuated by a picnic lunch. Ssu-ch'eng might climb about on roofs and rafters despite the fact that he was a semi-cripple. As a student he had had a motorcycle, long before modern traffic rules were understood. Inevitably he had a collision which broke his leg, but the bone had been set overlapping. This shortened the leg and eventually curved his spine and weakened his back. In later years he wore a back brace, somewhat as FDR wore leg braces. But Ssu-ch'eng was committed to his task and no discomfort could stop him.

After getting pictures and measurements, the Liangs then sought out the inscriptions, which usually gave the dating. Documents might be quoted on stone steles. Donors might add dates after their names.

When Ssu-ch'eng and Phyllis finally found a true T'ang building, the oldest then known, in the Wu-t'ai Mountains northeast of Tai-yuan, they knew its general age from the size of the brackets (called *tou-kung*) which carry the roof's weight down onto the columns. (These brackets get progressively smaller and more numerous as time passes. Those at Nara in Japan are the proper T'ang size.) But they found no date until Phyllis caught sight of an inscription high up on a beam, left by a donor. Ironically this discovery was made on July 7, 1937, the day the eight-year Sino-Japanese war began, putting them out of the business of North China field trips.

Ssu-ch'eng had learned to travel to his North China sites by taking buses, mingling with the common people who crowded into them, and we now proposed to do the same down the Fen River valley. But we found Yen Hsi-shan, the "model governor" of Shansi, was using his troops to convert the bus road into a narrow-gauge railway. Chiang Kai-shek urged him to use standard gauge but Yen, who had been governor since 1912, didn't want Nationalist (or Japanese) troop trains to roll into his bailiwick.

We also saw Ssu-ch'eng use the old upper-class approach with army officers and magistrates, for example, when we were competing with troops to use camping space in temples. He was a slight figure with a limp but a self-assured air and modern garb. He presented his card with its titles and institutional connections, all very low key, very polite and deferential, but using literati phrases and casually dropping names while the objects of his treatment became more and more respectful and began to think of many ways to help us. It was a demonstration of how to make your way from a standing start in the old China's ruling class.

With neither buses nor trains to go by, we fell back on carts and rickshas, mainly the latter, to carry our bedding and commissary and sometimes ourselves. The innkeeper in Ling-shih got us four pullers to take us to Chao-ch'eng in three days for four dollars, but they persisted in stopping every two hours for an hour's rest. We alternately traversed sections of railway roadbed, avoiding blasting areas, and other sections of swamp and mudholes alongside. I recorded how

we passed half a dozen International trucks mired and their Tientsin drivers cursing. Arrived at an inn ten *li* out of Huochou and were saved by a Tientsin driver who bullied the pullers into going on, helped by a small boy with a lantern and our flashlights fore and aft. Having a common province [i.e., Hopei], even of thirty million population, makes a kinship [in this case with truckers] where the local dialect is strange.

Reaching the shadowy outline of the Huo-chou wall as midnight came, we stumbled through the west gate, found a guide who left his opium and took us to the Nei Ti Hui [China Inland Mission], where old Mrs. Ch'ien made us fabulous noodle soup and we fell into bed at 1 A.M. after walking nearly twenty miles out of the thirty covered in the day.

In my rather wide-eyed approach to the Chinese scene, I had accepted the ricksha coolie as part of the landscape. Similarly several generations of Americans had accepted Negro slavery in its time in the Land of the Free. But sooner or later the evil strikes one. The day after our long trek to Huo-chou, I concluded:

Men ought not to stand in the same relation toward other men that animals do, and it is one object of the civilizing process to prevent this.

Modern industrialization in China, however, has brought about the utilization of manpower to take the place of animals and machines;—not to serve the machine, as the Western worker does in the factory. . . .

Pulling a ricksha . . . is . . . the simplest possible form of work. It requires only the muscular vigor which animals have and the horse sense necessary to stay on the road and avoid holes. The puller's brain is unused, and is not considered to exist. This is degrading. It is even more degrading, however, that the puller should be started, speeded up, and stopped by the will of another person.

Our ricksha boys today were partly conscious of this: the

more stupid accepted their situation and pulled, but the two who were more intelligent were surly and resentful; and on asking for tips when we paid them off they said, "We have been doing ox and horse work."

The ricksha in modern China takes somewhat the place which the horse did in nineteenth-century America: the city gentleman has his own private one, and in the hinterland, where transportation is spreading modern culture, the ricksha is the feeder for bus and railway lines and the surest means of travel in undeveloped regions. A coolie can travel faster than an animal and farther in a day, and on a relatively smooth road can pull a heavier load than a donkey can carry. Because there is in China a greater proportion of men to beasts than there is in America, the coolie has taken the place which the mule might otherwise have filled—the additional power needed for modern transport is provided by men rather than by more beasts.

Curiously the two major agencies of modernization in this ancient Shansi valley seemed to be unlikely allies—the government and the missionaries, one waxing, the other waning:

> The soldiers working on the railroad are largely Hopei men, well built and genial, and they appear to have a program of grenade-throwing and sports exercise in addition to working for the railroad company—in several villages and all cities both schools and camps (e.g., temples used for barracks) had basketball courts, and sometimes jumping standards. At Huochou I sat on the roof of the back building in a temple school and watched boys kicking a ball about for fun in the usual American bare-lot fashion—certainly a sign that the modern San Min Chu I students are getting the idea that exercise becomes study.

We were impressed with the hospitality and hostelry function of missionaries. There they were in each town, ready without notice to take us in at any hour, provide local news, guides, and connections, and accept only our nominal contributions of cash for expenses incurred. Even in the 1930s, past their heyday, they functioned in almost as many places as the China Travel Service of today and would tell you at least as much about local conditions. The Liangs, like us, were grateful for their help but felt a very lively chagrin to be depending on foreigners in their own country.

Huo-chou: Mr. E. G. Trickey of the CIM brought us back to his guest rooms, after we awakened, and blessed our English breakfast in a beautifully clear and expressive voice. His narrow eyes and long upper lip accorded with his religious consecration. Twenty years in various mission posts, now sent a year ago to revive Huo-chou, feeling silent opposition about him, father to three children (and three others in the Chefoo CIM school) while his wife nurses her heart, and carrying on the embattled tradition of Hudson Taylor with the outward and smiling graciousness which overcometh all, Mr. Trickey wears Chinese garb, abhors foreign-style houses, sees the student-officials as communistic enemies, and works and prays for and to a close personal god—a whole-souled way of life to express a literal and all-embracing, all-satisfying faith—strong in morale, adequate but not modernly-scientific in intellectual life—maintaining through the years the forms and standards of Wesleyan England from which he came—food of starches and pudding, reading of the *Times* as The Great Purveyor of contemporary fact, affectionately reverencing the King and preparing his children for English education—conservative politically, fitted to live and work in any clime but never cease to be an Englishman.

Dr. Hoyte was of the same stamp, nearly fifty and graying, a long face, narrow eyes, small mouth, strong jaw, with a sparkling interest in things and a forthright faith in his God. Our economic troubles, said he, are essentially moral questions, don't you think? Our hospital is run as a means of winning men to Christ. Therefore the nurses must be convinced men who will lose no opportunity to tell the patients of Christ and his message for them.

Mrs. Hoyte has had six children in almost as many years, is most devout, knows nothing of China, and made efforts to win Wilma to Christ. Dr. H. has a Trojan car, third hand, no differential, motor under seat, hand crank, and similar oddities, in which he came over the impassable road of which we had intended to warn him. Has a Leica in common with Ssu-ch'eng and London University in common with me: an able man, with ideas of a previous generation.

The CIM has 1,303 members and associates (chiefly of Scandinavian missions as well) and 80,000 communicants—i.e. 60 to a missionary. They may marry only members of the CIM; furloughs and salaries indefinite; controlled by Hoste *et al.* from Shanghai and London chiefly. Devolution gone far, all churches being in Chinese hands financially and foreigners as advisers only. Bible women are important in getting contact in homes with the womenfolk.

How to evaluate the contribution of Christian missions to China is a real poser. It is probably a nonoperable question: it cannot be answered in any conclusive way.

From this expedition the Liangs returned with energy unimpaired and data on several temples, one where Ming frescoes had been removed and sold abroad, no doubt by bribing the monks or others in charge. Our friendship had been forged from shared experience under stress. The adventures of the open road brought the four of us close in trying circumstances on an equal basis with no one host or guest. We remained close friends, saw each other in West China in 1942–46 and Ssu-ch'eng in the United States in 1947, and as I write this in 1981, Wilma is preparing an account of the Liangs' work in architectural history. It is a story of achievement in the face of disaster, tragedy valiantly surmounted.

10

SEEING THE OLD PORTS

VISITING THE EARLY treaty ports for research on my Oxford thesis, I found a China quite different from the plains and mountains of the arid North. The people were smaller and more wiry, the climate warmer and more moist. China in the 1930s was not yet homogenized by patriotic unity and modern conveniences for the traveler. The ports on the southeast coast were at the mouths of rivers, facing outward overseas. They were points both of foreign invasion and of Chinese egress to Southeast Asia and beyond, the locus, in short, of a maritime China which contrasted with the continental China of the northern plains and great river systems that underlay the old Chinese empire.

I began to see one of the long-term dynamic factors in China's modern history, a factor that would distinguish the Nationalists from the Communists, and separate Chiang Kai-shek's government that lived off trade from Mao Tse-tung's people who lived off the land. In the ports created by sea trade, British, French, American, and other intruders from abroad found a China quite unlike the one that the Mongols and Manchus had invaded overland from the north and west.

The heart of my D. Phil. thesis lay in the records of the British consulates at the five oldest treaty ports. They had been the front-line command posts, in daily correspondence with merchants and Chinese officials, the cutting edge of imperialism. Shanghai's records had been burned in 1870. The Ningpo records were kept at Shanghai. Files were largely intact at the other ports. (They are now at the Public Record Office in London.) At Charles Webster's prompting the Foreign Office librarian had written the Peking legation, which now circularized the port consuls authorizing me to see their early archives *in situ*. We toured the South China coast for this purpose from December 1934 to February 1935.

Our fortunes had turned a corner in April 1934 when I received a grant of $2,050 plus travel costs from the Rockefeller-supported General Education Board. Vice-president David Stevens had written me that I was trying to do too much (study Chinese, begin Japanese, travel, and do thesis research), "too many irons in the fire." I had replied, nailing my flag to the mast—those were the things I had to do. The awarding of the fellowship meant he now agreed with me that I had a future, even if an overambitious one.

In Shanghai in November 1934 we found rooms at 103 Nanking Road over the Chocolate Shop. The place was so rundown from use and so accessible at the businessmen's lunch hour we could not help feeling it had been accustomed to more rapidly transient occupiers than ourselves. When Wilma's sister Marian arrived to join us, fresh out of Radcliffe, she was duly appalled at our "rooms in a scabrous old building," and even more startled when Agnes Smedley came to see us, bringing her "atmosphere of conspiratorial paranoia and revolutionary zealotry."*

By day the British consulate gave me an office with a phone and an office boy's attention on demand, so that I could go through the Ningpo archives with Wilma's and Marian's help as copyists and précis writers, using the two typewriters we carried with us. I found thesis research hard work, partly because my subject as filtered through consular dispatches was sometimes very dull. The Canton consul, for example, had spent untold hours combatting the local monopoly in cassia, a plant that produced a purple dye. He was trying to reduce this ancient organized trade and its licensed guild to a free-for-all in which his British merchant-complainant fancied he could compete better. It was as futile as Mao Tse-tung's trying to wipe out the profit motive in China a century later. The consuls were

---

*Marian Cannon Schlesinger, *Snatched from Oblivion: A Cambridge Memoir*, p. 189).

ideological reformers just as much as the missionaries—all trying to get "the Chinese" to be more like us in our ideal form.

From this reformist tedium the seventy-five volumes of early Ningpo records 1843–58 were quite a relief. They were jam-packed with dirty work,

> the detailed lowdown on one of the greatest epics of the Triumph of Trade, escorted by piracy, blackmail, racketeering, slavery, assault and battery, squeeze, and efforts to amend the laws in order to fit the crimes. The Portuguese at Ningpo were called in against local pirates, but squeezed, and were only eliminated by calling in the Canton pirates, who squeezed, and while the two fought it out the British got the coast trade.

Ningpo in early days was rich in missionaries, but less devout British consular officers became more immersed than usual in the local Chinese community. At least three at Ningpo (J. A. T. Meadows, Sinclair, and Hart) seem to have had very close relations with Chinese women. Indeed one may speculate that Robert Hart got to the top in China because of his early initiation into the Chinese family system, aided of course by his headstart with the Irish family system.

To see Ningpo I took the night boat from Shanghai at 5 P.M. and next morning found a Methodist missionary couple who kindly took us in. (Wilma and Marian arrived by train from Hangchow.) We found the graves of some who figured in the archives. But instead of Apak and his Cantonese pirates of the 1850s, we now encountered the Chinese masses traveling by steamship, 3,000 of them standing or sitting on their luggage

> on the main deck on the waterline; above are Chinese second-class like railway passengers in cabins with bunks; and on the top deck ride we three, half a dozen officers, half a dozen stewards, and the Episcopal bishop of Chekiang, who is simply fascinated by Marian. Like riding on an ant hill. Piracy from below is discouraged by rows of spikes on turnable rods along the sides of the top deck . . . and big grills and gratings . . . also a squad of troops.

Returning to Shanghai our steamer threaded its way twelve miles down the Yung River past the old fort at Chen-hai. Like Canton, Foochow, Shanghai, Tientsin, and other old ports, Ningpo as an emporium for trade was at a head of navigation accessible to shipping but not easily penetrated by a high-seas fleet.

We found the same true of Foochow (with one unfortunate exception). After ascending the Rhine-like Min River for twenty-four miles, we reached Pagoda anchorage. There on the afternoon of August 23, 1884, a French ultimatum had expired and so a bigger French fleet (naturally) in a few minutes had sunk nine vessels of a new Chinese fleet moored nearby. They had also destroyed a shipyard built for China by French engineers. Going on up to Foochow, we soon got into the old treaty port atmosphere. It was more acerbic than anything we had met in North China.

In the foreign settlement on the island south of the walled city and river, first of all, we found lodging in a truly Maughamesque scene—

> an unbelievable house, ramified and gigantic, filled to the ceilings with bric-a-brac, gewgaws, tidbits, objets d'art, and junk generally. The house merely symbolizes the owner who built it, H. Shelley Brand, aet. 72, agent for Reuters, six tea firms, sexton, undertaker, and general old blowhard—a massive man with a mind cluttered like his house, a love for Foochow and his long silver ringlets that proclaim him the Oldest Resident, and a hatred for China and the Chinese.

Mr. Brand's profession was that of tea taster, as he demonstrated to us. As tea shipments came down the Min from the Bohea (Wu-i) Hills upcountry, large investments hinged on the appraisal made by the professional "expectorator," who graded the different lots ("chops") by brewing and tasting samples. Mr. Brand had also the recitative talent of a great ham actor. His personality made an impression on Marian as it had on Somerset Maugham.*

Foochow as an ancient capital of two provinces had been a hotbed of xenophobia. The Confucian scholars struggled long and hard to keep missionaries out of the walled city. The first missionary to arrive, in 1847, since the consul did not invite him, had to lodge with an opium ship captain, the only Britisher as yet able to sell anything.†
Sino-foreign animosity became better established as the two sides

---

*See *Snatched from Oblivion,* pp. 193–95, and *The Casuarina Tree.*
†See Ellsworth Carlson, *The Foochow Missionaries 1847–1880.*

found out more specifically what they didn't like about each other. In 1934 I found the British and American consuls still friendly enemies, trade and missions still the dominant foreign activities. "The foreigners despise and distrust the Chinese now as before," I noted, "but in a milder way."

We had become acquainted thus far with two types of Chinese:

> Traveling in the interior we have met the peasant and the villager, unsophisticated and close to the soil, the great mass . . . hard-working, simple, friendly on the whole. . . . In Peking we have met the Westernized returned students, most attractive as individuals but forced by their circumstances to stay with their own kind, between two civilizations. Now we are among a third type . . . the compradore type, who are after money from foreign trade. . . . I had lunch with the Rotary Club, which Gordon Burke the American consul started . . . an innovation still of doubtful success.

Three Japanese, half a dozen Westerners, and two dozen Chinese, each sat in their own group. They saw each other only on business. Friendship and mutual respect did not flourish. I sensed

> a distinct flavor of dislike of China in the Treaty Port atmosphere. . . . For one thing you can't talk to your servants here as man to man, not knowing the dialect, and so have to bellow at them in pidgin, "Boy, you catchee master topside chop chop talkee dinner."

Since treaty ports began for trade under gunboat compulsion,

> divorced from the soil and from local custom and public opinion both, no doubt the worst sort of Chinese gravitated to them—"Chinese traitors" as the Emperor used to call them.

In this context we found my fellow townsman Guy Thelin's agronomy school outside Foochow a bright relief. He said some students still dragged their feet at actually tilling the fields, but Guy set them a vigorous example in person. They eventually learned to get their hands dirty even though their education was bringing them into the upper class. This implied in fact a social revolution, though we could sense it only dimly as we passed through.

Our expedition down the coast to Foochow, Amoy, Swatow, Hong Kong, and Canton was not really what it seemed. To be sure, I spent long hours in the seldom-used British consular courtrooms going through some two hundred musty bound volumes of rare and sometimes worm-eaten correspondence, often flanked by my two typist assistants. But to the public eye it was a progress of two daughters of Cornelia James Cannon. Though accompanied by a male researcher, they were accustomed to painting or sketching surrounded by crowds of onlookers; playing tennis, swimming, and bowling with men of all nations; and engaging at all times in ceaseless repartee, badinage, and conversation. After all, they had been trained in countless Sunday-afternoon at-homes in Cambridge to put shy students at their ease and grasp the unintelligible remarks of foreign professors. They had learned that the most potent and available part of a male is his ego and that for practical purposes all men are brothers. Moreover, since the port communities were overstocked with males, an unattached young lady like Marian was every hostess's dream, especially when she came chaperoned, sort of, by her sister and brother-in-law.

The port consuls, Customs commissioners, bank managers, and business representatives uniformly inhabited well-serviced small palaces set in gardens and mini-deerparks. Their open-handed hospitality descended from a long tradition of inhabiting company rather than personal housing, and as part of a corporate service to travelers of their own class. We found them most hospitable at Amoy, where the very sociable community of foreign residents lived on the rocky and picturesque "Drum-wave Island" *(Ku-lang-su)* across the roadstead from Amoy city. We arrived for the Christmas season. Wilma and I were cordially taken in by the Hong Kong–Shanghai bank manager, David Allen Erskine Bell, very Scotch, whose grandfather had helped in the capture of Amoy. His father had commanded the Argyll and Sutherland Highlanders ("The Campbells"). He himself had represented the bank in Malacca, Tokyo, Tientsin, and Shanghai. Marian was invited to stay with the British consul, A. J. Martin, whose wife was American, in a spectacular cliff-top residence equally replete with servants and amenities. We were given club privileges and joined in banquets, balls with Virginia reels, carol singing, and other seasonal festivities for a busy week. We met a young archaeologist at Amoy University, Cheng Te-k'un (later professor at Cambridge and the Chinese University of Hong Kong) but otherwise saw little of modern China. Consul Martin took me along when he went to inspect a shipload of Chinese going under contract to work in Southeast Asia. Under the reformist legislation of the 1860s he had to guard against any revival of the evils of the coolie trade.

Our one-man two-women expedition took on a different cast when Wilma got us all three into one room in the Hotel Cecil in Hong Kong. It was advertised as quite cheap and turned out to be so in more ways than one. Lots of sailors and music. The room boy told Marian a nice gentleman would like to meet her. Soon a police sergeant summoned us to ask why we had not registered as aliens. Just at this low point, we got in touch with W. J. Keswick, through a Peking friend, the poet Harold Acton, and I was able to give the sergeant my Balliol card and say that we were moving out to Number 117, the Peak. Rags to riches, as usual. In a flash the sergeant metamorphosed from tyrant to servant. The address of the *taipan* of Jardine, Matheson and Co. was more esteemed in Hong Kong than 10 Downing Street.

Our salvation in this jam was a new-found friend from Peking, who happened to be a Cambridge classmate of Keswick. Gerald Yorke was a tall, dark, saturnine double-first, heir to a firm very big in bathroom fixtures. At first he had refused to be a director and for a time was cut off without a penny. He had gone into yoga, sat and meditated in a cave on the Welsh coast. He came to China third class across Siberia. In 1933 Yorke became a journalist and during the Japanese takeover of Jehol had departed from Peking for the front alone on a horse, cross country, wearing an enormous sheepskin like a latter-day Attila. Both the Chinese and the Japanese detained him as unusually furtive, since he spoke only English, but he filed a good story. Gerald Yorke was determined to participate in Chinese life and do what they did. For example, in a Shanghai theater he had signaled for a hot towel, which the hot-towel purveyors fire at you unerringly from twenty feet, but it gave him a rash of boils. A colorful man and excellent company.

In Hong Kong he stayed with his Cambridge friend W. J. Keswick (who is called Tony, but not having seen him for fifty years I hesitate to throw the name around). While staying in the big J., M. & Co. house on the Peak, Yorke was exploring the firm's archives. They had been collected in seven hundred tea chests in a godown at East Point.

Someone had gone through to remove historic postage stamps (the firm is Scottish), but otherwise the coast letters from opium captains and the main-office tea, silk, and chow-chow correspondence were all jumbled in fascinating heaps on the floor.

When I presented my letter from Harold Acton to Tony Keswick, he had me see Gerald and then invited me to come stay with him as a consultant on what to do with the archive. At dinner we used some of the plate and glass candle protectors (shaped like big brandy snifters) which J., M. & Co. had inherited from the East India Company's Canton factory back in the 1830s.

At about age thirty-one Tony Keswick was just taking over as head of the firm, in the footsteps of his father and grandfather. Family continuity as well as unremitting care no doubt had contributed to the firm's long survival. Automatically he would now be a director of some dozen local companies, including the Hong Kong–Shanghai Bank, as well as on the colonial Legislative Council and Defense Committee. He could obviously handle these responsibilities with aplomb. Evenings at home he occupied himself doing needlepoint.

After dinner I described to him the importance of the Jardine, Matheson records as seen by a historian, and urged that the firm establish them as an archive in London, get them organized and catalogued, and allow qualified researchers to have access. Next day I put this in a memo, and also drafted an announcement to send to a suggested list of academic people in the United States in order to find someone who would *at his own cost* take over the records of the American firm of Augustine Heard & Co., which were also in the J., M. & Co. warehouse.* Jardine's subsequently deposited its papers from East Point in the Cambridge University Library.

I met W. J. Keswick's younger brother, John Keswick, years later at the British embassy in Chungking, where he was in wartime intelligence as an interlude before getting Jardine's back into operation in the postwar world as a multinational firm. My particular bond with John Keswick was not only an interest in the firm and in Hong Kong but also a mutual appreciation of his book *What I Know about China.*

---

*The eventual taker was Professor David Owen, then at Yale. Later he joined the History Department at Harvard, the Heard papers found their way to the Harvard Business School Library, and in 1971 we published Stephen Lockwood's study, *Augustine Heard and Company, 1858–1862: American Merchants in China on the Eve of the Opening of the Yangtze.*

It was privately bound and distributed and went through several editions as Sir John gave copies away. Its special feature, that set it apart from all other China books, was its lack of print. It consisted entirely of blank pages.

The message conveyed by this Keswick volume was refreshingly straightforward and I have never ceased to admire its cogency. Over the years I have been able to send Sir John a number of blank pages for inclusion as appendices or as illustrative material. In all the China bibliographies I have compiled, I have regularly excluded this book, and in guiding others I have seldom failed to leave it out of account. It is the kind of book I wish I had thought of myself, even though by its nature it is not easy to describe in words.

When we moved on to Canton in mid-January 1935 we at first stayed in the New Asia Hotel on Taiping Road, but soon a wedding was celebrated by exploding at ground level a string of big firecrackers seven stories high. This bombardment took an hour and left the lobby looking and smelling like a Civil War battleground. We called on the Customs commissioner, L. K. Little of Pawtucket, Rhode Island, one of the Americans highest in the service. He and his mother invited Marian to stay with them while Wilma and I moved to the less nuptially-inclined Victoria Hotel. Later we also moved to the Littles'.

Shameen, the "Sandbank," just off the Canton bund, had been enclosed with a wall and filled in about 1859 to make a tree-clad, campuslike foreign enclave for residences, consulates, and firms, half a mile long and up to three hundred yards wide, reached by two bridges over a canal. When the revolutionary parade of June 17, 1925, marched with its flags and civic delegations along the Shaki bund facing Shameen, the canal was empty of the Chinese boat people who usually filled it and the British and French marines behind their sandbags had a clear field of view. When they were provoked to fire, killing fifty-seven, they practically blew up the treaty system. The Nationalist Revolution of 1925–27 scared five thousand missionaries out of the interior. Their later comeback was impermanent, on sufferance, but luckily for them China was soon hit by the greater evil of Japanese invasion. In 1935 the treaties, the missionaries, the Customs Service were all still in place.

L. K. Little, a Dartmouth graduate, had joined the Customs in 1914. As it became evident that he had the kind of even-handed judgment necessary for high office, he was given assignments to different parts of the country and of the service that built up a broad background of experience. These assignments took him to Peking as a language student; Shanghai, 1916–20; Amoy, 1921–24, in charge of Native Customs; Peking, 1924–26, in charge of the pension system; Tientsin, 1927–29; Shanghai, 1929–31, personal secretary to the I.G., 1931–32, 1933–34; at the League of Nations, Geneva, 1932; Canton commissioner, 1934–41; with home leave every six years, four times altogether. He later succeeded Maze as the last foreign I.G. from 1943 to 1950.

Mr. Little took us down the Pearl River to Whampoa in a Customs dispatch boat. We got an impression of where the East Indiamen used to anchor and where the British Navy repeatedly fought its way up to Canton.

Considering that I had a friendly reception and long talks with so many foreigners in the Customs at half a dozen ports, I fear I made poor use of the opportunity to study its current problems. Smuggling at the British free port of Hong Kong continued to be a lively business. Hong Kong did nothing to stop it. The Customs had only a small preventive force of three hundred armed guards on the Sino-British boundary. It could do nothing when Canton government gunboats regularly carried in sugar for the provincial sugar monopoly, which then sold it for a profit equal to the unpaid duty. Similarly the Canton-Kowloon Railway smuggled goods to deprive Nanking of revenue. Women smuggled silver dollars in their sanitary napkins. Where the boundary ran down the middle of a street, people simply threw things across. A barbed-wire fence anywhere would keep farmers from their fields. It was not easy to do the central government's work in the face of the twin local shibboleths—Cantonese particularism and British free trade. Peking had found the problem intractable in the nineteenth century just as Nanking did in the twentieth.

This journey through the old ports, as we were passed along from friend to friend, confirmed several ideas I had gained from the records. The ports did indeed constitute a single interconnected frontier community where foreign hospitality and individual enterprise flourished. Moreover, foreigners in their several lines of endeavor for good or ill, or just for business, found and depended upon Chinese counterparts to work with—compradores to handle the Chinese side of a business, colporteurs (distributors of tracts) and Chinese pastors to carry on mission work, and more recently Chinese educators and professional people in general. Yet this Sino-foreign cooperation went on in a context where aggressive foreign nationalisms roused a Chinese patriotic reaction. Thus Maritime China, the meeting ground for China and the West, was the place where modernization began. But in China as a whole the modernization movement could at first play only a minor role.

11

LEAVING CHINA THE FIRST TIME

AN AREA SPECIALIST is an onlooker, privileged to watch how the human drama unfolds without being caught in it. This gives him mixed feelings. The year 1935 was the climax and end of our four-year Peking idyll. I had to complete my dissertation and return to Oxford for my D. Phil. examination so that, armed with this British version of a Ph.D., I could find a teaching job. Meanwhile, for our Chinese friends there were new anxieties and imminent disasters to face. As we pulled ourselves out of the academic scene in Peking, we felt we were scuttling ratlike from a sinking ship.

The menace came from Japan's military expansion, as we found by going there. After Dr. Cannon visited PUMC and stayed with us in Peking, along with Mrs. Cannon and their youngest daughter, Helen, in June we all traveled through the Japanese colony of Korea and had several weeks in Tokyo and Kyoto. This first glimpse of Japan was colored by the overhanging threat of its militarism. Japanese family friends and liberal professors we met, oriented toward America, were plainly living on borrowed time, expecting the worst. For me as a student this powerful and modern yet exotic land was a further challenge, to be faced and studied at a later time, much further down the road. Its obvious power heightened our fear of the danger to China.

Japan's seizure of China's Northeast (Manchuria) had already posed the threat to take over all China that would eventually rouse the Chinese people to armed resistance and revolution. Unfortunately the two prongs of this response were not yet united. Chiang Kai-shek was building up his army at Nanking but mobilization of the rural masses was still in the experimental stage. Of the various efforts under way the best known to us as foreigners was the program set up by the charismatic Jimmy Yen (Yen Yang-ch'u). In December 1935 we went by train southwest to Ting-hsien to see his Rockefeller-backed Mass Education Movement for rural reconstruction. Yen had begun in World War II with mass literacy work among the Chinese labor corps in France where T. F. Tsiang had helped him. At Ting-hsien we went to villages where health clinics and reading classes were nibbling away at human problems so vast as to exhaust the imagination; even to think about them was an effort. We found that bringing literacy, hygiene, and scientific farming to the villages led inevitably to organizing farmers in associations that might begin to express grievances against government and landlords. In 1935 Jimmy Yen had the cooperation of a benevolent Ting-hsien magistrate, but when the Japanese invasion of 1937 forced him to Szechwan, the Nationalist government would be suspicious of anyone stirring up the villages. In 1935 his cause of rural reconstruction still shone brightly as an extension to China's villages of modern American knowhow. Forty-five years and several wars later, the cause is still valid but appears to be more complicated than any outsider could realize. Politics and class structure are imbedded in it.

Rural mobilization and army building were about to be combined by Mao Tse-tung and the Chinese Communist Party at Yenan, once their Long March of 1935 had brought them there. In Peking we heard only of Chiang Kai-shek's success in chasing Communist bandits from one province to another. But two new friends we met at this time were preparing to report this new development.

Edgar and Peg Snow, whom we had met in Shanghai, had come to Peking in 1934 as newlyweds and were now living near Yenching University. Ed was a talented journalist, trained at the Missouri School of Journalism. J. B. Powell, the American editor of the *China Weekly Review,* had sidetracked Ed's trip around the world in 1928 and soon made him assistant editor. At that time Powell supported the new Nanking government, still a red anathema to old Shanghai hands, and Ed Snow was detailed to tour China's railways and write up tourist attractions. This led him from the Lower Yangtze sites through Nanking to Peking and Manchuria and eventually by rail into the Northwest, where he ran into the terrible Northwest famine of 1929–30. Judging by his account in his autobiography *Journey to the Beginning* (1958), this experience of mass extinction completed Ed's fixation upon the cause of the Chinese people. He was a reporter, not an ideologue, but friendship with Mme. Sun Yat-sen and a host of others tied him to China.

Ed and Peg (Helen Foster Snow, who wrote as Nym Wales) were very different personalities—he relaxed and outgoing, led by a natural love of people, she tense and intellectualized, driven by ambition. We visited back and forth and went dancing on the roof of the Peking Hotel, the city's genteel night spot. Her obvious rivalry with Ed made me glad that Wilma and I worked different sides of the street. After Ed made his great coup of getting to the CCP area in 1936 and reporting Mao's career and the CCP cause to the world in *Red Star over China,* Peg also reached Yenan and did much basic reporting about the Communist leadership.

By late 1935 Japanese aggression was in the Peking air. The wily Japanese army was carrying on a campaign of psychic harassment. A company of troops preceded by a small officer on a big long-legged horse would march ostentatiously through our *hutung.* In field maneuvers the army would practice the "capture" of Feng-t'ai, the railway junction just south of Peking. They controlled the Peking-Tientsin area through puppet Chinese and still hoped to set up "North China-land" (Hua-pei-kuo) to add onto Manchukuo. They wanted to use Chinese of the generation who had flocked to Tokyo in the 1900s and spoke some Japanese, but twenty-five years later these men were either Chinese patriots or past their prime.

The Peking universities were led by a younger, Anglo-American-returned generation, imbued with the ardent nationalism of the May Fourth era. They were preparing to move their faculties and libraries south, shipping out books and equipment. The universities were being dismantled before one's eyes. I sat and watched helplessly as students (?) took unregistered books out of the Tsing Hua library.

As the Japanese pressure built to a climax, the students began to organize secretly to stage a great demonstration. The Snows helped the organizers, who seemed to be unconnected non-Communists, although of course many leaders (like Wang Ju-mei at Yenching, better known as Huang Hua) joined the CCP later. On December 9,

1935, university and middle-school students formed long columns marching in the streets, defying the police, protesting against the threatened detachment of North China. This event became a counterpart to the demonstration of May 4, 1919, a second assertion of Chinese nationalism. Liang Ssu-ch'eng's sister (Liang Ssu-i) was one of the Yenching student leaders. A policeman beat her heavily with his scabbarded sword. Phyllis's young brother joined in from his middle school and for twelve hours afterward was missing while Ssu-ch'eng combed the city's hospitals looking for him.

The students were demanding action from Chiang Kai-shek, whose troops were meanwhile taking control of Southwest China on the plea of pursuing the CCP Long March. "Unify before resisting" was the policy. Chiang's German military advisers were preparing his Lower Yangtze forces to fight the last war again, by positional warfare.

In the crisis our Chinese friends were between fires. T. F. Tsiang joined the Nanking government to do his bit in the cabinet of the Executive Yuan, as noted above. Liang Ssu-ch'eng contemplated dropping his life work in architectural history to confront the invader, but of course found no way to be useful in the absence of a modern mobilization. Phyllis had had another bout with tuberculosis. When the Japanese suppressed China's leading paper, the Tientsin *Ta Kung Pao,* to whose prestigious literary supplement she had been a contributor, she found herself lavishly invited to contribute to the puppet successor, the *United Asia Herald.* When she saw local relatives at her aunt's house, she found them still family-centered and ready to live under the Japanese. "Why do you get so worked up," they asked, "and plan to go south? What if there is an autonomous state here? That won't make any difference to us. Our houses will still be here. Peking will still be China and not Japan. And life will go on as usual." Some were even taking jobs in Japanese-backed enterprises. Phyllis and Ssu-ch'eng were in a rage made more bitter by treachery within the family network. They had already had to move from Mukden in 1931.

Patriotic modern-minded Chinese of an Anglo-American liberal background, the people most like ourselves, whom we esteemed and identified with, were thus a powerless minority in their own country. However, they were firmly aware of their role of cultural leadership and their duty as scholars to train China's future generation. They therefore stood together in mutual support.

The many Chinese academic friends we had met at Tsing Hua and through the Liangs and Lao Chin were leaders of their generation.* When we returned to China during World War II and after, in 1942–46, we found them in the Southwest. When we returned to Peking after the revolution in 1972 we would find some of them in Peking still in the status of scholars and teachers. (Chou P'ei-yuan spent part of the war years at Cal. Tech. and until 1981 was president of Peking University.) They had survived.

Fortitude is a pale word for it. Indeed, it doesn't express the half of it, for history split our Peking friends into two groups. One sizable group would be in Taiwan after 1949, still refugees.†

Both groups of these Peking liberal intellectuals would continue to be kicked around by history, but they kept on trying to serve their country as best they could under a party dictatorship during civil war and revolution. None of them exactly won his battle, but neither did he quit. Eventually someone will make a balance sheet for them all. They were a generation that met disaster but not a lost generation by any means.

In December 1935 no fortitude was required of us. Wilma and I were going on our way to a happier world. Just as the privileged status of extraterritoriality had smoothed our path during a four-year interlude in China, so our good fortune, not our superior merit, let us leave China's travail behind. We experienced the mixed sense of relief and of guilt that has tied so many Americans' sentiments to their less lucky Chinese friends.

Small human crises were all around us. Our chief house servant, Li, for example, had to bring his expectant wife in from the disor-

---

*They included two political scientists, Ch'ien Tuan-sheng (Ph.D., Harvard) and Chang Hsi-jo (Ph.D., Columbia, also at London); an economist, Ch'en Tai-sun (Deison Ch'en, Ph.D., Harvard); a sociologist, L. K. T'ao (T'ao Meng-ho, Ph.D., London); and a physicist, Chou P'ei-yuan (Ph.D., Cal. Tech.).
†They included leading figures like Hu Shih and Chiang Monlin, president of Peita; Phyllis's cousin George Yeh (Yeh Kung-ch'ao), a gifted professor of English literature, who became a principal postwar diplomat; Wen Yuan-ning, another littérateur who became a Nationalist ambassador; Fu Ssu-nien of Academia Sinica and Taiwan University; Li Chi (Ph.D., Harvard, in anthropology), who completed the study of the Shang dynasty capital at Anyang begun by Liang Ssu-ch'eng's brother, Liang Ssu-yung, among others.

derly countryside. His son and brother-in-law were already with us, trying to make themselves indispensable. We tried to ensure his future employment and Wilma counseled the wife about birth control. "Yes," she replied, "foreigners have ways of dealing with these things, but there is no way out for us."

Leaving friends like the Liangs was traumatic. We had learned from each other and given each other all we could. Phyllis had become the closest friend to both of us. Our departure was a real heartbreak.

From our first four years in China, 1932–35, we acquired an image of local conditions in the North, in the Lower Yangtze, and down the coast. We met the foreign establishment on its diplomatic, educational, and missionary levels in particular. Most important we found friends and made many acquaintances among the modern-minded Chinese academic leadership. Meeting on the Shanghai-Peking Blue Express, for example, we had a long talk with Fu Ssu-nien, head of the Academia Sinica Institute of History and Philology, who was later president of Peita and of Taiwan National University. The PUMC professor of physiology who had invited Dr. Cannon in 1935 was Dr. Robert K. S. Lim (Lin K'o-sheng). He had taken his medical degree at Edinburgh and was a thoroughly cosmopolitan scientist. But against Japan he organized a medical service for China's troops and I would meet him next as surgeon general of the Chinese forces. Such people would turn up in profusion in Southwest China during World War II.

PART THREE

●

LEARNING TO BE A
PROFESSOR
1936–40

12

AN OXFORD D. PHIL.

THE YEAR 1936 was a turning point for everybody. The Versailles settlement of 1919 gave way to the overtures of World War II: Hitler reoccupied the Rhineland, Mussolini finished the conquest of Ethiopia, they set up the Berlin-Rome Axis, the League of Nations collapsed, civil war began in Spain. Me, I finished my D. Phil. (Oxon.) and began to face issues of policy and livelihood.

Once away from China we made a stop in Tokyo. We found Burton Fahs and Hugh Borton, Japan specialists, were similarly in need of jobs in the United States, so we formed a "Pine Barrens Association," agreeing to settle on some no-account New Jersey land that Hugh owned and eke out our unwanted existences.

Actually, I had already begun to itinerate much the way missionaries used to do, though I didn't call it that. I arranged to stop at every existing center of Chinese or even Far Eastern studies on our route eastward to London, to meet the China people and ascertain the state of the art. This began in Hawaii and continued at Berkeley, the University of Minnesota, Wisconsin, Northwestern, Chicago, Michigan, Yale, and Columbia. I found not much going on in Chinese studies. Among the few individuals in faculty posts not many could use Chinese. But certain leading personalities were already in action, particularly at Chicago.

Professor Harley F. MacNair from St. John's College at Shanghai was newly installed there with his much older bride Florence Ay-scough, who was one of the genuine sentimentalists about the beauties of Chinese culture. On a prosaic street near the Midway she transformed an 1890s residence into The House of the Wu-t'ung Tree, complete with moon gates, fountains, lanterns, screens, and objets d'art that created a very Chinese, or at least Chinesey, atmosphere. With Amy Lowell she had translated T'ang poems as *Fir-Flower Tablets.* To convey the most from the characters, she stressed the meanings of their radicals perhaps more than the original poets had meant to do. Harley, who looked like a solid businessman (prose to her poetry), adored his poetic lady and her Sino-Victorian aesthetic style; their mutual affection set us all an example. Later I took my mother to meet the MacNairs. They were kindred spirits.

Herrlee Glessner Creel, another trainee of our time in Peking, was just beginning instruction at Chicago in Chinese history and language. Herrlee suffered all his life from looking very young. Actually he was older than most of us (born 1905), and had been a reporter in Oklahoma before he came into sinology. He wrote well for the public and had already published a book on *Sinism* (1929) and got his Ph.D. at Chicago. It really bugged him to be constantly taken for a student when professors met. I realized my sense of uniqueness was mild compared with his. He headed straight back to reconstruct the dawn of Chinese history from abstruse passages in early classics. He persisted in using the *Classic of Filial Piety (Hsiao ching)* as a language text so his students could start where the Chinese used to start. His book *The Birth of China* (1936) gave the Western public the first general account of the Shang dynasty findings at Anyang.

At Yale we met Kenneth Scott Latourette, who had taught two years at Yale-in-China before World War I and pursued as his main calling the history of Christian missions worldwide. However, at Yale he found himself also the successor in fact of Samuel Wells Williams (*The Middle Kingdom,* 1848, 2nd ed. 1883) and his son Frederick Wells Williams, who had specialized on China there. Dr. Latourette had moved into the China vacuum, doing his doctorate on early American-China trade and completing his two-volume successor to Williams as *The Chinese: Their History and Culture* in 1934. These were standard volumes of dispassionate knowledge, compiled by a fair-minded and indefatigable seeker after the facts. Ken Latourette was a benign bachelor, helpful to all who came to him. He covered mountains of sources and produced manuscript, I believe, every morning except Sundays. His presidential address to the American Historical Association in 1948 was on the Christian interpretation of history.

At Columbia we saw Cyrus Peake again and his senior colleague L. Carrington Goodrich, who had listened to me very helpfully when I sought his advice at the Language School. From his childhood missionary background in North China, Carrington had made himself a sinologists' sinologist. His doctoral monograph, *The Literary Inquisition of Ch'ien-lung* (1935), alone made him the risen star of American China studies, and there was much more to come over the next forty years.

At Harvard I found *in situ* Charles Sidney Gardner, a devoted scholar and Ch'ing specialist who thought in seriatim terms and therefore specialized in the bibliography of sinology—an unselfish friend, extremely knowledgeable, enthusiastic but curiously unable to generalize, a nonsynthesizer and hence a nonproducer. Graduate students became greatly indebted to him but he could not reach the undergraduates. At the opposite extreme was the engaging Bruce Hopper of the Government Department whom we had seen in Peking. He had been a World War I aviator, and spent three years in Russia as an early representative of the Chicago-based Institute of Current World Affairs that recruited talent to follow contemporary trends abroad, and alert the American academic elite. Bruce had traveled widely and could always fit the morning's headlines into a current background. If only Gardner and Hopper could have been scrambled!

My inventory of the China tribe scattered in universities across the country in 1936 was of course incomplete. Woodbridge Bingham, back from Peking, was beginning at Berkeley. Knight Biggerstaff was just getting started at the University of Washington at Seattle and would later go to Cornell. Earl Pritchard, who had come to Oxford when I was there, was at Washington State at Pullman and eventually would go to Chicago. Derk Bodde, who had married his Russian bride, Galia Speshneff, in Peking, would go to Pennsylvania to pursue his fruitful work in Chinese philosophy. Others would soon join this variegated company.

But on the whole this was the cohort of China specialists, baked, unbaked, and half-baked, that Mortimer Graves and David Stevens could mobilize to give America an understanding of China. For a nation about to fight three major wars in China or nearby during the next generation, it was not much. The knowledge of Chinese language among us was spotty, sometimes nonexistent. In general, those who dealt with the current scene lacked the language, those who had some Chinese were immersed in the ancient past. We generally lacked the capacity to grasp what today's Chinese were thinking about except as they would tell us in English. We were generally innocent of the concepts of social science (unless political science is included in that category). On the other hand we had usually had some experience of Chinese life or, rather, foreign life in China.

None of us had come out of the assembly line we later set up: two or three years in an American graduate school learning to read, followed by two years in the field (by that time it was Taipei) learning to talk and researching a thesis, concluded by two or three years back in the United States completing a thesis and learning to teach. Such a seven-year program later produced competent specialists but they had not had much contact with Chinese people and events. They were trained to be careful historians, not to sound off on public policy.

Wilma and I, during our four years in China, on the other hand, had been less focused on sinology, more in touch with current crises. I began making speeches as soon as I reached Sioux Falls, first Rotary, then Kiwanis, the YMCA, and Sioux Falls College. My offering was at the daily-life level of Chinese houses, servants, and food, but of course it got onto the Japanese menace. Wilma also gave a lecture on Chinese art. "The farther away we get from the scene, the more we know." We were already embarked on that missionary-in-reverse role of the area specialist, telling our fellow citizens about foreign parts in the hope of our mutual salvation from war. Of course it all worked out just the opposite way. Warfare is what put Chinese and Japanese studies on their feet in the United States.

When we finally reached Cambridge in January 1936 I was offered a job in the History Department as I had expected, to begin in September. My stops at other universities had not been jobhunting. I simply wanted to know the scope and personnel of the China field nationwide. We all had so much ignorance and opportunity in common, I felt it was my professional constituency. Meanwhile I had to go to Oxford to get my degree.

New York to London on the final voyage of the *Majestic* gave me a great nostalgia for other liners I had crossed the Atlantic on half a dozen times, especially the *Mauretania* in 1931. She was one of the few with four funnels (a sister of the *Lusitania*).

> She was launched in the world just about the time I was and for over twenty years held the North Atlantic record. . . . Used to get in promptly at the end of five and a half days, in time for passengers to get to the theater.

To challenge that pair the Hamburg-Amerika Line launched the *Imperator, Vaterland,* and *Bismarck* just before World War I, after which they became the U.S. Lines' *Leviathan,* the Cunarder *Berengaria,* and the White Star Line's *Majestic.* At 56,000 tons she was the biggest ship afloat in 1936 (the *Queen Mary* would soon be 73,000), and now she was going home to the junkyard!

We had a big A-deck cabin with beds. At once we succumbed to the grandeur that had been part of the come-on in the transatlantic liners' competition. We compared our faithful houseboy Li and wily cook Liu in Peking with the shipboard service of room steward, stewardess, and table stewards.

> Our two stewards are like Night and Day, one black-haired and square-faced, the other light-haired with a ruddy complexion. Both are smooth and agile young men, much better dressed than any of the passengers, white ties and tails every night, and much much better acquainted with etiquette, table manners, wines, and topics of the day—in short they are everything but gentlemen [we were back in Britain again!]. . . . They gyrate around us as though we were the Earth, Night unto Day bringing mayonnaise and Day unto Night returning the extra forks.

With all this service I did feel that we were drawing into the shadow of a great civilization. Once arrived in London we got hold of Tony Lambert at the Foreign Office, who at once found he shared many interests with Wilma. I was invited to talk to his shop club of young diplomats and rising officials, so I described the decline and fall of Ch'ing dynasty China, once the center of civilization, suddenly so invaded and kicked around, demoralized from within. My English audience applied it all directly to the decline of the British Empire.

Self-doubt was in the air though Munich was still two and a half years ahead of us.

In the London Underground stations and in the streets we saw the poster that Phyllis had designed and Ssu-ch'eng printed to advertise the big Burlington House exhibit of Chinese art. This 1936 exhibit was the pace setter for all those that have come later, a stupendous experience worth spending a week at. The Chinese government contribution brought in a British cruiser was safe enough from piracy but almost foundered in a Bay of Biscay storm on the way home. We saw without touching the marvelous jade circlet of dragons that we had handled in Peking when Larry Sickman was buying it, and a myriad of other treasures, including many we had not seen before. Wilma made friends with Percival Yetts and other moguls of art.

> Some of the remarks at the exhibit were priceless. There was one bronze dragon, Chou, very fierce, that always got the same reaction—"Oh, I say, St. George would have had a rough time with that one, wouldn't 'e?" And there was one pompous dilettante who constantly marveled to his companion, "And to think that thet bronze was cahst when we were still in a state of uttah bahbarism!"

Completing five legal-size copies of my Oxford thesis (three to submit) while traveling was a bit hectic. Five chapters had been published as articles.* These had been typed up in Cambridge, proofed on the *Majestic,* and now needed bibliographies and conclusion. For this purpose we found refuge in a small stone hotel with arched doorways and mullioned windows built in the fifteenth century on the main street of Burford in the Cotswold sheep country west of Oxford. Spring was in progress, rolling green fields were being plowed, and we fought the bone-chilling cold in the English fashion by wearing six layers of wool, eating enormous breakfasts, in complete silence, and tramping about in the afternoons.

When the Websters came for the weekend Hitler had just denounced the Locarno agreements of 1925 and reoccupied the Rhine-

---

*In the *Chinese Social and Political Science Review,* Peiping, in January and April 1935 and in January and April 1936; and in the *Nankai Social and Economic Quarterly,* Tientsin, in April 1936.

land (March 7, 1936) and Charles was "fiercely indignant" at the mild initial reaction of the British public. "It was just such wavering that let the 1914 situation drift into war . . . the only hope of peace in Europe is to make international legal obligations binding by backing them with the real threat of force."

Charles also told us of the last times he had seen Dr. Morse (who had died in February 1934. My obituary had appeared in the *Peiping Chronicle* for February 25). He had retained a keen interest in my efforts. We looked up his niece, whom I had taken to an Oxford prom during Eights Week, 1931.

The viva (oral examination) for my Oxford D. Phil. was the usual anticlimax. Sir George N. Clark, Regius Professor of History, had served as my nominal supervisor to submit the bulky transcript volumes. He said they seemed literate but were hardly his dish of tea. Since vivas are public events, Wilma accompanied me. We found the examiners were W. C. Costin of St. John's, who had just finished a solid summary, *Great Britain and China 1833–1860,* based on the Public Record Office files, and the brilliant Geoffrey Hudson of All Souls, who had used his Greek and Latin to survey China's relations with Europe since ancient times. The only cultural gap that emerged was an Anglo-American one when Mr. Costin asked me about British treaty port merchants acting as merchant consuls for citizens of minor states. Thus a Prussian would have as his consul the British merchant T. C. Beale of Dent & Co. "And now, Mr. Fairbank," said Mr. Costin, leaning back to conclude his point, "how about a Hamburger?"

In a source-conscious atmosphere my Chinese bibliography and references (practically all I knew) gave me an inexpugnable posture. I was already learning how to be a sinologist when among historians and, with a slight shift of gears, a historian when among sinologists—much like a Chinese bandit who is never caught because he stays on the border between provinces and when pursued from one side quietly fades across into the other jurisdiction. I passed the exam.

At Balliol I was taken to Sunday-evening high table by the master, A. D. Lindsay, a "massive, slow-speaking, gray-eyed, extremely intelligent person." When we came up the circular stair from the Senior Common Room below the hall, the undergraduates pounded the tables with their spoons until we all sat down.

I had forgotten this. The furor is on the whole pleasing to the guest, however. Also pleasing is the fact that the high table eats food of its own. . . .

The master, on my right, addressed Tyler, the semi-blind but brilliant law tutor, on my left, and opined that there should be a general course in law which could be added to the work of students of economics and social sciences generally, who were hopelessly ignorant, witness the theory of a brilliant Austrian economist which accounted for the trade cycle by supposing that all companies acted in such a way as to violate the English Company Law, which of course they never did.

Well, replied the law tutor, do we in this country also have this trade cycle you speak of? (This is a fact.) The Master replied in an even tone, yes, it is a universal phenomenon.

Back in the Senior Common Room I sat between my one-time tutor Humphrey Sumner and Cyril Bailey, the dean, who told how he got to the University of Chicago at night and was put up at the Quadrangle Club. He awoke the next morning and looked out the window to see, guess what, Magdalen tower on top of St. John's wall with Christ Church great hall right beside it. John D. Rockefeller's architects who built the U. of C. almost overnight had done a faithful job of reproducing Oxford on the shores of Lake Michigan.

The master (whom the Labour government made Lord Lindsay of Birker) had been on the Universities China Committee, which got remitted Boxer funds used to set up four academic posts in Chinese studies. But growth was slow because British education, like the French, was not bringing China into the curriculum.

The D. Phil. (Oxon.) was only halfway to my book, so we took a furnished flat in Bloomsbury and spent six weeks more in the PRO. After the consulates in China, Wilma found the home-side FO dispatches quite interesting. When she got information from a fellow searcher, the helpful gentleman turned out to be R. H. Tawney. Charles termed it a "real pickup." With the Websters we saw Eileen Power, who was more than ever a legend of brains and beauty, about to marry her economic history colleague at Cambridge, Michael Postan. Her legend already included a lecture on the medieval economy to Radcliffe students in a devastatingly simple and beautiful evening dress, as if to say to them, "See, you *can* put it all together!"

Yet in 1940 at age fifty-one, still on the way up, she suddenly died. Later in 1970 when Professor Mary Wright of Yale died at fifty-two, I thought of Eileen Power. Was it still too soon, too much of a strain, for a woman to master both *yin* and *yang* and yet survive?

Since memory usually recalls only unalloyed successes, it is a blow for verisimilitude to play up failures if you can remember them. We had a very lively visit with Gilbert and Helen Highet at St. John's College, Oxford. Later they migrated from despondent Britain to Columbia University during the year of the "phony war" in 1939 (come the Battle of Britain, Gilbert went back to help), and we invited them for a five-day visit to Harvard. I don't think any of us had ever participated in such an interpersonal disaster. Our bathing hours were discordant. They were night owls; we faded at 10 P.M. and were soon exhausted from social life. They were both very smart and lit'ry people, pursuing the American scene, and really not primarily concerned with China. It all wound up in a big argument about something on the subway train back to Harvard Square. Our paths never crossed again, though my mother was a fan of Gilbert's radio talks and kept in touch with him. Shortly thereafter Helen MacInnes became an institution in her own right. *Above Suspicion* came out in 1941.

It has sometimes occurred to me that an area specialist may be rather poor company for someone not interested in the specialist's area. But I don't know. I have never spent much time with such people.

We left England on the *Europa* for Sioux Falls in late May 1936 to be with my parents. In January we had found my father in good spirits but lacking white cells. He had aleukemic leukemia. Cortisone and chemotherapy had not yet been developed to handle it. He was eating liver extract etc. but felt restored to well-being only after a periodic blood transfusion. He was charmed by Wilma as usual and also relieved at my finally getting a paying job at Harvard. Occasionally he would remind us that for most people the main activity in life is making a living.

In June 1936 I went with him to his fortieth reunion at Illinois College, Jacksonville, where he got an honorary degree. (Curiously, just forty years later in 1976 Illinois College gave an honorary degree to Ambassador Han Hsu (Han Xu) of the People's Republic of China). In July 1936 we took a happy family outing across the South Dakota dust bowl to the Black Hills. My father died rather suddenly in September, and we had a very moving service out among the trees in the garden, surrounded by so many people who valued his friendship. I felt guilty at my long absence, but thankful to have got back in time for the summer together. My mother stayed on in Sioux Falls another seven years, but after we moved to Washington in 1941, she bought a house near us in Georgetown in 1943. By 1977 when I retired after forty-one years at Harvard, she was a senior Georgetown resident.

13

STARTING IN AT HARVARD

EVEN A BORN TEACHER has a lot to do to make himself a good one. Lecturing, tutoring, and conducting seminars are all crafts to be learned, mainly from the example of one's elders. Similarly, a pioneer in a new field soon conceives of the aids to research and the textbooks that are needed by his students as well as the language skills and knowledge of books that he needs himself. Once installed at Harvard I found a multiplicity of demands arising on all sides, some from the day-to-day environment, many more from my imagination. Building up my field had to include developing myself. This of course is what a university is for. The particular company of learned men that I joined was the History Department, and it soon became my professional home, the source of friendships and a guide to conduct and aspiration.

The History Department when I became an instructor in 1936 was just entering a golden age. Harvard had trained a generation of Ph.D.s whose Ph.D.s in turn would eventually help to flood the country. But the pecking order of libraries still had Widener at the top, and judged by the prevalence of presidents of the American Historical Association, which we took to be an excellent criterion, the History Department was also at the top. Ferguson, McIlwain, Morison, Schlesinger, Sr., Fay, Langer, Brinton were all past or future presidents. They might all be present at the regular Thursday lunch in Room 1 upstairs at the Faculty Club (the room with a chandelier in it)—all except Sam Morison, who found meetings a waste of time but occasionally turned up in riding breeches. Professors like Jim Baxter, Paul Buck, Fred Merk, C. H. Haring, Mason Hammond, Michael Karpovich, David Owen, Charles Taylor, Arthur Darby Nock, Kitch Jordan, Sterling Dow, Don McKay, Elliott Perkins were all singularly devoted to the department as their main focus of loyalty within Harvard.

In this happy era our in-group cohesion was promoted by fist-ball, a unique form of volleyball played only at the dingy and convoluted gymnasium of the old Sargent School for Women's Physical Education, located where the Law School now parks its automobiles. The gym shaped the game by having big columns around the floor and a circular running track overhead. In returning a serve, the team across the net could touch the ball three times (with a hand or a forearm only) to receive it, set it up for return, and return it. But unlike in volleyball we bounced the ball off the floor on each serve and return, with carom shots possible off the pillars and other tricks. The game could be fast. It required cooperation, ingenuity in interpreting the ever-changing rules, and sportsmanship over disputed plays. Participants included Austin Scott and Dean Erwin Griswold of the Law School (the dean was rather litigious), Percy Bridgman of Physics (who would dive for a ball halfway across the floor), Raphael Demos of Philosophy, and an economist, Seymour Harris. But mainly it was played by historians, usually led by Charles Taylor and Dick Leopold.

The department's Thursday luncheons were devoted not to history but to administration, the application of rules, an area where no one's ego was involved. The chairmanship rotated every few years and had no power of appointment. It was a service to the rest of us. Whether an Egyptian girl at Radcliffe could substitute Arabic for German in getting her Ph.D. might be debated at some length. Could the History of Science be counted as a course in the medieval period? How far could New Spain substitute for Colonial America? Such questions crowded out any discussion of historical substance. This solemn administration was a fraternal rite. We were all attached to the Main Story of Graeco-Roman civilization, medieval and modern Europe, and its expansion over the world, even to Japan and China.

After the first year I had a colleague in Edwin O. Reischauer.

Professor Elisseeff had happily found a peerless trainee in the son of educational missionaries at Tokyo Women's College. He already spoke Japanese. After graduating from Oberlin in 1931 he systematically acquired a basic sinological training, supported for successive years of work at Harvard and in Paris, Tokyo, and Kyoto. We did not meet until Ed had topped off his nonpareil training with a year at Peking and returned to Harvard in the fall of 1938. His thesis, translating the travel diary of a Japanese monk who went to China in the ninth century, four hundred years ahead of Marco Polo, was a major work of sinological scholarship, with 1,550 footnotes.

On our first meeting I recall Ed's look of oriental inscrutability, dead-pan, as if thinking, "Who is this Fairbank and what does he want?" No doubt I looked just as inscrutably at him, having had some practice at it myself. Typically, when Ed published his thesis he wrote a fascinating separate volume, *Ennin's Travels in T'ang China*, to convey the whole story to the modern reader. We at once found a common bond in our desire to educate the American public. My life would have been quite different without him as a colleague. Ed was immediately recruited for fist-ball, at which he was very good, and later on was made a voting member of the History Department, a real honor, at least in the department's view. As ambitious young academics in parallel fields we had a sort of sibling rivalry, but I always felt he was on the inside track in the establishment while I was more on the fringe. Since area specialists, according to one theory, take on the characteristics of the people they study, perhaps this accounts for Ed's establishmentarianism. The Japanese are the most prudently successful people of modern times, while the Chinese are still struggling to put their act together.

When I began tutoring and lecturing at Harvard I considered my preparation about half finished. My D. Phil. (Oxon.) had required no preliminary examination in fields of history. This sanction, which leads American Ph.D. candidates aiming at China to stuff themselves with books and ideas on ancient history or Ren. and Ref., was lacking in my case. As I have sapiently explained to so many candidates who didn't know the shortcuts I had taken, a knowledge of other fields adds perspective on one's own. I felt I had learned something from teaching the Renaissance, to say nothing of the Reformation, in clearly enunciated terms at Tsing Hua. So at Harvard I audited Professor Ferguson on Greece.

The other thing Oxford had not given me was a seminar. Since I planned to offer one on Ch'ing documents, I figured it might be wise to take one first. So I got Professor Langer's permission to participate in his on modern diplomatic history.

A dozen of us climbed to his upstairs study at his house in Cambridge once a week and sat all around the room in front of the bookshelves. He at his desk directed a systematic, efficient process that much impressed me. A student read his paper under a light at a table. Then each man around the room gave a critique of it—definition and value of topic, organization, sources used, style of writing, obscurities, lacunae—everything that could improve a good job or torpedo a bad one. After that Mr. Langer gave a magisterial summary of what he could offer, and finally the writer was allowed to speak in defense or explanation. Everybody had had a workout in serious criticism.

I admired the neatness of this strict, analytic exercise as contrasted with the customary seminar shambles: "Are there any questions?" asks the instructor. "What did you mean by so and so?" says one student. "I was interested in what you said about so and so," says another. "I found the paper very interesting since I know nothing about it," says a third. All batting the breeze, proving nothing, wasting everyone's time.

For Mr. Langer I prepared my paper on why Japan did not intervene in China during the revolution in 1911–12. I rounded up the British, American, French, German documentation and then looked at some Chinese and Japanese. Most of the students, some of whom were taking my course, let me off easily. Professor Langer suggested that since I was focusing on Japan I might best begin with their documents. Right on target!

One day after a reception Wilma had brought Felix Frankfurter, who was a family friend, and Harold Laski home to supper with us and some of her girl friends—a gay party. Come ten to eight, I excused myself "to go to Professor Langer's seminar." "What's he got that we haven't got?" asked our luminaries. I felt rather insufferably self-righteous and could only say, "It's part of a plan." I was still trying to qualify for the big time.

After I began lecturing in the spring of 1937 and found a graduate-student response, I wanted to offer seminar training. To check on my own efficacy as a translator, I worked informally with Professor James

R. Ware of the Department of Far Eastern Languages, an ex-Latin teacher with whose style I found a good deal in common. By 1940 I had a body of materials to use. The History Department assistant, a graduate student named John Morton Blum, helped me by duplicating them. He used the dittograph process, a predecessor of Xerox that marked its users with an indelible purple dye. I am sure this early Chinese experience not only left its mark upon John Blum but also, by the inscrutable ways of providence, contributed to his becoming a distinguished Yale Americanist and a member also during the 1970s of the Harvard Corporation. I got out printed editions of this Ch'ing documents syllabus in the boom years 1952, '59, '65, and '70.

Reading documents and translating them scratched a hole in the surface of the Chinese polity. One could glimpse all sorts of institutions operating underneath—the far-flung postal service, the salt gabelle, the grain transport that fed Peking via the Grand Canal, the Yellow River conservancy that tried to keep the Grand Canal from being flooded, the Chinese constabulary and Manchu banner troops, networks of land taxation and customs duties, all administered under the panoply of the venerable Six Boards at Peking. As a result documents were full of technical procedural terms in bewildering variety.

The newly published documents set up insatiable demands. We needed to know how they were produced and handled, how long it took to transmit them. In 1935 I had made the acquaintance of a skilled young bibliographer at Yenching, Teng Ssu-yü. He was just my age and had the myriad Chinese reference works at his fingertips. Knight Biggerstaff, who got to Peking two years before me, collaborated with Teng to produce a modern monument, *An Annotated Bibliography of Selected Chinese Reference Works.* When Teng came to Harvard to do his Ph.D. we collaborated in 1939–41 on a series of three articles—on the transmission of Ch'ing documents, on the various types and uses of them, and on the Ch'ing tribute system regulations and practices (all published in the *Harvard Journal of Asiatic Studies* and then in a combined volume as *Studies in Ch'ing Administration*).

The subject goes right on expanding. Harvard published Silas H. L. Wu's *Communications and Imperial Control in China* in 1970. Other revelations are now coming out in Taipei and Peking and at Yale and elsewhere. We are still acquiring a basis for understanding how the Chinese have organized themselves.

I have telescoped this growth of the Ch'ing documents field into a quick summary because, as things turned out, I acquired the franchise to exploit this gold mine at Harvard for some forty years, and something like sixty published volumes of monographic work came directly out of it.

Meanwhile my extensive experience in how not to study foreign languages was perfected in my study of Japanese. The easiest and most useless way to start a language is by exchanging lessons with a native speaker. I had begun in Peking with a crew-cut TR-type executive of the South Manchurian Railway Company. First, he spoke Japanese and explained it in English, then we both spoke English. Score: 1 to 3. I felt like a Detroit auto maker of a later day.

My second beginning of Japanese was at the Tokyo YWCA in the hot summer of 1935. The instructor was a lady so I learned some lady talk, super polite for a man. Third, I began the Naganuma course used at the American Embassy. The genial Mr. Naganuma had an American wife. His textbooks took one systematically through the necessary forms. One of his teachers went with us to Karuizawa, the diplomatic summer resort. I grew wise about the two kinds of phonetic syllabary *(kana)* and the two main kinds of Chinese readings (sounds for characters) plus the various Japanese readings of the same characters.

Back at Harvard I eagerly took the elementary Japanese course. To teach Japanese as a foreign language, it used the textbooks developed for Korean schoolchildren—mainly about birds, flowers, kite flying, and Japanese holidays. The equivalent of "Run with me to the tree" and "Rain, rain, go away; Come again some other day," which had begun my reading of English in Sioux Falls, was "Saita! Saita! Sakura ga saita!" meaning "They bloom! They bloom! The cherry blossoms are in bloom!" As a conversation opener this statement would obviously be more useful in March–April than in November–December.

Finally the new Elisseeff-Reischauer textbook came out in draft, bearing down hard on the moods, tenses, and other aspects of verbs, so I began the language for the fifth time with much profit. Professor Elisseeff, however, was a bit fussed at having a faculty colleague as a student. He seemed afraid to call on me lest I prove stupid and lower the flag.

Thus, by the time I got to Kyoto for Japanese language study in

1952, I was a pretty good beginner. Sure enough, the Kyoto language school used the Naganuma textbooks, and the teachers were profoundly impressed with my rapid advance through the first two. In eighteen years I had made distinct progress. I could ask excellent questions without necessarily understanding the answers.

In preparation for a period in Japan in 1960, I arranged to converse with a bright Harvard undergraduate, Tatsuo Arima. He was chairman of the Adams House student body and had also been the outstanding student in his class at St. Paul's School, truly bicultural (and now a top Japanese diplomat). "Sensei (professor)," he asked, "when did you begin studying Japanese?" "In 1933," I said. "My goodness," said Tatsu, "that's the year I was born."

In 1964 I gave some lectures to Japanese audiences in a combination of English and Sino-Japanese, that is, stringing Chinese phrases along in their Japanese readings. The topic was Kindaika (modernization), which some Americans were touting as an alternative to Marxism. The audience seemed to get my English, at any rate.

Since my object in reading Japanese was to find out what Japanese historians had written about China, I decided to round up the subject in a descriptive bibliography. In 1952 I found a partner in Professor Masataka Banno, a very lively specialist in the same field of China's foreign relations. His father was a businessman and Masataka had been born in New York City. He was teaching full time, so I took the lead in drafting the entry for each item and summarizing the contents while he corrected my drafts and summaries and added the insider's view of authors and interpretations that gave value to the resulting manuscript.

We were living in a tea-ceremony house beside a pond in a beautiful garden estate of the Hara family in Shinagawa. The teahouse was equipped with a gas heater and a refrigerator to keep us warm and the food cold. Every morning I took the fast, crowded municipal railway, circling halfway round the city to reach Tokyo University's Institute of Oriental Culture, where we had the use of a study and the library. Japan's postwar recovery was only semi-complete in 1952 and heat was a luxury, as at Oxford. I commonly wore overcoat, scarf, and even hat and gloves, and lunched on a peanut-butter-and-marmalade sandwich. In six months flat we covered a thousand items, making many discoveries, and Harvard-Yenching published *Japanese Studies of Modern China* in 1955.

Getting this manuscript finished had some illuminating angles. Since we were obliged to spell Japanese names in the English alphabet, we had to know how these names were actually pronounced. The Japanese characters may be quite ambivalent among alternatives but no one has to decide about it when writing or reading them in Japanese. Banno spent hours on the phone asking authors how they called themselves. Our friend Otake Fumio said he was often called Odake, sometimes even by himself, but it really *should* be Otake, not Odake or Kotake. Katō Shigeshi was usually called Shigeru incorrectly. Wada Sei was often called Wada Kiyoshi, and so on.

At first I assumed the multiple ambiguities of sound in Japanese writing, and their combining the unchanging characters with highly inflected verbs, would be quite enough of a handicap to hold Japan back. Since it didn't happen, one can only conclude this infernal complexity has prepared Japanese minds to outdo us.

Our manuscript had a long index and also a character index for authors' names. We happily persuaded Professor Sumiko Yamamoto of International Christian University to do these indices, but it proved to be a third leg of the book, very time-consuming, so we made her a co-author of the second printing in 1967.

I edited a supplementary volume of another thousand items done by Noriko Kamachi, *Japanese Studies of Modern China since 1953*, covering up to 1969 and published in 1975. We used mainly the Harvard-Yenching Library but got the guidance of our friend and teacher Ichiko Chūzō, head of the Center for Modern Chinese Studies at the Toyo Bunko in Tokyo.

On this subject I feel like Mao Tse-tung's "Old Man Who Removed the Mountain." All we have to do is keep at it.

In the time allowed, I doubt I could ever have become fully trained. I started Russian with a sweet, sad-eyed lady in 1958 and practiced it in Moscow and Leningrad in 1960 and 1972. But this language turned out to have too many roots from the back of beyond, not connected with European languages, impossible to remember at age fifty-one. It gave me still another capacity to ask questions in a foreign tongue and not get the answers.

This digression on my career as an always promising, never finished, language student is not meant to warn the young by an example of failure. I always felt that, given six months' intensive application, I could become quite fluent in whatever language I was working on. It was only that I could never find the six months, so much else took priority.

In my first years of teaching in Cambridge, I took Harvard U. for granted. It was like a gymnasium on whose barbells and flying rings an athlete could keep working toward his championship. It was an efficient environment in which to pursue books and ideas. Some specialists talked more, wrote less, and were often inspiring teachers. Others talked less, wrote more, and became top professors. At the last hurdle to tenure, the written word outweighed the spoken. This produced controversy, but to me the issue seemed simple. Writing is more durable, can be more influential if enough people read it, and can't easily be published if it becomes as repetitious as teachers may become. This suited me personally because in my new field there was a lot of basic data and new understanding to provide. Books were needed.

I remained aware, however, that in older fields one produced books less easily. After catching up with Rostovtzeff, Haskins, Burck-hardt, McIlwain, or other masters, what was the neophyte to do? He could rely on the fact that every generation has to look at history anew, but the history looked at is often hit and miss. Large topics may be put aside in the dustbin, including one's own.

My problem seemed quite different. I had every confidence that, if I could accomplish my own aims, the department would give me permanent tenure.

The appointment system had not always been reliable, however. In 1936 President Conant, new at his job, appointed as dean of the faculty a mathematician who was better at numbers than at people. When the Economics Department unanimously recommended the reappointment for three-year terms of two economics instructors, Ray Walsh and my Exeter roommate and close friend Alan Sweezy, they were turned down on budgetary grounds. Since both had been active in the Harvard Teachers Union, an affiliate of the American Federation of Labor, and were vigorously interested in the New Deal movement for the unionization of labor, a lot of us felt there might be some prejudice or bias at work behind the decision. In May 1937, 141 nontenured members of the Harvard faculty, after a lot of out-raged and concerned caucusing and resolutions, addressed a fifteen-page printed memo to nine full professors asking them to investigate the cases. Conant had the good sense to appoint this group as his own committee, and after a year's weekly meetings with oral and written testimony its report of May 1938 recommended that Walsh and Sweezy be reappointed because, although no bias was evident in the procedure, it had not adequately scrutinized their merits.* No more able and distinguished a group of citizens could have been found anywhere, and when the Harvard Corporation rejected their eighty-six page printed recommendation it diminished itself and under-wrote an injustice just as plainly to my mind as President Lowell had done in the Sacco-Vanzetti case a decade before.

Moreover, there was a specific loss to Harvard in the fact that Alan Sweezy had been an outstanding leader of the class of 1929, among other things as editor of the *Crimson* and class secretary, with the sort of loyalty that Harvard always depends upon among directors of the alumni association and the Board of Overseers. To be made a focus of heated public controversy, as I was to find out in the 1950s, is no fun. To be vindicated after a year, as to the facts, and then to be rejected ex cathedra was a depressing experience. As an able economist Alan went on, of course, to teach at Williams, work in the Federal Reserve Board, and then teach many generations of scien-tists at Cal. Tech. The Committee of Eight also continued for another year to scrutinize Harvard's entire handling of the faculty. Their detailed recommendations, once accepted by Conant, laid a firm basis for the Harvard faculty's excellence. I have always thought the resulting system should be known as the Alan R. Sweezy Memorial Appointment Procedure.

When I started to lecture at Harvard in February 1937, I was a new face with a lively and neglected topic. As warfare kept China in the news, one could invoke the national interest as a compelling sanction for learning about East Asia. "What this country needs," I reported to the class of 1929, "is a good course in East Asian history." Rather simple-mindedly, I assumed my job was to set forth the facts and let answers emerge of themselves.

Graduate students who attended the course soon shattered this excuse for not thinking. Three were Canadians who became diplo-

---

*This Committee of Eight (one of the nine having died) consisted of Ralph Barton Perry (chairman), W. S. Ferguson (Greek history), K. B. Murdock (English), Arthur Schlesinger, Sr. (American history), Harlow Shapley (Astronomy) and three Law School professors, E. Merrick Dodd, Felix Frankfurter, and Edmund M. Morgan.

mats—E. H. Norman, Ralph Collins, Arthur Menzies. (The last two were later ambassadors to Peking.) They simply asked not-simple questions. I soon realized that any "fact" set forth is already within a framework of assumptions. The fact stater's first job is to be aware of his framework. Usually it is the received wisdom of the field, what one's predecessors have worked out. First, one must choose among them, whom to follow. Second, one must try to go farther, what new can be said? For this purpose one should try to recast lecture headings and phraseology every time one treats a topic.

History 83 consequently began to expand in scope. "The Far East since 1793" had been set up by A. C. Coolidge and Stanley Hornbeck to deal with events since the "opening" of China and Japan. In 1793 Lord Macartney went as Britain's first ambassador to Peking in a gesture intended to make China accessible to British trade. It was ironic for this British move to provide the starting point of East Asia's modern history—almost as incongruous as China's taking the Opium War of 1840 as a starting point. The Jesuit chapter of Sino-European contact in the sixteenth to eighteenth centuries seemingly could be disregarded. After all, it had been merely religio-philosophical, not commercial-military.

Japan was also in the Far East and very prominent in 1937. In addition I found Korea, Inner Asia, and Southeast Asia had peoples and cultures galore, all in geographic habitats with long histories, all interacting. What a smorgasbord! No one seemed to know much about any of them.

The first necessity was to locate these places on maps. With funds from Professor Elisseeff I got the gifted cartographer Erwin Raisz to produce a series of topographical "Landform" maps on which Raisz's ingenious markings showed at a glance mountain heights, deserts, deltas, and other key features of terrain, but no names of places. For example, you can locate the Muzart Pass between Ili and Kashgaria when it figures in history in 1871. We made nine maps altogether. Raisz suggested putting my name below his as "editor," but I felt modesty was a better policy. It was he who had made the maps.

Lists of places could now be given each student; sample maps under glass in the library could show all places correctly; so our examinations included map questions.

Lecturers of course range between the shouters and the whisperers. Roger Bigelow Merriman, who was called "Frisky," I suppose because he looked a bit feline, had shouted at us in History 1. He needed to because the New Lecture Hall (anonymous gift of Abbott Lawrence Lowell, now Lowell Lecture Hall) in addition to hard seats had very poor acoustics in the pre-mike age. How to hypnotize five hundred squirming freshmen was a challenge. Charles Webster, when he stayed with us once before lecturing there, said it was the toughest job he ever faced.

The best whisperer was William Scott Ferguson. I attended his lectures to learn about Greece. No one dropped a pin, we were all straining so hard to hear his lapidary account. But for myself I believed in audibility, taking no chances.

Some lecturers, like Frederick Merk, talked precisely at dictation speed. From Tsing Hua I had got the habit of repeating each point in a paraphrase; one could seem to be going faster. One style of lecturing much admired was to speak without notes, shaping an oral masterpiece on the spot. James Phinney Baxter III did this while marching back and forth across the podium. I usually had a list of names and terms to convey, as part of a lecture outline, with bibliography added. Instead of using a blackboard for me to smudge over and copy on and for them to peer at and copy off, I gave students a sheet of paper, everything accurate.

A lecture as a form of dramatic art needs a shape—context, theme, development, climax, at the least. A reading assignment cannot take its place because the lecturer usually conveys more of attitudes, concerns, and possibilities than he would write down, and can make it all more timely. In the final analysis, the listener should have an experience of hearing "a mind at work." Whether he can actually have a vicarious experience of the past, "how it really was," is a further ideal seldom achieved.

In the late 1930s Radcliffe was still attached to Harvard like a dimwit sister hardly acknowledgeable in public. After lecturing to thirty or forty Harvardians, I would march across the common to Radcliffe and for an extra fee repeat my lecture to half a dozen or a dozen women. Since I can't abide verbatim repetition and was seated at a big table, not at a podium, the lecture would deteriorate into a sort of tutorial monologue, lacking wall maps and whatever histrionics one can put into a stand-up presentation. Some Cliffies would sense that they were being short-changed, but others would feel gratitude for the benison of Harvard instruction filtering down to them. It was a great day when Provost Paul Buck on the plea of wartime financial necessity opened the door to coeducation. Since that time some of my best friends have been women.

I also thought history should be full of mental images—not just the ladder of chronology, but also maps, sites, sights, and people. When Ed Reischauer and I in 1941 put our courses together to start a "History of East Asian Civilization," which later became a family of textbooks, we began using slides. The Fogg Museum and Department of Fine Arts had large files of glass 4 × 3 1/2-inch slides of monuments, paintings, and such. I began making slides from every book I came across, disregarding copyright on the grounds that within Harvard I was doing private showings only, not charging admission to the public. Slides can tell their own stories, and some topics can best be dealt with visually—like the loess soil in China's Northwest, or the succession of Ch'ing dynasty rulers, from the square, tough founders of the seventeenth and eighteenth centuries to the querulous skinflint Tao-kuang, Emperor in the early nineteenth century, and two successors who looked like girls, ending with the narrow-minded and ruthless Empress Dowager, who completely lost the ball game.

In 1973 I was lucky to find a meticulous production artist, Sumner Glimcher, who helped me voice my comments on fifteen filmstrips published by Harvard University Press as *China Old and New.* Since then photo albums have proliferated, with fine color and rare subjects.

Tutoring was part of Lowell's dream of combining the best of the European modes of education—lectures of French precision, Germanic seminars for graduate students, Oxford-Cambridge-type tutorials for undergraduates. Harvard had everything. The problem was to keep it all in gear. Tutoring couldn't get you tenure, but everyone was supposed to keep a hand in. Tutoring in my study in Kirkland House, I found it worked best in groups of three or four, even five, who could comment on each other's papers without having to do a paper each week. I avoided the laborious one-on-one tutorials that exhausted Oxford dons—except in the case of Theodore H. White.

That my most exciting student should be my first was a quirk of fate. Teddy was in the class of 1938, along with Arthur Schlesinger, Jr., but he didn't know many classmates or see much of Harvard because he was so busy making a living. His memoir *In Search of History* is a great saga of grit-and-intellect. It speaks kindly of me and Wilma. The only thing it can't convey is our excitement at meeting Theodore H. White—a not very tall bundle of energy with a world-wide imagination and eloquence to go with it. Teddy was already a junior and a top scholar when he became my tutee. Having come to Harvard from Boston Latin School in its great days, he knew his classics, and at night he taught Hebrew. He had a trained mind and also knew the "real world" of livelihood. All he lacked was social experience—balancing a teacup, presenting letters of introduction, being au courant with the theater and books of the moment, having made the grand tour of major European capitals, and the other superficial frills. These he picked up overnight when the time came.

Teddy did his honors thesis on Japan's Twenty-one Demands of 1915, a timely background for the war in China. His summa cum laude degree was assured in the oral examination by this colloquy:

Professor James R. Ware: "What's the BEFEO?"

T. H. White: "That must be a publication—why not the *Bulletin de l'École Française d'Extrème Orient* in Hanoi?"

Ware: "What's the BMFEA?"

White: "Sir, I haven't the slightest idea."

It was (need I say?) the *Bulletin of the Museum of Far Eastern Antiquities* in Stockholm, but the other examiners felt the question was nit-picking.

A session with Teddy was like Fourth of July fireworks. Ignite an idea and he would take off like a rocket. How come Confucius and Plato, Mencius and Aristotle were roughly contemporaries? Are civilizations really individual organisms—born, grown, productive, and senescent—like you and me?

Gibbon said Rome fell from "barbarism and religion." China was equally conquered by Buddhism and barbarian invaders from the north. How was China able to put it all together again in the great T'ang empire while Rome perished? Was it because Spain, France, and Britain developed as nations, while China lacked peninsulas and was unified by its rivers?

Or again: Japan and Britain, island empires on opposite wings of Eurasia, developed early nationalism, acculturated from the continent, sometimes invading it, living by trade and naval power. Did their Anglo-Japanese alliance (1902–22) extend the unequal treaty system for another twenty years in China? If so, was that a good thing?

Teddy White could have succeeded at anything (his brother became head of the Weather Service and the great monitoring agency developed from it) but he was cut out to be a journalist. Like a Chinese statesman, he turned weakness into strength—his short stature put him readily in a filial status to the great captains he interviewed. Talking to Teddy, Douglas MacArthur waxed more than usually philosophical. They were kindred spirits. Teddy had his own supply of grandiloquence.

Bright students enhance the life of a teacher. Another influence on me and Wilma was the yellow frame house at 41 Winthrop Street, facing the Owl Club, Lowell House, and the Indoor Athletic Building. It has definitely shaped our lives. We contributed some Chinese furniture and statuary. But the house has had more influence on us than we on it.

To begin with, it is a small house, built in the early nineteenth century, with fieldstones forming the basement walls. The entrance door originally opened into a vestibule, from which a cramped circular stairway wound up to the second floor and then to a third floor under the eaves, with two rooms symmetrically on either side. The two first- and two second-floor rooms each had a fireplace. The two-story wing added on the right, away from the street, had a steep narrow back stairs, and its first- and second-story rooms had fireplaces too—making six in all.

About the turn of the century the entrance stairway to the second floor was removed and the two first-floor rooms merged into one big room, fourteen by thirty. The back stairs became the only stairs to the second floor, while the circular stairway from the second to the third floor remained intact but with no support under it. This created a house, when we found it in 1936, with a big main room, lacking a vestibule, and a kitchen on the ground floor, three rooms on the second, and two garrets on the third. A bathroom with a short bathtub, where a sewing room had been, was suspended over the far side of the big room. The water tank for the toilet, however, was on the third floor; one pulled a chain that disappeared through a hole in the ceiling. Any third-floor occupant heard a sudden flooding sound.

The result was a certain lack of grandeur, favoring cocktail parties in the main room rather than dinner parties at one end of it, the masses rather than an elite. It was also a bit like living on one's yacht (I imagine)—closet and storage space rather confined, everything in its place, or else.

However, 41 Winthrop Street was only two hundred yards from Widener Library, across two arteries, Mt. Auburn Street and Massachusetts Avenue. I could be in my study in four minutes, after dinner, at 8 A.M., any time. In forty-odd years I saved commuting time equal to perhaps half a year of eight-hour days.

This proximity to the Yard and the Houses made it accessible to students. We began having an open-house tea at five on Thursdays. Omitting five years away in wartime and two on sabbatical, our Thursday teas continued for thirty-three years.

They were a multi-purpose institution. Foreign students practiced their English, girls met boys, visiting dignitaries were entertained, though they sometimes wondered in just what way they were being honored by this miscellany of cackling students. Cousins from Sioux Falls could not feel neglected. But primarily these teas helped to make my students into a community of friends. Some friendships indeed became marriages. Arthur Wright met Mary Clabaugh there. My classmate Bill Youngman met our onetime Peking housemate, Elsie Perkins. My colleague Myron Gilmore met Sheila Dehn. Teddy White stayed in the house almost alone on his first leave back from China in the summer of 1940. He says he learned a lot he wanted to know. Come the sexual revolution young couples have house-sat for us on weekends we were away. The house is completely adaptable.

Forty-one Winthrop Street also illustrates our umbilical relationship to Harvard. In 1936 cost accounting was not yet the American way. The amiable James Biggar, Caretaking and Real Estate Division in the Lehman Hall office of the Business Manager of Harvard U., showed us the house just vacated, which he could renovate and hold for our return in the fall. On February 11 we signed a lease. Rent at $50 a month would begin July 1. We can still be thrown out on a month's notice but it hasn't happened so far (1981).

The house was fifteen feet wide on a twenty-two-foot lot wedged in between a big boardinghouse two feet to the west and Merrill Hall, a three-story pile of brick on the corner of Holyoke and Winthrop. We planted an apple tree and lilacs in the narrow yard. But, when we tried digging, we hit cinders, toy automobiles, and other kinds of fill. The house had once been the Stylus Club, inhabited by Maxwell

Perkins, the editor of Thomas Wolfe, and by Van Wyck Brooks *(The Flowering of New England)*. Its history continued to unfold. After World War II Merrill Hall was demolished and turned into a grass plot. Then the landlady two feet away on the west complained one day of flying ants in her cellar. They were diagnosed as termites and within a week a large iron wrecking ball had smashed up the boardinghouse and it was carted away, leaving another grass plot. We hired an exterminator and were careful never to find a termite.

The steam heat came underground from the Indoor Athletic Building across the street, and then went on elsewhere. If we went down and turned the wrong wheel we could freeze up the Office of Placement and Career Counseling on the corner of Winthrop and Dunster. For years, until cost accounting prevailed, the steam pipes formerly under Merrill Hall kept a pleasant green passage through the winter snow.

Every seven years the house was painted, much as the university refurbishes professors by sabbaticals. As the clapboards dried and etiolated, the outer covering became almost as much paint as wood. Squirrels from the apple tree began to winter somewhere inside the eaves. Every few weeks in winter a radiator, in the heating system that had been piped through the rooms, would back up and start knocking like a jackhammer. The radiators had an early-model steam trap such that condensed hot water was supposed to flow down through the valve where the steam came up. Cognoscenti kept the valves fully open or tightly shut, but some guest, wanting just a little heat, would open a valve just a little. Knocking meant the radiator was filling up with water, but it could be removed by taking off the escape valve and catching the boiling effluent in a pail properly held. Water seepage every year or so would wet a ceiling and eventually drip from it. The ceiling would have to be replastered. By my retirement in 1977 the house was getting rundown and it was a question whether the tenants or the house would outlast the other. But then the university really renovated it—new clapboard siding, insulated windows, new ceilings—more than it or Geritol could do for the occupants.

One pleasure of Cambridge is its proximity to New Hampshire, a place where the early American character was formed by the laborious conquest of nature, only to find that life was more productive using machines to farm the Middlewestern plains. New Hampshire is essentially an outcropping of granite partly covered by trees and under snow all winter. But the summer is longer than in Siberia; nine months of the year it can be a weekend and vacation hideaway from Boston.

Wilma's family in 1910 began summering on a farm outside Franklin, New Hampshire, where Daniel Webster had welcomed the railway in 1842. Soon the family Ford supplanted the steam engine to get there, and then as the farming population continued to dwindle, the big interstate highways brought Franklin within two hours of Cambridge. Route 93 leaves one two-and-a-half miles from the New Boston Road, a dead-end road barely within the limits of city maintenance, that winds a mile uphill and now has been largely taken over by Wilma's brother and three sisters and their numerous offspring.

About 1914 Miss Ida Cannon, who was pioneering hospital social service at the Massachusetts General Hospital, bought a treeless sheep pasture whose topmost granite outcropping had one of the best views on the New Boston Road, looking at Mt. Cardigan twenty miles away up the Pemigewasset Valley. She built a forty-by-forty-foot summer cottage, which Wilma inherited. Rain collected off the roof provided washing water obtainable from a tank through a hand pump. Drinking water was carried up from a spring.

When I first saw Franklin in 1929, the hilltop was almost closed in by pine trees. Since the Cannons were from St. Paul, where trees were sacred, there was no help for it. But God intervened and the view was restored by the hurricane of 1938. By that time we had cut five miles of bridle paths through the surrounding forest and dammed a small stream for swimming. Endless miles of stone walls uphill and down still marked off the forgotten fields and pastures, but otherwise nature had reconquered the place and given us tree chopping as a necessary summer pastime. Chopping four-inch poplar trees, one can really impress city dwellers. The two secrets to using an ax are first to accelerate the ax head's velocity just before impact by wrist action, and second, to be able to hit the precisely same spot, like lightning striking twice in one place. Long arms also help.

Franklin also gave me a chance to see something of my father-in-law, W. B. Cannon, who was a gardener and a carpenter like my own father. When he was writing *The Wisdom of the Body* on the intricate capacity of the human system's self-righting mechanisms that preserve us in a steady state, we discussed the possible social implications. I had once written a paper for a Balliol discussion club on "Society the Superbeast," pushing the ancient analogy between the human and social organisms. I was fascinated to see how Dr. Cannon's scientific thinking cut the subject down to size, while salvaging what could be used.*

The summers in Franklin were integral to my five-year novitiate at Harvard. They allowed me to expand my D. Phil. thesis and integrate the British and Chinese sides of the story. It had started on the foreign fringe of China but wound up looking outward from Peking. *Trade and Diplomacy on the China Coast* was not finished and published until 1953. It completed my training for training others just in time for the postwar boom in Chinese studies.

---

*Walter B. Cannon, "The Body Physiologic and the Body Politic," presidential address, American Association for the Advancement of Science, 1940.

14

WAR AND POLICY PROBLEMS

WHEN I OCCASIONALLY lifted my eyes from Ch'ing documents and books on East Asia, the news had always got worse. Fascism was on the march. The German-Japanese-Italian anti-Comintern Pact of November 1936 had unified the predators. Disasters steadily ensued. The Spanish Civil War (after July 1936), Hitler's takeover of Austria (March 1938), followed by the Munich agreement (September) and his takeover of Czechoslovakia (March 1939), all provided the horrifying context in which Japan invaded China (from July 7, 1937).

The American reaction was continued isolationism—such a reactionary though often idealistic anti-war phenomenon that it now seems hard to believe. But there was a curious anomaly in our foreign policy. We actually had three policies at once: east toward Europe, no entangling alliances, "we keep out"; south toward Latin America, the Monroe Doctrine, "you keep out"; and west across the Pacific, the Open Door, "we all go in." In short, the soft underbelly of isolationism was in the Far East.

Of course no long-continued national policy is likely to be all bad, even if deficient in meaning or operability. The Open Door combined American idealism and self-interest in a classic fashion worthy of the British. The operative clauses in John Hay's original notes of 1899 came from Robert Hart of the Customs by way of his commissioner, Alfred E. Hippisley (to whom Dr. Morse introduced me in London in 1931). Hippisley drafted the memo for W. W. Rockhill that was used by Secretary Hay when he and President McKinley wanted an election-year China policy that would not overextend America in China. The European powers, after Japan's defeat of China in 1895, had grabbed concessions in 1898 and American expansionists were demanding we keep up. (So we did, in the Philippines, Guam, Hawaii, and Samoa.) The McKinley-Hay Open Door doctrine was a tour de force, the open door for trade of all nations on equal terms (what the Customs stood for), picked up from the British after they had abandoned it to join the imperialist scramble. It was our substitute for imperialism in China at the same time that we were practicing imperialism in the Philippines.

There were really two Open Doors, one for us and one for China. The original Open Door meant equal opportunity for trade and investment in China, in other words, an Open Season, under the unequal treaty system. But Hay's second set of notes in 1900 spoke of China's administrative and territorial "entity" (later the term was "integrity") in order to head off a breakup of China during the Boxer crisis. It was a declaration in favor of giving China a chance to remain (or become) a nation.

Thus the Open Door was protective of our unequal treaty trading privileges in China and in favor of China's survival as a nation, but it was non-operational—a unilateral declaration, not a treaty. It was an unenforceable sentiment with a built-in ambiguity, since it favored both China's continued sovereignty and the treaty system's continued impairment of that sovereignty.

Yet, in isolationist America of the late 1930s, China policy provided the best field for maneuver back toward an active role in the world struggle. The Western Pacific had succeeded our Far West as a frontier of expansion. Both missionaries and businessmen had a special and active role in China based on their extraterritorial status. In the late nineteenth century they had had such a role in Japan too. In both countries they remained involved in a way they were not in Europe.

Meantime, Japan's invasion of China created a plain moral issue of policy, whether to keep on helping it with war supplies or try not to. Out of this moral dilemma came the American Committee for Non-Participation in Japanese Aggression, the active beginning of a public lobby for the cause of China. It was an open, broadly based publicity organization solely devoted to stopping the flow of American oil, steel, and munitions to fuel Japan's war machine. America was supplying at least half of Japan's imported war materials.

The spark plug in this lobby was Harry Price, China-born son of a Southern Presbyterian missionary educator. He had done a Yale M.A. in economics (1932) and taught five years at Yenching. In May 1938, on leave in New York, Harry and his brother Frank brought a small group together who had mainly a missionary background. They decided on the longish name American Committee for Non-Participation in Japanese Aggression as the best way to show their concrete and limited aim, making use of the strongly isolationist mood of the country.

In August 1938 they mailed out 22,000 copies of *America's Share in Japan's War Guilt*. Harry Price and company did a truly exemplary job of organization. By Christmas 1938 they had an imposing list of honorary supporters. The national board of twenty-nine and the sponsors list of eighty-six included big names in all aspects of American life. For active chairman they got Roger S. Greene, who had had a distinguished career in the American consular service and then as head of the Rockefeller-backed Peking Union Medical College until 1934. We had known him as the top figure in the American community, who gave me moral support when I needed it. His brother, Jerome Greene, was secretary of the Harvard Corporation. Roger brought to the committee's work a wealth of experience and a very astute eye for policy.

The point about the non-participation committee was that during its two-and-one-half years of operation it mobilized and energized most of the American China hands who a decade later supported the Nationalist cause in American policy. By that time it was a habit. The ex-missionary and later Minnesota congressman, Dr. Walter Judd, made 1,400 talks on China during this period, and members of Congress could trace his peregrinations by the heavy non-participation mail they received from areas he traversed. Cooperation with leftists or on any other issue was avoided. In short, Harry Price in New York and Roger Greene in Washington mounted one of the most effective single-issue campaigns up to that time in our history. Chiang Kai-shek as the symbol of Free China was one beneficiary, because the committee tried to avoid touching upon the KMT-CCP conflict and spoke merely of "China's" great economic future and current posture as a democratic bastion like Britain.

While the committee's activists included many with missionary backgrounds, it was not able to win over the mission boards. These bodies felt responsible for mission work in Japan as well as China, and were generally against taking sides abroad lest it involve us in warfare. After the National Defense Act of July 2, 1940, marked the beginning of a tougher Japan policy, the non-participation committee eventually decided to go out of business and did so as of February 1, 1941. United China Relief had been organized in early 1941 but the KMT-CCP conflict had already produced dissension among the China hands.

As a Harvard instructor busy writing and lecturing, I took no part in the non-participation campaign. But events inevitably drew me into public activity. As the European crisis deepened and full-scale warfare hit both the Far East and Europe, Harvard professors organized in 1940 in order to mobilize American support of Britain and of freedom *vs.* tyranny in general. Professor Ralph Barton Perry and a large group of liberals, mainly humanists, foresaw an inevitable struggle with Nazism and set up a letter- and editorial-writing shop like a committee of correspondence. They called it American Defense: Harvard Group, hoping to see other groups arise elsewhere. Perry was chairman, my Roman History colleague Mason Hammond was treasurer, and Philip Hofer secretary. Also at the head were Sam Cross (Russian), Jim Landis (Law School) and Arthur Schlesinger, Sr. (American History). Among the eight committee chairmen my undergraduate tutor Donald Cope McKay (Modern French History) chaired the Press and Writing section.

I was still immersed in the China coast of the 1840s, but I was invited to an American Defense discussion of China *vs.* Japan. There I found an academic virtuoso in the person of Professor William Montgomery McGovern from Northwestern, who was at Harvard to lecture in the Government Department. He had an aggressive style and the self-confidence that goes with self-approbation. *Colloquial Japanese* (1921), *An Introduction to Mahayana Buddhism* (1922), and *To Lhasa in Disguise* (1924) were some of his rapid-fire books. We privately believed him to be a charlatan but if so he was a very smart one (later serving on the Joint Intelligence Committee under the Joint Chiefs of Staff), and he laid down the law about Japan in China in no uncertain terms. I tried to counter his oversimplicities but did it with many qualifications and humble disclaimers of expertise. Arthur Schlesinger, Sr., said to me later, "Don't be so modest, John. You really know more than he does. If you speak, say it with conviction."

This advice I often remembered. Enlightening and persuading others must begin at home with a view you believe in. A debater must have his case worked out. As I began to accept invitations to talk to the Foreign Policy Association and other groups, I was obliged to think more in policy terms—not only the vocabulary of national interest, public opinion, international stability, but also the convictions I could try to muster from all too little personal experience. It would take a long time because I found I was less a specialist on China than on the career of J. K. Fairbank, and believe it or not the two were not identical.

As American opinion crystallized pro-China, Cambridge developed a real climate of opinion. Dr. Elizabeth Boody Schumpeter, wife of the esteemed Austrian economist Joseph Schumpeter, had conducted a study of the Manchurian economy and could see extenuating or at least causal factors in Japan's expansion. When she boldly voiced these as facts to keep in mind, some Cambridge ladies hissed like geese and asked if I could not somehow squash this viper in their midst. China was becoming a moral issue, appealing to the springs of conscience, never mind the facts. As Hitler taught us there was evil in the world, American morality arose to combat it. Japan and China became all the blacker and whiter because people along Brattle Street knew so little about them.

Alleviating such ignorance called for the organized promotion of Far Eastern studies. Burton Fahs, in particular, as soon as he had a job teaching at Pomona, bombarded Mortimer Graves with proposals. In June 1937 Mortimer had begun to put out a concise and eloquent semiannual bulletin, *Notes on Far Eastern Studies in America*. It was a trade sheet reflecting the hopes and efforts of the two ACLS committees on promotion of Chinese and of Japanese studies. Burton and I and others contributed, seeking converts for the cause, debating over nuts and bolts.

In 1939–40 Ed Reischauer and I had reached across our departmental boundaries and set up a binary course, Chinese 10 on the Far East to 1500 and History 83 on the Far East since 1500. We each lectured in the other course, already part way toward a year-long survey of East Asia. As a climax to my first five years lecturing at

Harvard I joined Fahs in managing in the summer school of 1940 a Far Eastern Institute—a high-powered survey of history and bibliography aimed at a selection of a dozen young American teachers to start them off in preparation for teaching on East Asia. Graves (ACLS) and Stevens (Rockefeller Foundation) gave us the backing. This was actually the preparation at Harvard of an East Asian History survey course that later could be propagated nationwide. Reischauer and Fahs handled Japan, Bodde and I China, and Archibald Wenley of the Freer Gallery surveyed the fine arts. We all learned a lot, periodizing our subjects and refining our bibliographies. A hundred copies of the seventy-eight-page syllabus were finally distributed to everyone we could interest.

At the end of the six-week institute Burton and I presided over a conference at the Harvard Faculty Club with assorted colleagues, educators, and philanthropoids to plan further promotion of the field. This effort bubbled along in 1941 after we went to Washington. We got inside the educational apparatus and formed a Committee on Asiatic Studies in American Education appended to the American Council on Education. The chairman was the kinetic Howard E. Wilson of the Harvard Graduate School of Education. The members were Dr. Dorothy Borg, then on the staff of the American Institute of Pacific Relations, plus Fahs and me. We set up our committee on December 4, 1941. Within seventy-two hours Pearl Harbor showed history was with us. We issued a manifesto on the need for Far Eastern studies in the schools and propagated it through articles and presentations to meetings in the vast American educational network. We secured Rockfound money to keep Howard Wilson's energy focused on it. He held half a dozen big meetings around the country before our crusade got lost in the larger war effort.

This brush with the legions of American educators disclosed both the size and intricacy of their network and also their zeal for pure organization. Once in their hands, we were planning texts, maps, syllabi, bibliographies, visual aids, pamphlets, editorials, meetings, conferences, commissions, and convocations galore, with no idea where to find the trained people to do it all. The same promotion could have been planned for any other worthy subject. The missionary zeal of an earlier time seemed to live on among educators.

Back in the late 1930s I had been still seeking the China message that should be propagated, not only through education but even more in public policy discussions. It took quite a while for the issue of aggression to emerge as an international procedural matter that should take precedence over ideological considerations such as Christianity, communism, or capitalism. Spain gave us a fine example of how the Western democracies could help bring on World War II by trying to keep their skirts clear of warfare. When Franco rebelled against the Spanish liberal government elected in February 1936, there were only sixteen Communists among 473 members of the Cortes. Yet Hitler and Mussolini openly aided Franco militarily on the plea that he was fighting bolshevism, while Britain, France, and the United States withheld arms from the legitimate Loyalist government of Premier Juan Negrín on the plea of maintaining "neutrality." This gave Russia the golden opportunity to be the chief foreign helper.

Because my father-in-law Dr. Cannon had known and respected Dr. Juan Negrín as a fellow physiologist and democrat, he served for two years as head of the Medical Bureau to Aid Spanish Democracy. It sent more than a million dollars' worth of medical supplies and equipment. In this humanitarian effort Dr. Cannon tried to avoid Communist influence but in the free-for-all of American opinion of course some people called him a red.

I found that being a pundit, informing the public, required one to start with the public's inherited wisdom. For example, "China has always absorbed her conquerors" was an ancient cliché that applied, more or less, to the rather small groups of nomadic invaders of China from the northern grasslands. But in modern times China could not be expected to "absorb" her new Japanese conquerors because both countries had become nationalistic. Japan's aggression in China, I argued in a *Crimson* article of December 1937, could try to obviate China's growing nationalism by supporting puppet regimes, but Chinese puppets would be expensive and meanwhile Japan could not stop halfway. The *Crimson* headline was "Sino-Japanese problem still in its infancy, says Fairbank." A safe bet. The "problem" still had eight years to go.

By trying, I learned better how to bring history to bear on current crises. After Chamberlain's appeasement of Hitler at Munich in 1938 I wrote in the *Harvard Alumni Bulletin* on "Our Choice in the Far East." I asked, "If the Chamberlain government should decide to finance the Japanese development of conquered areas of China, how would American policy be affected?" The answer was that we always had acquiesced in and benefited from Britain's imperialist arrangements, and to head off a Chamberlain appeasement of Japan we must have a new and more active policy of our own: reduce our war supplies to Japan and Japanese sales to us, supply credits to China, prevent any British supply of capital to Japan, and not "allow England and Japan again to become partners."

By March 1940 in the *Harvard Guardian* monthly I suggested an American embargo on war materials to Japan would be effective only with the concurrence of several other countries. Our contribution to a Far Eastern peace should include giving up extraterritoriality in China, putting Sino-Japanese immigration on a quota basis, and giving Japan some access to the U.S. market. These were sound thoughts, no doubt, but academic in the sense of nonoperable.

My forays into print under American Defense prompting included a *New York Times* letter of October 3, 1940. The news peg justifying it was the new German-Japanese alliance treaty and Japan's occupation of Indo-China. My letter urged that we reopen the Burma Road and send American cruisers to Singapore as the best way to ward off Japanese expansion and keep us out of war. Aid to China would also do this. "If we want to avoid trouble with Japanese militarists, we have only to support the efforts of Chinese patriots . . . to keep Japan busy in China is merely good self-defense."

This questionable armchair logic brought a *Times* letter in reply from a certain Harry W. Knettel, Jr., who felt Japan and Britain were both imperialists, whereas the American interest was purely commercial and not worth war. His letter was captioned "Not Our Business."

I replied in a second letter that we were already, unfortunately, an imperialist power enjoying in China all the privileges secured by British arms. Japan's taking Singapore, "making the South Pacific and the Indian Ocean a Japanese lake," would be a mortal blow to both Britain and China, leaving us alone in our weakness and inviting attack.

I could see that polemics in the press demand an almost simpleminded assertion of broad facts, from which the conclusions deduced are likely to be broad and simple-minded too.

In July 1941 I wrote an article for the United Press. "If Russia loses to Germany, what will happen in the Far East?" I foresaw German use of the truck route across Chinese Turkestan, over which "Russian supplies until recently exceeded our own aid to China." The Nazis might thus by force and guile secure domination of Free China. They could also add Nazi airpower to Japan's sea power, "taking China out of the war and galvanizing Japan into action against us." Wild speculation of this sort reflected the extreme instability of the world we confronted in summer 1941.

This concern about American policy in the world crisis proved to me that historical knowledge was essential to mankind's survival—a simple faith that gave me a high self-approval rating. History was for me what the gospel had been for my grandfather the Congregational preacher, a way to make a living while saving the world. However, my rather jejune efforts at policy discussion, cited above, indicate what thin ice I was skating on as a would-be pundit. In 1941 I knew little about government procedures or even the national interest, but suddenly I was given a chance to learn.

PART FOUR

•

WASHINGTON,
CHUNGKING, AND SHANGHAI
1941–46

15

MOVING INTO WASHINGTON

FOUR MONTHS BEFORE Pearl Harbor I was recruited to join the buildup of academic resources being converted to war purposes under the U.S. government. For the next five years I was on leave from Harvard: first for a year in Washington (August '41 to August '42), then a year and a quarter in China (September '42 to December '43), then a year and eight months in Washington (January '44 to August '45), and finally another nine months in China (September '45 to July '46). This adventurous interlude, between the ages of thirty-four and thirty-nine, brought me into the world of affairs and undoubtedly remade me. Like so many others I came out of the war effort knowing more clearly what I thought and how I could function. This was because the war posed radically new problems of thought and organization. They required creative action.

In the summer of 1941 Colonel Bill Donovan as the newly-established Coordinator of Information (COI) was heavily engaged in setting up a secret service with both secret intelligence and secret operations worldwide. The Research and Analysis Branch of COI was a separate echelon designed to help the others. Its intellectual effort was based on the belief that the facts are not at all obvious and that knowing them can make all the difference in operations. Its staff, recruited mainly from universities, were asked to focus on the present and future with the same scholarly care that had brought them forward in their academic fields.

James Phinney Baxter III (president of Williams College) was asked to head R. and A. He invited Langer, who suggested McKay, who suggested me. The four of us from the History Department thus went to Washington in August 1941. On August 13 at 9:15 A.M. in the empty Apex Building, where Pennsylvania and Constitution avenues meet, I found Baxter, Langer, and McKay together with Langer's prize student Philip Mosely, a Russia specialist, having their first meeting to organize the Research and Analysis Branch. In order to bring scholarship to bear on problems of the war effort, they needed to have Army and Navy personnel working with COI researchers. The latter would need space in the Library of Congress (fortunately its new annex was just completed), but the products of these LC research sections would have to feed into the main office of COI on 25th and E Streets NW at the other end of town, where the SI (secret intelligence) and SO (secret operations) branches would also head up.

Baxter and Langer began recruiting academic specialists from all over the country. One principal recruit on the Far East was Professor Joseph Ralston Hayden, long-time head of the Political Science Department at Michigan. He had spent some years teaching in the Philippines, actually serving in the real world there as vice-governor in 1933–35. His big book *The Philippines: a Study in National Development* had just come out (1941). Meanwhile Don McKay took on the job of personally paraphrasing the State Department's daily flow of cables so that R and A would share in the lifeblood of current intelligence—much the way Dr. Frankenstein's lifeless figure, once sewn together, needed an electric current to give it vitality.

I was of course very junior, an instructor who had published only a few articles, but I represented the idea of using Chinese and Japanese sources to study China and Japan. I was given, as a first bone to gnaw, a naval intelligence report on Japanese shipbuilding and aluminum, steel, and plane production. It was a prize obtained the previous day from a trip to ONI (the Office of Naval Intelligence) and Colonel Donovan wanted it appraised. I spent the afternoon doing so. It was a "hodgepodge of observations by spies dressed as fishermen or pilgrims, plus statistics with no sources named and various lists of new airfields and factories." (We found out later it was British.) The level of sophistication was indicated by the news that Japanese engineers were "beginning surveys for a tunnel from Shimonoseki to

Pusan in Korea. That would only be 122 miles under the Straits of Tsushima."

I appraised the report as unintelligent. More could be learned by scrutinizing the Japanese press. Baxter and I presented this to Colonel Donovan. He impressed me as "smooth and rather flabby, not sure exactly what he wants to do." The latter was no doubt true, part of his creative effort. Flabby, however, he was not.

I was soon following two or three paths at once—helping to organize a Far East section at LC, where we needed reference materials as well as staff to use them, helping the new Donovan outfit prove the value of academic expertise among the established agencies of government, and getting acquainted with all the China hands in Washington. Every agency suddenly needed a China competence, and people we had known during our four years in Peking or elsewhere were soon sprinkled like seasoning over the city, with more arriving every week.

We found lodging for some weeks with my classmate Bill Youngman and his wife. Before her marriage to Bill, Elsie Perkins had lived with us for a while in Peking, and they had met in our house. Bill had been chief counsel of the Federal Power Commission during the New Deal and was now shifting into a law partnership with Tom Corcoran. They became active in the Chinese agency set up by T. V. Soong, China Defense Supplies, Inc. While Elsie's forebears had been in the Old China Trade, her husband was now developing a new kind of business for China. This lasted beyond the war and eventually T. V. Soong asked Bill to be executor of his estate.

In a few days Wilma found a neat house—two bedrooms, kitchen, and large parlor plus a small garden—at 1306 34th Street, N.W., conveniently located in Georgetown. We rented it at once for September 1 occupancy.

On August 14 I went to see Lauchlin Currie. Through an introduction from Isen (for Isabel) Bacon La Follette, Phil's wife, at Madison, I had met Lauch and his wife, Deo (for Dorothy) Bacon Currie, at Harvard in 1928 when he was an instructor in economics, still doing his Ph.D. Now he had moved from the Federal Reserve Board to be one of the six administrative assistants of FDR, who had sent him to China to see Chiang Kai-shek early in 1941 and put him in charge of lend-lease for China.

Dr. Currie was on the White House staff, with a big office and two secretaries in the State Department (now Executive Office) building on the second floor directly beneath the Far Eastern division (FE). He was full of the problems of the Burma Road, whither he had sent New York trucking-firm managers to try to organize the traffic. As China's principal lifeline for supplies, the road was an artery full of corruption. Drivers too ignorant to grease their trucks still knew how to smuggle private cargo. The New Yorkers were tough cookies but knew when the cards were stacked against them.

I found that Lauch was the home office for Colonel Claire Chennault and the AVG (American Volunteer Group), an unofficial mercenary air force with one hundred P-40 planes secretly training in Burma. Later I arranged to write up their origin as part of a COI study of *Aid to China,* using Lauch's files.

Since he had no budget for underlings, he and I by December arrived at the useful thought that I could be assigned by COI part time to do things for him. This would help him, me, COI, and the war effort. By Christmas I was using the small empty room 224 next to his. The phone number was simply "White House 80." How could one ask for a more exalted status symbol?

In this way I rose into the corridors of power, though I still had nothing in particular to do except drop around, see people, pick up information, and pursue minor projects. This was fun, and I soon got an impression of the *dramatis personae* making China policy in the climactic autumn of 1941.

This cast of characters after Currie continued with Stanley Kuhl Hornbeck, with whom I formally had a lot in common—we were both from the Middle West, members of the Alpha Pi chapter of Beta Theta Pi at Wisconsin and Rhodes scholars, and he had taught at Harvard the course on "The Far East since 1793" to which I had succeeded. Sometimes I have feared that we had even personal traits in common.

On August 15 I phoned Dr. Hornbeck to announce my arrival in Washington.

He sounded very gruff and wanted to know what Donovan's object was, what he thought he was trying to do, why he should get all these people down here. I claimed I didn't know, which is true, but I said I expected *he* would know, that of course I was calling him informally as an acquaintance, which was proper as I had not yet been organized under a chief and that I was hoping for advice.

We went to see him for drinks a few days later but advice I did not get. He obviously felt he was doing everything necessary about China policy. Currie was engaged merely in operations.

Stanley's study is a masterpiece of overhead pullropes and sliding writingboard contraptions, very efficiently organized for slow activity of a home-made style, rather like himself.

If one career could sum up the weaknesses in U.S. Far Eastern policy, it should be Stanley Hornbeck's. His experience of Chinese life had been four years teaching in Chinese government colleges (1909–13) just before and after the Revolution of 1911. This was after his Rhodes scholarship (1904–1907) and did not involve him with the language. His academic field was political science at a time when it had fissioned off from history and was still close to law. He took his Ph.D. at Wisconsin in 1911, and worked with Professor Paul Reinsch, who became Wilson's minister to China. Hornbeck published *Contemporary Politics in the Far East* in 1916. He taught at Wisconsin 1914–17. During World War I he became an army captain and then hit his stride by becoming a technical expert on the Far East in the 1919 peace settlement, and again at the Washington Conference of 1921. From being a specialist in government he moved to Harvard and for four years (1924–28) was a lecturer on Far Eastern history. In 1927 he published *China Today—Political* and then in 1928 returned to Washington as chief of FE, the Far Eastern division of the State Department. His forte was a mix of legality and moralism, well suited to the traditional American flatulence about the Open Door. This now outworn and feeble diplomatic doctrine suited both Dr. Hornbeck's legalistic punctiliousness on America's behalf and his rhetorical righteousness on China's behalf. In both respects he was a representative American, profoundly culture bound.

The strangest aspect of his role in State was that, as a civilian specialist not in the Foreign Service, after 1937 he sat above both the China and the Japan divisions of the Office of Far Eastern Affairs, whose work on matters of state had to pass through him and get his approval as PA/H (Political Adviser, Hornbeck). This unusual arrangement acknowledged that the Far East, unlike other areas, was indeed inscrutable to the uninitiated and required special handling by someone who "knew" the Orient.

Several things were wrong with this picture. Dr. Hornbeck was a very vigorous and assertive, also canny, person, and he worked the racket that all China hands have jumped or been pushed into—having esoteric knowledge denied to ordinary mortals. He had been in China and taught China's modern history, to be sure, but instead of disclosing to him how much he (and everyone) didn't know, this successful experience had given him intellectual self-confidence on a very frail basis of knowledge and understanding. Several kinds of revolution had occurred in China in his absence, quite beyond his ken, but never mind. His chief trait was a remarkable righteousness. He explained to me in one of our early encounters, "the United States Far Eastern policy is like a train running on a railroad track. It has been clearly laid out and where it is going is plain to all. The Japanese must take note of this. It is up to them." This asked for a big derailment.

Foreign Service officers who had actually been in Japan and China staged a revolt in August 1941 against the apparent appeasement of Japan and the arbitrary administration of FE by its director, Max Hamilton, a rather colorless individual who followed Hornbeck's lead. Several risked their careers by appealing to Under-Secretary Sumner Welles for more discussion of policy problems. This rift in FE was papered over until in 1944 the massive staff rebellion against Hornbeck charged him with withholding vital information from Secretary Hull; he was soon sent to finish his career as ambassador to the Netherlands. The barn door was locked.

One way that Stanley Hornbeck had tried to get strength out of weakness was by claiming that policy makers' direct contact with the field was unnecessary because all information came to the center, across his desk, and only there could one see the whole picture. This pernicious idea was echoed by his intelligent and attractive young lawyer assistant, Alger Hiss, whom I had not met before. Far from being a radical, Alger, some of us felt, went along too loyally, as Hornbeck's assistant, with PA/H's legalistic and conservative ideas. Not having a Far Eastern background, he seemed to contribute more on the side of procedure and protocol, at which he was undoubtedly efficient.

The brightest spirit I found in State's precincts was John Paton Davies, born in Szechwan, who after leaving Peking for a tour in Mukden had returned to the department. He enjoyed answering the phone with a crisp "Moshi-moshi" that made callers wonder if Tokyo had taken over.

At the Pentagon I found Dean Rusk, already a captain and momentarily in charge of the British Empire section of military intelligence. His predecessor had been a kindly old lady with no assistants who mainly kept a clipping file. We were not well prepared for operations in India and Burma. One of COI's contributions was to get maps and Indian railway capacities worked out by specialists.

At the Pentagon I found as G-2 for China a handsome and attractive individual, Major Frank Roberts, who had been a language officer in Peking and member of a study group we attended together. He had since been the hero of the *Panay* incident of 1937, taking charge of that Yangtze River gunboat when Japanese bombing sank it and all but killed the commander. In my capacity as a coordinator of information I told him about the files of basic Nationalist government data Dr. Currie had been given in Chungking in February 1941. These tables might be more imposing than they were accurate, but they were the only thing of their kind. I arranged to have copies made for G-2 and got Frank and Lauch together for lunch. They could meet informally through a mutual friend more easily than in official channels.

On Sunday, August 17, we lunched with Ambassador Hu Shih at his stately residence on its hill among lawns and trees. It was twenty years since he had led one wing of the May Fourth Movement. His social facility with Americans in the service of China had made him a high-level public-relations figure.

On August 18 I found another Peking friend and fellow language student, Major Haydon Boatner, who was working to supply China's military needs. He confronted the Chinese face that wanted only the latest thing—like tanks too heavy for the bridges—whereas he was stressing demolition equipment, far more useful as well as available. Haydon was in his element, doing what he had trained for, to help the Chinese war effort gain strength from the American.

Next day I called on T. V. Soong. Donovan had earlier called me in to meet T. V. and his adviser Dr. Ludwig Rajchman, a former League of Nations health expert at Nanking.

T. V. reminds me of Doyle Harmon, the star Wisconsin halfback, very quick on the ball and inclined to plow through between guard and tackle rather than waste time going around end. R. is a gimlet-eyed, hawk-nosed ferret-like little man. They both looked at me with penetrating gaze so I looked at them as penetratingly as I could.

Donovan explained that I was his Far Eastern expert. He showed me later Soong's letter, a hard-hitting plea for American planes to stop the Chungking bombings by the Japanese . . . at a time when we are hastening to aid Russia and still offering only words to China.

Within a few months, of course, the AVG, or Flying Tigers, would give Chungking this protection, but in the late summer of 1941 Soong was desperately seeking air defense for the Chinese capital. Donovan was one of several channels to appeal through. But Donovan was still in the process of setting up his own turbines in the Washington powerhouse. Being early on the scene, I served as his ad hoc "expert" for the moment, but he had little more power to provide air cover for Chungking than I, who had none. I noted, "Whether Soong's plea will ever be read by anyone but myself remains uncertain." (I was wrong, of course.)*

So it went, seeing a great many people but still with little to do. By September I got agreement on inviting Burton Fahs from Pomona College to handle Japan in our R and A section. Joe Hayden was taken onto the top-level Board of Analysts. Burton and I had had no experience as research directors, so we went along with Hayden's suggestion of Professor Carl (Charles) Remer of Michigan to be our Far East section chief. He had taught at St. John's College in Shanghai and published the standard work on foreign investments in China. He brought along his long-time research assistant, and we began to "get forward," as he would say, with the organizing of offices in the new annex of the Library of Congress. Burton and I, as juniors, felt the Remer leadership was a bit slow on the uptake but there was no lack of good will. Our trouble was to find talent, in competition with all the rest of Washington.

*Soong's plea is in R. E. Sherwood, *Roosevelt and Hopkins*, pp. 406–8.

I got a first glimpse of the intelligence-as-power game when Donovan sent us a hurry-up request for a memo on uranium in China. Fortunately we had a recent *China Year Book.* In the index was "uranium" and the text said there were deposits in Hunan and Kiangsi. Our cartographer drew a map featuring Hunan and Kiangsi with some xxx's on it and I rushed this chef d'oeuvre to a session Donovan was having with Thomas K. Finletter. This was my contribution to the Manhattan Project.

The LC Annex as yet had little going on, so I got Carl Remer's O.K. to pursue liaison with other agencies. After all, COI was supposed to be *coordinating* them. I collected friends from Peking and others scattered through the State Department, the Pentagon, and the new fly-by-night agencies like the Board of Economic Warfare. Soon we had an informal Wednesday luncheon meeting organized to bring together all the China specialists around town.

One pleasure in Washington was to get better acquainted with Mortimer Graves and his wife, Jane. With his usual foresight Mortimer got ready for the war emergency by compiling a list of all Americans skilled in East Asian languages, and he hired Wilma to make a directory of American organizations concerned with China (published in 1941).

Women had been banned from the ACLS office by fiat of its chief, Waldo Leland, whose early boss had had a woman secretary of the kind who carries the files in her head and so became indispensable. When she faltered it was like the electricity going out of the computer. Wilma worked in a back room out of sight.

Mortimer was a do-it-yourself man in any case, a lone operator not much interested in secretarial assistance. His imagination made him a pioneer in the development of weird-language competence among Americans. He especially promoted Russian and Chinese studies, and his tenacity and ingenuity got results on a shoestring—young instructors at major universities, a translation and monograph series, summer institutes, help for libraries and for training. The Hummel biographical project I have mentioned was only one among many.

Mortimer had been a World War I aviator and then a historian and humanist. One of his many hobbies was skilled woodworking. He was a foreknower in sensing the enormous need for language and what was later called area training in a shrinking world. Early on he was asked to head our section of R and A, but he kept free of government employ, which would have stifled the spontaneity and craftsmanship with which he worked.

On December 8, 1941, a Monday, the ACLS phone was jammed with government agency requests for names of Japan and China specialists, preferably male between twenty-one and thirty, field-experienced and fully fluent. Any such paragons as existed had of course already been picked up by the forehandedness of the U.S. Navy, which had scoured the country earlier in 1941.

As part of the general buildup in late 1941 the State Department's Cultural Relations Division (RC), hitherto devoted mainly to good-neighborism in Latin America, was empowered to set up a China section. Wilma became the first employee. When Willys R. Peck, an experienced China officer, became chief he began to teach her the bureaucratic precision and procedural sophistication to be prized in a drafting officer. She was on her way to a five-year government career and would wind up as cultural officer in the embassy in China.

The radio news of Japan's Pearl Harbor attack on that December 7 Sunday afternoon sent me like others rushing down to my office to be at my post in the crisis. Once in the empty, quiet LC Annex, however, I found no radio and so had to phone home to ask Wilma what was going on. General Marshall had been riding in Rock Creek Park, but when he went to his office at least he could receive communications.

War of course seemed to justify all our warlike efforts to prepare for war. But it did not lessen my feeling that in moving from Harvard to Washington, from a more individual to a more collective effort, I had moved from enterprise to boondoggle. Academic life gave me a strong sense of accomplishment from day to day—a book read for a purpose, a lecture offered as a brick in a larger edifice, a student conversed with responsibly to help his growth. One got results, whereas the bureaucratic life of Washington overwhelmed one with communications—phone calls, committee meetings, reading one's in-basket, seeing colleagues at meals and social events. Moreover, this constant communication was injected with competition and a low order of politics. A policy proposal seldom could stand on its merits; it had to be put across. Granted the stakes were sometimes higher, one's own achievement seldom seemed so.

Though disenchanted with official life I still succeeded, I think, in being a pretty good liaison officer for COI and Currie. I felt it my job to know everyone working on China among the many government agencies. I also helped distribute essential information. COI had a strong cartographic section and able geographers. We published topographic maps of road, rail, and river communications which had immediate practical value. We also put out a weekly, *The War in China,* and I produced historical studies of American aid to China. Finally, using Currie's big office as a meeting place, I convened an occasional roundup of China specialists from the major agencies for the purpose of mutual enlightenment as to the things we all were doing.

R and A of COI was given the task of producing the economic-social-political sections of the military and naval handbooks on which so much of the labor of G-2 and ONI was expended—compendia of data, maps, and generalizations that a field officer should have at hand. Thus the new agency won its spurs. From the same battery of specialists I could extract data ad hoc for Lauch to use in memoranda for FDR. At one point I became his

> expert on Indian transportation, using a phone to Dan Thorner of the Brit. Emp. section. Lauch asked me the number of trucks in India, and when I told him five minutes later, he was amazed and appalled.

These goings and comings on my part were about at the level of introducing people to each other. I had no strong policy convictions because I knew nothing directly of contemporary China. When FDR sent Lauchlin Currie to Chungking again (July 21–August 7, 1942) he came back to urge full support of Chiang Kai-shek, no strings attached, because we could rely on him "to go in the direction of our wishes in prosecuting a vigorous war policy and in creating a modern democratic and powerful state."* Obviously, Lauch knew nothing directly either.

Meanwhile, by June 1942 the Far Eastern section of R and A had twenty officers plus seven part-time consultants. Eight people worked on China. They averaged seven years' experience in the

---

*Michael Schaller, *The U.S. Crusade in China, 1938–1945* (1979), p. 235.

country. The section had put out seventy-five reports or studies. Few had even touched on policy. There was a great gulf of noncontact between these facts we compiled and the policy ideas of people like Currie at the executive level.

Since January 1942 Singapore had fallen, the Japanese were moving on Burma, and Stilwell's mission to China had got under way. Every agency in Washington felt the need of a Chungking outpost.

16

GOING TO CHINA IN WARTIME

THE FLUX OF wartime offered myriad opportunities for ingenious enterprisers. To meet unprecedented situations, utterly new efforts had to be made; some worked out and some didn't. I felt at the time that the roles I invented for myself were a logical combination that led to a consistent line of action, but no one gave me instructions or job descriptions that covered it all. I put it together on my own.

The starting premise was the need of the Far Eastern section of R and A to have a field representative or outpost in China to secure research materials. One of the first proposals that Fahs and I picked up, even before Carl Remer became our chief, was David Nelson Rowe's project for analysis of the Chinese press. From Harold Lasswell and other political scientists, Dave had become addicted to quantitative analysis (counting how often words were used) as an objective procedure that would make the cacophony of political discussion into a science happily based on numbers. He had sought foundation funds to go do this in Chungking. We commissioned him to represent R and A there. He reached Chungking November 27, 1941.

How to get COI started in China was no mean problem. Chinese-speaking Americans who recruited Chinese staff members had to assume they were double agents, reporting to Chinese bosses too. Anything secret drew flies like a garbage can and created exaggerated rumors, misconceptions, fears, false hopes, and jealousies moment by moment. Joe Hayden at age fifty-four was as experienced and level-headed a senior statesman as one could find. I believe it was on his recommendation that Dr. Esson McDowell Gale of the Chinese Salt Administration was recruited to represent COI in China.

Dr. Gale was an American scholar-official, having done a sinological Ph.D. at Leyden.* When we met him in Shanghai he was a very knowledgeable, slightly rounded sinologue with a small British-type mustache.

His career as the first COI representative in Chungking evidently did not go too well. Shifting from being a Chinese employee to heading an American office was not easy. Dr. Gale's printed card had him the agent of the "American Intelligence Office" (Mei-kuo ch'ing-pao chü), not a title to win Chinese hearts and minds.

While this was developing largely beyond my ken, David Rowe was also running into difficulties. He found he disliked the embassy and many of the Chinese. People kept giving him funny looks. He felt he was being followed and indeed conspired against and endangered. We feared he had gone bonkers and brought him back to see doctors; it proved unnecessary. I was suggested to take his place. On June 2, Donovan appointed me the chief representative of COI in China to be in charge of everything. His instructions were a remarkable prescription for getting me into one hell of a mess: "You are (a) to be the recognized head of the Chungking office, (b) authorized to represent the Coordinator in matters concerning the group as a whole and (c) authorized to exercise administrative direction over COI personnel in Chungking in matters affecting the general interests of the Chungking unit as distinguished from the particular functions of the representatives of the several branches." This meant I would be a front man with responsibility for but no control over secret activities—a poobah as well as a patsy. This was a fate to be avoided at all costs. Fortunately, though I received my formal signed instructions, the idea was stillborn. COI was reorganized on June 13, 1942, to cast off the Foreign Information Service, which became the Office of War Information (OWI). The remnants, R and A, SI, and SO,

---

*His *Discourses on Salt and Iron: a Debate on State Control of Commerce and Industry in Ancient China* was published in 1931, a translation of chapters 1–19 of *Yen-t'ieh lun,* reporting a debate in 81 B.C. Chapters 20–28 Dr. Gale published in Shanghai in 1934 in the *Journal of the North China Branch, Royal Asiatic Society.*

became the Office of Strategic Services (OSS). I at once set to work and created a much more narrow and concrete role for myself in China.

Simultaneously Dr. Gale was recalled and Joe Hayden in expiation for his failed advice was sent to Chungking to pick up the pieces. We traveled together very amicably in August-September 1942. The trip gave us a bird's-eye view of the wartime expansion of American technology, which was as usual outrunning the growth of our understanding of the world.

In 1942 Pan American Airways still provided the U.S. government with the pioneer transport facilities that were later to be expanded by the Air Transport Command. And Pan Am's workhorse was still the DC-3, twin-engined with a fixed tail wheel that left the plane, when on the ground, sloping down to the stern. Nose wheels, like jet engines, were still in the future. So also was air conditioning. Passengers in a DC-3 sitting on a tarmac in the tropical sun were soon frying in their own sweat. Once in the air they could freeze. Cabin pressure was not maintainable and crossing the Himalayas could be hard work for everybody. These are strictures from the 1980s viewpoint of tourists who aloft receive personal service and amenities beyond their daily fare at home. In 1942 Pan Am was achieving the impossible and we all felt like explorers.

On August 21, Joe Hayden and I started for China by air from Miami, going by way of South America and Africa, as roundabout as the sailing route from Salem or Baltimore to the "Far East" in 1842 via the South Atlantic and the Indian Ocean. We hopped first to Puerto Rico for refueling, thence to Port of Spain (Trinidad) for the night; second day across the Orinoco and the several broad streams of the Amazon to the old Portuguese city of Belém, three degrees south of the equator. Its fishing boats, pastel-colored houses, parklike plazas with white-painted tree trunks, and sidewalk cafés were all reminiscent of its contemporary at the other extreme of the sixteenth-century Portuguese empire, Macao.

> Belém . . . corresponds to Shanghai in being near the mouth of the great river, except that on this river there are no millions of peasants dwelling. We flew over a few shacks in the most surprisingly god-awful places on the banks of the Amazonian tributaries, set in clearings on the edge of the

swamp jungle. There must be a hinterland to a city as large as this, but I don't know where it is.

All the fields along here are busy with arrivals and departures from minute to minute. The Americans are doing an expansion job now which compares with the Portuguese expansion that built this place and Macao and old Malacca. . . . The Americans bring their shower baths that work and build enormous runways of concrete for their new weapons and carriers, just as Portuguese once came with ships and cannon and built wharves and forts.

From Recife on the coast of Brazil we crossed the South Atlantic all night in a four-engine plane and at dawn on the wide ocean saw a speck far ahead that grew to be Ascension Island, just halfway from South America to Africa, a solitary peak with a dusty landing strip still being bulldozed all across the top of it. I thought of my dentist working on a molar before he capped it.

Next stop was Accra (then on the Gold Coast, now Ghana), almost a double for pre-tourist Hawaii, with a big shallow beach good for surfboarding. In the bunkhouse you never wondered when the tan sheets had been changed. Who cared? From Accra the Pan Am route went east to another port, Lagos, and then took off northeast across Nigeria to Kano, where the railroad ended.

Next we came upon the pride of Pan American, the camp at Maiduguri. We began by driving fifteen miles from the airfield, from nowhere to nowhere, and entered a compound with a few new buildings. Inside one we all had Rheingold beer from an icebox made in New York City, plus Coca-Colas. We then showered in a porched bunkhouse fitted with large washstands, mirrors, metal beds and chairs, and flush toilets, and dined in a spotless dining room which had a white chef and served us something very near to Campbell's tomato soup, followed by fried chicken, veal and potatoes, and corn bread with peanut butter, jam, and mint sauce. Everyone on the line has talked of this place. How in hell, or through it, all this stuff was brought in, no one can estimate, but it is the nearest reproduction of home you could imagine, and about seven hundred miles cross country from the nearest source of supply. The moon came up, really large and African, and I listened for lions, but all I heard all night was the seven-foot electric icebox filled with ice water on the porch beside my bed, plus the flushing of toilets. It is hard to travel this way and keep Africa and Pan Am separate.

In Egypt and India, areas of the old British Empire, we ran into the Anglo-American alliance problem that we would meet also in China—a sort of sibling rivalry in which British pride, experience, and leadership, now stretched so thin, roused American knee-jerk suspicions of imperialistic and anti-popular designs. In decrying the remnants of Britain's empire, while also making use of them, the Americans had little sense of actually being Britain's inheritors. We were too accustomed to enjoying British arrangements in fact while sniping at them in theory.

On August 28 we came down the Nile from Khartoum to Cairo for six hours and landed in a Victorian monument, the old Shepheard's Hotel [now no more]. It had yellow marble columns, twenty-foot ceilings in the water closets, drownable bathtubs but no showers, buttons labeled Waiter, Maid, and Native, and a prize dining room on the walls of which are striations of red and yellow, ogee curves, endless knots set about lotus leaves, fluted impressions painted over doorways, cunningly wrought ironwork, lamps that look like floating junk piles, fountains with aspidistra, and all the other things that make Keble College and some other buildings into monuments. One expects to see Queen Victoria herself sitting inside her petticoats within one of the Moorish-arched, Roman-vaulted, Sienese-painted, English-made recesses.

We have been dining down in the garden, watching English officers dancing with their ladies in a subdued way, as though they didn't see why they shouldn't, since they could, although they didn't really need to. The Germans are out in the desert within three hours' car ride. On June 30, says a local informant, there was a gap ten miles wide for thirty-six hours through which they could have come in, but apparently they were too tired and Aussies arrived from Syria.

Eventually a British flying boat took us from the Nile at Cairo over the desolation of the goat-eaten Holy Land to the Tigris-Euphrates at Basra. Thence we went to Karachi and eventually on September 6 reached the Imperial Hotel, New Delhi. There I found Teddy White, wearing a big mushroomlike sun helmet, and he led me to a cocktail party that included Ed Snow, Arch Steele of the *Herald Tribune,* and Herbert Matthews of the *New York Times,* all dressed in the war correspondents' khaki shorts and shirt with a green shoulder band, very smart. Ed was just on his way to Russia via Persia. Teddy was flying around with a couple of generals.

I had not been in India before and the superficial contrast between Indians and Chinese was startling. In this wartime period before liberation the people in Karachi and New Delhi seemed like

> timorous cowering creatures, too delicate to fight like the Chinese. One never disputes a fee with them; they all salute and take it, at least around these military quarters, and they never smile at anyone. With Chinese coolies . . . if you pay too much, they try for more, if not enough they protest vigorously, and if the amount is right they still respond in some way. . . . These people are poor in the bitterest way, worse than in China . . . wearing rags in the midst of a modern façade of civilization . . . whereas in China everyone is poor.

This superficial tourist's impression, which Harold Isaacs caught later in *Scratches on Our Minds,* was very widespread among Americans who reached India and China in World War II. Somehow Indian servility before liberation fitted in reciprocally with British ruling-class arrogance, whereas Chinese and Americans met at this time on a plane of social egalitarianism—at least they could react to each other.

> In Delhi our British pals . . . have had an endless succession of itches and fevers, boils, dengue, malaria, prickly heat, and so on and on. In the summer it is dry and goes to 120 with constant wind, exhausting; then it rains and mildews and everything begins to crawl; now it is settling down for winter sunshine and clarity. You can understand the colonial way of life. All its outward shows and servants and empire are accompanied by fever and diarrhea.

It took us a fortnight to begin to see India, even if dimly. Going by train from Delhi to the American base at Allahabad, September 13, we found the countryside quite flat, not unlike Iowa, except there is no geometry in the landscape. The fields are all sorts of shapes; and crops—like corn—are in blobs and patches. Having lived here too long, the natives of India are bound to be a bit wornout by it and undoubtedly all need a vacation. The most amazing thing about them is how various they are, all poor and in shirt tails but no end to the diversity of individuals.

The India-China contrast was heightened by the suddenness with which one crossed the North Burma "Hump" of the Himalayas from steamy India to the arid Yunnan plateau.

From central India we flew to Assam and thence into China. . . . Going east one sees the Himalaya range standing out on the north, white peaks behind black ranges, and the streams coming down across the plain, and finally one reaches the Brahmaputra, a wide sandy meandering landmark like the Ganges, and follows it on east. We came down right in the middle of tea plantations, and found the Assamese natives working in the sun each carrying a big black umbrella—another army camp with boys from the Middle West who go to the movies twice a week and a post exchange (shop) selling Coca-Colas and so on in the midst of nowhere. . . .

Next morning [September 20] we went on east "over the Hump," rising steadily, higher than anything in Europe, over jagged green peaks, over desolate valleys until we were above northern Burma, and its high terraces of red earth—very spectacular among the green peaks and layers of cloud. Of course we all waited for Japs to turn up. No one (among the passengers) could see why Zeros should not come up from the south, not more than a hundred miles, and lie in wait for us, and there are some exciting stories of dodging them through the clouds. No doubt interception is more work than it seems.

We came over the Burma Road, a very thin red path winding about, in a rather short time, and soon slid down over the big lake which marks Kunming and the abrupt high cliff by the lake which is the landmark locally and beyond which are the Western Hills. Kunming is not big from the air and lies on the southern edge of a broad plain ringed by hills and dotted with streams and villages, a very pretty country-side well irrigated.

My first impressions of China on this second visit were most vivid.

1. I can talk to the people, phrases come to mind as needed as though I had been here all the time. 2. The people are vigorous and smiling, the greatest contrast to the lassitude and repression of the Indians. 3. Women are everywhere working like men and bustling through life with as much freedom as anyone else. 4. Square flat Chinese faces are somehow much stronger than the thin Indians, and their color is more robust.

Kunming as a sleepy provincial capital in China's far Southwest had first been invaded early in the century by the French-built railway from Hanoi in French Indo-China. In 1938 came the three refugee universities from North China. There followed in 1941 the big American airbase for the Flying Tigers (14th Air Force) and also to provide the China anchor of the new airlift over the Hump from India. All this influx of Chinese intellectuals and American flyers made Kunming a boom town, sprawled out and hard to get around in.

Since Dr. Hayden and I had to wait several days for a plane north to Chungking, we looked for friends in the university, beginning with President Mei Yi-ch'i. A physicist, he was acting president for all the three universities (Nankai from Tientsin, Peking National (Peita), and Tsing Hua) that formed Lienta, the Southwest Associated University during their wartime refuge in Kunming. He looked even more emaciated and wornout than I remembered him but was very cordial.

Food and housing, the bare necessities, were primary faculty problems at Lienta. My friends Y. L. Chin the philosopher, Deison Ch'en the economist, and F. T. Ch'ing (Ch'en Fu-t'ien) of the English Department, who was an American from Hawaii, were all just moving into makeshift quarters in the balcony of an old Chinese theater next door to the American consulate. Both establishments had been created by Yunnan's principal warlord from 1911 to 1926 (T'ang Chi-yao) at a time when the French-built railway from Hanoi was the chief artery between Kunming (Yunnan-fu) and the outer world. The theater balcony was of flimsy construction but rent free. As we sat talking,

> big rats ran over the ceiling paper and almost fell through it, so we discussed getting a cat but a cat would cost $200. I am invited to camp with them when I return. (Professor E. R. Hughes of Oxford also did so later on.)

I was alarmed at the professors' penurious situation and wrote:

> They are putting up a stout fight but can't go on much longer. You can imagine this situation—the despair, squalor, brave front, mutual support, and gradual weakness of thought and action.

In fact, as it turned out, they continued another three years and then went back to make do in postwar Peking.

Another Peking friend I found was Bob Winter, a fifty-eight-year-old American representative of I. A. Richards's Orthological Institute (Basic English).

> In air raids his clothes have been completely stolen twice and he now has a pair of monkeys in the yard, one of whom, on a wire, is a fierce biting beast and would have to be shot by an intruder. Bob has a courtyard full of flowers and a bookcase full of books, and knows all the ins and outs of local folklore and gossip.

All these men were bachelors except F. T. Ch'ing, whose wife was in Honolulu. For families life was harder.

> I hunted up the Lienta librarian, Yen Wen-yuan, who was understudy to the director in the National Library of Peiping. When I last saw Yen there, he was just taking over the Peita library and going ahead with a first-rate library program, getting in a complete Library of Congress catalogue (on cards), and making big plans. This time I found him lying half dressed in bed in a garret room over a cobbler's stall, half sick and wondering how to feed his three children. [Postwar, Yen joined the United Nations staff.]

Chang Hsi-jo, the Tsing Hua political scientist, had found lodging with his family in the Chin family temple, "where he lives in the hall of tablets in a lovely tree-studded garden." Our friend the Peita political scientist Ch'ien Tuan-sheng, however, lived five miles out in the country. Our closest Peking friends, the Liangs, had lived there too but then moved with Academia Sinica north to Szechwan. On Sunday Chang Hsi-jo undertook to guide us and Dr. Hayden secured an army Jeep.

We started out with six in the Jeep, I driving, over the usual chaotic stone roads through town, pounding on the tin sides to get the pole carriers out of the way, and bouncing among the carts and peddlers through the length of the city, policemen waving us on and the horn occasionally tooting mournfully. We then went out through the countryside on a corduroy road and wound about the plain onto its periphery and finally came down into Lung-t'ou, "dragon head," village, local name for Lung-ch'uan. There we parked the Jeep in a grove in front of a temple and walked over paths to the house of Ch'ien Tuan-sheng. It is next to the one that the Liangs built and Phyllis designed them both, they having begun the fashion of living in the country to avoid the bombing. The deal is to build a house and pay no rent on the land, the house reverting to the landlord in lieu of rent after five years.

So finally we brought Lao Chin and Ch'ien back with us, eight in the Jeep, all jammed together comfortably . . . to Dr. Mei's house at seven for a banquet. Dr. Mei has a big house and does the honors for all the faculty, who mostly live in garrets and can't receive callers. Dr. Mei according to Winter has a salary of under 600 a month, and the banquet cannot have cost less than 1,000. Foreseeing such a problem, we presented him with an inch-high bottle of Atabrine tablets for malaria, which ought to bring back the 1,000.

The inflation has produced amazing anomalies. Chesterfields sell at $10 apiece and Parker fountain pens for $6,000. Pens and watches and cameras are leading articles for the speculative buying and selling which accompany the having of too much money for any useful purpose. Consequently by giving a fountain pen to a Chinese professor you give him more than his year's salary. Kunming is especially the scene of wild prices for imports, with numerous Chinese and Americans cleaning up fortunes in business on the side of official life.

The Kunming faculty situation so appalled me that I lost no time in reporting it to Washington. I sent my views to Alger Hiss in terms intended for both Hornbeck and Currie. These papers stated points I often reiterated, so I reproduce them.

Kunming, Sept. 23, 1942

Dear Alger,

I have now been in Kunming five days waiting for a plane and seeing people, many of whom I knew in Peking, and without further delay I send you my first impressions: no. 1 is that the Chinese are so much more vigorous and enlightened than the Indians; no. 2 is that the British are being a good deal more active here than the Americans (twice as big a staff, a program of publications, a reading room with books, one Oxford professor in residence and more on the way, etc.); no. 3 is that the Tsing Hua faculty, part of the S.W. Associated University, are slowly starving both intellectually and physically, although they are the pick of the American returned students in Chinese academic life; no. 4 relates to our last conversation in which I believe you advanced the view that developments in China could be judged more effectively in Washington than in the field, because the reports are more complete in Washington, and that therefore a good man could be more effective by staying in Washington.

I regret to say, in friendly fashion, that I have come to the conclusion that this is one of the most pernicious doctrines in the history of diplomacy. The fact that it can be expressed in Washington strengthens my rapidly growing conviction that this is one of the laughable periods in American foreign policy, which will be held up to ridicule by future historians. You remember how Edmund Hammond, Permanent Undersecretary for Foreign Affairs, declared in 1870 after thirty years study of the European situation from Whitehall that he had never known the European diplomatic scene to be so quiet and unruffled; whereupon the Franco-Prussian War broke out two weeks later, and

Hammond has been frequently quoted since.

This period of our policy in Asia will be remembered, I am afraid, for its failure to grasp and deal with the essentials of the situation here. Whatever else it may be, this situation is one of combat, in which modern-democratic-western-ideal ways are directly opposed to old-authoritarian-Chinese-opportunist ways. You might call it a cultural struggle, in which values are being established and the future created accordingly. I need not paint in words the forces that are opposed, since you know them as well as I do. The point is that we in the United States are party to this battle, but that our foreign policy does not recognize the fact in practical fashion. We speak of the world struggle but avoid the issue in China.

This incompetence is exemplified in the case of the Chinese intellectuals, whom we have long known to be dying by degrees for want of support from their own government. . . . The Chinese intellectuals who have been trained in the United States and who think and speak and teach as we would do constitute a tangible American interest in China and are a not unimportant factor in the struggle going on here; and in the past year no solution has been found to the problem of helping them unless U.C.R. [United China Relief] can do something.

This particular failure is only an illustration of the fundamental evil in our policy, which appears to lie in the concept that we cannot mix into the affairs of another country, even though it is a battleground in the world struggle. The British are at least supplying books here, and before December 7 had also supplied more than we did.

There is another pernicious doctrine held in Washington and I regret to say I have heard it expressed by Lauch, from whom one would not expect evil any more than from yourself. This is that the main thing in China is fighting the Japs with military force, so-called cultural relations being an unimportant sideshow. On the contrary, I am coming to the conclusion that the main issue here is cultural. Lauch no doubt noticed that the arms which he expedited into this country have not been entirely devoted to fighting the Japs. The reason is a cultural one, in the broad sense of the term. The supplying of material things to China is only one aspect of the war, and unless the Chinese who use these things have the right ideas, the result may be evil and not good. American ideals, such as they may be, cannot be defeated here and the war really won at the same time; naturally the Chinese will always be different, but certain ideals we must get in common and make prevail if the world is to be organized. The amazing thing is that ideas are as easy to bring here as airplanes. Yet an idea-program for China has been delayed and frustrated by lack of imagination in the proper places in Washington. This lack of imagination springs directly from lack of contact with the realities of life in China. Reports can be collated and previously-held ideas supported at a distance, but one cannot respond to a situation forever without having more than literary contact with it.

You see that I have become an expansionist, because part of this country is a part of our world, and part is not, and we must all organize ourselves into one world—ours, not theirs. The fundamental problem here, springing from lack of comprehension at home, is that our representatives are too few. No one out here should be blamed for not doing three men's work.

Having expressed these opinions I have now to consider how to lay them before you. Fortunately I am informed that I have a "permanent" appointment at Harvard, assuming that there will always be a Harvard, and I can at any time come home and write letters to the *New Republic* if not through the Embassy pouch. I know you and Lauch will be flattered by this denunciation, at least I hope so.

[*Enclosure to Hiss*]

THE TSING HUA FACULTY

Summary: the American-trained faculty of Tsing Hua University, Kunming, represent an American investment and asset in China. They are seriously threatened with extinction, and means of help should be found.

Sources: the following account is based on conversations with Professor F. T. Ching (Ch'en Fu-t'ien), head of the English Department, an American citizen born in Hawaii; Professor Shiro Chang (Chang Hsi-jo), head of the Department of Political Science (both these men are elected members of the University Senate); Professor T. S. Chien (Ch'ien Tuan-sheng) of the Political Science Department of the Peking National University, a member of the People's Political Council; and President Y. C. Mei of Tsing Hua and the Southwest Associated University of which it forms a part. These men are leaders among the returned student portion of the faculty and I have known them since 1933 when I taught for one year at Tsing Hua under Dr. T. F. Tsiang, then head of the History Department. During a week in Kunming I have visited half a dozen places where faculty members are living and have discussed the situation with a dozen persons.

1. Tsing Hua University in particular represents an American interest in China because several million dollars of the returned portion of the Boxer indemnity have been invested in it. As in any leading university, the faculty are the more important part of the investment, and the Tsing Hua faculty, because of the prestige and resources of the institution, have been carefully recruited from the very best of the American returned students.

On the whole, these men are the elite among western-trained academic personnel in China, and therefore the living agents of American educational influence. The buildings and equipment having fallen to Japan, these teachers are all that is left of an investment made by the United States Government over a period of more than thirty years. Their situation demands special consideration.

2. The present Minister of Education, Dr. Ch'en Li-fu, in working toward the regimentation of intellectual life in China has made persistent efforts to gain control over the policies of Tsing Hua, as well as of other universities. In the Tsing Hua faculty, however, he has met the most convinced and determined opposition from the senior American-trained professors. The result is a continuing struggle, in which the power

of the Ministry and of the Kuomintang, with their financial backing, is matched against the determination of the faculty to preserve their freedom of teaching in the American tradition. This is an unequal struggle because the financial resources of the faculty—the store of books and clothes which they can sell off to support themselves—is rapidly being exhausted. Unless assistance is obtained, this struggle can have but one end—the continued malnutrition, illness, and eventual demoralization of those faculty members who stand for the American ideal of freedom in teaching, and their death, dispersal, or corruption.

3. Specifically, the effort of the Kuomintang and the Ministry has taken the following forms: younger faculty members have been urged to join the Party, and those who have shown interest have been entertained and given special favors and attention from Chungking; the assistance given to the University as a whole (and this applies to the S.W. Assoc. Univ. generally) has been less than would be justified by its academic standing in China—it has been aided by the Government on a quantitative rather than a qualitative basis; in Kunming the provincial Yunnan University has received extensive funds and is a good deal better off than Lienta although the latter contains the cream of the Chinese academic world in the faculties of Nankai, Peita, and Tsing Hua.

4. Examples of this struggle could be multiplied, and it is unnecessary to describe how the faculty members are living in bare garrets, selling their books and clothes, going into debt, and developing nutritional ailments. Whether or not they are victims of official animus or merely of the inflation, the fact remains that they are not receiving the help which their value to China and which their value to the United States demands that they should receive.

If it be admitted that China is one battlefield in the world struggle between regimentation and freedom in which we profess to be engaged, then it is clear that failure to help these people will be a shameful stain upon the American record in this struggle.

jkf

A reader of today will note that this call for intervention did not consider by what means American aid could be given to Chinese professors. In the end, however, a number of indirect means would be found. This and subsequent broadsides like it had some effect in Washington in the course of time, but not soon. This first crisis that I came upon in wartime China put me a bit out of step with the kill-the-Japs war effort envisaged back in the United States. I was already involved in a different struggle. It took on more significance as I made my way further into the Chinese scene.

17

GETTING SET UP IN CHUNGKING

DESPITE ALL THE difficulties of Kunming life, the great compensation for living there was the bright Arizona-like climate. When we flew north to the wartime capital at Chungking, we left the dry sunshine far behind. For the capital of one of the four Great Powers, Chungking was surprisingly hard to get to. Foreign allies could arrive only by air, and much of the year the air consisted of cloud cover. Yunnan is well named "South of the Clouds" and so is Szechwan ("Four Rivers," i.e., the Yangtze and others, each in its rocky gorge), because one can see the mist rising from the rivers to produce the clouds. We flew north from Kunming September 25

> over ridge after ridge of green mountains with red earth under the green, and rice fields half way up the hills. We got into clouds at twelve thousand and came down out of it to see the river and mist here.

Chungking's three airfields each challenged a pilot in a different way. First, the landing strip on a sandbank in the middle of the Yangtze could be used only at low water in winter. Pilots taking off there had a choice of going under or over a cable that swooped across the river shortly upstream. Second, another air strip (Chiu-lung-p'o, "Nine Dragon Slope") ran between a hill at one end and the Yangtze River bank at the other. Taking off, you might be over the water

before you saw any signs of being airborne. Third, the biggest field
(Pai-shih-i) was across a mountain range in a valley where planes
circling in the clouds often had to circle down below mountain
height before breaking out of the mist to see the strip. A four-engine
C-54, finding itself twenty feet off center and having to side-slip
while landing, would look like a dancing elephant. Sometimes planes
couldn't get in and would have to go back to where they came from.
(Often after the war C-54s after seven hours' flight from Shanghai
might circle over Chungking for an hour and then return in frustration to Shanghai.) In 1942 we had no trouble. On landing, naturally,
we met General Chennault and also John Ford, the movie producer.
Wartime personages concentrated at airports.

Chungking struck me at once as "an amazingly unfortunate site
for human habitation, since there is no level land. One becomes a
goat in the effort to get anywhere." The rocky peninsula between the
Yangtze and Chialing rivers had only "a few new streets strung along
the hillsides on which modern traffic can go." Everything seemed to
be "under a quarter of an inch of mud."

During the fifteen months I spent in the Chinese wartime capital,
neither the Cold War nor the Chinese Revolution as yet bothered us.
The menace was still the Germans and the Japanese. World War II
was only half over. Japanese bombers on clear days could still drive
Chungking's ragged citizens into their stone-cave air-raid shelters.
But the Chungking rock pile on its long peninsula was usually under
clouds, so our daily problem was not bombing so much as humidity.

People in Chungking in 1942 were curiously confident of victory
in World War II, now that the United States was mobilized. My
presence in fact was proof of the mobilization—a thirty-five-year-old
Harvard professor arriving as a civilian to work under the American
embassy distributing microfilm from the new China section of the
Cultural Relations division of the State Department while collecting
Chinese publications for the Library of Congress. This was, as I announced to all and sundry, my respectable academic cover for my
less publicized effort to win the war by finding and microfilming
Japanese publications for use by the Office of Strategic Services in
Washington.

OSS's first-born in China, Dr. Esson Gale, before he left for home
passing us en route, had prepared a house if not a home for OSS in
the compound of the Ch'iu-ching Middle School, a couple of miles

out along the city's rough spine not far from where Chiang Kai-shek, his brother-in-law the Prime Minister, H. H. Kung, General Stilwell, and others had their headquarters, a neighborhood of power if not fashion. Within the school compound were several civilian offices— for the Red Cross, the China Foundation (dispensing American Boxer funds), and Nanking University, among others. Our house had twenty-five rooms on four floors within good stone walls, but only Clyde Sargent (who had once rented our rear courtyard in Peking) to represent OSS, left behind by David Rowe. Into this vacuum accordingly had moved the U.S. Office of War Information, a sibling of OSS, since it also was the descendant of COI.

OWI had a great deal more going on. Mac (Francis McCracken) Fisher, a journalist friend formerly in Peking, had been drafted after Pearl Harbor to handle the American news output in Free China. For psychological warfare (PW), i.e., leaflets for planes to drop, he was assisted by Jim Stewart, who had grown up in Japan. They already had a staff to take down, duplicate, and issue the daily OWI news broadcasts. With Dr. Hayden's concurrence I invited OWI to move in further. Soon their specialists from New York were sending and receiving news pictures on special equipment. Our combined offices were also blessed with a car.

Since I had been given the title of Special Assistant to the American Ambassador (though on a special, not a diplomatic passport), I journeyed to the tip of the peninsula, descended the two hundred or so stone steps, crossed the Yangtze in the small steam ferry that always pointed upstream into the six-knot current, and climbed up to the American embassy on the south bank. There I spent two days explaining my roles to Clarence Gauss, the ambassador, and John Carter Vincent, his counselor of embassy. It took some time to lay out my handiwork.

I was determined first of all to operate under and through the ambassador, without my own code or special channels. After all, I was a very small potato in the war effort, connected only with research and the handling of publications, no secret intelligence or operations. My office budget and payroll would be handled by the embassy. It came from funds of the Interdepartmental Committee for the Acquisition of Foreign Publications, known first as Indec, then as IDC.

This worldwide collection service was managed by a young library specialist, Frederick G. Kilgour, under the wing of William L.

Langer as head of R and A. Fred had graduated from Harvard in 1935 in chemistry but went into Widener to microfilm foreign newspapers. Langer drafted him in March 1942 to handle the collection of printed materials, mainly from Germany, needed for intelligence work. His committee was a bundle of agency interests, and since Fred was only twenty-eight, he had to be diplomat, scientist, and office boy all at once. East Asia was the least of his worries. I had a Leica camera and film so I could send back microfilm of Japanese, Chinese, or other documents I hoped to obtain from Chinese intelligence agencies. For example, Burton Fahs was eager to get the press, yearbooks, and ministry reports from Tokyo.

Since I hoped to send back Chinese publications also, to open up the normal pipeline closed by China's being cut off over the Hump, I was designated the China representative of Archibald MacLeish, the Librarian of Congress, with little budget but plenty of good will, from Dr. Hummel of Orientalia in particular.

Finally, I felt it most important, if I wanted to get something from Chinese sources, to give something. This was simply the ancient idea of reciprocity, not seeking something for nothing. I was therefore the informal agent of RC, the Cultural Relations division of the State Department, in whose China section Wilma was helping to select and ship to me American academic and technical publications on microfilm. I brought with me a model projector, invented by a scientist in Washington, and a supply of electric bulbs and lenses with which to manufacture others.

In order to make reciprocity my *raison d'être*, in drafting my instructions of August 12, 1942, from MacLeish and of August 18 from Colonel Donovan, I had inserted in each a special paragraph: "Your primary objective is to aid in reviving the flow of printed matter in both directions between China and the United States."

I explained myself fully to Mr. Gauss because I deplored the fragmentation of the American presence in China under the military and wartime agencies that left it a multiheaded monster incapable of unified policy. The ambassador had been bypassed first by Lauchlin Currie's personal mission from FDR to CKS (Chiang Kai-shek). Dr. Gale had been given his own code and had run a separate show like the military. I wanted to be sure my three-headed academic venture did not threaten the ambassador's already anemic authority.

Ambassador Gauss was a solid square peg in a very round hole.

After a reception he came back with Mac Fisher and me and regaled us for an hour

> with tales of his Shanghai consulate days when he broke drug
> rings and enforced the letter of the law. As he says, he plainly
> would like nothing better than to be a district attorney some-
> where at home where the rules could really be executed. He
> wishes he could have retired and done this before the war
> began. He is a Connecticut Yankee, he says, and he can't bear
> to see public waste or inefficiency. He was determined to be
> on time for the Generalissimo's dinner even though John
> Carter tried to dissuade him gently.

The ablest American diplomat was Gauss's counselor, John Carter Vincent, a Georgian with a long experience in China. He struck me as

> very quick of speech and even quicker of comprehension,
> buoyantly interested in any situation and yet objective about
> it at the same time that he is very personal. Says H.E. turned
> down chance after chance to end this farce of trying to repre-
> sent the country across a river from a treaty-port hillside. The
> one thing that broke his heart was not being able to get the
> present magnificent FO place when he could have if H.E.
> would only ask for the money. Says this has been eternity out
> here, even in a year and a half. It is amazing how he lives with
> that large, slow, legal-minded, antisocial viewer of the past
> when he himself is so quick, lively, and all for action. It is
> exhausting. He does it by expressing himself. One sits and talks
> to the two of them and forgets H.E. and his cigar are there at
> all, white in the corner. J. C. has the kind of genius that flows
> fast around obstacles toward objectives without seeming to
> try. If he had had to use willpower on this situation of constant
> opportunities and failures, he would have broken up long
> since; only temperament could put him through it.

In October 1942 Mr. Gauss had just undergone another snub from Washington in the person of Wendell Willkie, recent GOP candidate for President, who brought to town the circus of American presiden- tial politics. He was running for office in Chungking a few days after we arrived. Nothing could have demonstrated for us more dramati-

cally the cultural gap between China and America. The visitor, full
of bounce and gusto, projected his personality American-style to gain
favor and win votes from people who were not voting. It was like an
African chief performing his tribal dances before Eskimos.

On October 5 I joined our Peking friend Edmund Clubb, now at
the embassy, and we followed the dynamic Mr. Willkie

> on the run through four colleges, the technique being very
> simple. March in through the flag-lined student-packed be-
> decked approach under the arch with the flowers and mottoes
> of welcome, welcome, etc., suddenly stop and shake hands
> with a small baffled cheerleader, stop again and cross-examine
> a student selected at random, as to his work, objective, father,
> routine; double into the reception room and cross-examine
> the principal on the numbers, classes, ages, subjects, and funds
> (he left the saintly Chang Po-lin in a dither) and appear on the
> steps before the massed throng and speak. Theme, how I spent
> four years in college trying to make it difficult for the teachers.
> Subjective remarks, about himself as a personality, changing
> halfway through to the seriousness of war and a dedication as
> the representative of the whole people to the task of seeing to
> it that world order will prevent war again. Nothing specific of
> course but plenty of dedication, including part of the Gettys-
> burg address. All accompanied by excitement, wonderment,
> and enthusiasm from the crowd of students, who showed real
> interest, considering that most of them looked thin and tired,
> like everybody else in Chungking. The morning ended, after
> a good deal of long-live-democracy and flag waving with a
> reception at the library where I met the Ch'en brothers
> [Ch'en Li-fu, Ch'en Kuo-fu], each of whom looks more diminu-
> tive than the other. The Education Minister [Ch'en Li-fu] is a
> little guy with a Presbyterian cast of countenance who pro-
> nounced much on educating for democracy and freedom.

Mme. Chiang gave a tea for Willkie at which she

> made a speech on the theme that he was very disturbing and
> had taken everyone by storm, and she did such a neat job that
> it appeared she had him tied, but he countered with the crack
> that speaking against his great opponent [FDR] was nothing

compared to following her on the program, and so on and on
—a good verbal performance, before the New Life crew who
are the specialists on such occasions.

October 6. Dr. H. H. Kung gave a lawn party for Willkie,
a good-looking sight on a grass plot behind his house which sits
up on a hill. I sat near the head table, which read as follows:
Wang Ch'ung-hui, Chennault, Ho Ying-ch'in, Mme. Sun,
Willkie, Kung, Mme. Chiang, Gauss, Stilwell, Pai Ch'ung-hsi,
and Sun Fo.

This assemblage of leaders in the Sino-American relationship exemplified the cross-currents in it. On the American side Generals
Stilwell and Chennault outgunned Ambassador Gauss as power holders but Stilwell represented George Marshall, who sat at the center
in Washington, whereas Chennault was a soldier of fortune backed
by Mme. Chiang on the basis that airpower is all. The two ladies,
Mme. Chiang and Mme. Sun, were of course sisters, but the latter was
a humanitarian sympathetic to the left and not a careerist enjoying
power; in fact she was kept city-bound by the rest of the family. Of
the other family members, H. H. Kung functioned as a brother-in-law
dependent on CKS while Sun Fo as Sun Yat-sen's son by his first
marriage was a possible but ineffectual rival to CKS, kept on partly
for his legitimizing value (to show CKS was Dr. Sun's successor).
Among the Chinese generals, Ho Ying-ch'in was the leader of the
Whampoa graduates loyal to CKS whereas Pai Ch'ung-hsi, a more
able soldier, was from the sometimes separatist Kwangsi clique and
so symbolized unity under CKS. Wang Ch'ung-hui, finally, was a
revolutionary who had become an internationally recognized jurist
and so represented the American-trained echelon.

The picture they generally presented was one of the military
dominating the civilians, as not unusual in wartime, and of coalition
under CKS the leader, who was on the level of FDR and so did not
appear with the defeated Willkie.

The occasion was colored, however, by the fact that General J. L.
Huang was master of ceremonies—a very large man, effusively genial, whom we had first met in Nanking in 1934. He was a key
operator in Mme. Chiang's entourage, active first in the Officers
Moral Endeavor Society, then in the New Life Movement, and now
in the War Area Service Corps that provided the food and housing

of American troops. On social occasions with Americans she had him act the court buffoon, which he did with a good deal of prancing about and backslapping bonhommie. He was said to have trained early on to be a heavy or "big painted face" (ta-hua-lien) in Chinese opera. Combined with the American collegiate style of the 1920s, the result was pure corn. Wilma probably witnessed a high point of General Huang's performance between the cultures at a Christmas party in 1946. He came in as a dead ringer for Santa Claus and presented gifts, including one for "Georgie, who has been such a good little boy." The recipient was George Catlett Marshall, General of the Army, who showed no sign of being amused.

On the other hand General Huang had to suffer a good deal of incivility from the American officers his Service Corps was trying to please. He told me the American "troops were always frank and honest but the officers who had been in China before and felt they knew all about it" were very hard to deal with, both demanding and suspicious. It made him almost anti-American.

Chungking was full of people we had known a decade earlier in Peking: Edmund Clubb in the embassy, John Davies attached to Stilwell, Mac Fisher heading OWI, and an equal number of Chinese like Franklin Ho from the Nankai Institute of Economics in Tientsin, now doing postwar planning. This continuity of personnel made for continuity of understanding and a useful perspective. Everitt Groff-Smith was doing Customs business even though it was now non-maritime. The I.G., Sir Frederick Maze, was still interned in Shanghai. In 1943 he would be succeeded in Chungking by L. K. Little.

I also found that T. F. Tsiang lived nearby. I had written him more than a year before, as isolationism in the United States gave ground to war preparation. His reply in July 1941 had stated China's aims and his own hope to get back to scholarship—after the war. From Washington I wrote him in September outlining our problems in injecting academic researchers into government. I stressed our lack of published materials from China and the need for reports on conditions and on the Nationalist government's social and economic programs. His reply of October 11 offered to supply "quantities of material, some statistical," especially to correct the over-rosy picture put out on the CCP areas. I replied November 12, enclosing a letter from Baxter introducing D. Rowe as our agent to microfilm materials. I also outlined the new RC program for China. On December 6, 1941,

T. F. wrote back enthusiastically, suggesting where university reading rooms could be set up and how scholars might be exchanged. He foresaw the need for an embassy cultural attaché and several trucks to bring books in from Burma.

Nine months later, here I was on his doorstep, fostering part of the RC program. But in the meantime I believe T. F. had got a poor impression of COI. He had me around to supper and bridge occasionally but no flow of materials developed. Presumably it was not in his line of work.

One September evening I stopped in with the U.S. Treasury representative on the Stabilization Board, Sol Adler, and

> T. F. told some more tales of his life as CKS's budget maker. Weng Wen-hao wanted to build steel plants which would produce at $40,000 a ton, useless after the war and ineffective during it. T. F. argued it down. Someone else got CKS to agree to a railroad or road to Siberia, at great expense, and T. F. laid the details before CKS by wire and got a reversal in the end. His whole idea is to cut out inessential investments in this crisis period so as to keep the budget and therefore the inflation from running away. He and Adler agreed on the Army and key government organization being the essentials. I disagreed because I think the Army will have little to do now and the intellectuals will be very essential as soon as fighting stops, at least they will from the view of American interest.

In early October the former librarian of the National Library of Peiping, T. L. Yuan, came out of a year's incarceration under the Japanese in Hong Kong. He was an academic entrepreneur of the first magnitude, with a new project idea every day. Operating on a shoestring, T. L. had created in 1934 the *Quarterly Bulletin of Chinese Bibliography*, which gave us what little news we had of new Chinese publications during the war years.

T. L. Yuan had been librarian of Tsing Hua, taken a Columbia B.A. in 1922 and a B.L.S. at the New York State Library School in Albany in 1923, helped catalogue the Chinese collection at the Library of Congress, become librarian of Peita in 1925 and of his own National Library above-mentioned in 1929. From that post of leadership he had trained Chinese librarians abroad, begun interlibrary loans and international exchanges, and started union catalogues, several indices of publications, and serial lists. In 1935 he began a printed card service for Chinese works, like that of the Library of Congress. He sent 2,800 Chinese rare books to LC for safekeeping in wartime. He even fostered museum development in China and represented his country in the field of international intellectual cooperation.

In short, by age forty-eight T. L. Yuan had made himself China's librarian. His reappearance in Chungking was for me an auspicious event. We joined forces immediately. Soon he had set up the International Cultural Service of China under the Ministry of Education to give proper official auspices to the distribution of RC microfilm from my office. Films with indices of contents were packed in bright red boxes and sent out to reading rooms at major university centers. We found that our neighbor, the dean of engineering of Nanking University, could assemble the microfilm readers to go with the film. Faculty specialists were starved for American publications in their fields. To break the transport bottleneck by using microfilm was the latest marvel of technology, promising and much appreciated.

T. L. also gave my office its Chinese name, Service Center for Academic Materials *(Hsueh-shu tzu-liao fu-wu ch'u),* under the American embassy. "Academic" and "service" were golden words and put me at some distance from secret intelligence. In English we christened it the American Publications Service.

I had inherited from Dr. Gale a business manager in the person of Mr. Ch'en Sung-chiao, formerly of the Salt Administration, who was not only an able fixer but was known personally to Dr. H. H. Kung. In fact Ch'en reported to H. H. regularly on my office's activities. When we became well acquainted he would tell me when the premier (H. H. was head of the Executive Yuan) particularly approved of my work. I was thus tied into the Chinese network of official auspices and personal relations.

I went to see Dr. Kung in January 1943:

H.H. and I sat in some easy chairs while I told him my forebears, status, and intimate purposes. He is a shrewd man and looked at me for a long time to decide whether I was honest. He concentrated on this point, and also listened to what I said, so when I got around to it, he said, Yes, I could have the confidential documents.

Arthur Boyce Fairbank 1873–1936
and Lorena King Fairbank 1874–1979
(*pencil portraits by Wilma Fairbank,
1936*)

Age 7—my mother dressed me nicely

Age 10—my father built me a fort

Age 18, at Phillips Exeter Academy—
winner of a trip to England, 1925

Sir Charles Kingsley Webster, professor of international history, who suggested I study China

Wilma at a temple in the Western Hills, Peking, 1934

JKF—horseman   My reluctant teacher Kuo Yu-hsiu

Foreigners on Mongol ponies exploring the Peking countryside (*watercolor by Wilma*)

Peking's muscle-power water supply, delivered in barrows and buckets (*WF*)

Informal portrait, Peking, 1935 (*WF*)

At the feet of a Buddhist guardian of the rock-cut caves at Lung-men, Honan Province, 1933

Chinese friends: Liang Ssu-ch'eng and his wife Phyllis (Lin Whei-yin), historians of Chinese architecture, on a field trip, early 1930s

Chou En-lai's aides Kung P'eng and Ch'iao Kuan-hua, married in Chungking, November 1943

Kung P'eng interpreting for Tung Pi-wu, a party founder close to Mao, Chungking, 1945

Teddy White—war correspondent

Wilma Fairbank, cultural attaché of the
American Embassy, in Kunming, 1945

The house on Winthrop St.—our home since 1936

Professor Ch'ien Tuan-sheng on our Cambridge doorstep, 1948

Holly and Laura visiting their grandmother in Georgetown, 1955

Leaders in Chinese studies (conference on China's traditional polity, 1959, at Steele Hill, Winnisquam, N.H.). From left rear: A. Doak Barnett, Joseph R. Levenson, Hans Bielenstein, Judith Shklar, Franz Michael, Edward Wagner, Mary Wright, Benjamin Schwartz, Edward Kracke. Foreground: Albert Feuerwerker, Fritz Mote, Charles O. Hucker, Lien-sheng Yang, T'ung-tsu Ch'ü, Chou Tse-tsung, John M. H. Lindbeck, Edwin O. Reischauer (*Photo, JKF*)

Our long-time friends Eleanor and Owen Lattimore with Japan's eminent historian Tatsuro Yamamoto, Rome, 1955

With Professor Mary Wright of Yale in my seminar on Chinese documents, Widener Library, 1959

Peking, 1972: with Vice-Minister for Foreign Affairs Ch'iao Kuan-hua and Premier

Taking a bow at Peking University, 1979. JKF and Assistant Secretary Richard Holbrooke; foreground: President Chou P'ei-yuan and Joan Mondale

Osborn Elliott, right, and Teddy White giving me immortality if we can raise the money, 1977

Sometime later I tried to picture the working of the personal-relations network by recording

A DAY IN THE LIFE OF CH'EN SUNG-CHIAO

The business manager and Chinese secretary, Mr. Ch'en, is the oil surrounding this bit of the American ship of state which alone prevents its foundering daily and hourly in the seas of Chungking. He is not very tall and of uncertain age [actually thirty-two] but always wears a long gown and somehow has a presence, deferential toward his superiors, persuasive among equals, overbearing toward inferiors, like a good car with three gears shifted instantly to accord with the terrain. The Americans like to go shopping with him to see the performance when he goes into low, racing the engine, and overwhelms the luckless shopkeeper with a torrent of vigorous verbiage, the American embassy, Dr. Kung, possible rebates, the face of China, friendship, high-placed relatives, money, future trade, and pure reason. Frequently he is implored by OWI and by other friends to come and "negotiate." When something is stolen, or we run out of coal, or someone is arrested, or the toilet overflows, or we need envelopes or a new house, Mr. Ch'en is brought into action.

After a day out in the world he comes back and reports, Well, Dr. Fairbank, I went to the Liquid Fuel Control Commission to see about gasoline. Well, you see, Mr. Wu, the secretary of the vice-chairman, is a cousin of my brother-in-law, Mr. Tseng, the number one painter in China, and he said we could renew our 50 gallon ration—20 Kansu gas, 20 substitute, and 10 alcohol. Well, you see, we got more than the usual ration of 20 gallons because the OWI was here; but it is in our name, so I told Mr. Wu he should continue it, for the American embassy. Well, I saw also the vice-minister of food, Mr. Hsu, who used to be in Salt Administration, and he gave us a permit to buy rice at the official rate for Chinese government offices —well, you see, the staff is mainly Chinese people here—so I have arranged with Mr. Paton to sell rice to the Chinese staff mess at less than they can buy it and we will put the difference in the staff medical fund. Well, here are your calling cards, there is a small mistake, Universitiv for University, and the printer does not wish to charge you for them, so I gave him a small gift. Also I brought back some paper, which is very hard to get now but I got a permit from Mr. Wang, the chief accountant in the Ministry of Finance, who used to live at my uncle's house. The driver, he says he must get another can of brake oil and his friend in the Yuan Tung Repair Car Co. will sell a rusted can for $2,000. Well, I told him he must reduce the price to $1,200 and I would ask Dr. Fairbank. I also stopped at the Military Council to see Mr. Kuo, who is sick in the country, but Mr. Hsi, his assistant, said that he would be glad to lend us his file of confidential studies and I gave him your card with a copy of the Microfilm Guide and will see him next week. Well, here is your visa from the Foreign Office; you see, they stopped issuing visas last week, but I saw my cousin Mr. Li, in the secretariat, and explained that you were going to leave last week and he said he would make a special note.

Having received this report, I then restock Mr. Ch'en's supply of negotiations as follows: the water which runs into Mr. Raichle's room from the bathroom is really from the outlet pipe of the bathtub; if you will have a brick put under the pipe to hold it up against the tub, it may stop. Also the hospital reports that the staff cook, whom they finally examined, has trachoma, worms, and syphilis (a true story, that handsome young man!), so they must get a new cook. But the staff mess should not use the kitchen coal, they must get their own, as we arranged last month (also the month before). Please buy two notebooks, and I wish you would have Mr. Yang get a separate bill for each book he buys, in duplicate. If he gets three copies of a book, then he needs six bills. I want to see General Yang sometime next week. This hinge must have a screw bought for it. We must return to Standard Oil the two drums which Mr. Bothnerby lent us when he took their drums to lend to the Salt Administration last year; although it is true that Driver Wang took one away before we fired him, we must recover it (a true case). Please make out checks for the book boxes, and give me another statement showing where you think the revolving fund is. . . .

Since this goes on day after day, broken-field running with

occasional off-side penalties but numerous scorings, some fumbles, and no time out, you will see why I cannot really describe Mr. Ch'en's duties.

The basic fact, in any case, was that Mr. Ch'en, as a Chinese bureaucrat assigned to look after and keep track of an American office, could invoke the shadowy authority of the prime minister and so expedite the foreigner's business while keeping an eye on it. It was in the ancient tradition of barbarian taming.

Thus based, I began to scour the city for materials of interest to IDC. Ch'en Sung-chiao arranged appointments for me with heads of offices and ministries and I called on them to explain my function, offer assistance, and ask for help. Each time I sent Fred Kilgour at IDC a memorandum of my adventures through the embassy pouch with a drop copy for the ambassador. On occasion I sent memoranda to the ambassador with copies to forward to State. I also wrote personal letters, some direct to Lauchlin Currie but mainly to Wilma for her to pass on as she saw fit, and sent them through the Army Post Office.

In Army circles I had the assimilated rank of a "field grade officer," whatever that meant. I used Army planes and medical services but did not work in Army channels. The few times I saw General Stilwell reinforced my appreciation of his favorite motto as one clue to his populist, can-do character. The motto read "Illegitimati noli carborundum," which in U.S. Army Latin meant "Don't let the bastards grind you down."

This multichanneled operation suited me very well, as an observer who liked to meet people and write about them. Only a few things were wrong with the picture. First, the bare-bones model of a projector from Washington was murderous on the eyesight. It cast a bright light on a white wall and scholars, who often needed glasses or an ophthalmologist's attention in any case, found themselves blinded, crying and with headaches in no time. The projector also overheated dangerously and moreover could not be used on its side. We needed commercial models developed from experience with what users could stand.

Second, my own provision of film for the expectant researchers in Washington proved completely illegible. Many Chungking materials including newspapers were being printed with oily ink on the cheapest kind of paper, made by coagulating the fibers floating in a pan of water and lifting them out to dry on a screen. The resulting paper, usually gray or green, was of doubtful value even for the toilet. Catching the ink spread upon it in a picture, black blobs on a dark background, would have baffled everyone from Mathew Brady to Cartier Bresson. Moreover the Chungking electricity varied in strength over a wide range from moment to moment. I could not take a photoelectric cell reading, adjust the Leica and shoot before the current would have changed its brightness perceptibly even to my untutored eyes. Nobody could make head or tail of the film I sent back. But it didn't much matter. What I had to photograph at first was junk anyway.

Since what I supplied to China at first was almost as worthless as what I supplied to Washington, my function as an intellectual go-between boiled down mainly to a public-relations job. This did not bother the bigshots I dealt with because their jobs also were mainly public relations. None of us was an end user of the materials we talked about so knowingly.

In time these deficiencies were caught up with. Better projectors and useful films came out, and after six months Kilgour sent me Gus Paton, an indestructible film technician, who got steady current out of his own transformers and also by that time had materials worth filming. By the end of 1943 IDC in Washington was distributing a twenty-two-page subject index to its Chinese publications on film and was handling some seventy Chinese periodicals. Printed matter was flowing both ways.

18

MARY MILES AND OSS

THE AMERICAN PUBLICATIONS SERVICE, operating at the innocuous level of professors and librarians, left me out of the secret war effort to which OSS was primarily committed. No secrets of intelligence or operations came my way. (I liked Mortimer Graves's remark, "If *I* know it, it can't be secret.") My impression of the OSS struggle to spread its particular war effort around the globe is unresearched and after the fact: in brief, the Donovan organization seemed an upstart rival to well-established agencies like the Office of Naval Intelligence. OSS like OWI (the Office of War Information) was effectively excluded from MacArthur's Southwest Pacific Command, for he brooked no Washington rivals in his theater. OSS succeeded in getting into China in late 1942 only by supporting what the U.S. Navy was already doing there.

One day in October 1942 a super Jeep of the type called a weapons carrier arrived at my office in the Ch'iu-ching Middle School and disgorged a youngish man in khaki shorts and shirt who looked like a Boy Scout troop leader. His face was not only handsome but actually rather pretty, producing two dimples when he smiled. His name was Milton Miles but everyone called him Mary because when he was at the Naval Academy, class of 1922, Mary Miles Minter had been the toast of Broadway. Now commander, USN, Mary Miles had the personal backing of Admiral Ernest J. King of the Joint Chiefs of Staff, head of the U.S. Navy, who had made Miles head of U.S. Naval Group China.

At age forty-two Miles, like me, was just setting up his own personally devised operation in China, feeling his way, battling to define his official status and to get his supplies flown over the Hump from India. The resemblance ends at about that point because his supplies were TNT and tommyguns and his mission was to work with Chiang Kai-shek's chief of secret service, General Tai Li. This was probably the most potent and terror-producing name in wartime China. In brief, if CKS wanted anyone watched, investigated, arrested, or exterminated, Tai Li's organization did it. General Tai had risen as CKS's chief of security with a positive flair for assassination. He was Nationalist China's J. Edgar Hoover and William J. Donovan rolled into one, because his people performed both FBI- and CIA-type functions. Miles's rare photos of this legendary and secretive figure (published in his memoir *A Different Kind of War* (1967) after they were both deceased) show an intelligent man certainly much more handsome than J. Edgar ever was.

How Miles and Tai Li got together—and how China's secret police got U.S. Navy guns and training—makes a major case study in the Chinese-American pas de deux. First of all, Miles was romantically entranced by China. After graduation in 1922 he spent five years on the China station cruising among Chinese ports. His bride, Wilma (called Billy to match his Mary), found things Chinese similarly fascinating. In 1936–39 he had another tour of duty in China, commanding a destroyer, and on return managed to take his wife and three boys out over the Burma Road.

Second, Miles rose in Navy circles by technical competence. He had done a Columbia M.A. in electrical engineering and in 1940–41 served as recorder of the Interior Control Board, which kept the specifications of equipment used in the many control systems of Navy ships. Board members he worked with included leading officers in the various Navy bureaus. Naturally gregarious, Miles maintained, he says, a sort of *Kaffeeklatsch* where fellow officers dropped in for a break.

History began clicking when this vigorous and competent romantic technician found a warm friend in the person of Major Hsiao Hsin-ju, assistant military attaché at the Chinese embassy in Washington. By 1940–41 China-concerned naval people foresaw the need for naval observers in China both to monitor the weather that thence came out over the Pacific and to watch Japanese shipping along the coast. Major Hsiao turned up frequently to discuss such problems. Soon he and his wife were intimate friends of the Miles. They often dined together.

Shortly after Pearl Harbor Admiral King instructed Miles orally to go to China, set up some bases, and prepare for eventual Navy landings on the China coast. His written instructions merely made him naval observer under the American embassy, where the naval attaché, Colonel Jim McHugh of the U.S. Marines, was a classmate of Miles. (We had known McHugh in Peking.)

Next step: Admiral King, Miles, Admiral Willis A. Lee, who was Miles's sponsor, and Colonel Hsiao met secretly in mufti at the Washington Hotel. Hsiao made a sales pitch. He got King's tentative approval. Soon he had CKS's clearance for Miles to go to China and work with Tai Li, whose Washington representative all this time had been none other than Colonel Hsiao.

"And who," Miles asked, "is General Tai Li?"

Miles's memoirs go on like this, recounting how he was inducted step by step into a seemingly close and certainly sentimental relationship with China's J. Edgar Himmler. He found the American intelligence reports all gave Tai Li a very bad reputation indeed, though Colonel Hsiao on the contrary said he was a very fine man. Considering what Miles's project accomplished, one must give Hsiao high marks as a fisher of men. Problem: to find as a conduit of American aid one highly connected and resourceful natural leader, a real "friend of China," full of the latest technology and quite oblivious of broader policy concerns. Miles had just the right mixture of fine personal qualities and insensitivity to abstract political considerations.

His impresario Colonel Hsiao I recall as a rather beefy gladhander, whose geniality would, I felt sure, be the same if he was offering you more wine or impaling you on a meat hook. He explained to the OSS China specialists in Washington that Chinese patriotic humiliation over the unequal treaty system of the past was so great that it would be insupportably embarrassing to have any American now come to the new Free China who had been to China before. Such a person would be a reminder of China's shame. His mentality would have been poisoned by his earlier experience. How could Nationalist Chinese of today and such Americans from the past possibly work together? In the name of this nonsensical doctrine, Colonel Hsiao saw to it that Miles's merry men in Naval Group China were nearly all innocent newcomers, ignorant of Chinese speech and writing.

In April 1942 Miles took off over the trans-Africa air route in company, as it chanced, with Edgar Snow. By June he had been accepted by Tai Li and was with him behind Japanese lines near the Fukien coast. When an informer was discovered, says Miles, "an immediate trial was ordered." " 'The general,' explained his interpreter, 'is in charge of executions, but not of trials.' " The general, Miles concluded, "never had anyone shot without proper authorization. So there went another colorful bit of Washington intelligence."

After visiting India in July-August 1942 to get supplies moving (and being knifed but not quite assassinated by a Japanese agent), Miles began developing a sabotage training center, "Happy Valley," about eight miles outside Chungking. The Americans lived Chinese style and worked closely with Tai Li's men on terms of real equality.

Suddenly as of September 22 Mary Miles found himself appointed "coordinator of the OSS in the Far East." General Donovan had rushed to capitalize on Miles's success in getting in with the notoriously suspicious, secretive, and anti-foreign General Tai. The ripples of this opportunist plunge reached me when Mary Miles marched into my new Chungking office early in October 1942, as above noted, and announced with a grin, "I'm your new landlord." He handed me a letter from Donovan to the effect that I was under Miles's authority as chief representative of OSS in China. I didn't know of Miles's Tai Li connection, but I explained my setup and made plain that secret operations were not my line. If Miles or his people came around too much or tried to use my premises, I might as well resign. We agreed to leave each other alone. With hindsight I can see my activities could have contaminated Miles almost as much as his could me. He asked me not to seek Japanese materials from General Wang P'eng-sheng, the chief possessor of such things in Chungking, because his military intelligence agency was Tai Li's rival.

By May 1943, however, my microfilm lab manager from New Jersey, Gus Paton, and I were exchanging dinners with General P. S. Wang and filming dozens of his Japanese publications. Materials received from Miles were comparatively old and trivial. Meantime the American Publications Service had distributed two thousand different items of stateside microfilm with a catalogue and seventy projectors to a score of reading centers and had collected several thousand publications for the Library of Congress. This activity for LC and State's RC program, I reported, gave us "access on friendly terms in many directions, the office staff are proud of their work, and we are out from under the shadow of secret service."

Meantime, at Chiang Kai-shek's request Miles and Tai Li had codified their international relations in an agreement that Miles drafted by December 31, 1942, to create the Sino-American Cooperative Organization or SACO (to be pronounced Sock-O! in the best comic-strip fashion). Tai Li as commander and Miles as deputy commander each had a veto over operations. Their respective contributions were spelled out. Approval was required from the top on both sides. Miles took it back to Washington. In February 1942 the Joint Chiefs of Staff planning committee recommended approval. By April 15, 1943, President Roosevelt had signed the SACO agreement. The Navy–Tai Li operation thus ensured its independence from OSS and even the Army theater commander, General Stilwell. SACO got half a dozen planes to bring in its own supplies, regardless of Stilwell's statutory monopoly control of lend-lease for China. Tai Li on his part distrusted the OSS as politically unreliable and possibly anti-KMT. He "vigorously opposed the expansion of OSS activities in China."* Donovan's grabbing onto the Navy's coattails to get further into China didn't work out. At the end of 1943 OSS abandoned the relationship and Miles ceased to be its man in China. During four days in early December in his talks with Tai Li and CKS, Donovan, as he told me himself, said he "would either work with them or would if necessary go through them; if they did in his crowd, he would do in theirs, and he hoped there would be no trouble." (My note of December 17, '43.) This tough talk was of course far from the spirit of SACO. It was also partly bluff. As it turned out, OSS did not get very far alone in China.

Service rivalries were of course primal motivations in the war effort. China was such a massive Army show that Admiral King, with the Navy conquering the Pacific, was determined to support the SACO program of weather stations, coast watching, and commando

---

*Michael Schaller, *The U.S. Crusade in China, 1938–1945* (1979), p. 235.

training. But in the summer of 1943 SACO began a program of "what General Tai called 'F.B.I. school instruction.' " This was to train and arm Tai Li's secret police for work among the Chinese people. The embassy, the State Department, Stilwell, OSS, and others all objected to this use of American aid. The feeling was widespread that the Chinese war effort against Japan had been superseded by preparation for civil war against the CCP. SACO did indeed harass the Japanese and prepare for Navy landings. The pernicious aspect of SACO was that as the Nationalist-Communist civil war developed in 1945 it put American aid to use actively on the KMT side. This amounted to a "premature" initiation of US-anti-CCP activity that the CCP bitterly resented and properly enshrined among the iniquities of American imperialism.

My knowledge of all this secret story, so briefly sketched above, was accumulated only in later years, especially from the publication of Miles's posthumous memoir *A Different Kind of War* (1967) and Michael Schaller's eye-opening research study of the official documentation, *The U.S. Crusade in China, 1938–1945* (1979). The story of SACO is a high point in American-Chinese collaboration and also a scandal in the history of American China policy. After a third of a century it is still unresearched in full detail. Miles's eager success in helping Tai Li's guerrilla army also involved the United States as a partisan in China's domestic politics. To this policy consideration was added a full measure of interservice rivalry—Army and others *vs.* Navy.

Luckily for my operation, I had instinctively had minimal contact with Mary Miles, even though I was only vaguely aware of what he was up to. John Davies, I find, had opposed SACO on Stilwell's behalf in Washington in 1943, but it was a really secret operational matter and did not reach my ears. Like most Americans in uniform, Miles was fighting to defeat Japan by all means. My small office in Chungking was on a different track. Like many civilian China hands, I was concerned about China's future and the American role in it.

The ungovernability of modern societies and the insolubility of social problems had not yet been brought home to us. Fresh out of the New Deal, many Americans (like Lauchlin Currie) envisioned our helping the postwar industrialization of China. Postwar planning became very popular among Chungking's frustrated bureaucrats and a chief subject for RC microfilm to deal with.

I found an avid interest on the part of C. C. Ch'ien (Ch'ien Ch'ang-chao), a leading figure in the National Resources Commission. This agency had built up a hundred industrial plants in Free China. Ch'ien was Mrs. L. K. T'ao's brother-in-law, an engineer, and "of all the people I have seen here the most like a *genrō* in the making—a compact, square-built, ageless, alert man, working constantly and with precision. Every day he reads from one to two after lunch and from ten to eleven in the evening. He spends the week in his office," seeing his family on weekends. (Meeting Dr. Ch'ien again in Peking in 1979, I found him very lively at eighty. He had left China in 1947 to study in England, returning after the CCP takeover to continue to work at China's industrialization.)

C. C. Ch'ien's supervisor as head of the National Resources Commission was the long-time minister of economic affairs, Wong (or Weng) Wen-hao, formerly head of the geological survey. On October 18, 1942, he gave me a ride into the city.

> He is about four feet tall, thin like a grasshopper, has a large depression in his forehead from an accident on the Shanghai-Hangchow road, and has a very very lively quizzical cast of countenance, gnomelike and quick. He wants to see microfilm especially on postwar. He may be the rebuilder of China sometime.

Wong Wen-hao had been teaching geology at Tsing Hua when the national crisis made him, like T. F. Tsiang, one of the Peking scholars who in 1935 joined the Nationalist government at Nanking. He was from Ningpo, a Chekiang man like CKS, and in the scholar-official tradition. In 1943 Dr. Wong did indeed pull together an outline for postwar industrialization that would use state and private capital and foreign investment, which the KMT accepted in August. (Like C. C. Ch'ien he did not stick with the KMT but resigned his premiership (head of the Executive Yuan) in 1948 and went abroad. In 1951 at age sixty-two Wong Wen-hao returned to the mainland and geology, heading several PRC expeditions to prospect for uranium and other minerals.)

These leaders' interest in China's industrialization was something my office could help to meet. But I suppose Tai Li's preparations for killing his domestic enemies was a more portentous stream of history at the time. American technology to kill people could be brought into

China more quickly than information to improve their lives. Soon the supertechnology of the atomic bombs of 1945 would put word-purveyors like myself even further behind. I still wonder if we can ever catch up.

19

ACADEMIC CENTERS
AND THE AMERICAN INTEREST

MY PRIVATE WAR aim had now emerged—to help preserve the
American-educated Chinese professors, some of whom were old
friends from Peking. This was my personal response to the situation
around me, in which the war effort in China against Japan was practically monopolized by the Chinese and American military. Rather
few professors were mobilized. Even students were considered a
rare national resource that must be preserved for the future, not
squandered in battle. Some American civilians in wartime China
consequently felt disillusioned and relieved their boredom by collecting women, boys, or Ming blue-and-white. Personally I was not
against the anti-Japan war. It simply seemed less urgent in Nationalist China than the survival of liberal education.

Having dreamed up and put together the three roles advertised
on my calling card—special assistant to the ambassador, representative of the Library of Congress, and director of the American Publications Service—I was a free agent able to travel around Free China.
I had seen the three major universities in their penury at Kunming.
A fourth, National Central, I saw outside Chungking, together with
the Nankai School of Economics. This gave me a basis for visiting the
main institutes of Nationalist China's national academy, Academia
Sinica, now quartered out in the boondocks up the Yangtze. My
ulterior aim of course was to see our friends the Liangs, but I felt this

combination of public duty and private desire was not outside the Anglo-Saxon tradition.

Not far from T. F. Tsiang's house was an Academia Sinica dormitory, and there on September 26, 1942, I found our friend from Peking days, Liang Ssu-ch'eng. "He held my hand for five minutes with excitement." He had come to the capital to raise money from the Ministry of Education and the British Boxer Fund.

Since we had parted at Christmas 1935, he and his family had gone south in the academic migration from Peking to Changsha on the railway in Hunan. There the Japanese bombed them out and they trekked by bus and on foot for two months to reach Kunming in the Southwest. When the Japanese bombed the city, the Liangs moved out into a village and built the house I had seen there. Dr. Fu Ssu-nien as head of the Institute of History and Philology had decided to escape possible invasion or at least the bombing and high prices in Kunming by moving north into the cloud cover of the Szechwan countryside. The institute's valuable sinological library and its Shang dynasty archaeological artifacts from the Anyang excavation, all had to be trucked north to the town of Li-chuang ("Li Village") on the south bank of the Yangtze some twenty miles east of the head of navigation at I-pin (Sui-fu). There, in the cold mist of winter and the steamy summer, books and artifacts were safe, but the staff risked their health. Liang Ssu-yung, the excavator of Anyang, was dying of tuberculosis. Liang Ssu-ch'eng's Institute for Research in Chinese Architecture had had to come along with the rest, and Phyllis Liang was in bed with tuberculosis too.

Ssu-ch'eng discovered that I had foolishly abandoned the Chinese name he had given me in Peking, Fei Cheng-ch'ing, because Mac Fisher of OWI was also surnamed Fei. I had shifted to the Chinese name used for the movie star Douglas Fairbanks, Fan Pang-k'o. "That sounds like a phrase meaning 'the barbarian kidnapper,' " Ssu-ch'eng told me, "whereas Fei Cheng-ch'ing means 'Fei the upright and clear' and Cheng-ch'ing approximates the sound of John King. With such a name you might be a Chinese." He was quite correct, of course. I recalled how often foreigners had unknowingly accepted pejorative Chinese names, ever since Lord Napier, the British envoy at Canton in 1834, had found his name "Lao Pi" meant "laboriously vile." Chiang Kai-shek had taken the name Chung-cheng, "central and upright," a figure people could rally around. My "upright and clear" well suited a historian.

In the second half of November 1942 I arranged to visit Li-chuang and took ship up the Yangtze by river steamer, with Dr. L. K. T'ao (T'ao Meng-ho). Since our first meeting in Peking in 1932, his Institute of Social Research had been taken into the Academia Sinica array of institutes. He had brought his ill wife to Chungking and put her on a plane for the dry sunny climate of Lanchow in the Northwest, hoping to allay her T.B. To travel with him was a rare opportunity. We were both fascinated by the human condition we met with, first of all on the steamer itself.

The vessel is a sort of tenement-boat, shaped like a three-deck pullman the color of an army truck with a great tree growing from the top, being branches camouflaging the smokestack. Washing flutters over the sides and the deck is perpetually crowded with people at the rail. These are the outer layer of people who are *traveling* at the rail. We have a no. 1 cabin six by eight feet with two berths and a desk, and the deck leading here is just enough for one stout person to traverse. But this provides space for two thin people to lie on the floor, leaving interstices in the pattern of limbs for the traverser to place his feet in, and occasionally where it is considered that the two people are unusually thin, or merely resilient, a third person wedges himself down sideways. This pattern of continuous quilt-and-limb topography is carried over all the decks in from the rail, fills all the passages and the dining room and afterdeck. There is nothing quite like sitting in a toilet and staring through the wooden door slats into the cherubic face of a Chinese lady who is asleep on the deck immediately outside the door. [The boat deck toilets, I may add, operated by gravity, being cantilevered out over the stern of the ship, which however seldom went into reverse.]

We boarded ship late on the 10th and sailed at 8 A.M. after the dawn had penetrated the mist which hangs over the confluence of the Chialing and the Yangtze. We tie up at night and if we get to the next big town a little after noon, we probably tie up for the rest of the day. The crowd is like the subway, but not the hurry. Our cabin is a good place to talk and sleep, which is all we have done.

My traveling arrangements consist of a new oilcloth which has a much-prized stale-vomit smell which terrifies bugs but supposedly not humans, unless they dream they are bugs. We also keep the light on all night to cow the bugs. There is a particularly efficient-looking kind of roach which has wide hindquarters and tapers over the withers to a mallet-shaped proboscis. It approaches my oilcloth but flees in dismay. On top of the oilcloth I have a machine-sewed blue cloth bag seven by five feet into which I get. The theory is that no bug can get in except past me, although of course it is true that bugs once in might never get out. With this system one adds extra covers from the bottom inside by mysterious contortions. Graham Peck heard of a missionary lady who undressed, or was thought to undress, inside a sleeping bag. Over my head I can spread Mother's thin scarf, which has been most useful, and this makes me unrecognizable to man if not to beast.

For food we have three square meals a day Chinese style and no banquet-like monkey business. Two bowls of rice morning, noon, and night will make my lion-stomach into a cow-stomach. One merely shovels it in at the top and waits for gravity and osmosis. We also have good round, hard Szechwan oranges. Sleeping on my overcoat and raincoat on a board produces a somewhat compressed feeling but already seems very natural.

Meanwhile the Yangtze goes by. Unlike the Mississippi, this river has high banks all the way, through Szechwan at least, and seems seldom to change its width. The hillsides above the banks have a charming silhouette of trees standing alone and houses clustered against the horizon. At some places we have passed extensive factories in the river bank, as they are at Chungking, with small buildings on top emitting the smoke. The most interesting item is the boat life, big junks with sixteen people rowing hard *down* stream in perfect time, a woman holding the tiller with a baby on her other arm and giving orders like a virago; gangs of upstream trackers who chant even when some eddy pulls them all backward. We invariably tie up at a dock where one or two other boats have got ahead of us, so that going ashore is like playing hide and seek in a garret full of old furniture, over bodies, up companionways, and across narrow planks above the water. One then climbs a big flight of steps to the town.

Our first stop was at Chiang Ching, "River Ferry," no more fragrant a name than Pottsville. Our second was at Ho Chiang, "River Junction," where the Ch'i enters from the south. Both these towns were quite amazing, each with a big paved main street running the length of the place parallel to the river, the pavement crowded with people and devoid of vehicles, and this main street lined with a multitude of shops each with its electric light wanly gleaming and a great variety of goods on display.

The mixture of old and new is most fascinating—last night we passed a Taoist funeral ceremony in progress, one priest in a fedora, then an obelisk erected by the San Min Chu I Youth Corps just recently with slogans painted on it, followed by a fortune teller with an acetylene lamp to dazzle his audience, wearing Harold Lloyd spectacles, with a sign "The truth will be told and nothing suppressed, if you get angry, you will not be accepting fate."

On a rather deserted side street we suddenly came upon a man lying crumpled on the thoroughfare and breathing with difficulty, whether ill, drunk, or victimized. "Don't touch him!" Meng-ho said to me sharply. His reason was that this body might be a trap; touching him could incur responsibility; people could emerge from nowhere and accuse us unless we paid them off.

Four days brought us to I-pin (formerly Sui-fu), the head of Yangtze steamer navigation, and we took a smaller boat downstream to Li-chuang. This

town of about 10,000 has the usual long paved main street with shops full of goods and a crowd of people. It is on a stretch of plain about half a mile wide, high enough to avoid flooding. The Yangtze here has its typical setting, a long valley with hills rising some two to four hundred feet on either side and a narrow plain running along the river's edge, all cultivated. The river has a very definite rocky bed and never wanders anywhere in Szechwan. The most amazing thing about it is that you look across at the peaceful terraces on the other side, and then you notice that the water between, more than a quarter of a mile wide, is all sliding out of the picture.

The Liang household is in the same courtyard as the Architectural Institute, which in turn occupies part of the compound used by the National Museum. From the edge of the town, one walks on the narrow stone paths that circle the rice fields. The Liang house is under big trees at the foot of the hill which is crowned by a watch tower and covered with oranges and tangerines. From being in Szechwan it gets more water than sunshine and is damp and dirty with the accumulation of years of wetness. This gives rise to the damp urinous smell which hangs over Szechwan like a cloud. Often there is a cloud layer all day and a rather lazy rain all night.

A dozen young draftsmen come to work in the institute in a big room on one side of the inner courtyard and Phyllis lives in a big room on the same courtyard, so that she hears everything going on. But there is usually more going on where she is, so that the young men hear more than they contribute.

Chinese scholars out of office traditionally lived close to rural nature. But these modern-trained academic leaders had their noses rubbed in it. The final trek to Szechwan had further degraded their living standard. They were now at the peasant level—water carried in in buckets, rice as staple fare, charcoal heat if any, no plumbing. Japan's bombing had rusticated them as effectively as Mao's peasant rebellion was to do later.

Life in the Liang household is full of complications as it always was, except that the drop in standard of living has made the complications more elementary and less complicated. First, servants. They are expensive and so are largely dispensed with, except that the maid while very dumb has a nice disposition and so was not changed for another more efficient because no one wanted to make her feel bad. So Ssu-ch'eng does most of the cooking himself with advice from the Patient. Second, personalities. Lao Tai-tai [Phyllis's mother] has her way of doing things and can't see why she left Peking anyway, S.C. likes things peppery and Phyllis likes them vinegary, etc. Third, friends. On my arrival I found an air officer from Sui-fu had come for a visit, a friend of Phyllis's brother [an aviator shot down by the Japs]. Before I left, Ssu-chuang [Ssu-ch'eng's sister] arrived from Yenching via Shanghai, Hankow, Hunan, and Kweilin, the usual route through the lines on a Jap pass, not having seen the family for five years.

Phyllis is very thin but for the moment quite full of life and runs everything as usual by thinking about it before anyone else does. Meals occur by degrees and after them we discuss things at length, she doing most of the talking. At night, after 5:30 one lives in candlelight, or the similar light of a wick in veg. oil, so that 8:30 gets to be bedtime. There is no telephone. There is a gramophone with some Beethoven and Mozart. There are thermos bottles but no coffee, plenty of woolen sweaters but few that fit, sheets but not much soap for washing them, pens and pencils but not much paper to write on, newspapers but always several days old. As though one shot holes through one's daily life and took out some things and not others; the result is a hit-and-miss sort of life.

Staying for a week, much of the time in bed with a severe cold, I was impressed by our friends' tenacity in continuing to function as scholars. Americans, I imagined, would have forsaken their books and turned to reconstructing their living conditions. But this highly trained Chinese community accepted the primitivism of peasant life and went on with their work. The scholar's role was deeply ingrained in the social structure and everyone's expectations. If our friends had broken out of it by becoming amateur carpenters, bricklayers, or plumbers in their own interest, they would have been subverting the social order and soon become déclassé and targets of local suspicion, if not abuse.

After visiting Fu Ssu-nien's library in a remote temple, I made the trip back 150 miles to Chungking. But first I had an afternoon in I-pin waiting for the Chungking steamer, so

I hunted up the local missionaries. The head of the local Baptist establishment is Dr. J. C. Jensen, who (naturally) comes from Spink County near Watertown, South Dakota. He came to Szechwan in 1911 and now has several schools, a hospital, and thirty outstations which he visits on foot twice a year, walking twenty or thirty miles a day for weeks at a time. He is a vigorous man of definite ways, sprung from the farm and naturally interested in helping local agriculture as well as evangelizing. He says the local populace are definitely well off, there are fewer poor and they are better dressed than he can remember. There has been a marked fall in the use of opium, cut down 90 percent in the last few years since the central government moved in.

It was plain that China's modern-trained and displaced intelligentsia were special victims of the wartime inflation, along with the lower levels of officialdom at the capital. These segments of the ruling class were being squeezed more than the common people. On January 19, 1943, L. K. T'ao's wife

> died in Lanchow from a sudden attack of pneumonia. She is the first one of our friends to go. Our plan to get Phyllis up to Lanchow will now seem useless. The nurse that we are sending up is a stout girl [this project petered out], but there is not much help possible when the shadows begin to close in like this.

Many others also became concerned about the welfare of Chinese faculties. United China Relief addressed the problem, and its administrator set up faculty committees in twenty-two institutions to handle UCR grants for medical aid, education of children, and destitution from war. He included both government and private institutions. Unfortunately he announced the UCR funds would pay for "living expenses." Someone objected to having American charity support Chinese government professors. It appeared in the newspaper. CKS blew his top and vetoed the idea. One day in Chungking,

> Chiang Monlin came in before lunch and I talked to him about the UCR fiasco. He is very much like Y. C. Mei in form—tall and thin and graceful, but a man of ideas rather than of feeling. The two of them, as leaders of the Kunming faculties, are impressive ascetic-looking figures. Chiang has not done much about Peita lately. He is down to bedrock, having pawned or sold his last bit of clothing and books, and his wife is now going to get a job here while he goes back to Kunming to be Chancellor of the greatest Chinese center of learning. He is better off than Mei, whose wife took a job under another name, was discovered, and had to stop.

Dr. Chiang got a hot protest from the Lienta faculty when he reported to them; they saw no disgrace in taking American aid, in view of lend-lease and their own poverty, and he had a hard time to restrain them from writing in retaliation. The real issue, says Chiang Monlin, is whether the cadre of teachers in Chinese higher education can be preserved for the future, or whether China will lose the trainers of men during the war and fall that much further into chaos. He thinks the hurt already is very serious.

The Lienta faculty kept going, from hand to mouth and by all sorts of private efforts that in total were far beyond any one person's knowledge. I can report only on one corner of the battlefield. By August 1943, we were helping the Lienta faculty by privately shipping in drugs. Through Currie I got a big shipment of Vitamin B-1 from the Hoffmann-LaRoche Co. that allowed Lienta medics to counter a widespread vitamin deficiency (bleeding gums, etc.) among the student body. Wilma kept a flow of drugs and valuable hardware (pens, watches) coming to the Kunming consulate for clandestine distribution as salary supplements through Professor Deison Ch'en next door. By late 1943 RC had got six professors to the United States; Harvard-Yenching at my urging had given $1,000 to each of six researchers and $500 to eight others, total $10,000; ACLS was moving along similar lines.

At my prompting also Currie persuaded the Army Special Services to set up a fund of $5,000 to pay Chinese professors to lecture to American troops at Kunming. In setting up this last arrangement I had a spectacular blowup with General Frank Dorn, Stilwell's closest aide among the China-trained officers—a handsome soldier of artistic talent with a short temper, called Pinky, I suppose because of his high coloring. When I started reporting my lecture arrangements with his subordinates, he blew his top at civilian interference with his command. Who in hell did I think I was, coming from the embassy to push the military around? This was so off base I raised my voice in reply, producing authorization (as I should have done first) from Stilwell's chief of staff. Pinky calmed down and the incident made us good friends from then on.

In the Kunming lecture series to GIs I teamed up once with Chang Hsi-jo and again with Ch'ien Tuan-sheng and also arranged a lecture by Major General Robert Lim, Inspector General, Medical Services, on "the Chinese soldier's fighting efficiency." (Out of 6,000 doctors in China in 1937, he had got 1,200 into the army; 30 hospitals grew to 750 but equipment was a bottleneck. In six years they cleared 3.5 million casualties. Troops supplemented their rice and salt ration by growing their own vegetables. It sounded like Sisyphus gradually winning his struggle.)

The Christian colleges gathered at Chengtu, the old provincial capital of Szechwan, where I went January 26, 1943, were a striking contrast to the purely Chinese establishments I had seen at Kunming and Li-chuang. Nanking University, Ginling College for Women, Cheeloo University from Tsinan (Shantung), and Yenching University from Peking, all missionary institutions, had moved onto or near the spacious campus of their sister institution, West China Union University—

> big gray buildings with Chinese roofs, rows of trees, playing fields, and missionary houses set inside walled gardens, a Baptist row and a Canadian row.

I found the missionary teachers we had first met in Nanking in the 1930s: Frank Price, Andy Roy, Bill Fenn, also the young archaeologist Cheng Te-k'un we had met at Amoy in 1934, now organizing the museum with an art student from England named Michael Sullivan. It was a friendly community only bedeviled by the missionary vice of continual committee meetings. The students were mainly well off, intent on being better off. Most studied economics, money and banking, the better to make their way in the continuing inflation. "The KMT Youth Corps is thoroughly organized on the campus with Frank Price to advise them."

Away from the orthodoxy of the Nationalist capital, however, I found a different view of politics. After six weeks in Chungking I had opined to Lauchlin Currie in October 1942 that "the chances of civil war after the war are not great. . . . There may be a crushing of the Communists by the KMT" but little chance of a real "internecine peasant struggle as in Spain." In January in Chengtu, however, I found the most "pressing sentiment in local minds is the dread of civil war in China—the missionary leftists are sure of it and the foreign military assume it." So also did local gentry leaders, big landholders in their sixties who had studied in Japan about 1905, opposed the Szechwan warlords, and welcomed CKS into the province in 1935.

> They will follow Chiang as the leader, but they can't abide the KMT party and its politicians, they exterminate Communists and they want Szechwan for the Szechwanese (landlords). Just another group at odds with all other groups.

Yet all these prophets foresaw the KMT crushing the CCP in six months when the time came.

Anti-British sentiment was also strong. Ginling's gracious president Dr. Wu I-fang (who after 1949 would serve as the CCP's educational commissioner for Kiangsu province) stated a general disillusionment:

> The Chinese trusted their wives and fortunes to the Hong Kong and Singapore fortresses and when they folded with British troops still unkilled there was intense frustration. Britain failed to perform according to British claims and when the claims are still maintained, anger results on the part of the bystanding Chinese.

The governor of Szechwan, Chang Ch'un of the Political Science clique, with whom I had a session, saw the British and Americans as

> fundamentally different—having a monarchy and a democracy, respectively. He reiterated the slogan that China and America must work together, meaning America must be Santa Claus forever.

The great variety of insights that I obtained on these travels led me to tilt again at the Hornbeck windmill in Washington. I sent Currie a memo on cultural-relations policy to present to Hiss for Hornbeck and Hamilton. It was an interventionist piece, arguing:

> Programs must be based on policies. The Cultural Relations program for China suffers because the policy behind it is inadequate to the occasion. China is a battleground where we should seek to make our values prevail, insofar as they are suitable to Chinese life. But the Cultural Relations program so far has dealt with means instead of ends.
>
> Specifically, it stands at one end of a spectrum of informa-

tion services which seek to tell China How the Americans Do Things. Thus the army communiqués say This is How We Fight, the Information Service proper explains This is How We Live, This is What Happens in the United States, and finally the RC microfilm and the RC technical experts explain This is Our Science and Technology. The whole program is informational, on the theory that our way of life can sell itself, if it is good China will take it, if it is no good there is no use in our saying it is good.

This view is too superficial, of a piece with nineteenth century free trade ideas, now out of date. We cannot leave the American way of life to sell itself; the result will be the propagation of Main Street all over the world, picture magazines, contract bridge, American slang, and collegiate manners. We are not ashamed of these things or of Main Street. The point is that we have much more than this to offer. Main Street which sells itself is not enough, and to a sophisticated intellectual class in China it is often repugnant and disgusting. We must seek contact at a level above that of Life Magazine. This higher level deals with values, Why We Do Things, not How. It is conveyed through the arts, literature, drama, through "cultural" media. It appeals to the creative people who are seeking new ideas and new art forms, not to the bankers.

The recent RC grant to the Sino-American Cultural Institute illustrates this point. This Institute is the creation of Dr. Kung and exemplifies the collegiate-compradore way of life in modern China. It is managed and frequented by Chinese who are chiefly from the business class and who picked up in the United States the rah-rah aspects of college life. The Institute is for members only. It is a going concern, but it does not appeal to the Chinese student class, to the creative people who seek more ideas than Time Magazine has to offer.

In contrast, the Sino-Russian Cultural Institute has art exhibits which attract hundreds of people. It has a public teahouse and makes a conscious effort to present the best that Russia has to offer in the arts and in ideas and literature.

The Chinese can accept our technology as the Japanese did. Their absorption of modern science may not bring us together. It may merely give China the means of opposing us.

Certainly it is not our object to make China be like the United States, which is impossible, but it is our object to build a common ground between us. Japan developed Bushido and battleships simultaneously. China is receiving our help to create a heavy industry and her Minister of Education believes in *Pen-wei wen-hua*, China's Own Culture, a doctrine reminiscent of Chang Chih-tung's "Western studies for use and Chinese studies for the fundamentals." We cannot object to the growth of nationalism in China, which is a local necessity, but it is in the American interest to foster an internationalism here also.

In short, we Americans have been slow to formulate the values of our own culture, which we now call the democratic way of life. But we are being forced to appreciate it and believe in it, and we are trying to find in it principles of universal application. If we have anything to offer out here, we had better offer it.

For example, a young Chinese leader in dramatic work, who was trained at Yale and is producing plays in Chungking now, says that he knows all about the Russian stage and contemporary Russian life, but he has heard nothing of the American stage for two years. What can RC do about this? (December 4, 1942)

Stanley Hornbeck's comment of January 5, 1943, illustrated very neatly the myopia in Washington.

C

  O

    P

      Y   DEPARTMENT OF STATE
           ADVISER ON POLITICAL RELATIONS

January 5, 1943

PA/H   AH

I am inclined to agree with Dr. Fairbank except as regards the opening paragraph, second sentence—which happens to be, for the moment the most important sentence.

The *current* Cultural Relations program for China seems to me utterly appropriate, as far as it goes, "to the occasion"—the occasion being the present situation. The United States happens to be at war; China also happens to be at war; both countries are fighting on the same side; the most important thing for each and for both at this moment is to win the war (without undue prejudice of other values); and to win it, we need to do to the maximum those things which will contribute toward the winning of it. It is important at this time for us to send to China materials, instruments, agents, etc. that can and will contribute toward the winning of the war. It is *not* important at this time, comparatively speaking, for us to send to China people who will tell the Chinese about "the American stage" (*vide* the concluding paragraph of Dr. Fairbank's memorandum under reference). I have urged, I do urge, and I shall continue to urge that we send to China men who not only can tell the Chinese something of the theories of engineering, of industry, of agriculture, etc., but who, even more, can and will get right down into the shop, the mine, the field, and apply remedies where remedies are necessary, and show the Chinese how the *most practical and resourceful* of Americans do things—and who can and will learn from the Chinese something about how the extraordinarily practical and resourceful Chinese do some similar and some other things with less of materials and with less of expense than Americans do them.

I note Mr. Hiss' statement that Mr. Currie has stated that Dr. Fairbank asked that the memorandum be shown only to Mr. Hamilton and to me. Notwithstanding that, I hope that, with Mr. Currie's permission, Mr. Fairbank's memorandum and my memorandum of comment will both be shown to Mr. Peck.

S. K. H.

Max Hamilton agreed, adding that "values" were being put forward by OWI and the statements of American government leaders. Willys Peck, chief of RC, also agreed with PA/H.

In my view, PA/H's first yes-but-no sentence was classic bureaucratese. His bland assumption that the two countries were equally engaged in a war effort disregarded reality. He remained oblivious of the domestic struggle in China that I wrote about. His reiterated "urging" sounded forceful indeed but was quite unnecessary—men were already being sent. His balancing of Americans and Chinese as "practical and resourceful" was sentimental. The last paragraph was overpunctilious.

These comments from FE, though I saw them only later, illustrated my belief that Washington was unaware of Chinese reality. I kept brooding over this and wrote to Alger Hiss again.

> I have been for the past five months in a state of mild shock. It arises from the fact that the American representational activity in China appears to be inadequate, and yet in Washington it appears to be considered adequate.
>
> This country is struggling to modernize itself, but it is not impossible that it will retain from its own past more vices than virtues, and fail in our lifetime to become a stable and contributing element in world affairs. We can expect our Chinese problem to grow greater with the years. In self-defence this China must industrialize and do it rapidly. This can only be done effectively with American help in capital and technique.
>
> We will continue to be mixed up in the fate of China for some time to come. China will continue to be one of the weak spots in world organization. Many many brave and intelligent Chinese people are making changes in the old ways and resolutely making changes in themselves, but they are drops in the ocean. The American interest requires that we help them, but it will be a long-continuing process.
>
> In this situation the very minimum is that we should have *knowledge*. We need to know who is who.
>
> The Embassy is too busy to maintain a who's who file. The who's who file in the Department is very sadly in arrears.
>
> In the present system, knowledge of China is largely obtained by conversation in English with Chinese officials. This is excellent for immediate situations. When it comes to long-range studies, this is like hopping on one leg. The Chinese government publishes an official statistical abstract, in English and Chinese. It is published monthly and the current number is number 72. I may be wrong, but I believe its existence has not been known to the Embassy. In any case, the Embassy staff is already fully occupied. The thing to be criticized is the system which does not provide for serious study of Chinese publications.

The one thing that really seems incredible is that officers in highly responsible if not decisive positions concerning this area have not come here during the war period. Someone or other has believed it unnecessary that such officials should have first-hand contact with the area which they are expected to understand. The thing that shocks me is to find that my respected and intelligent friends believe that they can maintain an understanding of modern China through the existing means of communication in words. I could not do it over a period of years. This is my fifth year in this country, and my understanding is genuinely superficial; given every advantage of official information while here and after my departure, I could not keep myself really in touch for very long through communication in words. The new type of drama which is now being produced, the spate of subsidized magazines talking nonsense about culture, the proportion of people wearing western dress in small towns, every sort of incommunicable impression must go to form a balanced judgment as to which way the tide is running.

Our long term interest here must be to encourage the development of Chinese personnel who can provide leadership in our direction. No one has thought it desirable to keep track of the returned students, but it is plain that they as a class are leaders and constitute our chief human investment in China. They form the bridge between us and China. Without them we would be in an unhappy situation more like our situation vis-à-vis Russia.

Here are things to do. (1) Put the Cultural Relations program on a higher plane than the merely technical. (2) Send out a person directly from RC to execute the RC program. (3) Study Chinese education (the field of "culture") scientifically. The RC man should visit the universities and know their staffs. The British Embassy's Cultural Attaché, J. Blofeld, did this last year; an American could do it much better. The objective is a practical, interventionist one, to find people who are on our side and find ways of helping them. Don't let anyone tell you they will muddle along all right. Some are already ill and some have left academic life to feed their families. (4) Put American exchange professors into the four or five leading university campuses—Kunming, Chungking, Chengtu, Kweilin. If this is a total war and if the Army operates here, why not act on the intellectual front also?

The shrinkage of the world requires us to build up more of a governmental mechanism for relations with China. The Department should create a special grade of Research Officer, to be filled by men recruited from academic life. The day is past when a Foreign Service officer can do everything, like a Chinese mandarin.

We must support American interests rather than merely defend them. Liberal education in China is an American interest.

[*Chengtu, February 1943*]

This general view, though not always stated precisely in my terms, was I think in the cards. The war effort was moving us toward a greater intellectual if not ideological assertiveness to accompany our great logistic effort. Wilma spread copies of my memos around among key people in Washington. Gradually I think they began to have some influence.

Working my civilian side of the street, I rounded out my reconnaissance in Chungking by attending a meeting of the People's Political Council (PPC), a body set up by the Nationalist government in 1941 to offer a promise of representative government. Its powers were only advisory but its membership did indeed represent the nonparty intellectuals. My friend Ch'ien Tuan-sheng from Kunming, chairman of the foreign affairs committee, got me a pass to attend a session.

The room was a not very big hall, two stories high with fans above, white, and plain. Chang Po-ling and others sat on a high bench behind, councilors on one side of the place packed in chairs, and guests, many military, on the other side. Many vigorous-looking people, women mixed in with the men, seats being by lot.

From everything I have seen, I doubt if the PPC is a flash in the pan. The members seem to have a feeling of their own significance, and many regard future development as assured.

This liberal hope, to see representative government transplanted into the Chinese political system, proved unfortunately stillborn. Assemblies of worthy people from the governing elite became an occasionally useful act of public relations, but little more. Legitimacy continued to derive from the security system, the very practical capacity to intimidate dissidents and destroy opponents. Tai Li outweighed the PPC; and liberal values, like the liberal professors themselves, were losing ground.

20

1943—CKS BEGINS TO LOSE
THE MANDATE

AFTER ANOTHER YEAR in wartime Chungking I came to a very definite conviction that our ally the Nationalist regime was self-destructing and on the way out of power. The KMT decline was gradual and so was my coming to my conclusion about it.

First of all, I had more chance to contemplate my impressions of people and places because I stayed in bed more. Illness is part of most overseas assignments, and in the late winter and spring of 1943 I had in succession a heavy cold, which merged into hepatitis and wound up with amoebic dysentery. The cold developed after Bill Fenn and I rode back from Chengtu to Chungking in freezing weather on top of the mail truck. Passengers atop the mail bags were an established custom, though what postage was paid on us I have forgotten.

When no Army planes had turned up, Bill Fenn took me to call on the Postal Commissioner and we got passage. The public buses are described in terms suitable for a 6 P.M. Bronx Express on a roller coaster in a high sea. Some compare bus travel to making the Middle Passage in the Black Hole of Calcutta. Western man, having conquered Nature, is face to face with the Machine; but Chinese man is beset both by Nature and by the Machine, fore and aft. So sometimes the bus carries the passengers and sometimes the passengers push the bus.

We got to the Post Office at 4:30 (A.M.). The other passengers stood eyeing each other suspiciously to see who would make a break for the cab of the truck. No use doing it unless your status is enough to hold the position. We finally started at 6:30 with baggage for eight persons on top the top of the mail and Bill and me and five others on top of it. It was cold and in these circumstances for real comfort there is nothing comparable to a large, well-padded, resilient Chinese lady.

Chinese history at Harvard and the United Board for the Christian Colleges, which Bill Fenn later captained, both are indebted to the lady against whom we snuggled for body warmth that kept us from actually freezing.

After a fortnight the jaundice set in. So I did not eat anything for a week, at least not with any success, and gradually became yellow. A great number of people, some of whom I knew well and some of whom I had not seen before, dropped into my room. When I did not want to see them any more all I had to do was sigh deeply or make a low moan. The cook, who is a master at producing food without nourishment anyway—cabbage with fish taste, cardboard carrots, potatoes with cabbage taste, and all bound together by a common grease— also got sick, and the local yokel who assists him was hard put to produce greaseless food. He could more easily have produced foodless grease, but finally he obtained four squabs at CNC124, apiece (US$6), which he boiled. This was a feat.

Then John Carter Vincent as chargé d'affaires had me brought to the embassy and put in the ambassador's bed, His Excellency being on home leave. There I rapidly improved.

From the Ambassador's Bed. From the ambassador's point of view, which is now mine, this is the least attractive city in the world. This house stands about one hundred feet above the water, with other gray stone houses below and above helter skelter, connected by winding stone staircases which appear and disappear among the roofs and rubbish heaps. Every inch of the hillside has been improved; native cement covers all flat surfaces, like that in front of this house or of the Chungking Club next door. There are also trees, now in bloom, and flower gardens laid out in the middle of the cement. But the effect is the same, gray and hard.

Foreigners and Chinese from downriver generally shared this dislike of Chungking as a cold hard place. The ambassador's bedroom gave me a particularly somber view of it.

From this half-mile distance across the water, Chungking looks like a junk heap of old boxes piled together. It sounds like a constant riot in the distance, since every sound of the boatmen hauling, the coolies carrying stone and water up endless steps, and the vendors crying their wares comes right up here. Of course what we see is the bombed and burned-over area, since rebuilt with shacks. There is no color. Nothing grows out of the rock, the stone is all gray and slightly mossed; people, houses, pathways all blend into gray, with the gray river swirling between. It is a hard place. Every downriver Chinese hates it. Every local person seems to have a surly temper.

The river is no relief, merely another problem. When low it recedes from this shore, which develops a sandbank soon half built up with bamboo shacks and boat shops. So the smaller stream flows just as fast in half its bed along the city front, and the ferry boats are swept down with the current four hundred yards before they can get across, while on the return they sometimes puff for half an hour against the stream inching their way painfully back to the landing stage. The Yangtze is no man's friend. Every single boat that comes down, rowing with eight or ten oars to keep away from the rocks and flats, must sometime go back up again, pulled by human muscles every inch of two or three hundred miles. The river junks pass upstream in front of the house here in an endless series. Every one must get a line and its trackers on a certain rock ledge now exposed, and pole itself into the whirl of the river and stretch and strain gradually upstream. The whole business is unlovely and painful to look at, no one is happy, no one can get ahead, and the swarms of shoeless, hatless working men with their doleful chants and sores and body itches and big swollen feet all seem to lead gray lives in a gray anthill. Staying here I can understand the ambassador better.

My present plan is to remain in the ambassador's bed until someone kicks me out or it gets too full. The room is beautifully decorated with photographs of ladies, all of whom are Betty Vincent.

In April, however, the dysentery saw its chance and set in slowly but persistently. The U.S. Navy doctor was baffled. When I visited Kunming again in May, I got admitted to the Army base hospital, where a vigorous team of Chinese nurses kept the wardful of GIs properly medicated and supplied with ice cream between movies. Nobody could get a fix on my disease but it ended after I returned to Chungking and took a course of emetine shots, a German drug that required its recipients to avoid exercise and heart strain. So I went slowly up the eighty-nine steps to the Army clinic each time.

In the second half of 1943 the ineffectiveness of CKS's government became widely apparent despite (or because of?) his efforts at tighter control and personal leadership. As inflation got steadily worse, malnutrition and despair riddled the salaried class. To foreign observers the left began to seem like a viable alternative. My own mood, now that I was healthy again, progressed through stages not unlike other Americans I knew in the embassy and press hostel: distrust of the KMT, disillusion as to liberal potentialities, and admiration of the local leftists. By August 1943 I saw

> little hope in the present regime because it cannot trust the mass of the people emotionally and is too inefficient to help them much practically. It may stagger along with appalling suffering and calamities dogging its trail just because there are not enough people with guts to do something about it.

This swing of opinion in 1943 in which so many shared was part of an old Chinese political phenomenon, the slippage of the mandate of Heaven (tacit popular acquiescence in the regime), part of the mechanism of Chinese politics. Early in 1943 I tried to describe the factors then at work, beginning with the censorship that let Americans see China only through rose-colored glasses.

> Feb. 5, 1943. *The coming American disillusionment:* the Chinese propaganda line about the gallant Chinese resistance is being undermined by American observers, who note that China is not a country at war, although it is in war circum-

stances; the place is not mobilized because the facilities for mobilization have not yet been created. The Chinese publicity abroad is therefore creating a dangerously hollow fabric.

To bolster up Sino-American relations Mme. Chiang went to Washington in March 1943 and addressed a session of both houses of Congress. Her smart appearance and emotional appeal made a great hit and further inflated the Free China bubble. I noted on March 10, "Mme. Chiang's salesmanship is lushly reported by Central News here." Some time after her return I went to see her. I got the impression that pride led her to play-acting.

Chungking, Sept. 16, 1943
My small hour with the great lady: I have just come back from an hour's talk, with a number of mixed impressions, and since many others have got their impressions, I record mine. The sum is that she is trying so hard to be a great lady. Conversation too cosmic to be real. An actress, with a lot of admirable qualities, great charm, quick intuition, intelligence; but underneath, emotions that are unhappy (I always find unhappy emotions in ladies, especially if beautiful), bitterness about something, a penchant for acting a part which produces falsity. Usually the beautiful but sad expression and the well-modulated tones with pauses for effect, upper lip pulled down in a strained way; but occasionally a real laugh, with a round relaxed face and higher-pitched voice, which seemed natural and at ease and made all the rest seem forced and tragic.

I was guided over by Pearl Ch'en and passed numerous saluting gendarmes, winding up in a small room with Tagore and a panda on the wall, to which she descended shortly from upstairs. I explained I had an interest in trying to educate the Americans about China and had been in Kunming and worried over the Army life and helped start some lectures which were getting a response, but much more must be done. She asked some pertinent direct questions about this. Then she got my life history and China connections, which I carry about ready to serve; then we got onto general topics, how to give the Americans perspective and counteract their materialism. I used the word first, since I find the boys referring the state of China to the statistics on bathtubs and refrigerators, assuming the two are equilibrated. So she did a few vigorous phrases on American materialism. (The chief complaint is usually, I think, based on the fact that the Americans have so damn many more things than anyone else, in other words, it is jealousy, and to express one's feeling of irritation at these fat-living Americanos one hits them for materialism; also, they *are* materialistic.)

Out of this we got a good idea, which I shall memorialize —to encourage RC to collect the real impressions of Chinese students in America, what they felt first, when they got angry first, when they were first moved to awe, when they were first humiliated—personal impressions, if they can be got hot off the individual's mind without mincing. This, she thought, might give the Army boys cause to think; I didn't query how we could bring it to their distracted attention.

Then the acting set in, on a cosmic level with a bit of you-and-I thrown in. I brought up the censorship problem but she sidestepped. Looking into the distance, she said that Life is a combination of keeping your ideals, keeping your sense of humor, and meeting the circumstances that come up; and she also said something about seeing ourselves as actors in a great experiment of which we do not know the dénouement. Now if she had left out the phony part, I would have retained the admiration I first felt when she was thinking about Who is this, what does he want, and is he for us or against us.

She was tired and her head shook a bit as old men's do. I get the impression that she was unhappy about many things and in spite of her philosophical remarks has not been able to make peace with the fact that China is backward, the material backwardness being associated with spiritual backwardness, each causing the other. Also, she has no particular solution for the problem of Sino-American understanding (neither do I), but hopes to give the Americans a sudden awakening and true perspective (esteem for China) by the use of parables and comparisons which will make them to think. (My line is to do it with syllabi. No doubt it will be done with postwar sales of steam engines. She and I can issue parables and syllabi contemporaneously and all rejoice, if we live that long.) She asked me why I didn't take on the job of educating the troops, but

I replied we had to educate Washington. I still think the first step is to cut down the censorship and deflate China to the level of reality.

Free China's inflated image in the United States was in very real danger of exploding like a balloonful of hydrogen. This was because the government was peculiarly dependent on its reputation, or as we of the TV generation say, its public image. This in turn was because of its actual superficiality.

Chengtu, Feb. 7, '43: It is hard to realize how many people there are here on the land and what a very small ruling class there is above them and the local gentry. Peasantry and gentry are the inheritance from old China, and new China consists of a thin, thin crust of people who maintain the whole fabric of modernized life. The equipment of the modern China is also very meager here, and the whole modern paraphernalia could be obliterated by cutting off all contact for a few years, if someone at the top wanted to do so.

The governor of Szechwan is almost the second man in the country but he lacks a secretariat comparable to that of a business executive in Iowa, has less foreign news to read, has no way of traveling faster than a few miles a day in a few directions, is not at the top of a closely articulated administrative machine, does not need legal advice, has no regular representatives of the people to consult seriously and therefore receives little criticism, and is not able to budget and control more than the general outlines of provincial finance. When conflicting interests emerge, he harmonizes them and the rest takes care of itself.

These observations were in a de Tocqueville-in-China tradition in which hundreds of foreigners had preceded me. They came from a fusion of reading, teaching, and now observation that gave me my fix upon the situation.

The essence of the problem is illustrated in the Ministry of Education's attempt to control the content of courses in the curriculum of each college and university. On the one hand, the ministry issues its commands that certain subjects are to be taught. On the other hand, the people teaching the courses go ahead and teach what they think best. The principle is not contested that the ministry should dictate. The principle is also not contested that the teacher should take orders, but the orders are not taken. So both sides acquiesce in a situation which is inefficient and help to make it more so. If the ministry has a good idea, it still cannot be applied with certainty. The situation rapidly deteriorates into a personal one—the minister wanting certain things done, his supporters and friends doing them and others avoiding the doing of them.

My impressions were reinforced by foreigners I talked to, as we created our own climate of opinion. One old-timer who had done mission work since before the 1911 revolution (Dr. Daniel Dye) told me:

> During the first three years of the war after 1937 there was a great growth of student enthusiasm. Singing teams toured the country and there began to be a popular movement. This is the period of gallant China, which has been made known to the West. Mr. Dye went home on furlough for a year before Pearl Harbor. He came back to find the spirit gone out of things a bit. During the past year it has deteriorated further into intellectual stalemate. The CC [Ch'en brothers' clique] and other government people are afraid of an unchecked movement which might sweep the country and sweep them out. The situation is one of apathy, such as Andy Roy found on his trip to seventeen institutions lately.

As the government's standing came more into question, its leadership felt increasingly embattled, confronted by nonsupporters and suspicious of them. As we now know, Chiang Kai-shek had responded to the European success of fascism in the 1930s by setting up his own secret movement of young officers loyal to him personally.* The New Life Movement so publicly promoted in the mid-thirties had been an outward manifestation of this secret effort to revitalize the revolution under a leading personality. Ch'en Li-fu and his brother Ch'en Kuo-fu at the Central Political Institute had been the top organizers of

---

*See Lloyd Eastman, *The Abortive Revolution*.

KMT loyalty to CKS as party director in succession to the canonized Dr. Sun Yat-sen.

Ch'en Li-fu's operation represented China's transition from government by a dynastic family to government by a party dictatorship. Both systems rested on personal loyalty of inferiors to superiors at all levels up to the One Man who still had to be the Top Authority. Emperors had used their wives' relatives, who were utterly dependent on them, and kept their own brothers, as possible rivals, under scrutiny. The new party leaders depended on their loyal organizers of party personnel. The two Ch'en brothers, Ch'en Kuo-fu and Ch'en Li-fu, together led the CC or organization clique within the KMT. They were from Chekiang like Chiang Kai-shek, and their uncle (Ch'en Ch'i-mei) had been CKS's revolutionary mentor as well as their own—almost a family relationship. Ch'en Kuo-fu had managed the recruitment of seven thousand of the cadets CKS trained at Whampoa; they formed the personnel basis of his power. Ch'en then worked to organize the KMT as a Leninist party. Come the split with the CCP in 1927, he knew whom to kill and where the bodies were buried. He remained a guiding light in the KMT organization department and the Central Political Institute for training civil servants. When I went there to give a lecture in 1943 I found it extremely neat and orderly, in a beautiful setting.

Younger than his brother by eight years and thirteen years younger than CKS, Ch'en Li-fu had qualified as an American-trained returned student by spending two years to get his M.S. in mining engineering in 1925 at the University of Pittsburgh. He even joined the United Mine Workers. But counterrevolution called, and by 1926 he was in Canton as CKS's confidential secretary. Then from 1928 to 1938 he headed the KMT investigation division responsible for spotting and eliminating all Communists in the party. Tai Li worked under him. When Ch'en Li-fu was made minister of education in 1938, it was about like appointing J. Edgar Hoover to be chancellor of Berkeley with budget control over all the state universities in the United States.

When I called on Ch'en Li-fu in October 1942, I reported deadpan to the ambassador that

> he was most affable and explained to me the manifold ways in which bamboo is used in China and also recited some early

mythology, as examples of Chinese cultural material which might be injected into the American school system in the process of exchange of materials. I informed him of the general interest in microfilm and of the fact that Dr. Koo [his vice-minister, Ku Yu-hsiu, formerly dean of Tsing Hua] was working with a group of Chinese on that subject. The minister was a bit vague as to the nature and use of microfilm, inquiring whether projectors could take pictures as well as show them.

I had a longer session with Ch'en Li-fu a year later.

MEMORANDUM FOR THE AMBASSADOR

Nov. 3, 1943

Subject: *Conversation with the Minister of Education*

Through the arrangement of his brother-in-law, Dr. M. H. Chiang (whom I once failed on his Ph.D. examination), I called on Mr. Ch'en Li-fu at his house last night, in the capacity of adviser to his committee known as the International Cultural Service, and had a lengthy conversation with him on various aspects of cultural relations. Mr. Ch'en seemed to be in disappointingly excellent health and good spirits, and was as usual charming in manner and filled with a general euphoria and naïve enthusiasm regarding educational matters.

He inquired as to the progress of the microfilm program and asked whether microfilm was likely to be used on the same scale after the war, expressing the view that for scholars there could be no substitute for a book, which could be taken home, read in bed, and marked up. I informed him that this view was not confined to himself, but that film had been used recently for its facility in transportation, which he acknowledged.
. . .

Ch'en Li-fu then expressed an interest in securing educational films from the United States, which I informed him I understood the Division of Cultural Relations was even now preparing for Chinese use. He would also like cartoons, which are able to express more than the human figure can express. He feared, however, that the complicated machines required for projecting moving pictures could not be successfully maintained in China, and inquired as to the availability of a "reflectorscope" which would not require the use of electricity. With sustained enthusiasm he envisaged the installation of 80,000 "reflectorscopes" in the 80,000 villages of China, where the masses could be shown pictures of the world, incidentally remarking that he believed Sunday, not being a day of religion in China, should be regularly devoted to education of old and young. Remembering his query last year as to whether microfilm projectors could take pictures as well as project them, I did not press the Minister for a description of the "reflectorscope," but reminded him of the existence of the United Nations Filmstrip Library and its program, of which he seemed to be only vaguely aware.

My strongest impression, from this and earlier conversations with the Minister of Education, is that his interest in and understanding of education is extremely superficial, as though he seldom had found time to contemplate any of the topics which we discussed.

                                                                    jkf

I had noted in March that

as the attrition of the inflation continues, the government more and more seems to be impelled to concentrate on the holding of power. Ideas, reforms, programs are all secondary. Thus the Generalissimo, as one friend put it, has turned to the CC as the group that can organize some kind of nucleus which will hold together during the big blows likely to come from within or without. The CC are a type interested in power and regimentation to preserve it. They are not capable of much innovation. Their men are yes-men, not big people, usually, and do not bring much strength to their jobs. The effort to tighten up the organization does not produce results that can command public respect, so that the CC may well be sapping away the claim of the Party upon the Mandate of Heaven. The Party in a crisis might find itself without many friends outside its ranks, and with turncoat opportunists scattered within.

To put Ch'en Li-fu in charge of education was a step toward politicizing it and was resented accordingly by the Peking liberal educators, who had seldom been enthusiastic about the KMT in any case. CKS's refusal to let American private aid through United China Relief go to government university faculties was stated as a matter of national pride, but the implicit message to Kunming was, Go ahead and starve.

Conditions among the scholar class had reached the point where CKS's ill-conceived efforts to provide strong leadership only led to further alienation. CKS tried, for example, to counter the inflation by fixing meat prices by decree. It didn't work, and Li Chi remarked to me that

> it was most unsound for the Gimo to put himself behind the price-fixing fiasco, as though his personal request would change the laws of economics. My student Hsiang says they have had no meat nor cooking oil for a month. All our meat at the house here has been bootlegged. The immediate reaction was for meat to leave the market, all pig owners et al. waiting for better prices. Li Chi says people are really starving now. He has lost two children in these years and T'ao has lost his wife. The intellectuals would not mind starving if they felt they were mobilized or if all classes were taking it together. But they see gross inequality and lavish spending in high places. A lot of intellectuals will therefore get lost, some will die, and others will become revolutionaries.

When I went to Kunming in May 1943 I found *China's Destiny*, the power holder's book, was taken as an insult to the professors whose forte was book writing.

> The bitterness here against the Gimo since he began to be a Sage as well as a Hero is very intense and to me quite outspoken. Lao Chin has refused to look at *China's Destiny* and the social scientists call it twaddle, with mixed scorn and shame. The scholar class do not and will not lightly forgo their prerogatives, and CKS now affronts them.
>
> Kunming, May 17: I must say I am appalled after reading more of *China's Destiny.* I never saw a more pernicious use of history for political purposes. Much of the book is in the guise of straight history, the woes of China beneath imperialism, on which everything is blamed. E.g., the Chinese legal system could not develop because the treaty-port courts set it

such a bad example. The book is a tract unworthy of a states-man, and I can now see why everyone connected with the English translation is having chills and fever.

One can guess that *China's Destiny* is more than an expression of personal bigotry. It may be calculated not only to bring credit to the Party and Gimo for ridding China of the imperialist monster, but also to rekindle the anti-foreignism which is one source of patriotism and internal cohesion.

The professors here are discouraged, and foresee the growth of an unbreakable police control over all China, with liberal education extinguished and economic life regimented as well as thought. They see nothing to stop the process. I have argued in return that the regime lacks the personnel to do the job it wants to do, and hence will have to compromise with the people who seek the development of the country, rather than mere political control over it.

American disillusionment as to Free China came with a bang in the summer of 1943 through three articles—Pearl Buck in *Life* for May 10, Hanson Baldwin of the *New York Times* in the *Reader's Digest* for August, and T. A. Bisson in *Far Eastern Survey,* an IPR publication of limited circulation that was nonetheless taken very seriously in China. Bisson categorized the CCP as "democratic" compared with the KMT as "feudal." Baldwin and Buck were nonideological, trying simply to give realistic appraisals of China's true condition. Baldwin as a military correspondent reflected the long-standing GI disillusionment from Kunming. It was Pearl Buck who particularly tried to counter the hyperbole of the fleeting vogue of Mme. Chiang. As the guest of President Roosevelt she had in fact behaved like a petulant princess. Pearl Buck, whose Nobel prize for *The Good Earth* in 1934 had made her the best-known American China watcher, later told us one symptomatic incident. She received a hurry-up call from Madame's entourage at Hyde Park, saying, "Please come right away. Madame wants to see you." Pearl Buck therefore hastened from Perkasie, Pennsylvania, to Hyde Park but found herself embarrassingly unexpected. Mme. Chiang had actually wanted to see her attendant Pearl Ch'en. So sorry!

I repeat this story only because there were so many others like it, indicative of a truly self-destructive egotism. Psychologically, I suppose one skates faster as the ice grows thinner. A precarious situation leads to overcompensation.

T. F. Tsiang with his usual forthrightness told the CC clique's minister of information that he should not be upset when "out of a hundred articles on China half a dozen are critical." Give and take was the American custom. China's censorship might be the real fault; "if more truth were allowed out, it might help to counteract misinformation."

My own theory about the Chinese publicity bubble in July 1943 was that

> the rosy picture given to the West, so harmfully, is merely an offshoot of the rosy picture which any Chinese administration must maintain at home. The Publicity Board and Holly Tong [information director] are not out to pull the wool over our eyes, at least not to the point of blowing up a great bubble which may someday burst and drop China into a position of contempt. They are only answering the pressures of the moment, among which the greatest is the tradition of government by prestige. No official, who is of course in jealous competition with many other officials, can publicly proclaim an evil, a failure, or a misstep in his administration; one such admission would be a club for his enemies to beat him with. No government can point to evils in the land in the same way that we can at home, because the government, or traditionally the One Man at the top of it, is felt to be responsible for all such evils. We distinguish between Nature's problems and Man's efforts to combat them. The Chinese tradition is different, Man and Nature forming parts of a natural-social-ethical continuum. In the time of Darwin and Marx the Emperor here was still kowtowing to Heaven when it rained too much and issuing penitential edicts to the people taking personal responsibility for the floods. If he did not take responsibility, he would be abdicating his office.

But all remedies were now too late. The mandate (meaning the public confidence) had begun to shift. I proceeded to work out a lengthy rationale of what was happening. The following constituted my clinical analysis at the time:

Two Chinese customs should be understood: 1. The government has the monopoly of organization, and everything organized must in some way be under the government, or it is assumed to be a rival to the government and therefore dangerous. The historical types of nongovernment organization have been secret societies and merchant guilds. But organization arising from the people is too full of dynamite. The government has never been more than a thin veneer of officials and magistrate's, scattered at wide intervals over the masses and depending on their prestige as rulers rather than on their physical power, and so any new creation of an organization which can command the movements of a mass of people is a threat which can only be countered effectively before it comes into existence. This is partly also because organization is on a personal basis, like the loyalty of the citizen to the ruler, and a new organization means a new personal leader, who is ipso facto a rival to those already governing. The result is that from a long time past all new organizations have come under the government, including the Catholic missionaries in 1898, and down to the Chinese Industrial Cooperatives just last year.

The modern mode is to have movements and national organizations, and so such things have been started from official quarters, like the New Life Movement and the women's division of it under Mme. CKS; but these things exist primarily to supervise, as well as to organize and lead. They have two faces —one is the movement in Western terms, to educate or lead or put across; and the other is to prevent the growth of rival bodies not under official control, which would create a threat to the official monopoly of organization. The Youth Corps, for example, is used on some campuses to do things and on others to prevent things, but usually just to keep track of things; so Westerners call it a spy system.

2. Criticism is not nice in China. It is indulged in against the background of personal relationships which hold together the social fabric, and so it is taken personally, rather than as an expression of difference of opinion. This is part of the face complex—if one lacks the confidence of others, one soon lacks the confidence of a lot of other people also; loss of others' confidence is a direct threat to the person, whether he is a

government official or a merchant or a ruler, because most positions in Chinese society are maintained on the basis of confidence, usually personal confidence. So if you criticize, it at once becomes a question whether you still have confidence. The correspondent who really lets fly at some part of the Chinese situation is likely to be persona non grata. The evil in this situation is that we in the West don't understand it, or give a damn, and believe in progress by criticism. The Chinese cannot bring themselves to put out any criticisms, which would be worse than an obscene exhibitionism.

The main problems lie in the provinces among the mass of the people. Frank Price took a trip through nine provinces last spring and saw the governors and twenty *hsien* magistrates. He makes the point that the Kuomintang is indistinguishable from the government, and it would be impossible to separate the two and retain either one. It is perfectly natural that the local primary school teacher should be the local party head and the *hsien* magistrate should lead the party in the *hsien* — you cannot tell party from government, any more than you can separate the government and party ministries in Chungking. This is a party monopoly so great that it is not comparable to the Democrats or Republicans being permanently in power with the other chafing to take over. It is a structural arrangement. There is no way of giving place and opportunity to minority parties without either changing the system fundamentally from the ground up, or else weakening it.

My effort at political analysis of course bore a message for American policy. If I was correct in thinking that in 1943 we were seeing the Nationalist loss of Heaven's mandate, then Ambassador Pat Hurley's nailing the American flag to the mast of the Nationalist ship of state after FDR's death in 1945 would be both futile and disastrous. Such it proved to be.

In 1943 my analysis continued as follows:

Two factors are little publicized, but I believe they are the fundamental stumbling blocks to Chinese progress. One is the lack of good men. Of the group who have the ability to rise to the top layer, only a rather small proportion are really vigorous in principles or character. Ability is not the same as honesty and courage. Labor and sincerity do not bring the American reward of modest success in life. Life must be wangled here more than elsewhere. Virtue does not get results unless combined with cunning. The American copybook maxims which led our great men to the heights would have killed them off in this country before they could grow up. Washington would never have been able to pay off the debt for the cherry tree. Every administrator is therefore handicapped by a lack of men to work with who are both able and honest. It is not honesty in our sense. It is having courage to take responsibility, and having taken it to discharge it for the assigned purpose and not make the job into something for oneself.

The other difficulty is the tendency to factionalism. Doing anything on a national scale as we do would be at the present time almost impossible—people would not be moved by the national issues of policy and would require the customary personal bonds. The first thing is survival and in political matters it is survival through helpful personal relationships; the political questions in the Western sense, concerning the polity, the state, and the nation, are secondary. They are luxuries.

Democracy in China?: This society is democratic in the sense of individualism. There is opportunity in China for the strong, and a certain amount of social fluidity, and people rise from obscurity by their ability; and this is known as democracy.

The gentleman is recognized as such, on account of his virtue. This form of individualism is also democratic, recognizing a man for his merit, or moral virtue.

But when it comes to administration, the democratic process is not customary. An administrator has the mandarin tradition behind him. The mandarin had no check upon his authority except circumstance; he could do almost anything he could get away with. The two powers to check him were his superiors in the chain of rank, above, and the populace, below. Between them he could steer his own course without consultation. He was judged by what happened afterward.

Many administrators are autocrats nowadays, partly because it is expected. When I try to consult my Chinese secretarial staff, just as when I used to try to get the opinion of students, they become at once very polite, because they realize how polite I am being in giving my orders or instruction; I go to the trouble of seeming to consult them.

China's tradition of arbitrary government, in short, now reinforced the modern mode of authoritarianism. The crowning insult offered by CKS to the Lienta professors was the requirement that before the half dozen who had been invited for a year in the States could depart they must receive ideological training at the Central Training Institute in Chungking, "where a course of five or six weeks gives Chinese bureaucrats of all types calisthenics, orderly routine, and edifying speeches."

A psychological turning point came in the beginning of summer. I went to Kunming again in July 1943 and reported the

Latest round in the Lienta battle. The two delegates who went to Chungking to present the requests of the Lienta faculty for adequate subsistence, following a faculty meeting late in May, got nowhere. They presented several propositions. One was that the rice subsidy should be paid partly in cash at the market price of rice; thus a unit of rice rated at about CNC 900 by the official rate would count for about 2,400, the market price, and the recipient could get the cash value. Another proposal was that salaries should be increased in proportion to the increase of prices locally. In Kunming salaries have been increased about five times while prices are said to have gone up three hundred times.

The main issue in all this is whether Lienta can break the doctrine by which the ministry is strangling them, namely that the same monetary treatment should be meted out to government institutions in all parts of the country, without regard to local conditions. So far Ch'en Li-fu is ahead.

One proposal was that the university here should make use of its laboratories for commercial production, such as the making of electric bulbs and radio tubes. Capital would be required to get the project started, and the delegates got a promise from Dr. Kung of CNC 3 million for the purpose, and the Gimo is said to have approved. But when the proposal came up in the Executive Yuan, Ch'en Li-fu brought in a proposal to do the same thing in all the government universities, with a budget of 17 million. He had not had the idea before. The catch is that on the pro-rata basis, Lienta can get only CNC 800,000 from the 17 million. Thwarted again. This move on the part of the minister appears to have been the final proof, for any who still needed it, that CC is bent on the destruction of the Lienta faculty. Various professors declared that they no longer had any obligation to the authorities and would try to keep alive by any means they could.

This attitude was confirmed in late August when I visited Kunming and then Kweilin in Kwangsi, an American forward base that was also a center of provincial aloofness from Chungking with a very active cultural life. I stayed partly with the consul, Arthur Ringwalt, and partly with Graham Peck of OWI. Opinion in these intellectual centers outside Chungking was more outspokenly anti-KMT, but still there was no mobilization of the universities. Outside Kweilin I visited the Academia Sinica Institutes of Geology, Physics, Chemistry, and Physiology "all grouped under the masterful leadership of J. S. Lee (Li Ssu-kuang), head of the Geological Institute, one of those outstanding individuals who arise in this country and do wonders"— big buildings, cottages, a power plant, manufacture of chemicals and precision instruments, and so on. (J. S. Lee later stayed to work under the PRC.) Many scholars were waiting for a new opportunity. In Kunming I had seen "the Chou Pei-yuans, very charming Tsing Hua people; he is a physicist and they are about to go to California to work with Milliken."

In Kweilin I found an Australian Rhodes scholar and physiology professor from Hong Kong University in the person of Colonel Lindsay Ride, head of the BAAG (British Army Aid Group) that handled the flow of intelligence via the "underground railway" from Hong Kong. I promoted cooperation in the use of publications between him and OSS. (Postwar, when he headed the university we became warm friends and stayed with him several times at the vice-chancellor's lodge overlooking the mountainside campus below the Peak.)

By mid-September I was writing Currie,

the liberal-type American-trained men of Tsing Hua and Peita, the best exemplars of the American system and scientific standards, still have little dynamic to offer China. On the CP question, the real issue, they are mostly reactionary.

They have no particular direction in which they wish to move the country. They are very very patiently waiting for the good old liberal-education days to come again. This may never happen.

The longer I try to figure out what I would do about the general Chinese mess, the more I come to the conclusion I would do what the CP are doing. Nothing not radical will succeed in moving things.

To Currie on September 22, 1943:

The people who really want to fight are the people who want to rouse the masses. The fighting policy for us would be to back them a bit, get into North China and be friends with the revolution. An observer in the North is the first thing needed. I hope J. P. Davies' idea can get somewhere. [The U. S. military observer group, or Dixie mission, went to Yenan in July 1944.]

Once the desertion of the intellectuals set in, it was quickly transmitted to the sprinkling of foreigners with whom they had contact. In my case, I went around to meet and interview a number of key people and wrote up my impressions for the embassy and for Wilma to distribute in Washington.

Writers and artists were least likely to be interchangeable as officials, yet they too traditionally had had to live on official patronage. After the decline of the second united front in 1938, many creative people had been given sinecure rice allowances and shelter in Chungking. This group was headed by the versatile Kuo Mo-jo, who is properly listed in the major biographical dictionary as "poet, playwright, novelist, essayist, translator, historian, paleographer, Creation Society leader and Chinese Communist propagandist"—a real literary powerhouse. Trained in medicine in Japan, he had become famous as a spark plug of the Creation Society in the 1920s. He had become a Communist, helped in the Northern Expedition, and then spent a decade in Japan 1927–37 in archaeological studies, which gave him a reputation among Western scholars. In July 1937 he escaped from Japan and was accepted in Kuomintang China, where he became director of anti-Japanese propaganda under the Military Affairs Commission. After holding this position for two years, he was forced out of active war work and organized the Cultural Work Committee.

The committee is in effect a sort of corral or stockade into which have been herded a number of leading writers whose departure for Yenan would be a calamity for the united front. Thus three leading members, Hu Feng, Mao Tun, and Shen Chih-yuan, were coaxed back from Hong Kong by invitations from the Generalissimo, Hu Feng being offered a stipend of $2,000 a month to keep him in Chungking. . . . Their complete freedom of movement and expression is felt by the authorities to be undesirable.

In September I drove out to the farmhouse used by the Cultural Work Committee in the summertime.

We were received by Kuo Mo-jo and his main colleagues and with them had a banquet, consumed several bottles of excellent wine, and became very chummy. I presented him with the complete Microfilm Catalog and Microfilm Guide of the RC program, which is now formidable, as well as a special list of IDC microfilm on the American war effort which has great interest for research people here. We arranged for his office to receive a projector from us, and use our facilities here.

In October I was invited to Kuo Mo-jo's fiftieth birthday party:

I took Bill Sloane of Holt and Co. to this affair, a really lively occasion where a lot of people who looked thin and bright enough to qualify as critics of the established order swarmed through a suite of rooms, in the big mansion below the British Embassy which is occupied by the Cultural Work Committee and its rats and spies. Mr. Kuo wandered about looking very bright and gentle, young and receptive as usual, and his guests, who included a lot of the people who had turned up in public at the Russian Embassy reception, it being the only open affair in Chungking, wandered about too and looked at photos on the walls and a big layout of copies of his books. The book display was amazing, sixty or seventy-five volumes of various kinds, thin, and variegated in subject, while the photos showed him in Japan with half a dozen children quite different from the two that now followed him about, not as old as the war. A lot of these people looked as though they could be enthusiastic and even creative, especially if they had a couple of square meals first.

For his birthday I sent him some razor blades and sulfaguanidine, not having any art or letters available, and he replied in a very friendly fashion. Bill Sloane told him about books at four cents apiece.

Come the revolution Kuo was made head of the PRC's Academy of Sciences, while the leading novelist, Mao Tun, was made Minister of Culture.

In October 1943 I had a chance to talk with Mao Tun.

He has a small mustache and looks rather Japanese, a rather slight little man, very nice but not very colorful, named Shen Yen-ping, probably the leading short-story writer now extant, under the pen name of Mao Tun ("Contradiction"). He says everyone is publishing more and more translations because they are easier to get past the censors. They may still be cut up (Victor Hugo has been censored, etc.), but one is more likely to make enough to eat, whereas if you write an article or short story in the effort to feed yourself and the wrong idea slips in, there goes your rice. He says the censorship and secret police are now annoying nearly every writer he knows or has heard of. Himself he has always been a loyal supporter of the Kuomintang, but he does think there is a possibility of more than one interpretation of Sun Yat-sen, and the present party product does not entirely agree with his ideals. Sun was very broad (I agree) and one should have a right to interpret him.

My attempt to canvass the Chungking political landscape led me also to one of John Dewey's most active disciples in China, Dr. H. C. Tao (T'ao Hsing-chih). I went to see him on November 19.

He studied at Illinois and Columbia during the First World War and went abroad lecturing in 1938–39. Before that he had experimented with the idea that anyone who knew something could impart it to others. In Kiangsu at Ta-cheng hsien near Shanghai about 1933 he was running a school and got the students, schoolchildren, to start teaching their illiterate peasant parents all they knew, as they learned it. The idea spread very fast and all twenty-five villages in the area were soon doing it, with thousands becoming interested. The provincial commissioner of education took it up with excitement and after a year there was a sizable movement. But at this point the then governor of the province, who was, it seems, none other than the worthy Ch'en Kuo-fu, dismissed the commissioner. The movement was criticized because, while it educated, it seemed to demean the standing of the teacher as a professional monopolist on the meaning of these written signs used locally. If small children could be teachers, what were teachers good for?

In the Hankow period, says Mr. T'ao, there were hundreds of children's organizations and the Little Teacher movement spread to twenty-three provinces in a year, the idea being that the school was the powerhouse and every child a wire reaching out from it to electrify the minds of the people. T'ao Hsing-chih is entitled in this movement to wear seven stars because he has taught someone to read and that person has taught another person to read and so on for seven stages. T'ao's pupils can wear six stars, and so on.

The Gimo when he first saw T'ao's work had praised it, so after the war began T'ao saw him and got an O.K. to keep it going and expand, but the Minister of Education, H.E. Mr. Ch'en Li-fu, called him in and offered him the headship of an agricultural college. T'ao said agricultural colleges were out of his line, and how about the people who lived by the agriculture? But the minister felt it would be better for him to do something else, so T'ao opened a school for orphans, which he now runs at Peipei. The orphans are picked up from Madame's camps or elsewhere and if bright and promising are put into various arts and crafts and given a chance. They do well, being selected and appreciative. I saw some here in an art class, drawing copies of busts from Greece very faithfully but still looking a damn sight better off than most orphans.

The school of course has no funds from the government to speak of, but T'ao begs it from local businessmen and charity such as UCR. Here is a man in no sense ever a Communist, but he wants to open up the minds of the people, first by teaching them to read, and that is evil in the minds of the authorities. From such examples one gets the impression that the only hope of the country is the revival of industry and business to decrease the power of the fascists, and if that fails then a bang-up revolution.

These various impressions, selected here from a large corpus recorded at the time, added up to one conclusion: that Chiang Kai-shek as the symbol and forefront of the Nationalist regime had by late 1943 lost the confidence and allegiance of China's literate leadership.

21

DISCOVERING THE LEFT

UNTIL 1944 the American war effort in China was confined to the Nationalist area. The CCP part of the nominal united front was heard about only indirectly. Its capital at Yenan became a sort of political Shangri-la from which only a few visitors emerged, usually starry-eyed as though fed on honey dew.

The CCP at Yenan were fortunate in who reported on them. Who could be a better witness than the head of the Peking branch of the National City Bank of New York? Mr. Martel Hall had been in the Navy in World War I and was still a lieutenant in the U.S. Navy Reserve, a student of the Chinese language in 1919 and manager of the Citibank's Hankow branch under the Japanese in 1938–41. He was caught in Peking by Pearl Harbor but made plans to escape with CCP help. He made a practice of taking long walks all over the city, longer and longer every day, until he finally walked off into the beyond. He came out to Yenan through Wu T'ai Shan in the uniform of the 8th Route Army. He wore Chinese shoes, carried soap but had little chance to bathe, got lousy, but had no major troubles. He reported:

> At Yenan they have dances once a week on Saturday nights with gramophone music. He dropped in for lunch with General Chu Teh and ate up much of the millet, but when the general asked the cook for more, the cook offered cabbage and told him he had had his grain ration for the day. In all his time

in the area he could find no evidence of graft or scandal, either financial or sexual.

Hall's main reactions are two. First, the people in the Communist area are much more alive intellectually and are filled with an ideal still. He addressed a hastily collected school body and was asked questions for two hours afterward. The people there are a selection, and include many of high training. Second, Hall finds the people in Chungking are blindly self-confident of their ability to mop up the Communists when the time comes, just as the Japs were about mopping up China. He believes the people here are likely to try a little six-week campaign to liquidate the Communists, and find themselves in trouble aplenty as a result.

The armies facing the Communists are sodden with commerce, as are the Japs in some areas, trading with each other, and as Graham Peck found a year ago the officers in Honan are great merchants. The fortification system is also built against the Communists and not against the Japs.

The sunny vitality and homespun egalitarianism of the CCP at Yenan were already famous from Ed Snow's *Red Star over China*. Every traveler confirmed the picture—Michael Lindsay, Consul Ray Ludden, medical people. Yenan glowed in the distance.

My major achievement in late 1943 was to find new friends on the left who gave me in a few months some understanding of their revolutionary cause. With health restored and a successor (Dr. George N. Kates) designated to relieve me, I was preparing to leave Chungking for Washington. It would take five months, as it turned out, for Kates to arrive. In this period I became acquainted with Chungking's scattered leftist community, but especially with two very articulate young women.

The first was Chou En-lai's liaison with the Press Hostel. As the Chungking representative of Mao and the CCP at Yenan, Chou symbolized the united front, which both CCP and KMT wanted to preserve in form. Chou En-lai's headquarters therefore received news from Yenan and offered it to the foreign press. In June 1943, after seeing so many cabinet ministers and educators, and garnering little in the way of Japanese publications, I told Teddy White I felt I should approach the CCP and see what they could offer. As a result a very intelligent and attractive young woman named Kung P'eng came to see me. She was just at the start of a brilliant career as Chou En-lai's press officer. (At the time of her untimely death of a massive stroke, in 1970, she was one of the best-known women in the world of journalism.)

Kung P'eng agreed to come around periodically and give me Chinese conversation practice. Her personality combined the freshness of youth with the certainty of her faith in the CCP cause plus a good deal of sophistication about war correspondents and a refreshing sense of humor. Amid the dispirited drabness of 1943 Chungking, her vitality was a breath of fresh air. What she put forward was a liberal bill of particulars against the KMT—its assassinations, press suppression, smashing of printing plants, railroading of liberal critics, refusal to permit demonstrations, denial of the right to strike, and so on. When denouncing the KMT for denying civil liberties that the CCP also denied, Kung P'eng became extra-righteous. She knew the lingo of both sides because she had lived on both sides of the KMT-CCP struggle.

Kung P'eng's biography as I recorded it:

> [She] was born in Yokohama in 1915, grew up in Canton and after 1925 in Shanghai. Her father was one of the first Paoting Military Academy students and became a general in the 1911 Revolution. She was very much attached to him as a child and was fascinated by his tales of revolutionary work, and developed a romantic interest in Chinese Robin Hood fiction. At the same time she grew up in the atmosphere of the May 30 (1925) anti-imperialist movement in Shanghai. In 1928 she went to St. Mary's Hall, the girls' missionary school connected with St. John's, largely a finishing place for Shanghai middle-class Chinese. She became at one point deeply religious as a Christian and also deeply interested in English literature. Her name in school and college was Kung Wei-hang.
>
> In 1935 she went to Yenching and was one of the leaders of the student movement of December 1935, which made her a revolutionist in conviction; after graduation in 1937 she spent six months in Shanghai, teaching at St. Mary's and working in relief projects, but finally decided to leave her family and go to Yenan. Her trip to Yenan was during the height of

the era of good feeling in the united front, through Hankow. Getting used to life in Yenan was a bit difficult, her individualism requiring discipline to be merged in the group. About the end of 1938 she went into the field to help organize peasant villages and spent two years in North China leading the life of the guerrillas and village organizers. She worked with the peasant women, helping them to organize and resist male tyranny, sharing their daily lives and concerns including their head lice and body lice. She had been an aide to General P'eng Te-huai and admired him immensely.

In late 1940 she married a Communist several years older, a returned student from Germany, but after three weeks departed under orders to go to Chungking, where she arrived in early 1941 after crossing the Jap lines. Party plans to send her abroad were hindered by the New Fourth Army incident, her health broke down and she was in the hospital for six months with complications from an infected inoculation needle. Her father died in sad circumstances in this period and her husband, whom she had not seen again, died in the North late in 1942. In Chungking she was assigned as a liaison, informally, with the foreign community, especially the press.

Kung P'eng made trips down the street to the Press Hostel with carbons of the latest Yenan broadcasts in her handbag. The Western journalists, battling the KMT censorship day by day, welcomed the opposition's story. Her attraction for these activist word users bereft of family life lay partly in her intelligent personality but also in the role she was playing as the voice of dissidence in a city of yes men and time servers. She was the spokesman of the outs, whose ideals of betterment exposed the evils of the ins. Chou En-lai, moreover, was the legitimate Chungking source of news on the CCP part of the alleged united front. In Chungking his headquarters symbolized the ambivalence of the united front—such an extraordinary place that I tried to preserve a verbal picture of it.

Chungking, November 8, 1943
"The Palace of the Duke of Chou (Chou Kung Kuan)." This is stamped as a receipt on the chit books of messengers who make their way there.

This "palace" is a very interesting place. One goes up a dead-end street running to a cliff edge, and passes by the Chiu-ching School, where fifteen cultural and relief bodies live and the chancery of the American Embassy; and you also pass by the entrance to CKS palace, and the Executive Yuan, and at the end of the dead end you pass the big white house lived in by Tai Li and duck into the little alleyway that runs along the edge of the cliff, jam-packed with stalls and shops and sewers and sweetmeats on either side. This you follow through the slippery ooze for fifty yards—it is always crowded with people—and suddenly you duck into a doorway and there you are.

You must understand that this palace has a peculiar composition. It is a sandwich made up of Communists and secret police, alternating. First, there are two courtyards; the KMT secret police live in the first courtyard and the Communists live in the second. Further, there are in the main building between the two courtyards, three floors: the Communists live in the bottom and top floors and the secret police live in between. In addition there are features that make for even greater intimacy: around the inner and CCP courtyard there are three floors on one side, two on two sides, and a sun porch on the fourth or cliff side, looking down over the Chialing River two hundred feet below. The secret police, having the second floor, can walk out on the two sides and use the sun porch, getting between the Communists and the sun. If one listens hard, one can sometimes hear the secret police people talking, just as they can hear you talking, and sometimes they talk English. There is no need for a common entrance; the second floor is entered by a special stairway from the front courtyard, and the Communists do not exactly live with their KMT friends, but they are never more than a few feet or whispers away.

Also, the Communists have a back entrance down onto the cliffside, which is nothing less than a trapdoor in the floor of the entrance to one suite of rooms, frequently open and around which you step cautiously in the murk. But lately some people have built a house on the cliff *under* the palace, so that this trapdoor exit goes right by their door, there being nowhere else for it to go. This house may help to keep the Chou establishment from collapsing into the Chialing some dark night, but it completes the barbed-wire encirclement from which the CCP hostages would have trouble in escaping.

The people who live in this house of mystery, as Brooks Atkinson [of the *New York Times*] calls it, seem to be happy most of the time: there is a crowd of Little Devils *(hsiao kuei)* who were with the 8th Route Army but many of whom have now grown up and are rather husky young men; they hang around in the entrance room, where the little foot-square speakeasy window opens onto the dark entrance from the front courtyard. In this room are big hand-drawn maps of the Russian front and the Chinese front, with battle lines, and various posters on the wall. The boys play a flute or a game and make plenty of normal noise. All the rooms are rather bare, like any Chungking room, with bits of plaster missing and the cane chairs sagging soggily. Recently the campaign of discouragement has eliminated electricity at night, so it is even more dusky and dim a place than usual. But a rooster still crows at times from the woodpile in the courtyard, the foreign embassies still try to make themselves heard on the roaring telephone, the local comrades still produce mimeo'd translations of the latest Yenan diatribe against "Mr. Chiang," and the battle is not yet over.

I called at Chou's to meet his aide Ch'en Chia-k'ang, a bright little man very full of ideas, with whom I had more talk on Ming-Ch'ing history in half an hour than all winter with the rest of Chungking. Two press and two embassy came to dinner there, so there is plenty of company in this stealthy contemplation of revolution. One cannot get very worried over the concept that the CP is working on us all like missionaries, inasmuch as they may get into a dungeon any day and we cannot be hurt.

In short the CCP in Chungking was still an isolated group of underdogs and no sense of menace attached to them. Their containerized town house was compensated for by the barbed wire and strongly guarded Chungking headquarters of the 18th Group Army situated on top of a hill outside the city, where a radio kept contact with Yenan and no KMT or foreigners were ever admitted—an indispensable vestige of the second united front.

Chou En-lai's charisma struck me at once. Here was a handsome black-eyebrowed aristocrat who stood for the masses, a rarely intelligent and intuitive individual who served collectivism. I told him my mission to find Japanese materials. He said he would send a request, but nothing ever resulted. We both tossed a few English words into our Chinese conversation, while Kung P'eng filled in the gaps for both sides.

Later she introduced me to her fiancé, Ch'iao Mu (Ch'iao Kuan-hua).* Ch'iao was tall, almost my height, with the large spectacles and long hair of a student, plus a broad toothsome grin and a really irreverent sense of humor. He had been at Tsing Hua when I taught there, taking his B.A. in 1933, and then studied German philosophy at Tübingen as the Nazis took over (Ph.D., 1936). Back in Wuhan he did propaganda for the KMT in 1937–38 but joined the CCP, and in 1938–41 was a writer in Hong Kong until he escaped from the Japanese and reached Chungking in 1942 to edit international news for the CCP news agency. His articles in the *Masses (Ch'un-chung)* I found eloquent and fervent, not a joke in a carload. Revolution was both his philosophy and his religion. I said to him, "You seem to have studied the totalitarians." He said, "I *am* a totalitarian."

In September 1943 the KMT was rumored to be considering a short, sharp attack to wipe out the CCP at Yenan, but generals who knew the terrain opposed it and Chungking feared to undertake it lest dissent break out in other provinces. Police surveillance of Chou En-lai's staff increased. Kung P'eng and Ch'iao Mu, intellectuals with a faith, home missionaries, never went out alone. They expected arrest and possibly martyrdom, and this enhanced the drama of seeing them.

> *September 9, 1943:* The Communists who live up the street in Chou En-lai's headquarters do an excellent job of contact with the Americans, with whom they can discuss things critically and realistically. They now expect to be closed up and

---

*He was sometimes identified as "Southern Ch'iao-mu" in Chungking to distinguish him from "Northern Ch'iao-mu" in Yenan (Pei Ch'iao-mu, whose name was actually Hu Ch'iao-mu, in 1981 head of the PRC Academy of Social Sciences). Both of them came from Yen-ch'eng in eastern Kiangsu.

concentrated at any moment, but carry on with their own amazing esprit de corps and faith in the movement. Their line now appears to be to act just as much like modern American liberal democrats as possible, which to some extent they are; they play down the totalitarian side of the movement, and are all set to be martyrs and heroes if the KMT is foolish enough to martyrize them. Our impression of them generally is very favorable, because the group here consist of Yenching and Tsing Hua students who speak good English and know their Western ideas; they study regularly, have discussion and self-criticism groups, live all out of the same pot, and are more like one of the religious communities of a century ago than anything else I can think of. Bedbugs may drop off the mat roof and rain fill the beds in the Chou En-lai garret, but the religious enthusiasms and ideas go right on as though they would even be able to wake up this country. We all wish them well, even though our knowledge of the North Country is vaguer than ever.

Just what goes on in Yenan, what they are able to maintain there, is lost in fog. No really sound efforts are being made to find out, as by putting a consul in Yenan by forcing it down CKS's throat. This is a serious failure in American policy, since Yenan is a major observation post. We could get Jap publications from there, for instance. As time goes on and we get more and more fully set up in this country by air and outposts, I hope some modern imperialist will come along and really meddle in Chinese affairs, instead of taking a ringside seat for the catastrophe. We should have consuls and observers in the North, a plane service, and airbases, and make Chungking like it. It would save us a lot of trouble, and would not hurt China.

Kung P'eng and Ch'iao Mu were married quietly in November. Shortly after, their meager wardrobe was stolen by a thief who inserted a pole with a hook on it through a window grating. Since we were of similar height and I was trying to pack lightly for air travel home, I gave Ch'iao a 1936 Oxford-tailored blue serge suit and prevailed upon him to accept it as a token of friendship. He replied, "Material things are to be used by human beings. It's the people who use them that matter. . . . I believe the ideas in my articles are shared and appreciated by you. We are pursuing similar ideas and are fighting on the same front, aren't we?"

In this atmosphere Kung P'eng became a symbol of freedom of speech, indeed a glamour girl admired by most of the young Americans in the embassy and Press Hostel.

> Our Communist pal, Kung P'eng, got dysentery, so I told Brooks Atkinson, who got her to the Navy doctor (a secret), and she is OK, only bacillary which sulfaguanadine kills quick. Met her on the street as I was taking mss. back to the Chou En-lai firetrap and being incipiently on the receiving end of a purge she offered to pass without recognition, in case I didn't want to be seen in public with the party—gave me rather a start. She and her pals live and work in momentary expectation, because it has been done before here and elsewhere.

To Wilma I described Kung P'eng as

> the official appointee for contact with barbarians and I discover she has a taming effect on everybody I know. Brooks Atkinson feels the same enthusiasm, to say nothing of J. Alsop outrageously, Eric Sevareid brilliantly, Phil Sprouse secretly, part of the British embassy, and I don't know who else. The point is in large part that she has your quality of being communicative.

As Kung P'eng freely admitted, however, "I am very superficial. I do not think very deeply. I like to touch many things, but I do not know one thing. I do not read much. There is the danger to be a most superficial propagandist, talking nothing but the slogans of the time" —a shrewd self-appraisal.

The other young woman from whom I learned something about the springs of revolution did not have Kung P'eng's glamour or play a public role as a Communist but she probed the Chinese dilemma more trenchantly and in broader philosophical terms.

Yang Kang when I met her in mid-1943 was thirty-eight and the literary editor of the influential *Ta Kung Pao*—much like being editor of the *Times Literary Supplement*. She had grown up, she said, in an atmosphere of marital discord that tended to make her a feminist. She was born in Kiangsi in 1905, named Yang Ping. Her father, a native of Hupei, had an official career as chief secretary to the governor and then as commissioner of finance in Hupei-Hunan, and even acting governor of Hupei for a time in the warlord era before the Nationalist revolution of 1927. "He was a collector of books, scrolls, porcelain, etc." Revolutionary peasants burned his house and books and divided up his land. He was jailed and after release died in Szechwan in 1939.

Yang Ping's mother was the youngest daughter of a big landlord, illiterate but clever and stubborn. She had eleven children but her marriage was unhappy because her husband took a concubine. She took refuge in Buddhism and died in 1921. What a catalogue of the old social evils!

Yang Ping studied the classical curriculum at home with a tutor until age seventeen in 1922 and then went to the Baldwin Middle School at Nanchang in Kiangsi until 1927. The next year she entered Yenching and graduated in 1933. In this period she developed a very close and filial relationship with Professor Grace Boynton of the Yenching University English Department, a truly humane and compassionate teacher, who had a deep influence on her young Chinese students and played an important part in Yang Kang's life and the growth of her literary interests. She began to support herself by translating English books into Chinese for the YMCA, including Jane Austen's *Pride and Prejudice* and Reinhold Niebuhr's *Moral Man and Immoral Society.* She also edited the literary section of the monthly magazine *People's Knowledge,* published by the early ethnographer Professor Ku Chieh-kang of Yenching.

She had married in Peking in 1933 and had a daughter. Yang's husband was a banker, and when the Japanese invasion began in 1937, she decided after four years in Peking to go to Shanghai; he stayed in Peking. She was on the staff of the *Ta Kung Pao* in Shanghai in 1937–39 and moved with it to Hong Kong, where she fell in love with another man, got a divorce from her Peking husband, and married him. In this period in 1940 she lectured on literature at Lingnan University. When the Hong Kong *Ta Kung Pao* moved out to Kweilin in 1941, however, she stayed with it and

> refused to sacrifice her career to domesticity, which is a laborious drudgery; so they are now separated. Her daughter in Hong Kong was reported disappeared or sold as a slave girl but is now reported safe again.

Slight of build and comely rather than beautiful, Yang Kang was fluent in English, highly intelligent, and thoroughly devoted to her literary work. She solicited or accepted prose and poetry for her literary page and wrote poetry herself as well as publishing short stories, many articles, and especially booklets of reportage. For example, her collection of first-hand accounts of the Chekiang devastation after the Japanese campaign there in 1942 was esteemed by the American military attaché as the best account he could find. She was a leftist but not openly Communist, in fact an "outside cadre" urged by the CCP to pursue her career in the outer world, keeping clear of CCP connections. But her allegiance was evident in her change of name about the time she left Yenching—Kang was the character for "steel" (shades of Stalin himself!).

We found agreement first in a critique of H. G. Wells's "The Chinese Outlook" and of Lin Yutang's *My Country and My People*. As she wrote me in August, "I think the Chinese persistence in life can explain something. . . . We seldom commit suicide. . . . We seldom go intentionally lazy. . . . We don't change readily and wholesale. We adapt but don't absorb wholeheartedly. . . . We are more 'realist' than metaphysical. . . . All these can be traced to the economic background.

"For me, if these points are true with us, they should be changed . . . cowardice, paralysis, meanness, lack of daring thinking, earthly practicality rather than imaginative realism, readiness to compromise, slavish obedience to arrogant autocracy, all these must be removed before the Chinese people can be real human beings. This is what I mean by reviving ourselves. And the first step is to break all shackles."

This had been the vision of the May Fourth Movement of the era about 1920. One could hear the voices of influential thinkers like Ch'en Tu-hsiu and Lu Hsun. Yang Kang had absorbed the ethos of China's modern revolution in culture and values all the more readily and completely because she had grown up in warlord China and seen the evils of the old society from the inside. She was in fact a very serious and devoted observer of China's old society and the struggle to remake it. As we continued to meet and talk or exchange letters, she could give me an analysis from the inside of the complex role of intellectuals, their customary dependence on authority, their function as moral critics, their current struggle for survival as personalities, their need for an ideal of service to humanity. For me this kind of discussion was a godsend. Finding such a friend was a lucky circumstance.

My closest Foreign Service friend was Philip D. Sprouse, a southerner with a spotless record for protocol, prudence, and wisdom, a very proper bachelor with a strong streak of benevolence. When I arranged for Yang Kang to apply for a Radcliffe fellowship, Phil wrote in support, Miss Boynton did the same, and in 1944 she was awarded a grant and came to America. Her getting a passport was the work mainly of her publisher, Hu Lin, a stalwart of the Political Science clique.

In conversation and correspondence I found these two women intellectuals' Marxism was marginal. They were graduates of Yenching and knew as much about English literature as about historical materialism. They were concerned for creative expression as much as for material uplift. They were Leninists in their faith in the party and their acceptance of its discipline. But this faith was essentially practical, in that individuals acting alone could do little; in unity lay their strength. No supra-rational miracles, no dogmas of virgin birth, divinity of the savior, or resurrection were necessary. As home missionaries they seemed to me well prepared to gain converts.

Once regarded as friendly, I found myself cultivated by the left, which I on my part enjoyed cultivating in response. This was as much a personal as a political activity. Ch'iao Mu brought around the playwright Hsia Yen. At Mme. Sun Yat-sen's (Soong Ch'ing-ling's), I met her German assistant Anna von Kleist Wang (wife of the later PRC ambassador Wang Ping-nan).

> Mme. Sun was very frank, expressed very great interest in a recent ruling Chinese without passports cannot go on Army planes. She is not allowed to leave Chungking even for a change of air in China, much less go abroad. She said, What would the secret police think if they saw me coming to see her, but I said I knew people even worse than she was. (A man was squatting watching as I came out.) . . . These people like Mme. Sun are so pathetically grateful (unexpressed) and encouraging to people who rather naïvely and late in the day turn up with a desire to help.

(After the war she reportedly returned to Shanghai in the plane of the American Air Force commander, General Randall.)

When John Davies and Eric Sevareid arrived, fresh from their enforced parachute drop among the Naga tribes of North Burma and their long hike back to Assam, we demonstrated our frustration with Chungking by staging a dinner party. Phil Sprouse and Jim Penfield of the embassy, Eric Sevareid of CBS and I took Kung P'eng and Ch'iao Mu to the Kuan Sheng Yuan restaurant and had a lively and ostentatious banquet as publicly as possible.

> Alas, no public was there but enough secret police to get the point, take the car number, etc. Kung and Ch'iao are a handsome couple but very full of religiosity and set for martyr-dom. Lately they have been shadowed everywhere, and when they talk to someone the police turn up and intimidate the someone. Reminds me a bit of Agnes Smedley in Shanghai, getting a neurosis from the police trailing. The difference is that these people might really disappear—hence our demon-stration.

This was symptomatic of the growing American annoyance at China's domestic politics. None of us was concerned to support com-munism. We wanted a normal acceptance of political opposition instead of a party dictatorship.

This was part of a tidal movement that soon split American policy. But it was a side current of the major Chinese phenomenon, the passing of the mandate of Heaven. In essence the CCP did not sub-vert us all and steal the mandate. On the contrary CKS had to lose the mandate first. Nineteen forty-three was the year when he visibly began to do so.

Another site for political demonstration was the Soviet embassy at its November open house.

> The Russian embassy is an enormous ducal mansion on top of the highest hill, where the north and south roads running downtown from this region split and go by on the two sides of it; the mansion looks out over the CNAC landing strip in the river and is most imposing, after one climbs up to it. On the Russian anniversary recently a gang of us from the embassy went and rubbed our way about through the jam. Kiev had

just fallen [been retaken by the Soviet Army] most appropriately, but the press attaché USSR solemnly assured me it was not specially planned that way. There was not the traditional caviar, but a lot of local wine and cake, and an enormous crowd of maybe a thousand people all told, in the half-dozen big bare rooms on the ground floor, most of them wan-looking leftists (leftists are usually starved for being leftists and go further left the more they starve). These people all greeted one another with excitement and greeted us also, since we all felt that, being in the USSR embassy, we could act a little more leftish than on the streets among the gumshoes of Chungking.

An occasion like this, far from being a social affair, is a truly political affair and everyone present was a political animal. Chou En-lai's secretary, Ch'en Chia-k'ang, that fascinating excited little man with a quick ferretlike mind, greeted me with unusual clamor because Holly Tong happened to be passing just at that moment. Dr. Sun Fo reached across the table to shake hands and made a long speech about sending me something the next day, which never arrived, because I happened at the time to be talking to Wang Shih-chieh [another KMT minister]. General Ho Ying-chin did likewise.

As my departure drew near I found my daily routine tilted toward dissidence. I borrowed the title of Mrs. Roosevelt's column to record

My Day, Sunday, October 25, 1943. Arose and fought off the cook's demand for another $5,000 for the mess (meals are running about CNC $95 apiece now), and slid through the mud up the street to see our Communist girl friend (Kung P'eng), who soon produced a pamphlet in which the CP does a royal job of cursing out the KMT, printed excellently on beautiful white paper—how in the devil they produce such things is a mystery. Having given me several copies of this tract, half translated by herself, this very admirable missionary then explained that the Kuomintang secret service, considering that she distributes too much to foreigners, are planning to kidnap her sometime, and she cannot leave the citadel so frequently. I assured her that her clientele would easily create a convoy system.

Last week, for example, her older sister [Kung P'u-sheng,

B.A. Yenching, 1936; M.A. Columbia, in religion, 1942, who had worked with Mrs. Roosevelt] arrived in Kunming with a box of drugs and clothes and wanted to deliver them without becoming marked as Communist, so she gave them to the correspondent of the *New York Times* (Brooks Atkinson), who happened to be in Kunming, who gave this large bundle to the naval doctor of the U.S. Embassy, who brought them to Chungking by Army plane and gave them to the correspondent of *Time, Life,* and *Fortune* (Theodore H. White), who sent them to the American Publications Service, where the recipient picked them up—all a strictly legal proceeding in every respect.

Since one of General Stilwell's aides was coming to take her out to lunch, I left the young lady's rat-infested fortress and came back through the mud, noting that a callow uniformed agent slipped out of the watching teahouse ahead of me and loitered down the alleyway, waiting for me to pass. I therefore loitered in a most loiterous and supercilious manner behind him, until he finally stopped entirely, I stopped, and he turned around and went back to look for another customer.

I then went to see one of the leading members of Academia Sinica, who inveighed in no uncertain tones against the Ministry of Education and its policies, and expressed the hope that I was not too thoroughly disillusioned.

I returned in time for dinner with Jack Service and the Wang Ping-nans, who went deeply into the minor-party situation until after ten, so I sent them home in the car. The Kansu gas having eaten holes in the gas pump metal, we have put in a new one (second-hand) for CNC $4,500.

The themes of this life appear to be prices and revolution. With PDS [Philip D. Sprouse] I entertained the CP member of PPC [People's Political Council], old Mr. Tung Pi-wu, who talks an incomprehensible dialect, and Ch'en Chia-k'ang, Chou's secretary, who has an idea a minute. To atone for this I saw the War Zone Party Affairs bureau of the Ministry of KMT Organization next morning. By having the chief Jap expert of CKS headquarters to dinner Wednesday, I figure I can see the CP Thursday, a sort of rough justice, so as not to get biased.

I had bad luck in not coinciding in China more often with Jack Service. We barely overlapped in Peking in 1935 and he was in Chungking before I arrived in 1942 but absent till late 1943. I found him always to be the political officer most in touch with the Chinese people. Although I was not privy to his prescient reporting for Gauss and Stilwell, my impressions ran parallel.

I had experienced more of China in 1942–43 than had many other China specialists, and I was quick to record and distribute what I had to offer. But my experiential base was nevertheless extremely narrow. I had had no personal, man-to-man contact with the common people. I had not even talked much to students. My formal acquaintance was among officials and administrators and necessarily superficial. Aside from my own observations, my personal experience with friends gave me vicariously my basic evaluations, and my friends were of two kinds: Westernized, genuinely liberal professors met first in Peking in the early 1930s and now seen again as old friends indeed; and a few younger friends newly found on the left, products of Western education in China who however had embraced the Communist cause. As 1943 wore on I began to realize that the older liberals were stuck in a social role that made them helpers, not holders, of power. They could not themselves lead the way. The younger leftists, on the other hand, were as yet equally impotent; but they had hope, resourcefulness, and perhaps a future chance would come to them. Both these groups of friends I regarded as moral heroes locked in a mortal struggle with the people in power.

Curiously, the common people were not principal parties to this struggle. Farmers in Szechwan, for instance, were generally well off while those in Honan were starving, but the political struggle within my narrow view did not involve them but was rather within the ruling stratum. There, the issue was CKS's leadership in the face of terrible difficulties, like the inflation, for which he seemed to have no solution. Keeping the U.S. dollar exchange rate at 20 to 1, when the black-market rate was more like 400 to 1, alienated Americans who were eager to help China; it also held down their influence. Things that the KMT could have done were demonstrated, we discovered, in the CCP area—literacy campaigns, small industrial-production cooperatives, village mobilization, women's emancipation, and so on, but all in a context of revolution. Instead, CKS trusted his organizers, the CC clique and Tai Li, and they sought to build up consent by suppressing dissent, which didn't work out as they hoped. Manipulation and intimidation eroded the government's legitimacy in the eyes of upper-class patriots. Official corruption did not win the loyalty of corrupt opportunists. It was a tragic process, out of control inside China, beyond control from outside.

The anti-foreignism that accompanied it stemmed from the humiliation felt by oversensitive patriots. Foreign aid, like my year-long efforts to help the Lienta professors, could be best understood as a form of intervention, a new aspect of the imperialistic aggression that had increasingly pushed China around. To receive aid and not be able to reciprocate was a blow to one's (Confucian) sense of self-respect. One needed a new, supra-personal and supra-Confucian attitude, above considerations of face and reciprocity.

> *What they think of us:* This is from a good observer, the literary editor of the *Ta Kung Pao* (never quote anyone), who says the little people on the street in China regard foreigners as unspeakably favored and incredibly accoutered with material goods, so that their feeling is one of jealousy, which easily turns into anger at the discrepancy which has occurred in theirs and our fortunes. Similar feelings are felt toward Chinese plutocrats, but they are better understood, as persons. This reaction I can understand, since it is what mine might be. Since it will be called for forever, inasmuch as material standards in China can never catch up with American, we can expect trouble.

As I packed for home I again tried to sum things up and again sent it to Alger Hiss. I had got no feedback from him, but with Currie devoting less attention to China and Hornbeck too exalted and protocol-minded for me to address directly, Alger as Hornbeck's assistant seemed my best point of contact in Washington. I also sent a copy to Wilma.

Chungking, Nov. 9, '43

Dear Alger,

It is so long since I last wrote you that it is now difficult to do so without attempting broad and perhaps pointless generalizations. During the year that I have been here, I have gradually understood more of the situation, I believe, and at the same time the situation has got worse, so that my fullest understanding, such as it is, coincides with the worst situation.

At present I see little possibility of the country avoiding serious internal political disturbance after the war; this is because the regime now in power has got itself into a situation which can be described as "proto-fascist," in the sense that a small political group hold tenaciously to power in the government with hopes of using industrialization as a tool of perpetuating their power and with ideas which are socially conservative and backward-looking rather than aiming to keep up with the times. For example, it is plain that industrialization will further upset agriculture, which is the body of the country, but I have found no political leaders who have any kind of program for the land except to let the present system drift along.

Again, it is plain that the development of communications in the process of industrializing will bring the mass of peasants closer into touch with the new western-type society, but the politicians in power are too busy to start a program of mass education and frankly do not believe in it—they distrust the people as all the thinly scattered groups which have ever governed this vast mass have done in the past. In short, the day is around the corner when the Chinese masses will be directly and vigorously stimulated by the impact of modern industrial life, but the present leaders of the country, i.e., the politicians in power, cannot understand this and see only the power-side of industrialization, not the social-side. They do not have a social program. The formula of western science and ancient Chinese virtues will never meet the situation.

Having no ideas, their only alternative will be to hold the situation together by force, which they are now preparing to do. Secret police and censorship is now the system, in a widespread and vigorous form, and when American arms and military power have been sufficiently assimilated, they may well be used also. The authoritarian organizers can use an increasingly xenophobic nationalism as one means also; it is increasingly difficult to have contact with minor government employees in a friendly way and I am inclined to believe the stories of orders from the Generalissimo advising against too great contact with foreigners. At present the political outs have everything to gain from foreign contact, and I believe the left-wing opposition in particular finds a good deal in common with Americans, as most Americans are inclined to do with them.

This left-wing opposition includes both the Chinese communists who take a public stand, for which the government is now trying to intimidate them, and a large fringe of intellectuals who do not acknowledge communism but agree in criticism of the censorship and secret police system. During the past year, in fact, there has been going on that "desertion of the intellectuals" which some historians see preceding every great revolution, and I can testify that many liberals who formerly were strongly anti-red and pro-American are now making the same comments as the communists and, also, most of the Americans. I do not believe the more objective communists think their movement can do much in the near future, nor arouse the Chinese peasantry with the dogma of Marxism, but they have importance far beyond their numbers or power because they are the only organized minority and protestant group, and toward foreigners they depict themselves as reforming idealists. Consequently the government, in so far as it is actually becoming more authoritarian and despotic, is no doubt well advised to try to keep foreigners away from itself. Unfortunately it is not efficient or strong enough to keep foreigners away from the opposition, and the result of its xenophobic policy is to drive us all into the arms of the critics.

Many of the Kuomintang personnel I believe feel hurt at the critical attitude of their American friends; they are caught up in a movement, as were many Germans and Japs, and the movement carries them along into positions they had not foreseen or desired. This, however, is nothing that worries me, because I have gradually formed a rather low opinion of the average Chinese character in politics, and I consider it lucky that these politicians are amoral opportunists rather than fanatics. At present the country does not have the moral fibre even for fascism, because the people have too long been clutching at every straw to keep themselves alive and still feel they cannot let any straws escape their grasp. Moral fibre here goes into patience and stubbornness rather than what we would call courage, so that no situation is ever quite as bad as it would be with us, and also no situation can ever be as good.

I am more than ever convinced of the necessity of trying to help the good people, whenever we can find them out, and letting the bad people at least not fatten off us.

From what I have said you will understand why I do not look forward to talking to people in Washington, since I have seen something of the Kuomintang effort to keep all critical Chinese out of the United States and to have all Chinese who are allowed to go put up a patriotic front of pseudo-democratic propaganda. Between the anathema of the materially-civilized American soldier and the calculated front put up by the official representatives of China, we are going to have a tough time explaining this mess to the American public, and I look forward to losing my status as a "loyal friend of China" as soon as my friends begin to repeat my utterly confidential remarks.

The problem here is essentially one of ideas and ideals, even more than of economics or mechanics. If the government or the top class could adopt a genuine ideal, they could make great changes through leading the people, but these changes would not strengthen their personal position—the result is that we must wait for the Great Chinese Revolution which may some day eventuate. How will this sound on 17th Street?

I wish you were coming out here. As I may have remarked, the failure of persons in responsible positions to keep in touch with the field through personal experience in the field is, I believe, most unhealthy intellectually and represents a considerable danger to the success of American policy. In fact, it is to me really incredible that it could happen. I think the American establishment here does a superb job, considering its resources and the confusion of wartime agencies dumped in the lap of the Embassy, and I do not see how Washington can keep up its end without looking at China as well as reading about it.

Yours ever,
jkf

I left Chungking with General Donovan on December 8, 1943, long overdue for transfer, but it was not easy to get out of the arena of Chinese politics. Since wartime travelers commonly carried personal mail, Chou En-lai's secretary Ch'en Chia-k'ang turned up and ostentatiously handed me a letter to post in India. Meantime Mme. Sun sent me a letter to take to Mrs. E. C. Carter in New York. This friend-pidgin circumvented Chinese censorship and was no doubt noted by the Tai Li agent, whoever he was, among my office servants. The fact was that Donovan had broken off the OSS connection with Miles and Tai Li, though they came amicably enough to see us off at the airstrip. But, once gone, I was rumored to have been yanked and sent home for too great intimacy with the left. When the story reached me in Washington in April, 1944, I countered it by getting a letter to the contrary from Bill Langer as director of the Research and Analysis branch: "This idea is so preposterous that everything possible should be done to squelch it . . . you did an admirable job in China and got much further with the work there than anyone could have reasonably expected. . . . I know of no instance when you exceeded your instructions . . . you were recalled to Washington solely because you had already been in China longer than seemed desirable" etc.

This, however, cannot have been Tai Li's view. He had his own record of my guilt by association.

In retrospect I can see that my interest in the Chinese left followed the pro-underdog liberal orientation that family connections had given me. Through her brother-in-law, Gilbert E. Roe, my mother quite early became a devoted friend of the La Follette family. In our political pantheon Senator La Follette and Belle Case La Follette were sacred figures. They fought for the rights and welfare of the common people against the vested interests of big business. This populism, anti-establishment and pro–civil liberties, fed into the progressive movement to which my aunt and uncle, the Roes, in New York were deeply committed. They admired Emma Goldman. Lincoln Steffens was a close friend.

I had seen Steffens at Harvard in 1928 at the Liberal Club, which occupied an old house on Winthrop Street where the Lutheran church now stands. Lincoln Kirstein had painted murals of industrial machinery in the main room. In 1928 I represented the Liberal Club in a debate at Tremont Temple with a team from Tuskegee Institute on the subject of racial miscegenation. The chief black speaker, Richard Hirst Hill, became a good friend. A decade later Dick Hill stayed with us in our Winthrop Street house. He was fighting to expose the incidence of black lung disease in southern plants. Had he lived, he would have been a leader in the rights movement.

With this kind of background I was prepared to consort with rebels against the established order, although I had no faith in any doctrine except the supremacy of law and individual rights. I felt reform was needed on all sides but not an all-embracing ideology. Yet in China I could see clearly how reform was stultified and this left rebellion as the only way out. The CCP as the living embodiment of the cause became the parental figure in the life of the believer.

The primary conviction that I took back to Washington in 1944 was that the revolutionary movement in China was inherent in the conditions of life there and that it could not be suppressed by the provocative coercion of the CC clique and Tai Li police. The ideals of liberation for the peasantry and of science and democracy inherited from the May Fourth era twenty years before were patriotic and kinetic. CKS had nothing adequate to oppose them.

This sense of conviction to some degree partook of faith in the manner of a true believer except that I was not organized or tied in in any way and was not primarily concerned about the revolution in my own life and work. It was all vicarious. I was a kibitzer at the revolution. But I felt I knew which way the wind was blowing.

22

WITH THE OFFICE OF WAR
INFORMATION IN WASHINGTON

AT THE END of 1943 I returned from "the field" (meaning the place
of struggle or practical work) to Washington, the administrative metropolis where all field interests came together in competition for
central attention. I could sympathize with a congressman rushing
back to the capital from a constituency ravaged by flood, tornado, or
other disaster of man or nature. How could the urgent needs I had
seen in the field be put forward in Washington's pandemonium? I
found myself obliged to shift gears from the very interpersonal life
of Chungking back to the impersonality of the Washington bureaucracy. However, my knowledge of China's politics was no longer abstract. It was attached to concrete persons and situations. This helped
me raise questions about American policy.

Coming out of wartime China required a transition, which began
in Kunming. Reentry into the PX culture of the U.S. Army was like
our later experience in 1972, going from the austerity of Mao's China
into the material opulence of upper-class Hong Kong—one was trans-
ported suddenly from monastery to fleshpots. Life lost a certain vir-
ginal simplicity. In China material poverty made the spirit and moral
qualities of friends stand out more starkly. In contrast American GIs
fed their spirits on a diet of abstract sex—pictures, stories, movies—
while the *Time, Life,* and *Newsweek* newsmags gave them a view of
world happenings abstracted from feeling. They gave me a sense of

sexual nonsatisfaction and of mental clutter about world events. I learned about so many things going on in the world but couldn't remember any of it. Taken in through the eyes only, it was not experienced.

Travel was also a spectator sport. I crossed the Hump westward in the plexiglass nose of a B-26 bomber, suspended in bright moonlight over the eastern end of the Himalayas.

> Being all plastic, on steel ribs, a bomber's nose puts one really forward into space. Straight down below the full moon crossing a little lake or a paddy field seems to be rushing violently through the earth just under the thin surface, like an underground headlight, appearing in the brief interstices between tunnels. The moon above is stable like oneself in the chill thin air, the moon below is plowing furiously through the land surface. But about this time I felt dizzy and crawled up through the trapdoor into the flight deck, where I got hold of my oxygen mask just in time.

On a number 3 priority it took me three weeks to cross the Mid-East and Africa. Wilma met me at Miami and we took a couple of days off to reidentify ourselves.

Back in Washington I enjoyed six weeks' popularity as the latest witness from the field. Many in the ten or a dozen groups I talked to had read some of my letters and memoranda. I mainly answered questions, trying to give these colleagues a vicarious feeling of Chinese reality. Not easy. But the distrust of CKS's regime was already widespread. I was only confirming with new examples the themes that had already begun to form a consensus among American China specialists. This was not offset by the persuasive presence and speeches of T. F. Tsiang and Wang Shih-chieh, who visited Washington and New York in early 1944 to rebuild confidence in the KMT government.

Amid all the proliferation in Washington during my seventeen-month absence, that of Fred Kilgour's Interdepartmental Committee for the Acquisition of Foreign Publications seemed the greatest. He had taken over a theater, the old Washington Auditorium, and had a staff of a hundred handling materials in some fifty languages coming in from nine outposts abroad. Fred still looked quite young, very trim in a naval ensign's uniform, but his administrative talent kept him a bit aloof; IDC flourished because he always kept his authority clear and intact.

For two months, following up on projects, I used Lauchlin Currie's office as a base, but he was now active in the Board of Economic Warfare and no longer doing much on China. I investigated what I should do next. Neither IDC nor OSS had a job waiting for me, and the various offers I received seemed woefully confining. I was interested in ideas more than operations. As I wrote Mac Fisher, head of OWI, Chungking, I concluded that "OWI is doing more good work than any other American agency except, perhaps, the 14th Airforce; the Washington Office is the livest place in the city." It inhabited a stone-and-glass behemoth, the Social Security building, where the Far Eastern section had four rooms, "air-sound-and-light conditioned."

OWI had been put under Elmer Davis, whose Hoosier twang on the nightly CBS radio had become a warranty of truth as seen by an incorruptible individual. The shock to this individualist of suddenly heading a worldwide staff of many thousands had been mediated by his alter ego–business manager Ed Klauber, whose close assistance allowed Elmer Davis to carry on his calling as a first-rate newsman free of busywork and politicking over contracts. Ed Klauber's guardian role was enhanced by his looking like an experienced mafioso, heavy-set and hard-bitten, not a man to cross. When Wilma and I dined with him and his comely young bride on D-day 1944 he explained that his thirty-five years or so seniority to her, as a business proposition, would leave her free and well off soon enough. They were both charming and their union of youth and age seemed quite harmonious.

Under Elmer Davis as director of OWI was a deputy director, Ed Barrett, who was on leave from being editor of *Newsweek,* and his deputy, T. L. Barnard, on leave from the J. Walter Thompson advertising firm. Assisting them as a sort of Holy Ghost was Jim Linen of *Life.* This trio had both the editorial skills and the business connections to represent the private news-media conglomerates in their eternal vigilance against any growth of government control over the news. They were three young and vigorous watchdogs on the home front all the time they fought the totalitarians abroad. Thus OWI's domestic news output to the American public was kept carefully restricted.

As assistant deputy directors there were three area representatives: for the enemy area in Europe, Wallace Carroll of the New York *Herald Tribune;* for the British commonwealth, Ferdinand Kuhn. Both had been top-notch correspondents, Ferdie as the *New York Times* bureau chief in London during the onset of Hitler and the Battle of Britain. For the Far East the assistant deputy director was an academic, George E. Taylor, who invited me to head his China section.

George had come from England (M.A. Birmingham, 1928) on a Commonwealth fellowship to Johns Hopkins and had gone thence to Harvard, where he secured a Harvard-Yenching fellowship to Yenching. We had met in Peking, where he had written a pathbreaking article on the "Social and Economic Background of the Taiping Rebellion" and then spent some years teaching at CKS's Central Political Institute in Nanking.

George was a natural leader, imaginative in starting new projects, solicitous for his staff, a capable manipulator who could keep on good terms with the front office and keep peace among prima donnas in his own group. I jumped at the chance to work with him as his number two. When he was away I occasionally got a whiff of power by signing myself as Acting Assistant Deputy Director, OWI, certainly the bottommost appendage of the topmost management. I knew George was out of touch with wartime developments in Free China, and that he also needed help to follow up on administrative details. During 1944 and the first half of 1945 in Washington I think we made a good team. What we actually achieved is of course another matter.

One of George Taylor's leading ideas was that the social-science disciplines must be applied to China and take account of the Chinese case. In fighting Japan he felt it imperative to get social anthropologists and psychologists to understand and explain Japanese motivations. He enlisted Clyde and Florence Kluckhohn and Alexander Leighton in this enterprise. They encouraged an early classic tour de force in this line, *The Chrysanthemum and the Sword* (1946) by Ruth Benedict.

In the China section with me were Derk Bodde, on leave from the University of Pennsylvania, and Randolph Sailer, who had returned from many years of teaching psychology at Yenching. We added up to a good deal of competence, but how could we apply it to winning the war or anything else in far-off China? Every day we had a flow of pink copies of cables from various quarters, often quoting some publication but classified confidential, presumably because our seeing it should be kept under wraps. We were a think tank with the task of guiding OWI's output. But we professors in Washington, telling the professional word producers in New York, San Francisco, London, and other world centers how to slant their statements, were small voices in a noisy world. We could compose guidances, scrutinize scripts, pass upon the themes and subject matter proposed by others. But we never really controlled what happened in America's war of words. Too many other able people were involved.

I took on the job of representing Area Three at the weekly OWI Review Board meeting that hammered out, or more often squeezed out, the central directive. Like a weekly newsmagazine's editorial meeting, this was an occasion for surveying the state of the war and enunciating news and propaganda lines to be followed by the Voice of America and our other media. The Far Eastern contribution dealt mainly with what to say to Japan, and when I arrived to sit around the long table, this section was usually supplied in no uncertain terms by Captain Phillips, USN, who came with an aide to represent the Office of Naval Intelligence. After all, ONI had been geared to fight Japan for a generation. What had it to learn from fly-by-night professors? When I quickly took issue with the captain on some point I can't recall and loudly established my case, he was amazed. My OWI colleagues seemed delighted and thereafter we had more of a dialogue.

But as soon as I visited San Francisco (SX), where the Voice of America (VOA) for the Far East had its staff and operation, I found Washington's central directive, including ONI's commands, carried little weight. SX was locked in battle with Tokyo radio. The listeners to our transpacific broadcasts were mainly the enemy radio people, who almost alone had receivers to listen with. Unlike the radio war that Wally Carroll masterminded for our European front, our Far Eastern audience was quite limited by the lack of receivers among the public. The verbal struggle was carried on between the broadcasting stations' staffs. Yet each country desk, for Burma, Thailand, Indo-China, the Netherlands East Indies, etc. manfully kept turning out its daily hours of broadcast directed at its homeland.

The other OWI subempire, equally out of control, was Overseas

News and Features on Fifty-seventh Street in New York. ONAF was a monster with a distinct ethos. The European country desks vibrated like microcosms, reflecting the rivalries of refugee intellectuals who were determined to make their own truth prevail. Even if they read Washington's central directive, which we often wondered about, it still had to be conveyed in the native tongue of each country by first a translator and second an announcer. Influencing this process from another city was like shouting at an airplane propeller. Not much got across, and what did was often disregarded. George had previously lacked the manpower to deal with ONAF but I found the news people interesting. For a time I went to New York every other week and harangued the ONAF staff to elucidate the capital city's Far Eastern wisdom. They were polite in a sardonic New Yorker way, but I felt they seldom bought much of my verbiage.

The central directive mainly helped Wally Carroll in his phone discussions with New York desks from day to day. It also gave themes to our columnist ghostwriter Irwin Wexler, who turned out scripts to be broadcast as from Admiral Yarnell, Raymond Gram Swing, or others of our stable of names.

ONAF was a humming hive, which spewed out news and commentary, feature stories, news photos (newly transmissible by radiophoto, television's predecessor), photo exhibits, and other things. The main content of all this was the Projection of America. This produced the slick photos of well-fed, well-dressed school tots to whom refugees in Europe's rubble found it difficult to relate themselves. It was of course very natural to celebrate the American virtues, especially when transplanted Poles and Bulgars were beaming it all back to their former countrymen. But when these products were aimed at Asia, across a wider cultural gap, they often seemed uncomprehending and even aggressive.

In July 1944, as I outlined the state of OWI operations to Elmer Davis and Ed Barrett, we were active in the Central Pacific (Nimitz), the Southwest Pacific (MacArthur), and the China-Burma-India theaters (Stilwell). In Washington we maintained contact with State, War, Navy, and OSS. Within the Washington office we produced *directives* for SX and New York and *plans* for work in various countries; we also handled *personnel,* and pursued *stockpiling* of printed matter and films for future needs.

In July I also inaugurated a circular letter ("Washington Weekly

Intelligencer") to our outposts in Honolulu, Brisbane, New Delhi, and Chungking in order to give them a common budget of central office news. For the psychological-warfare teams producing leaflets for air drop over enemy territory, I also started a weekly "coordinator" telegram. But these efforts to keep things in an overview were hardly more than a housemaid's tidying up. I doubt they had much effect.

In developing our weekly contribution to the OWI central directive, we met on Friday with the British and then with our own drafting officers; at 11 A.M. Monday with our regional specialists; and at 3 P.M. with the Review Board, where the whole document was put together. The effort was to set a tone of confidence on our side while sowing doubt and discord among the enemy. We could not really do more than events were doing for us, but it seemed smart, when we knew the enemy was about to lose Karkhov, say, to "commit them to hold Karkhov" so as to magnify the loss when it came.

Meanwhile in China, American contact with Yenan had been opened up by a group of journalists in the spring of 1944. The journalists found eager readers among the American public, some of whom began to attach to Yenan the rosy glow that had formerly accrued to Chungking. After the Dixie Mission settled in the rebel capital in July 1944, we began to get the meticulous and eye-opening reports of Jack Service and John Davies on Mao and the CCP there.

For OWI's problem of inducing Japanese surrenders, Mac Fisher found in Yenan the extraordinary group of almost two hundred Japanese deserters who had been won over by the Japanese Communist Nozaka Sanzō. We knew the only Japanese prisoners taken by American forces had usually been unconscious at the time. No Japanese would consciously surrender to us. Mac sent back a valuable series of reports on the CCP's POW program. Kaji Wataru, the elfin little Japanese who worked for the Nationalist military and helped the OWI leaflet operation under Jim Stewart, had nowhere the same forcefulness and leadership capacity as Nozaka.

Our policy debate over how to treat the Japanese Emperor hinged on the question how far he was an essential prop to militarism. In general the Japan specialists felt he was essential to keep Japanese society in order and secure acceptance of the peace terms. Non-Japan specialists wanted him under some kind of constitutional control, not above it, i.e., no longer divine and sacred.

In early summer 1945 OWI beamed to Japan half a dozen commentaries by Admiral Ellis Zacharias, who had many acquaintances in Japanese Navy circles. They implied that the imperial institution would be respected in a peace settlement, something that could not be said officially under the "unconditional surrender" formula. This was a highly classified operation at the Washington end. Zacharias recorded his texts in Japanese and they were flown to Saipan for broadcasting.

As the Pacific War moved to its finale, OWI began intensive planning for the stockpiling and shipment by sea of newsprint; printing presses; libraries of books on technology, the United States, and the postwar international world; and other equipment for constructive peacetime information work. OWI's stockpiling (and often shipping forward) of materials for use locally, after occupation of various countries, was handled by special teams and bureaus in the different media operating under various directives. The materials included, for example, for China 45 commercial feature films (in four copies) plus 46 commercial shorts and 50 OWI documentaries; picture exhibits; feature materials for the press; musical recordings for radio stations (15,000 discs on order); radio scripts; publications including complete libraries.

When George Taylor went off on a much-needed trip (May–August 1944) to see the CBI theater, leaving me in charge of his job, I was in a good position to innovate, coordinate, and get credit topside, using the staff and setup that he had pulled together. But, instead of becoming a wheel geared into the Washington merry-go-round, I wanted to go back to China.

There the withdrawal of General Stilwell as theater commander in late 1944, just after we had got into contact with the CCP at Yenan, had seemed to put the Americans on the KMT side of China's domestic conflict. Many of those who sensed the growing power of the CCP felt that if we lined up against it we could get into endless trouble. This prudence, however, did not register with the new ambassador, General Patrick J. Hurley, who as a would-be mediator soon was in over his head, bamboozled by CKS.

Wilma departed for Chungking in May 1945 to be an embassy officer in charge of cultural relations. In Chungking she found our Peking friend Professor Knight Biggerstaff handling the Chinese correspondence in the embassy. Knight was big, competent, and quite unafraid of the Foreign Service, a big help to her. She stood up to the mettlesome poobah-ambassador and soon had her sphere and function clearly established as the China end of the RC (now CU) program.*

With Hornbeck and Hamilton gone, FE (the Far Eastern office in State) was under the new management of John Carter Vincent and other Foreign Service officers with long experience in China. Their absorbing problem was how to avoid being sucked into further intervention pro-KMT if the KMT regime continued its collapse, and then how to make the transition to a new relationship with the Chinese revolution if the CCP came to power. FE did not believe U.S. policy could determine the outcome in China. Presumably at American behest, the Nationalist government included in its delegation to the founding of the United Nations in San Francisco in 1945 a CCP representative in the person of the aged, undistinguished-looking, and very quiet Tung Pi-wu. He had been a founding member of the CCP along with Mao and was one of his most loyal and trusted followers. When he came to Washington John Carter arranged one day to see him privately at my mother's house on 33rd Street in Georgetown. (After Wilma's departure for China we gave up our 34th Street house and I stayed with my mother.) This was thoroughly proper, since Tung was a delegate, but it also reflected the Nationalist sensitivity over the least evidence of State Department neutrality in China's domestic struggle.

In May 1945 I had agreement from the front office that I should go to China to assist the director there, who was now William L. Holland, a New Zealander who had recently acquired American citizenship. Bill was known to all Far Eastern specialists as the longtime executive secretary of the Institute of Pacific Relations (IPR), skilled at organizing its big international conferences and calling forth its research publications. This combination of qualities and experience made him an able successor to Mac Fisher, who had been on the job four years in Chungking. Bill Holland invited me to come handle the OWI information program as it expanded in China, leaving the psychological-warfare (leaflet) operation to Jim Stewart. I proposed on July 30 to leave in late August or September. By August

---

*Wilma's official history of the CU program, *America's Cultural Experiment in China, 1942–1949* (Washington, D.C.: Department of State, 1976) hardly mentions herself, least of all her success in setting up the embassy's cultural section.

6 I had agreement to leave September 15. All this was suddenly changed by the peace.

The war ended in a considerable flutter of round-the-clock work. Secretary of State Byrnes's reply to Japan's acceptance of the Potsdam surrender terms (accepted on condition that the imperial prerogatives be retained) was worked out among the allies (who refused to retain the imperial prerogatives). This reply was released at 11:30 A.M. August 11. However, the Japanese government had not made its negotiations known to the Japanese public and might conceivably prolong the war. OWI therefore had the task of getting the facts and our terms before the Japanese people. We did it as follows:

1. The Byrnes text was broadcast from SX at 8:29 A.M. (Washington time) on our cable-wireless news service in Morse code and on short-wave radio in English, with news bulletins in Japanese on short wave from Honolulu and medium wave from Saipan. It was about 4 A.M. in Japan.

2. SX lashed all its voice transmitters together to make a single transmission in Japanese and English on all beams, repeated steadily for fifty-two hours; Saipan ran it on medium wave around the clock.

3. SX Japan section translated Byrnes's statement into Japanese and cleared it with State on the OWI tie line. SX then put it out by cable wireless in romaji (English letters) and sent it to Honolulu, Manila, and Kunming by Army Signal Corps.

4. We then cabled OWI psychological-warfare outposts to make up Japanese leaflets to drop locally and proposed to 20th Air Force at the Pentagon that they prepare B-29s to drop leaflets on Japan. To ensure the correct translation SX read the romaji version to Washington on the tie line. The leaflet heading was cleared with Pentagon and State (Archie MacLeish suggested inserting "every Japanese has a right to know") and then we read it to Honolulu in clear by commercial radiophone.

5. Honolulu used its short-wave transmitter for radiophoto and sent the leaflet text in eight pictures to Saipan, where they were reduced and reassembled to make plates. Three million leaflets were run off on our high-speed Webendorfer presses (don't ask me to identify one),

> the 20th loaded them into bombs and B-29s were dropping them on Tokyo and six other main cities twenty-nine hours

after we started the project in Washington and six hours before the Japanese government received the Byrnes statement through diplomatic channels.*

Lest this seem a mere mechanical achievement by a well-coordinated team of skilled operators, note that in translating "Emperor" into Japanese we used the customary Tenno Heika (Exalted Heavenly Emperor) in the text of the Japanese offer but merely Nihon Kotei (Emperor of Japan) in the text of Byrnes's reply. In this case operations reinforced policy.

From OWI Washington I indeed learned a good deal about news operations but not much about China. This made me particularly eager to get back to Chungking.

---

*Ed Barrett, *Truth Is Our Weapon,* pp. 13–14, gives a slightly different account. Mine is from a summary I made at the time, not published.

23

IN POSTWAR CHINA

MY NINE MONTHS in postwar China from October 1945 to July 1946 was a time of mixed hope and disaster for the Chinese people and also for American China policy. The Nationalist government of CKS and the KMT was already far gone from inflation caused by excessive note issue and from the corruption caused by the inflation. It bungled its takeover of the coastal cities evacuated by the Japanese and yet believed its superior American armament could defeat the CCP in battle. The CCP expanded wherever it could and mobilized for civil war. In this crisis the Americans, having proved incapable of realistic forethought and a rational China policy in the years before the Japanese surrender, improvised the best policy they could and sent General George C. Marshall to mediate between those bitter enemies, the KMT and CCP.

I had the experience in this period of building up an American information program in a gradually worsening situation. Like a house of cards, the more we built it up, the more precarious it became. Our problems began with the disintegration of the American war effort. When peace broke out in mid-August 1945, the two hundred-odd Americans working in China for OWI lined up to depart for home. Many joined in hiring a steamer to take them from Chungking through the Yangtze gorges down to Hankow and Shanghai. Bill Holland, as director in China, saw his wartime operation decay and vanish overnight. He wanted help. The need to expand our informa-

tion offices to the main cities of "liberated" China, i.e., areas reoccupied by the KMT, finally provided the sanction for my leaving
Washington at the end of September.

Unlike my flying to China in 1942, pioneering by air across Africa,
in 1945 I had a tour of war-racked European capitals under the
auspices of ATC, the Air Transport Command. First a Pan Am clip-
per took me from New York to Ireland. It was "a flying boxcar, twice
as big as a Pullman inside, probably the last of its kind," too slow and
feeble to fly the Atlantic in one hop. In London I found it was old
home week. I spent a night with Sir Charles and Nora Webster. After
helping to create the United Nations at the Dumbarton Oaks conference in Washington, Charles at sixty was now a "special assistant for
preparation of conferences in the Foreign Office." Geoffrey Hudson,
my Oxford examiner, took me to lunch at a Whitehall club. I also
stayed with my brother-in-law Arthur Schlesinger, Jr., in a Mayfair
mews he was inhabiting.

The ATC tour then took me to Paris, Marseilles, Rome, Naples,
Athens, and Cairo, with bus rides, GI food, and hotel billets all laid
on. Thence to Abadan, Karachi, Delhi, Calcutta, Kunming and on
October 12 Chungking, where Wilma met me with an OWI car. We
were together again in China but the situation was fluid. Our agencies were trying to move from Chungking downriver, and travel
would keep us apart much of the time.

When I reached Chungking in October 1945 the blow-hard Ambassador Pat Hurley had fortunately departed for Washington. He
had previously gone to Yenan, uttered his Choctaw war whoop, and
fulsomely inaugurated the American mediation to help the KMT and
CCP achieve a coalition government, which both then felt it expedi-
ent to claim they wanted. With the supine Stettinius of U.S. Steel as
Secretary of State, after the death of FDR the forceful Hurley had
opposed the considered judgment of his Foreign Service staff, who
wanted to avoid taking sides in China, and announced that our policy
was to support CKS. This unnecessary and foolish step, as it turned
out, moved us toward the Cold War (anti-communism) as a "solution"
to our foreign-policy problems. It left us less room to maneuver and
committed us to being ousted from China as soon as CKS was defeated, as most of us had foreseen he would be.

For me this sojourn in China was a very different experience from
1942–43. First, the war against Japan was over and the United States

was picking up the pieces, sending the Japanese troops home while trying to suppress the KMT-CCP civil war. December '45 to January '47 was the year of General Marshall's mediation, negotiating to set up a coalition government and so save our Nationalist allies from being overwhelmed by the CCP revolution. I was there during the happy phase, when agreements were made and fighting was stopped.

Second, I was no longer a one-man office with time to meet all political persuasions as an observer. Instead, after I succeeded Bill Holland as director, I was the operating head of an entire echelon of the U.S. government, with a central office in Shanghai and ten branch offices reaching out to the Chinese public through all the media. In the course of nine months we pulled our OWI operations out of West China and expanded them into reoccupied China. Right after the peace the entire PW (leaflet) side of OWI, some 150 Americans, folded up and went home. The information program of OWI was metamorphosed by stages into the new U.S. Information Service (USIS) to operate more closely under the embassy and include cultural relations.

In the first half of 1946 we continued and expanded our activities while making them ready for the transition. American personnel dropped from 125 in September 1945 to 25 by April 1, 1946. Chinese personnel declined from 706 to 342. Branches at Yung-an (formerly behind Japanese lines in the Southeast) and Lanchow had been closed, Kunming was reduced to an agency under the consulate, Chengtu was put under Chungking and Tientsin under Peiping. Meanwhile branch offices were opened in Shanghai (as well as the general office there), Canton, Hankow, Peiping, Nanking, Taipei (Taiwan), and Mukden. Production and control were centralized in Shanghai. The first stress was on (1) Chinese and English news files, (2) feature material in Chinese, (3) pictures, exhibits, and posters, because these were on hand to put out. Filmstrip had ceased, and movies were delayed as well as libraries. Cultural relations waited upon the libraries and surveys of each community. The CU (formerly RC, Cultural Relations) exchange-of-persons program was being handled by Wilma in the embassy.

Facilitating all this activity was the radio network that OWI had developed under U.S. military authority to handle war correspondents' news reports. We now expanded it as a quick communications system by Morse code or Chinese number code tying all branches to Shanghai. It meant that we could not only move the news, and continue to send the messages of war correspondents and of UNRRA (the United Nations Relief and Rehabilitation Administration). We could also communicate personally on our own business in a way that no other civilian agency could do. And we could send messages for others in cases involving life or death, financial disaster, or the national interest. Communication was power. People cozied up to us. We had lots of friends.

Reoccupied China was intellectually starved for much of what we had to offer. They needed news of the world and books of all kinds. While the fate of China remained politically obscure, the need for information seemed to me just as urgent as the material supplies being brought in by UNRRA. It was such a challenge that I deferred my return to Harvard from April 1 to August 1946. If I couldn't stay and see it through to that point, how could I expect others in USIS to stick to it and keep on functioning?

October 18 I went to Shanghai with Bill Holland (I being now his deputy director for information). We stayed at the Park and ate at the Cathay,

> the Ritz of Shanghai, now run by the Navy, where our offices are. The streets teem with buses of troops, rickshas and pedicabs, which are rickshas with bicycles attached behind or in front, taxis, marching Chinese troops, wandering shop clerks crossing in front of antiquated streetcars, little girls selling newspapers in the very midst of traffic, a few bearded Sikh policemen, soon to be sent home, and sundry GIs, long-gowned Chinese collaborators, speculators returned from upriver, White Russian dancing girls, stranded Germans, wandering Jap soldiers, and tubercular coolies.

This street scene reflected the fact that Shanghai was still one of the most international cities yet could still be dominated by whoever had his gunboats in the Whangpoo. Heat was scarce that winter in Shanghai and we Americans, though in the most posh living quarters, commonly wore extra sweaters and socks and our overcoats at all hours. The challenge was to expand our information work in the midst of shortages and lack of services. As I wrote Paul Buck when I postponed my return to Harvard, China was in an uneasy state of countrywide truce, in which assassination, beatings, strong-arm and police methods and mass demonstrations are likely to multiply. Modern Chinese intellectuals and liberals are struggling to seize this opportunity to establish democratic practices, and many will lose their lives in the effort.

But the work of USIS might help reason prevail and possibly somewhat mitigate the disaster.

After Bill Holland went back to the United States and I became China director, my essential problem was how to keep enough special talent in the Shanghai central office so that it could service the ten branches. For this purpose I had a lucky break. Four ONAF (Overseas News and Features) specialists, all women, came over the Hump from OWI Bombay. They preserved the quality of the Shanghai operation. The news file was handled by Ruth Lewis and Alice Ford; the feature service by the head of the OWI Chinese staff, Liu Tsun-ch'i, and Amy Schaeffer; and the photo department (posters, picture exhibits, and news photos) by Helene Pleasants. These were skilled people who believed in their work.

My other lucky break was to find and promote Bradley Connors, a photo editor from ONAF who had set up his photo lab in China. I made him Director of Operations in Shanghai. Brad was from a well-off and cultured background but didn't look it. He had the acuity and energy sometimes found in a large physique. Greatly overweight, with a cigarette dangling, he could pass for a tough New York expediter, maybe a gangland enforcer. The main thing was that he knew everything and everybody and was a master of nuts-and-bolts logistics. He knew the managers and even the pilots at the airfields and when planes were going; he knew the secretaries and all the higher-ups in the consulate general across the street and what his superiors specially needed or wanted. He could get things done. Everyone came to him for help. But his skills encompassed the regulations too, and he kept strictly within the rules. His forte was to catch newsbreaks in the late wires from early-morning Washington and tell officials at bedtime in China what they needed to know. (In Washington in June 1950 when the North Korean tanks rolled south of the 38th parallel at dawn in Seoul, Brad spotted it on the State Department ticker as he was closing up for the night and alerted Dean

Acheson. When I saw him last, shortly before his sudden death, he was minister in London.) I was fortunate to have him running the show at the center.

USIS, China division, as we finally got it set up with the help of administrative experts of various kinds I forbear to mention, proved my belief that most operations require two-man management. While Brad kept things moving and under control, I maintained a fitful presence in the Nanking embassy and traveled to various branches. In the transition period (until July 1 when Brad as my successor became chief public affairs officer on the embassy staff), my embassy liaison was John Melby, a thoughtful career officer with Latin American and Moscow experience, who quickly became adjusted to China.

Having to give official guidance (authorizations, limitations, requests, suggestions) to ten branch offices, I naturally thought, "What would Robert Hart have done?" The result was that I sent out between Christmas and June 1, 1946, a series of forty-four circular letters. They dealt with all aspects of USIS work and often were drafted by my Shanghai specialist colleagues so that we all would understand our multifaceted operations. Thus, for distribution of news pictures (circular letter no. 34, April 24, 1946) we had a list of 110 publications in China that had photoengraving facilities, so we prepared 110 prints and captions and sent them out instanter. Our feature output (background information as opposed to the news file received by radio from SX) was selected by the head of the Chinese translation department (the same as under OWI since 1941) and approved by the Director of Operations at Shanghai. Ordinarily we translated only materials already published for the American public and received from San Francisco, New York, or Washington by mail or radio. Items translated formed a weekly periodical, *News Materials (Hsin-wen tzu-liao),* of eight sheets per issue with eight to ten articles, sent out in 5,000 copies (2,750 on a direct mailing list and the rest to the branches).

In circular 20 (February 11) on the "Purpose of USIS in China" I offered a personal definition under the headings of

1. *Information, not propaganda.*

2. *Action as well as understanding.* "We want to present evidences of American experience in facing and overcoming modern problems in such a way as to stimulate the Chinese people to face and overcome their own problems."

3. *Modernization, not Americanization.* "What we have found good for us will not necessarily be good for China. The Chinese problem may be formulated as one of combining science and democracy and applying them to the life of the masses in the context of the Chinese cultural tradition."

4. *Realism, not salesmanship.* "Present a thorough, complete and truthful picture of the American scene without attempting to tone down or underplay the difficulties, problems and failures. To maintain our credibility, things that count against us should be reported by us first. We do not want to oversell our audience. Another reason for realism is that we are trying to provide a sound basis for independent action. For instance, the initiative, referendum, and recall are not a panacea for political evils in China when they have not proved so in the United States."

While we were thus institution building in China, George Taylor and his China desk chief, John C. Caldwell, were fighting the less glamorous battle of Washington to give us the budget, personnel, and directives USIS needed for its Chinese future. Caldwell (who was born of Fukien missionaries) paid us a six-week visit to see the problems. We held teletype conferences with Washington in Army channels and exchanged sapient bons mots with George.

My administrative crises were largely personnel problems—how to keep together the nucleus of skilled people. A major flap came with the announcement of General Marshall's mediation on December 15, 1945. John Carter Vincent, Dean Acheson, and Marshall had carefully phrased a public statement from Truman to CKS to avoid affronts to Chinese pride and give Marshall a balanced posture. When the chargé d'affaires Walter Robertson and I in Chungking received this, it was accompanied by a news story datelined Washington that characterized Truman's statement as one of the harshest reprimands ever delivered to another head of state, etc., etc.—way out of line with Washington policy. What was this?

I soon discovered it emanated from our Shanghai office, so I took the next plane to Shanghai and investigated. (I didn't want to meet General Marshall just yet.) The author was not a Communist saboteur but simply a staff reporter who felt he was supplying a rewrite or news story such as he claimed any newspaper might give its readers to beef up the news. Such a custom was news to me. Fortunately this man had received an invitation to join the United Press in Hong

Kong. After working it out with him, I convened a meeting of the American staff who were the key to keeping our work going in China. If I seemed to mistreat their colleague, they might go home. I therefore expatiated on (1) his innocence of evil intent, (2) the delicacy of Marshall's mission, (3) the fact that we were government employees not expected to counter state policy. Solution: Our colleague had resigned to join UP and I would recommend him; I would also try to reassure General Marshall that we knew our job. After some discussion, this was accepted and I reported to Robertson that the perpetrator was no longer with us.

My other most memorable contribution to General Marshall's mediation was when I figured out, for reasons that now escape me, that the course of events had made it unnecessary for him to hold a 2 P.M. press conference (USIS arranged the conferences for him) and so canceled it. Liking a 2 P.M. nap, I evidently put myself in his place and did him this favor as one professor to another. I was having lunch when he caught me on the phone, very much annoyed. His message was clear, concise, and so crisp that to remember it still chills me. There would be a press conference.

I had about an hour to produce the press. I started all the bells ringing that I could but several key Chinese reporters had gone home to lunch. With no time to spare I set out by Jeep for their addresses. My driver found his way in the cold Chungking drizzle to some of the saddest habitations I ever saw, and I beat upon doors, ascended rickety stairs, and roused hapless tubercular-looking men from their post-lunch naps to our mutual humiliation. But I invoked Ma-sha-erh's name and got them to the place on time. When the general's aide, a smart young colonel, said, "Maybe you don't need to attend," I agreed and slunk home. Harvard is poor training for the Pentagon.

The OWI compound in Chungking had grown to total seven or eight buildings, including a dance floor, most of them now empty. Wilma and I had a corner room with a fireplace, very enjoyable, but travel distracted us. In October Wilma went by truck to Chiating and Chengtu and then in November flew to Sian, while I flew to Kunming, Canton, and Shanghai again, and again to Shanghai in December and in January. In February Wilma flew to Kunming and went by Jeep down the Burma Road to Tali, while in March I went in the opposite direction to Peking, twice. In April the embassy finally accompanied the Nationalist government moving from Chungking to Nanking. Since Nanking is overnight by train from Shanghai, Wilma was now more available to meet writers and artists in the metropolis.

All this moving about heightened my sense of China's confusion. But the stronger position of the CCP seemed evident from conversations with Chinese intellectuals as well as other Americans, especially the correspondents covering General Marshall's year-long mission.

The beginning of negotiations had given a more definite status to the CCP and facilitated American contact with them. In Chungking we had Ch'iao Mu and Kung P'eng to dinner one night and the Joseph Kus from the Nationalist FO the next; each side saw the other as insincere. C. C. Ch'ien of the National Resources Commission agreed that China needed *both* industrialization, which the KMT was attempting, and agrarian reform, such as the CCP was pursuing; but he soon took off for Europe.

Just as the negotiations seemed in early January 1946 likely to bear fruit, the CCP Chungking delegation gave a dinner

for USIS, two tables with Chou En-lai at one and Yeh Chien-ying, the commander in chief, at the other, both wound up with nervous energy, Chou swaying to the singing, which we soon started, and Yeh beating time with chopsticks on the table and glassware. They sang Yenan songs, after a number of toasts, and we tried to sing something equally spirited and found the comparable songs were those of our own Civil War —the recent music is too sweet or soft or sentimental. Mrs. Chou, who uses her own name, Teng, wears trousers, very simple and charming.

(In 1980 Teng Ying-ch'ao was still a leader in Peking, Yeh Chien-ying was still the commander in chief. Chou En-lai died in 1976.)

The CP delegation did a vigorous social job with meetings and negotiations thrown in day and night—a big cocktail party in the main hall of Chungking's best hotel, Victory House, to which Everybody and a lot of other people went. Wilma and I wound up at a very tipsy dinner party with Kuo Mo-jo and his wife and our two best friends among the CP here. All this enthusiasm and really carefree letting go bespeaks, I think, the relief of the Communists at getting some kind of settlement, based on a sensible American policy, which gives them opportunity to work in the future. Added to that, they are vigorous because they are a selected group of believers and workers for a social cause.

In Shanghai I went out with Koji Ariyoshi from Honolulu, a Japanese-American expert on Yenan, who had been there with the military-observer section. We had dinner with the widow of China's great satirist, "Mme. Lu Hsun and a friend—very sweet and devout ladies who had faith more than cleverness, reminding me a bit of Christian converts as a type." Through Ariyoshi, who had been a leftist longshoreman in Honolulu, we put Yenan on our USIS distribution list.

In early 1946 the Executive Headquarters set up in the PUMC in Peking sent out truce teams to stop the KMT-CCP firefights that had erupted across North China. Among the three staffs—Nationalist, American, and Communist—the only woman was Kung P'eng, handling General Yeh Chien-ying's public relations. She was very smart, Phil Potter of the Baltimore *Sun* reported, in a blue gown and American-style hairdo, but she said, "There's no aggressiveness to these Peiping people." Like other Press Hostel denizens, he played her up. As the early euphoria fell away, I saw Ch'iao Mu and Kung P'eng in Shanghai at her family's place, where their baby boy, Paris (named for the first liberated capital), was taken care of by the grandparents; soon they were transferred to work in the safer environment of Hong Kong. Chou En-lai was obviously stockpiling his key personnel for future use. (Ch'iao Kuan-hua came to the UN as PRC ambassador in 1971 and was foreign minister in Peking in 1975–76.)

USIS had its share of involvement in the civil conflict through the case of Yang Ch'ao, an intellectual employed by Christopher Rand (later of *The New Yorker*) when he was director of the OWI office at Yung-an at the end of the war. Chris had sent Yang Ch'ao on an OWI mission during which he was seized by the Nationalist war zone commander and jailed at Hangchow as a suspected Communist. Rand tried to get him out, since he had been doing American business, but the old days of extraterritoriality, which might sometimes cover Chinese in foreign employ, were gone. Yang Ch'ao died in jail, apparently of illness and presumably neglect, but foul play was naturally suspected. His jailer tried to induce his widow to leave Shanghai, fearing she would cause trouble. Rand and I and other Americans tried to protect her. The left took up the case. At length a large memorial service was held, where Kuo Mo-jo and others made impassioned speeches. I attended in order to show the American concern about an employee but I refused to speak, though called upon, because the United States government had no standing in a purely Chinese case. I did not want to be used by the CCP in its campaign against the Nationalist government. One complication was that Yang Ch'ao was the brother of my friend Yang Kang, who was then in the United States.

As USIS tried to develop a cultural program in contact with writers and artists, we found ourselves dealing with so-called liberals and leftists in a bewildering mixture. The issue of political loyalties was in our view extraneous to art and letters and moreover quite beyond our capacity to ascertain if we had wanted to. The U.S. policy to favor coalition government left us strictly outside Chinese party politics. We tried to deal with individuals on their merits all across the political spectrum.

As events unfolded in later years, the strength of the CCP organization in 1946 seems surprising in retrospect. The much-respected head of our Chinese editorial staff in Shanghai, Chin Chung-hua, after 1949 became vice-mayor of Shanghai (he killed himself during the Cultural Revolution). The editor of the newly founded paper *Wen Hui Pao* (Huan Hsiang), to which OWI had given some hard-to-get newsprint in order to foster a nongovernment press, became the first chargé d'affaires (i.e., ambassador) to London. (In 1981 he is vice-president of the Academy of Social Sciences.) My friend Yang Kang herself after 1949 became assistant editor of the *People's Daily* in Peking (until her suicide in 1957). Such positions of trust could presumably have gone only to long-time party members. Another outside cadre, the stalwart head of the entire OWI Chinese staff was Liu Tsun-ch'i, a newspaperman recruited by Mac Fisher; his cool judgment had been of tremendous help to Mac as the Chinese staff mushroomed in size. After 1945 Liu came to the United States, hoping to get help for mass education, procure modern presses, and set up an independent publishing business in postwar China. This did not work out. He had been a party member since the early thirties, but from 1957 on he spent twenty-one years in labor camps in Manchuria, in exile, and in prison, both in Peking and in Hunan. (He is now editing the English-language *China Daily* in Peking.) Volumes could be written and I hope will be on the very mixed careers of such people since the mid-century. Perhaps the adage will stand up, that the revolution first of all devours its own. The university graduates who went left in the 1930s were part of the world intelligentsia of the time, educated people. Red Guards and others cast up by the policy struggles from 1957 to the 1970s were another type.

When I visited Peking early in March 1946 it was again a lodestone that drew people from all over. F. T. Ch'ing had returned from Honolulu and was helping Deison Ch'en and others from Kunming put Tsing Hua University back together again. Our Harvard graduate students, Arthur and Mary Wright, had come back from their three years of manual work in the self-run internment camp at Weihsien in Shantung. True to their calling they were resuming their studies in the fine Chinese house of a former puppet in the north city. It had those big brass-studded chests, polished wood tables, carved window woodwork, and other touches I remembered, plus the old type of professional servants. Mary was about to start building the Hoover Library collection on revolutionary China. They introduced me to a fellow student from the USSR, young Sergei Tikhvinskii, who was later to rise high in the Soviet power structure. I also lunched with George Hatem (Ma Hai-teh), the American doctor who had performed wonders in public health at Yenan. Graham Peck had found a house in the west city and was writing his classic memoir of China in wartime, *Two Kinds of Time.* Two CCP liaison officers came to call at USIS—Huang Hua and K'o Po-nien. (In 1981 Huang Hua is foreign minister. His son is a student at Harvard.) I was there helping the incoming director of USIS Peking, John Burt Foster, who had come to our Far Eastern Institute in the 1940 Harvard summer school and married a fellow student. What a mixed network of friends and acquaintances!

In Shanghai also the mixture was growing difficult to handle. In April we used the new USIS quarters in Hamilton House, a high rise opposite the consulate general, to stage three cocktail parties for the Shanghai community—a curious mélange of foreign military, official, and business people with Chinese officials, as well as editors, artists, and writers, most of whom were long since disaffected. Every week some Chinese acquaintance would come to say goodbye as he or she prepared to slip away to the North.

One day Kaji Wataru, the poetic-looking Japanese intellectual who had translated OWI leaflets into Japanese for Jim Stewart, came to see me in Shanghai hoping to get passage back to Japan. The U.S. Navy was shipping his countrymen, our late enemies, by the hundreds of thousands, but Kaji was held up evidently by security. I wrote a letter to the American military suggesting that someone who had helped us in the war deserved as good treatment as those who had fought against us. This intervention got Kaji back home but gave me a black mark. We were already afraid of the Communists, who were already afraid of us. Security was at work.

In Shanghai I favored USIS assisting the translation of English-language writings for a Chinese audience. To do this we had to interest the Chinese scholars who could make good translations. From Chinese, Japanese, Korean, or Vietnamese, any English translation has to be a re-creation of the original. I was sure this applied in reverse. If we wanted real literature we had to find Chinese Fitzgeralds to translate our American Omar Khayyáms. I sought advice from the omnicompetent scholar Cheng Chen-to, and encouraged the efforts of Yeate Feng (Feng I-tai) whose wife Anna Mae Cheng helped in our USIS cultural contacts. We also enlisted Chao Chia-pi, Hsu Ch'ih, and others, but nothing was achieved before my departure. Along the way I was privileged to attend a meeting of the Writers League, the vestige of the League of Left-Wing Writers that had made history in the 1930s. Being so deficient in Chinese literary capacity, I functioned mainly as a symbol of good will.

The USIS branch office in Peking had special problems. Forty thousand U.S. marines in the Peking-Tientsin area to give political stability were natural targets for CCP agitation as representing "American imperialism." Setting up a Sino-American Cultural Institute was not easy because the collapse of Marshall's arrangements was imminent. Civil war and the repression of cultural workers seemed just around the corner.

In early June 1946 Wilma made an effort to have CU carry out General Marshall's policy of even-handedness in China's civil conflict. She secured his agreement to invite the CCP's North China Associated University at Kalgan (Chang-chia-k'ou) to send four academics for a year in the United States under the exchange-of-persons program. A couple of dozen such persons had gone to America from the Nationalist area.

To select these people she had embassy orders to go via Peking to the CCP capital, which had been moved from Yenan to Kalgan. Since I was in Peking troubleshooting during my branch director's illness, I attached myself to the expedition, but it was her show. She even cozened an Air Force colonel into flying us over the Great Wall and along the border of Mongolia, dry, sandy, and dust-blown like Arizona. "We reached Kalgan in forty-five minutes and a week later took sixteen hours to get back by train and mule cart." We stayed at the Liberation Hotel as guests of the Border Region Government. Wilma did her official business and we watched drama teams dance the "seedling song" or *yang-ko,* a chain-step folk dance very popular in the process of "liberating" peasants. We talked to a number of groups. Their main question was, How can a democratic America have a policy to oppose the people's movement in China? Not easy to answer.

We had a luncheon with the literary czar Chou Yang (one of the four they had chosen to send). He was flanked by the woman writer Ting Ling and an old Creation Society leader (Ch'eng Fang-wu). The poet Ai Ch'ing said simply, "We look for help from Walt Whitman's America; we hate Hurley's America."

I had never been able to dream up an adequate reason for a trip to Yenan, so this week in Kalgan was my only exposure to a CCP area. The university seemed about at middle-school level with mainly mimeographed study materials. We met the top man, General Nieh Jung-chen, and at one point Wilma and I jointly addressed a theaterful of eager youth. I never felt so inadequate. My Chinese was good for travel, dinner talk, and modern history but empty of Marxist lingo. I was acutely conscious of the very different world images in my mind and my audience's. All I could offer was platitudes of the sort they were already full of—friendship between peoples, let us have peace, and so on. I couldn't disown the American policy of supporting CKS, nor could I invoke it as the road to a New Jerusalem with justice and plenty for all. If this was the high point of my 1945–46 visit to China, I was ready to pack up and go home.

The wall slogans in Kalgan read, "Firmly establish democracy and build a new life." Coming back we took a mule cart across ten miles of no-man's-land, waited with a CCP outpost for the Nationalists to stop their shelling, and reached Nankow and the Great Wall gate with its slogan "Follow the leadership of Chiang Kai-shek." In the end the four CCP nominees were refused Nationalist passports, and a few years later, when the McCarthy era got under way, we all quietly forgot the episode.*

I left Shanghai after a fine leftist sendoff, a banquet of some fifty intellectuals at which Kuo Mo-jo and others made speeches of appreciation and I replied with the thought that "within the four seas, all men are brothers" and other expressions of admiration for the struggle for freedom, etc. It was more than perfunctory and I was glad to have the little booklet of signatures customary on such occasions, bearing many illustrious literary names. Alas, I forgot the unwritten code of loyalty and gave this treasure to the office boy, a capable expediter whom Brad had christened "MacDougal," to mail to me in the United States along with some papers. The booklet never turned up, and I realized I had forgotten how obligations cease when a relationship ends. "Mac" may have sold it but probably it went to Tai Li's files.

I left Shanghai July 7, 1946, and did not return for twenty-six years. Wilma, however, stayed on in the Nanking embassy another nine months in order to complete the integration of the CU and USIS programs.

My nine months in "postwar" China in 1945–46 were actually a prewar experience. I watched the Nationalist government with its American arms spread itself out to the major northern cities while its carpetbagging politicians despoiled and alienated the reoccupied areas of East China. Corruption and inflation eroded even the normal upper-class support for the KMT. I hoped that USIS could somehow help to stem the disintegration but we really had no chance. The trend toward civil war, which Marshall had miraculously checked in January, resumed in the summer. Our China policy was on the skids but the American public didn't yet realize it.

---

*For details see Wilma Fairbank, *America's Cultural Experiment in China 1942–1949*, pp. 106–109.

PART FIVE

•

THE FALLOUT
FROM WORLD WAR II
1946–52

24

CHINA POLICY AND AREA STUDY

ONCE RETURNED FROM China to Harvard I began riding two horses
—teaching Chinese history and speaking up on China policy. Both
were in demand, and they went together naturally, serviced by the
same Dictaphone and secretary. From OSS and OWI I knew a lot of
officials and journalists. I became an articulate member of a growing
minority. My usual self-confidence was buttressed by recent field
experience and continuing historical study. In China and Washington since 1941 I had been mainly dealing with people, using words
for the purpose. From 1946 the words became more important because I was dealing with the subject of China for a larger audience
and from a distance. I had to explain how it was not America, and
how English words when applied to China might not mean the same
thing.

My article "Our Chances in China" in the *Atlantic Monthly* for
September 1946 was precipitated by events. I had hardly reached
Washington in early July and become a private citizen again when
the uneasy truce in China was shattered not only by the renewal of
Nationalist-CCP hostilities but also by an especially blatant political
murder.

On July 15, 1946, a leading liberal professor at Lienta in Kunming
was assassinated in broad daylight. Wen I-to had studied English
literature at Chicago and was well known also as a poet, a man of
culture and of the spirit, a leader in the faculty protest against civil

war in China. Phil Sprouse as Kunming consul had had Wen around to a great dinner party when I was there in late '45. Shooting down such a figure escalated the Tai Li–CC effort to intimidate dissent by force and to eliminate both the liberals and the CCP. This headstrong use of violence posed very acutely the question whether American support of the Nationalist government in civil war was a wise idea. My article suggested it was not.

As usual this article at once became a brickbat in the continuing struggle within China. At least three different Chinese translations were made, with various subheadings inserted. The playwright Hsia Yen wrote a sentimental appreciation of me. I began to confront the phenomenon of having a public persona which I could not control. People made of me what they chose to.

Ever since 1943 I had believed revolution was probably unavoidable in China. The collapsing urban economy and the KMT corruption and repression visible in 1945–46 confirmed me in this view. When the Marshall mediation began to collapse too, it became urgent to warn the American public not to back CKS and his right-KMT, who were so busily digging their own graves and trying to pull us in with them.

This is one of the oldest problems in American foreign policy—how, as a pluralistic polity, to relate ourselves to one-party or one-gang dictatorships abroad. We continue to confront this problem all over the world—in Latin America, Africa, the Middle East, Eastern Europe, and East Asia. Seemingly each generation has to wise up to it anew. The hardest thing to learn is that we alone from the outside cannot decide the outcome.

The Chinese case, as always, had special features. We had been allies of the Nationalist government. It had many American friends from its early days of promise. The Chinese domestic rebels were not democrats we could identify with, but avowed Communists seeking a new party dictatorship. What's more, the United States was slipping into a worldwide anti-Communist Cold War, in no mood to cozy up to any CP abroad.

So what could one say to the American public, short of giving them a course in Chinese history?

But of course it was not that simple. My posture was really conservative because I backed Secretary of State Marshall's experienced conclusion that we must not further intervene pro-KMT. Yet we had already intervened part way, giving CKS's forces training, equipment, supplies, and transport, even American marines garrisoned in North China to keep out the Russians.

My *Atlantic* article, which I reprinted with modest pride in 1974 in *China Perceived,* stressed our liberal faith and aims in China, China's authoritarian political tradition, and the CCP effort at economic betterment and "liberation" among the peasantry. "Must we not prepare sooner or later to come to terms with Chinese Communism?"

I asserted the CCP was not a Moscow puppet. "If we oppose the revolution blindly, we shall find ourselves eventually expelled from Asia by a mass movement."

In taking this pro-administration stand, I felt purely professorial, reasoning from the facts. During five years as a government official I had been trying to formulate an understanding of Chinese politics and work out an American posture for dealing with the Chinese revolution. I was fortunate to have my then brother-in-law Arthur Schlesinger, Jr., at hand in Franklin, New Hampshire. He was deeply involved in the organizing of a "non-Communist left," which took shape in ADA (Americans for Democratic Action) as a counter to the PAC (Political Action Committee) that Henry Wallace was naïvely supporting. I could see at once that the only effective basis for our China policy must be a non-Communist one. In other words, I could state the merits of the CCP effectively only if I was anti-CPUSA at home. This was, plainly, my natural posture; I had been absent in China during the leftism in America of the early 1930s and had never found much hope in Marxism. I had no CPUSA connections and felt the ADA's anti-communism was a necessary part of its liberal posture.

In this stand I was denying the universal nature of communism as an ideology which claimed to be the same everywhere and was being so acknowledged by fearful Americans. Liberals do get themselves between fires! I was committed to viewing "communism" as bad in America but good in China, which I was convinced was true. This led me to claim China and America were different "cultures" or "social orders"—also true. It followed that area specialists like me had esoteric knowledge of these cultural-social differences between China and America. The question was whether we could impart it to our fellow citizens and make them all area specialists (in the sense of understanding cultural-social differences). It was a tall order but the only way to keep American policy on the right track.

This present personal narrative could not survive if I weighed it down with a historical analysis of the Chinese revolution plus a dissection of American China policy. Those are monographic subjects so much bigger than I that I would need extra volumes to treat them properly. For those who came in late, however, let me simply explain that we Americans let ourselves get involved in opposing the Chinese revolution, to our mutual nonbenefit.

The fault was partly in our heads. Much of the argument was what communication specialists like to call "noise," expression devoid of meaning to the listener; so much of it was simply patriotic rhetoric. But even more of it was ambiguous. For example, by accepting Western terminology, some of it Marxist, to characterize the Chinese scene, we got ourselves thoroughly confused as to what was going on there. As a result the American public debate over China policy dealt partly in make-believe. Take the question of class struggle by the proletariat against the bourgeois capitalist class. Recent studies by M. C. Bergère, Parks Coble, Lloyd Eastman, *et al.* have made clear that the KMT after 1928 was not pro-capitalist in the sense of being pro-business-enterprise. It was simply pro-KMT, a new faction, gang, or power group coming into control of the Chinese government much as a dynastic family would have done. By calling it "capitalist" and accusing the Nanking government of representing the Shanghai capitalist class, the CCP Marxist ideologues set up a false assumption and caused everybody unnecessary confusion. Their class analysis played them false—another proof that theirs was simply the latest effort to apply to China foreign ideas that didn't fit reality there.

The fact was, as we now know, that CKS's Nanking government from the very beginning used strong-arm methods to shake down the Shanghai business world in an entirely parasitic and exploitative way. The KMT did not help business, but squeezed it for money. Business leaders were abducted and held for ransom, even assassinated, in a gangster-run reign of terror. The KMT lived for itself as an organization in power, and to call it the supporter of the capitalist class was simply unreal. Worse, it built the KMT up in Western eyes as an ally defending Western free-corporate-enterprise values.

Confusion was increased when American-educated political figures like T. V. Soong claimed to be capitalist entrepreneurs struggling for the same principles as those that founded Wall Street. A realistic equivalent to T. V. Soong's role in China would have been Bobby Kennedy's becoming head of the Bank of America, Chase Manhattan, National Citibank, and the Federal Reserve Board all at once while JFK was in the White House. The only capital investment possible in China was either through a government agency or an official or under their protection. Law was no safeguard. Personal relations *(kuan-hsi)* were necessary.

No doubt we are all aware by now that similar lack of realism clouded the term "proletariat." The CCP revolution was led by intellectuals who became professional revolutionaries. Their efforts to organize industrial labor were largely futile. The "proletariat" they had to settle for consisted of poverty-stricken farmers. The "class struggle" in the countryside, in the general absence of big estates, was a matter of organizing poor peasants as a majority to dominate "rich" peasants. The class struggle that Mao precipitated in his Great Proletarian Cultural Revolution of the late 1960s was in the first instance an attack by restive urban youth on party bureaucrats and subsequently often a civil war between factions.

Behind this misfit of terms lay the fact that nineteenth-century Europe, from which the studious Marx and Engels derived their class categories, had little counterpart in twentieth-century China. The principles of centralized organization that Sun Yat-sen, Chiang Kai-shek, Mao Tse-tung, and Liu Shao-ch'i picked up from Lenin and Stalin were useful in China to form party dictatorships as they have been elsewhere. But their utility cannot hide the bankruptcy that overcame Sun's Three Principles of the People and seems to be threatening Mao Tse-tung Thought as guides to China's future.

My second public statement was a review of Teddy White's book in October 1946. As Teddy had written us two years before (July 24, 1944), "I have made the big decision—yes, I am going to write a book. I feel now that there is no good to come of this government; that someone must once and for all lay the full picture before the American people." The strain of this decision is vividly recounted in his *In Search of History* (page 49). *Thunder Out of China* was written with his *Time-Life* colleague Annalee Jacoby, and published by Bill Sloane. It is still a classic account of wartime China. My review of it for the *New York Times Book Review* (October 27, 1946) was printed on the front page. The message was stark:

> Chiang Kai-shek's brand of democracy is not ours, any more than is Mao Tse-tung's . . . between the two, China may eventually decide for the latter even though we support the former.
>
> The underlying issue in China has not been communism but good government. . . . We have let our fears of Russia and of communism, on which the right-Kuomintang plays so skilfully, drive the Chinese revolution further into dependence on Russia and upon communism.

I concluded that if *Thunder Out of China* was an accurate picture, "then the lid is really off and the American public can see what kind of dictatorship they are backing in the name of democracy."

Another chance to disillusion American readers came with the final publication of the official English version of CKS's *China's Destiny* and a separate volume, *China's Destiny and Chinese Economic Theory,* also by CKS but not authorized, which I reviewed in the *New York Times Book Review,* February 9, 1947. The unauthorized volume had highly critical commentaries by the then left-wing editor of *Amerasia,* Philip Jaffe. The "economic theory" was both jejune and chauvinist, really a scandal to come from a chief of state.

For the Foreign Policy Association's *Bulletin* of November 19, 1948, I capsulized my rather negative message. It amounted to saying: Don't just do something, sit there! As the association later recalled, I "presented a view that was widely condemned as heresy at the time." Part of it read as follows:

> The Chinese Communist program may indeed be cynically ruthless, economically unsound, swayed by Moscow, and feared by many Chinese. Compared with the overall Kuomintang program, however, it remains preferable from the point of view of the great majority of poor peasants.
>
> The demoralization of Kuomintang China is likely to become accelerated. Material aid from the United States cannot stop this process. Foreign arms and food for the police will not maintain a Chinese regime once it has so clearly lost the tacit acquiescence of the population—in old parlance, the Mandate of Heaven. The fact is that Chiang Kai-shek has had twenty years in which to compete with communism for the support of the Chinese peasantry, and he has lost.

It is most important that the United States retain a certain measure of diplomatic flexibility with respect to Chinese politics. Any commitment to deal only with a recognized Chinese government-in-exile, or with Chiang Kai-shek bolstered by American aid in a South China or a Formosan base, can only handicap our cause. Without indulging in much hope that we can work with Chinese communism, we must avoid accepting claims to legitimacy by Chinese political figures who have lost credit with their own people. The Chinese Communist success helps Russia, but cannot be equated with Russian conquest of China. We have to face up to the fact that the Communist movement is not only genuinely Communist but also genuinely Chinese.

Critical attacks on the KMT record and capacity came from many others too in this period after General Marshall returned from China in January 1947. His parting blast blamed both sides, but especially the KMT right, for the failure of his mediation. His returning to the post of Secretary of State ensured our staying out of a military intervention against the CCP—one of his greatest services to the American people. The pro-Nationalist agitation of CKS's supporters in the United States did not get into high gear until a bit later, when the Republicans made the "loss of China" an anti-Democratic issue in the election of 1948.

My senior colleague, Professor Arthur Holcombe, who had surveyed the Chinese Revolution in the late 1920s when the Nanking government was its great hope, was shocked by my low opinion of CKS and the KMT (some years later he wrote to tell me I had been right). Others responded according to their experience. The particular China they had known, whether in warlord days or the hopeful early thirties or the heroic resistance of 1937–38, gave them their basic posture. I realized my own experience in China was dated. My observed truth came from points receding in time too. I had to substitute new study for continued observation.

One help at this time was to have our old friend from Kunming, Professor Ch'ien Tuan-sheng, as our house guest in Cambridge from December 1947 until his return to China in September 1948. He was a visiting lecturer at Harvard on Chinese government and politics at the same time that he was finishing his English manuscript on the same subject for the Institute of Pacific Relations. The study was based on his and others' work in Chinese but of course the English version was a new book put together for the foreign reader. Tuansheng worked very hard, aided by a devoted American secretary, and Wilma and I went over the manuscript to help. It was a remarkably objective and informative account of the KMT government. By the time Harvard University Press published it in 1950, the author was back in Peking under the new regime and wanted no copies sent to him. He had gone back expecting to be assassinated by the KMT in a final bloodbath as it went out. (In 1946 they had fired over his head as he addressed an anti-civil-war rally at Lienta in Kunming.) But he survived to be used by the PRC as a democratic personage, as head of the College of Law and Government and on good-will delegations abroad. We continued to correspond until in late 1951 the Sino-American war in Korea made us break off. Needless to say, we were each later accused of having known the other. Liberals became suspect on both sides of the bamboo curtain.

As our national debate on China proceeded, it was increasingly overshadowed by the rise of the Cold War in our foreign relations and the onset of the Great Fear within the country. I borrow David Caute's book title *(The Great Fear: the Anti-Communist Purge under Truman and Eisenhower,* 1978) because in a 542-page record of this pervasive subject, hardly a score of pages are devoted to the China issue. No doubt China took more than its share of the headlines but we can see now it was only a lightning rod on the top of the iceberg. China specialists found themselves unusually newsworthy in the era of Joe McCarthy. But in fact they were only one facet of a widespread social malaise. McCarthyism battened on atom spies, USIS libraries, anything exploitable. China proved to be a gold mine awaiting exploitation.

Partly this was the achievement of Ned Carter and Bill Holland, whom we first met in Peking in 1932. Edward C. Carter had worked in India for the YMCA. After the Institute of Pacific Relations (IPR) was founded by YMCA and other people in Honolulu in 1925, he succeeded in taking over as chief executive and soon moved the IPR into the big time. Ned was a handsome New England type and a sometimes rather Jesuitical operator, adroit in being able to agree with almost everyone and bring the most disparate groups together. He evidently sensed that after World War I the Council on Foreign

Relations in New York had become so entwined with the East Coast establishment that it let Asia go by the board. Its counterparts in the British commonwealth—the Royal Institute of International Affairs at Chatham House in St. James's Square, London, and the similar institutes in Canada, Australia, and elsewhere—all had Asia in their sights. Ned Carter's success was to make them all members of the International IPR, which consisted eventually of eleven national councils in all the Pacific powers—Britain, United States, Canada, France, Australia, New Zealand, the Philippines, India-Pakistan later, the Netherlands, Japan, China, even the USSR. Only the American IPR was different. Instead of being part of the Council on Foreign Relations it was a smaller New York show that tended more to the left, partly under the patronage of Frederick Vanderbilt Field, who was executive secretary 1934–40 and who, weighed down by his name and money, became a CP member.

Remember that between the two world wars travel was by ship, truly international conferences were few, and no think tanks or university centers researched the contemporary scene abroad. The IPR was alone in getting businessmen, scholars, and (after 1941) government officials together biennially or triennially for a fortnight's discussion of international problems and national interests. Bill Holland, an economist, became Carter's right hand in this intricate task of mobilizing national delegations and bringing out research studies.

For my generation the IPR was a magnificent institution. Its conferences were held in glamorous settings.* They were staffed by smart young women like Barbara Wertheim (Tuchman) and Marian Cannon (Schlesinger). I readily agreed to become a trustee of the American IPR in 1947.

From 1933 to 1941 Owen Lattimore edited the IPR journal, *Pacific Affairs,* with a keen eye for controversy. He and E. C. Carter among others believed in contact and exchange of views across the political gap with the USSR. Its Soviet unit, once set up, contributed hardly anything, but the IPR kept it proudly on the list and developed what Soviet contact they could—I suppose you could call them premature believers in détente. Meanwhile, the IPR executives tried

---

*Honolulu, 1925, 1927; Kyoto, 1929; Shanghai, 1931; Banff, 1933; Yosemite, 1936; Virginia Beach, 1939; Mont Tremblant, 1942; Hot Springs, Virginia, 1945; Stratford-on-Avon, 1947.

to secure participation from everybody active in the area of East Asian studies. Through its correspondence files they were all "associated." Any believer in "guilt by association" could have a field day.

For twenty years I also had tried to meet and know everyone on all sides of the China field. It was like virtuously accumulating kerosene and kindling against the winter cold only to find they could be used by arsonists. The China policy issue did not heat up until 1948, or explode (for me) until 1951. Until then it was a sideline and occasional occupation. My real postwar challenge was in Regional Studies at Harvard.

Regional Studies–China was one of Harvard's responses to World War II. The common, generic name was "area study." "Regional" was Harvardese, a special name to go with a special place. Both terms meant multidisciplinary study, more specifically, focusing the skills of the social sciences to study a certain part of the world.

For a time there was a mystique attached to area study, an assumption that a combining of disciplines would somehow produce a super-discipline, a new intellectual grasp. Some had visions of panel discussions in the classroom by a team of geographer, economist, political scientist, sociologist, psychologist, and historian, leading to an Illumination or Enlightenment. Such happenings might indeed produce a new level of academic ego frustration, if it could only be measured. But the field of battle was not a classroom dais but rather the mind of the student. What could he take in? Any multidisciplinary synthesis had to occur in his head. Piling professors into a classroom might be simply confusing to him.

In the end one had to agree that area study was not a new discipline of organized principles. It was only an activity, something one did. So it could be approached through an M.A. program but not through a Ph.D.

To guide this new venture Don McKay chaired a faculty committee on International and Regional Studies.* This was the group I now

---

*It was composed of leading lights: W. Y. Elliott and C. J. Friedrich, leading personalities in the Government Department; Rupert Emerson, who studied colonialism and nationalism; Talcott Parsons, of Social Relations, who had a special interest in China through Fei Hsiao-t'ung; Edward S. Mason of Economics, who had been a center post in the Research and Analysis Branch of OSS, and others.

worked for in launching the China program, but it was a support and watchdog group, not a center of doctrine. We were all feeling our way.

The Regional Studies–China seminar met five days a week 3 to 5 P.M., and also (which in retrospect seems insupportable) on Thursday *mornings*. Such eager-beaver-ness reflected our feeling that we were doing something utterly new. The seminar members had few other courses except in language. Only later did we decide history like language could best be picked up in a history course, which meant Rice Paddies, the survey course. Our sense of contact with recent reality was heightened by the presence in the late 1940s of a distinguished group of former war correspondents who came to Harvard as Nieman Fellows in journalism or on other funds.* All had been in China at the end of the war and/or immediately after it.

This China-centered community was still small enough to be knit together by discussions and cocktail parties. I believed also that mature minds subjecting themselves to beginning Chinese deserved special forms of relief. Stunt parties with skits and parodies could offset the academic authority structure by staging a different show occasionally, in which all wits were on an equal footing and all personalities fair game for satire. A lot of our academic generalities verged on the pompous and platitudinous. Given a slight twist, they were laughable. At our party celebrating the end of the first year, I presented a mock paper on "Water Control and Personality" which caricatured two of the large theories we had been offered: first, that irrigation and flood control required a buildup of central bureaucratic authority; second, that toilet training at an early age prepared individuals for parental authoritarianism. This fused macro- and micro-scale topic offered a satisfying succession of *double entendres* involving dikes and diapers, rates of precipitation and absorption, runoff, silting, movements of many kinds, upward and downward mobility, and so on.

Until the advent of beards in the 1960s I was also able to startle students and colleagues by imposing some false whiskers on my very bald appearance. Not even whiskers, really; just an ancient switch,

---

*They included Tillman Durdin *(New York Times),* Christopher Rand (OWI, later *New York Herald Tribune*), Robert P. (Pepper) Martin (CBS, *U.S. News*), Robert Shaplen *(The New Yorker),* Albert Ravenholt (Universities Field Staff), George Weller, Richard Lauterbach, Graham Peck (OWI), and others.

found in a trunk, made of bunches of hair strung on a cord, originally used to pad out an 1890s coiffure. This device, mounted around my face, destroyed my dignity, which is one objective of authority figures in a stunt party.

The first two years of Regional Studies were a focal point where many things came together, for me at least, in an incandescence of exciting ideas. Partly it was the graduate student seminar members, a dozen young men who could fuse their book learning with their practical wartime experience. Most of them had seen service in the Pacific, China, the Philippines, or the initial occupation of Japan. Benjamin Schwartz became a distinguished professor at Harvard, Marius Jansen at Princeton, Rhoads Murphey at Michigan. Bill Nelson rose high in the CIA. Partly it was the novel postwar environment in which potentialities seemed less limited and innovation was demanded. I also experienced within myself a synthesis of theory and fact, from my five years teaching and five years in government, especially of course my two-and-a-half years in China. After the first year I began putting this new synthesis on paper.

The United States and China (1948) was a home run with the bases loaded. I mean that it climaxed a buildup to which many others had contributed. I wrote it mainly in the fall of 1947 by dictation to a typist while shroffing over piles of notes. Government service had elevated me from the level of the scribblers to that of the talkers, and since 1941 my mouth had been open much of the time dictating.

The book was a survey, but much more condensed than a series of lectures. Its multidisciplinary treatment of China was guided partly by my notes on what various leaders in the disciplines had said to Regional Studies–China. I had asked three members of the committee, C. J. Friedrich, Edward S. Mason, and Talcott Parsons, to summarize the principles of political science, economics, and sociology, respectively, in a few well-chosen words and then apply them to China even more briefly in a couple of lectures apiece. Other faculty members also contributed. The result for me was not only a learning experience but an increase of self-confidence in treating things I knew little about. These leaders of their disciplines gave us the essence of each approach. After my six years in China, I could be my own informant and supply the illustrative examples of the principles they set forth.

In addition to rounding up the disciplinary concepts (which naturally formed an "analytic framework"), 1 also tried to round up the books thus far available on China. This produced a descriptive bibliography of "Suggested Reading" at the back of the book. (Perhaps for accuracy I should have added: "Estimated reading time, ten years.")

The United States and China was an early product of area study such as a well-situated historian could pull together, but it was also a brief history of American China policy. It was part of the American Foreign Policy Library that Don McKay was editing for the Harvard University Press to reach that foreign-policy public I also wanted to reach. Appearing in 1948 before the CCP victory in '49, it was an unfinished story. The second edition in 1958 had a further drama to recount, an upbeat one of revolutionary reconstruction, on the whole. In 1971 the third edition (500 pages compared with 384 in '48) had a sadder tale to tell—of the Cultural Revolution and the Vietnam War—while the fourth edition of 1979 (606 pages) could afford to be a bit more hopeful. The "Suggested Reading" of 1948 in 18 pages had grown by 1979 to total 100 pages with its own author index. I had not taken full account of the almost 1,200 books described, but each edition had required a good deal of rewriting, and I suppose a comparison of editions, if anyone ever makes it, will show up the author as both impressionable and pig-headed.

When *The United States and China* came out in July 1948, it was reviewed enthusiastically by Annalee Jacoby (noblesse oblige!) on the front page of the *New York Times Book Review* (July 8). The book's few pages on recent China policy opined that the Marshall mediation had failed because we continued "to build the Kuomintang dictatorship up materially at the same time that we tried to get it to tear itself down politically." I foresaw the danger of a population explosion as the death rate dropped more rapidly than the birth rate. (This is, of course, what happened as population roughly doubled between 1949 and 1980.) "Such an outcome would make the Chinese social scene one of continuous turmoil and uncertainty." I argued that "the choice in China is not between the American way of life and Russian communism, but between the old KMT dictatorship and the new CCP dictatorship. . . . It is a choice which the Chinese people must make in China, and we cannot make it for them."

During 1947–48 I reviewed a score of books, including works on American policy by Harold Isaacs *(No Peace for Asia)*, Robert Payne

(China Awake), Richard Lauterbach *(Danger from the East)*, Freda Utley *(Last Chance in China)*, Gerald Winfield *(China: The Land and the People)*, and others. I also joined in a dozen or so radio discussion shows—"Crossroads of the Future," a series on WEEI, Boston; "America's Town Meeting" on the ABC network; and "The Round Table" on the NBC network. On this last, seated about a little table in Chicago on November 28, 1948, with Congressman Walter Judd and Professor Donald Lach each with his own mike, I set out to best the congressman's famous machine-gun delivery that usually left his opponents speechless. Talking fast into my own mike, I tried to drown him out. It was aggressive high school debating of the sort that was in Walter Judd's background as much as my own. A small skirmish no one else will remember.

An instructor of graduate students, in addition to being as smart as they are, should be able to guide them with his knowledge of bibliography and source materials—what has been done, what can be done. I set out in late 1946 to survey the modern Chinese history books at Harvard-Yenching. By great good luck I got the help of my student Kwang-Ching Liu. He had come from a Christian family in Foochow and graduated from Harvard in 1945 in English history magna cum laude, with an honors thesis on the philosophy of T. H. Green. K. C. had a genius for bibliography, especially for imagining what historians could do with available materials. Our journey through the collection on modern China was a voyage of constant discovery. In the course of three years we canvassed 1,067 works and produced *Modern China: A Bibliographical Guide to Chinese Works 1898–1937* (Harvard-Yenching Institute Studies, volume 1, 1950) in 608 pages. I still get excited reading this volume. As long as I had it at hand I could give any student the knowledge of Chinese sources that he ought to have and show him how to proceed. It was like having an extra section of brain one could carry around; and a lot more reliable.

Since my 1938–41 collaborator S. Y. Teng was back at Harvard for a year's postwar refurbishing, we decided to pull together in English translation the key Chinese documents or essays that would tell the story of the oft-cited and misnamed "opening" of China. We formed an advisory committee, secured IPR and Rockfound funds, got the suggestions of some thirty scholars, and produced in 1950 a massive

mimeographed draft of *China's Response to the West 1839–1923.*
Two very competent scholars, Chao-ying Fang and E-tu Zen Sun
joined us as sub-authors, and we finally published the volume in 1954.
Of the sixty-five key documents, Teng drafted most of the translations and compiled most of the data on authors, which I edited, and
I then wrote the final text that links the documents together. Corrected in turn by our colleagues, this narrative gave me another
invaluable education.

Another collaboration was to produce *A Documentary History of
Chinese Communism* in 1952 with two then graduate students, Conrad Brandt and Benjamin Schwartz. They were researching the history of the CCP for their Ph.D. dissertations, and were sophisticated
as to the "bloc within" strategy, to say nothing of the "bloc without"
and other twists in the party line. Schwartz's *Chinese Communism
and the Rise of Mao* (1951) was the granddaddy of a continuing tribe
of Mao books. Brandt's *Stalin's Failure in China 1924–1927* (1958)
later used the Trotsky archives at Harvard. We selected forty documents and wrote twenty-three critical commentaries on them. The
result, a connected history of the CCP party line traced through
seven periods from 1921 to 1950, illuminated a confused area.

These works of bibliography and documentation, like the two
Japanese bibliographies and the Ch'ing documents syllabus I have
mentioned earlier (chapter 13), all seemed to be needed foundation
stones for the monographic studies my students were soon erecting.
Getting them done required systematic effort with collaborators, and
demonstrated how, in the current state of the art, our Chinese studies in America stood on two feet—one consisted of the able scholars
from China who were available to help us cover the ground.

The one that got away was an annotated survey of Russian works
on China. I invested several thousand dollars for preliminary work
but could not find a ball carrier who would see it through. My own
study of Russian began too late, and my enthusiasm was undercut by
a feeling that Soviet scholarship on modern China was, after all, of
marginal merit. Yet, of all the bits of national literature that we
Americans should try to comprehend, I suppose the Soviet view of
China might claim top priority. In short, we failed.

In this way my academic and policy interests reinforced each
other. At Harvard we had embarked, as many others would also do,
on study of the background as well as the foreground of a great

contemporary event. China's great tradition and modern disasters, the origins of her revolution, all had a bearing on her future and on what American policy should be. I felt more fully prepared for public disputation.

25

FIGHTING McCARTHYISM

THE CHINA-POLICY debate heated up in 1948 as part of a general crisis. In 1947 we had had what seemed like positive moves: Churchill's iron curtain speech at Fulton, Missouri, the Truman doctrine for defense of Greece and Turkey, and the Marshall Plan announced at the Harvard commencement. But 1948 brought a lot of bad news: the Communist coup in Czechoslovakia, the Berlin blockade and airlift, and Governor Tom Dewey's fruitless use of the China issue in his campaign for the presidency. In the midst of all this came the Hiss case in August 1948.

If you don't know about the Hiss case, how can I tell you here? For a year and a half (through an indictment in December 1948, a hung jury in July 1949 and a conviction for perjury in January 1950) Alger Hiss—a Harvardian paragon of apparent rectitude, secretary-organizer of the UN founding at San Francisco, and retired from government as president of the Carnegie Endowment for International Peace—figured in whodunit headlines on the losing side. It became evident that he, like others, had had Communist connections in New Deal Washington of the 1930s. This was amazing and appalling news to me, because it showed CP subversion and duplicity to have been an operational fact within the U.S. government. Whether or not Whittaker Chambers's "pumpkin papers" (copies of State Department documents) were genuine (they seemed to me remarkably inconsequential in content), and whether or not Alger was finally railroaded through "forgery by typewriter" as he claimed, the fact remained that he had had an extensive relationship with this Communist Chambers, which he at first seemed in 1948 to try to cover up. I never saw any proof that Alger's conduct had damaged us. But his conviction gave us Richard Nixon from California as our savior from Ivy League traitors. Unfortunately Mr. Nixon did not absorb the chief lesson of the case, which was: in a nation raised on cops-and-robbers fiction, don't try any coverups.

Things did not improve in 1949. The CCP entered Peking in January, Shanghai in April, and Mao proclaimed the People's Republic of China in October. By that time NATO (the North Atlantic Treaty Organization) had been set up and in September the Soviets had broken our monopoly of the atomic bomb by exploding their own. Nineteen fifty brought sensational disclosures of atom spies, and in June North Korea invaded South Korea. Within five years of World War II, we were at war again. General MacArthur proved himself one of our luckiest military geniuses but was fooled by Chinese "volunteers" who doubled for goats, traversing impassable North Korean mountains in the winter night. Finding no available substitute for victory, the general contemned his commander-in-chief and was recalled in April 1951. In July began a full year of congressional hearings on the IPR.

Many have analyzed the ingredients of that extraordinary period, the McCarthy era, ca. 1950–54. From having been around at the time and read a few of the books, I am impressed with the variety of factors that contributed to it.

1. In general, the Great Fear of the early 1950s was an illness in the body politic induced by a pervasive feeling of insecurity about national defense and American values and of vulnerability in liberal institutions. Totalitarianism, the police-state enemy so recently defeated in the biggest of wars, seemed to live on in Stalin's Russia. Communism was active, and had been active, in the United States. Secrecy, deception, espionage, ruthless party discipline, united-front tactics, manipulation of free institutions, all menaced our carefree way of life. The incredible destructiveness of the atom bomb had threatened human survival since 1945; its acquisition by the Soviets in 1949 evidently through espionage had been a triumph of ideology, of the alien Communist faith burrowing secretly in our midst. It was no joke. We must act in self-defense.

The key point, it seemed to me, was that this sense of ideological danger had a paralyzing effect on the old liberal credo. People could no longer be taken at face value. At a meeting of the American IPR board of trustees, of which Hiss was a member, I recall expressing the view to Arthur Dean, the chairman (a very substantial and square-cut partner of Sullivan and Cromwell, later the doughty American ambassador at the Korean truce talks at Panmunjom), that I didn't see how we could turn inquisitors and interrogate Alger. "Every man has a right to his own opinions." Very soon I had to accept a different formula: "Every man must be accountable for his own actions." The liberal guideposts were confused. Your neighbor might be a spy precisely because he didn't seem to be one—wasn't that just what a spy would do? So whom could you trust? An individual's ideas could no longer be his private concern alone. Fear of ideological subversion led on to fear of intellectuals generally. Alger Hiss, as a symbol, was handsomer and better educated than his accusers, but the common man won out against his Harvard connections.

2. There was enough Communist infiltration to justify setting up a government loyalty-security apparatus. The CPUSA in 1928 had stood for world revolution to be led by alienated intellectuals, whereas in 1935 the united front shifted to a strategy of enticement of liberals through front organizations: "Communism is twentieth-century Americanism." In New Deal Washington, Communist cells, study and/or espionage groups, were organized in several departments or agencies. The House set up an Un-American Activities Committee in 1938. The Senate Judiciary Committee later followed suit with an Internal Security Subcommittee.

Through such committees, the Congress could express the public concern by investigating. Its right to investigate as a basis for enacting legislation stretched further to let it act directly by "prescriptive publicity," to destroy the evil by exposing it. Congressional vigor could thus make up for the alleged laxity of the executive branch. The door was open for careerist enterprisers.

3. This apparatus became active when the "normal" alternation of parties in the two-party system went out of kilter. The Republican party with its big Eastern industrialists and Western small-town businessmen and farmers had managed America from the Grant through the Hoover administrations, except for the Democratic interludes under Cleveland and Wilson. Then, however, the depression had

brought that man FDR, whose "treachery" to his class (while he was busy saving it) lasted not two terms but *four!* When the fully expected Republican comeback under Governor Tom Dewey was frustrated by the 1948 election of Truman, it was more than many could accept.

The Republican Congress after 1946 thus had complex motives—to make up for Democratic "perfidy," take the law into its own hands and defend the realm by exposing the traitors in our midst. The opportunity was seized most notably by the chairman of the Government Operations Committee, Senator Joe McCarthy.

The ensuing controversy of course operated through the media and absorbed the morbid attention of the public, much as Watergate did a quarter of a century later. All the participants were in a national drama, but for real. Yet it is almost impossible in the 1980s to recapture and convey (in mere words) the atmosphere of suspicion, paralysis, and underlying fear that spread among the American public. It was far from our finest hour. Our democracy was saved by its established legal institutions, not by the courage of the political leadership or of the public.

The "loss of China" is a laughable phrase in literal terms but it had a historical reality in the American public psychology. Nearly a thousand China missionaries had been on furlough in America every year after World War I. Each one was likely to be active day by day among his supporting constituents, eagerly seeking to maintain their interest in laudable Christian work in China. The result was often a proprietary, sometimes patronizing attitude toward the Chinese, but a warm and supportive one nevertheless. United China Relief became a big operation. By 1943 the gallant virtues of Free China had been oversold. But the myth lingered on, cherished as a positive thing in the world.

The times bring men forth. Alfred Kohlberg, a rich New York importer of lace from Amoy, Changchow, and other Fukien ports, from 1943 began frenetically attacking the IPR as soft on communism. Friends of the Nationalist government in its Nanking decade, 1927–37, many of whom had rallied to the Committee for Nonparticipation in Japanese Aggression, soon formed a loose group or "China Lobby" supporting CKS and the Nationalists. The political split pro and anti the right-KMT in China set people against each other in the United States. As the Nationalist government began to lose its grip among the Chinese public in 1943, it became more active to cultivate its American friends. Receptivity increased for the idea that the "loss of China" was due to failure of American support, engineered by "Communists in the State Department." McCarthy saw his chance.

After considering other targets, McCarthy denounced Owen Lattimore as the top Soviet spy in America on March 23, 1950. Owen was in Kabul, Afghanistan, at the time on a UN mission. I phoned Eleanor immediately and suggested she must engage a capable Washington law firm without delay. She went to Arnold, Fortas and Porter, the top firm for the purpose. Owen would take some defending because he had lived mainly abroad, knew several foreign languages and scads of actual foreigners including Soviets, had corresponded with lots of people over many years, loved controversy and not the Establishment, and had been writing a column which often verged on punditry and sometimes favored the Soviet view. Having heard and read him for so long, I felt I knew how Owen's mind worked. Thinking about Chinese-nomad prehistory, he conjectured how it must have been, given all the known circumstances. Thinking about some current news item, say Stalin's purge trials, though he was not a deeply versed Soviet specialist on top of all the data, he still conjectured anyway.

Owen Lattimore was not an organization man and to call him a spy was asinine. Quite the contrary, he was a fighting individualist who claimed descent from Bishop Latimer, burned at the stake as a heretic in Oxford in 1555 where the Martyrs Memorial now stands. He was not a passive and meek witness. His book *Ordeal by Slander* (1950) tells his experience better than anyone else could.

While Owen was finishing his work in Kabul, Eleanor moved all his files to Abe Fortas's office in Washington and requested a hearing before the Tydings subcommittee of the Senate Foreign Relations Committee, which the Democratic administration had set up to investigate McCarthy's charges of "Communists in the State Department." Eleanor had to get away from her home phone in Baltimore and stay somewhere in Washington. My mother invited her to stay at 1318 33rd Street, N.W. As Eleanor wrote later, "The mother of an old and good friend invited me to stay with her in her charming little house in Georgetown. She knew Owen wasn't a Communist. She didn't have a job to lose. She lived alone and no one need know I was there. It was perfect, and will always be remembered gratefully."

Owen's forty-two page answer to McCarthy at the April 6 hearing dealt with the Kohlberg–China Lobby charges, which McCarthy had peddled, in hard-hitting and eloquent terms. McCarthy had Louis Budenz testify April 20. Other ex-Communists followed. Owen had a final hearing May 2, 1950. By May 30 he had written an intimate account of the whole experience and Little, Brown published it in July. *Ordeal by Slander* is still worth reading. The Lattimores had stood up to Joe McCarthy in ringing terms and finished clearly far ahead on technical points.

McCarthyism, however, had far from reached its apogee. The Tydings committee report issued July 20, 1950, exonerated Lattimore but the Republican minority on the committee refused to sign it. The Korean War had erupted in late June. Just before the 1950 elections, China entered the Korean War. Even Senator Tydings was swept out of office. The public were ready to accept theories of conspiracy, always so simple to grasp, as explanation of our troubles.

Senator Pat McCarran's Internal Security Subcommittee (of the Senate Judiciary Committee) got ahead of McCarthy's Government Operations Committee and in February 1951 seized the IPR files that E. C. Carter had conscientiously collected in his barn at Lee, Massachusetts, so that he could work on an IPR history. The McCarran staff spent five months delving into these records and then for eleven months (July 25, 1951, to June 20, 1952) held more or less semi-weekly hearings. They called sixty-six witnesses (most of them not connected with the IPR) and printed a transcript of over five thousand pages in fourteen volumes plus a fat index. Needless to say, *everyone* was in there. Graduate students can still fall into those fifteen volumes and not emerge for a year.

Later, Bill Holland, who was never accused of much, wrote a commentary on *The Committee's Methods of Investigation* under the following headings: "presumption of guilt, display of bias, sensational publicity, illegal seizure of files, reliance on untrustworthy witnesses, denial of cross-examination, unfairness to individuals; *The Committee's Methods of Analysis:* distortion of evidence, quotations out of context, favorable testimony ignored, hearsay vs. direct knowledge of IPR, expert opinion: 6 vs. 161; hundreds of important witnesses disregarded." Over a quarter of a century the IPR had issued about 1,200 books and pamphlets in 116,000 pages plus 18,500 pages of periodical articles. The committee referred to less than 2 percent of this output (5 books, 5 pamphlets, 21 articles, and 6 book reviews). The IPR investigation was a great fishing expedition. It thoroughly muddied the waters, broke some careers, and perhaps inspired a suicide, but didn't catch many Communist fish.

Before taking off for China in 1942 I had written Professors Merk, Buck, and Schlesinger from Washington, foreseeing a postwar need for Harvard to supply "trained personnel for administrative purposes" in East Asia, and especially instruction in Asian history, both through an undergraduate survey course and through a special institute or program for graduate students. To teach on modern Japan I recommended Dr. E. Herbert Norman, a Canadian diplomat, who had been rated excellent (an unusual grade) on his general examination by Messrs. McIlwain, Elisseeff, Gilmore, and me. His thesis had been published by the IPR as *Japan's Emergence as a Modern State*. Herb Norman was soon a rising Canadian diplomat. Witnesses with Congressional immunity testified in Washington that he had been a Communist. The accusation kept coming up. In 1957 Herb stepped backward off the eighth-floor roof of the Canadian high commissioner's office in Cairo and killed himself. This tragedy still seems hard to explain.

It seems evident, to me at least, that right-wing Republicans who were pushing Senator Taft for nomination in 1952 believed the "loss of China through Communists in the State Department" could be hung on the Democrats and would help swing the election. For this purpose they had to "get" Owen Lattimore, whom McCarthy had already denounced, and the IPR investigators set out to do so. Between February 26 and March 21 the McCarran Committee spent thirteen days or more (675 pages of testimony) interrogating Lattimore back and forth on a multitude of details in order to entrap him in inconsistencies that could be called perjury. The senators badgered him by the hour—"What do you mean by 'assiduous'?" "When will you answer my question?" A typical snare was the question "Did you know in 1940 that your friend so-and-so was a Communist?" An unwary answer "No" would imply that your friend was indeed a Communist and you didn't know it. Meanwhile they kept denouncing Owen's self-defense as disrespectful. They accused him on seven counts of perjury, all of which when put before the courts and attorney general were thrown out as insubstantial.

However, they had made his name a household word for treason. They sought to collect on their investment by parading three signs at the Republican convention of 1952: *Lattimore, Acheson, Truman.* When Eisenhower was nominated instead of Taft, the effort subsided. But Owen and Eleanor, driving across the United States, found motel managers who figured they couldn't afford to let them have a room, once they learned their names. Later Johns Hopkins, under Milton Eisenhower, where Owen had no permanency, let the Page School, of which he had been director, die out. In 1960 he became head of a China center at Leeds, England.

By this time McCarthy, though finally censured by his colleagues in 1954, had got his results (he died in 1957): liberals became cautious about the principal people he defamed. Owen had a host of friends who defended his integrity. On March 27, 1950, before his return from Kabul, I circularized some forty China specialists, all I knew, urging them to send Senator Tydings their views on whether O.L.'s writings had been "pro-Soviet" or not. If he remained "publicly besmirched as of doubtful loyalty . . . we can all be put on the defensive. . . . If American scholars are intimidated or put under public suspicion, in their study of Asia, it can contribute to great disasters for the American people, in their difficult relations with Asia." When I referred on the radio to "my friend Owen Lattimore," it was considered courageous. But when I also took care in radio debates to state that I didn't subscribe to all his pronouncements, I was acknowledging the overriding importance of ideological orthodoxy, which was the last thing we needed in our state of national ignorance about Asia. It became second nature to indicate at the beginning of an article, by some word or phrase, that one was safely anti-Communist. This of course was the mirror image, in subtler form, of the Soviet custom of quoting Marx, Lenin, or Stalin in the first footnotes of any publication.

The issue was whether we were to become ideological, putting such credence in various forms of words that we in effect joined in righteous bands as men have done throughout history to fight others of equal but opposite ideological conviction. This is still a principal posture among human beings, and there is still a good chance that mankind will righteously destroy itself.

The working of ideology was illustrated by what happened to our friendship with Karl August Wittfogel, an imposing, rangy Teutonic

ex-Communist savant whose work *Oriental Despotism* makes him a
successor to both Karl Marx and Max Weber in the theoretical analysis of Chinese society. After migrating to the United States and then
breaking with communism in the late thirties, he embarked on a
gigantic project for translation and analysis of the Chinese standard
histories, with working space in the Low Library at Columbia. When
I invited Karl August to lecture in Regional Studies, he mesmerized
my students with the vigor of a prophet, tracing the effect of water
control in irrigation and canal transport as the basis for China's all-
powerful bureaucratic despotism. Karl August's utterly committed
denunciation of theoretical errors concerning Marx's briefly cited
"Asiatic Mode of Production," over which he had once waged a
polemic in Moscow, gave us a taste of the Germanic intricacy of his
ideological way of thought. In October 1948 he praised *The United
States and China,* and he and his wife stayed with us in Cambridge
when he came to lecture in November. They did so again in December 1949. He came again to speak in March 1951.

By that time, however, ADA had set up under Reinhold Niebuhr
a study group on Asia, especially China, including Harold Isaacs,
Wittfogel, Arthur Schlesinger, Jr., and me. We had found it hard to
agree on what we were discussing since we purely American types
could not follow Karl August's long-winded concerns. The projected
commission was still-born.

When the IPR hearings began in July 1951 with new and juicy
quotations of correspondence and denunciations of dozens of people,
Karl August evidently got the wind up. He had not liked concentration camps he had been in in Germany and was determined to stay
out of those he expected to begin operating here. He testified that
when he was still a covert Communist talking to Owen Lattimore in
China in 1935–36, he could tell that Owen was also a secret Communist, though nothing was explicitly stated between them. Later on
Owen had helped Wittfogel enter the United States as a non-Communist refugee intellectual, but this innocent helpfulness was used
against him by the recipient of it. When I was accused in August
1951, Arthur Schlesinger, Jr., asked Karl August to write in my behalf
but he backed off, saying he had never been clear as to my position,
and then I had supported Lattimore and in fact still invited him to
Harvard, and so on.

This Wittfogel incident suggests two things, about him and about me. His thinking made theory the ultimate truth. Abstractions were the basic facts. (That it had to be *his* theory was just egotism.) This seemed to me essentially a religously fanatical cast of mind, a logo-mantic faith in words.

I seemed to have an entirely opposite weak spot. I couldn't take theoretical formulations seriously enough. All proofs depended on prior assumptions. I had no faith in Biblical writ or any form of words as ultimate truth, not subject to change through redefinition of terms. This made me no doubt too tolerant and relativistic. Man, the word-using animal, is motivated only in part by reason or belief. If an ideological-minded ex-Communist turned accuser out of fear, he would rationalize it to himself on ideological grounds as a patriotic duty to warn us of the danger. I would say he was fearful but not hold it against him.

My not getting mad at anyone, when others would, no doubt indicates some kind of weakness, but I prefer to ascribe it to self-confidence. As late as 1967, presiding over a session of the International Congress of Orientalists at Ann Arbor, I joined the audience while Karl August was speaking, as a gesture to give him face and offset what struck me as definite paranoia. Owen was at the Congress too, and said to me, "John, it's hopeless to be nice to those people; they don't change." I guess he was right.

In my loyalty-security case I was slightly peripheral. I did not come before McCarthy's Government Operations Committee but was dealt with by one of its rivals, the Internal Security Subcommittee of the Senate Judiciary (McCarran) Committee, which had seized the IPR files before McCarthy could. Unlike the Foreign Service officers in China, I had not been in the main line of making reports and policy recommendations. Unlike Lattimore my rather academic output and lower visibility left me less promising to victimize. Unlike his 675 pages, my testimony fills only 107 pages in the published IPR Hearings, volume 11. I have never felt in need of vindication, in fact I would have felt neglected if uninvestigated. What interests me in retrospect is how it occurred. What can we learn?

My case was an exception in that my job was not at stake, only a trip to occupied Japan, for which we needed U.S. Army entry permits along with our passports. We applied for them in April 1951. By mid-July we understood the decision rested in Tokyo, so we put our baby daughter, Laura, in our station wagon as a play pen and drove across the continent seeing family and friends. By September we were lodged with Arthur and Mary Wright at Stanford, waiting to embark.

Meanwhile the eager investigators had not been idle. In the IPR files since February they had found a wealth of mysterious messages, dubious activities, and questionable associations, enough to make any sleuth's mouth water. Ex-Communists like Louis Budenz and Elizabeth Bentley had "identified" all sorts of CP members and fronts. McCarran's IPR hearings began on July 25. Bentley testified August 14 that I had carried a message for a "spy ring." Budenz, ex-editor of the *Daily Worker,* testified August 23 that he knew me to be a Communist, "not by personally meeting him but by official reports, particularly in 1945." On September 4 the news reported I had been denied a military permit to enter Japan.

I phoned Provost Paul Buck. He put me back on full-time salary for teaching. I wired the McCarran committee asking to testify. We drove back to Cambridge. Paul Buck suggested I see Dean Erwin Griswold at the Law School about getting counsel. Erwin suggested the major Boston firm Choate, Hall and Stewart. There I saw Richard Wait, an unpretentious, firm, and clean-cut New Englander. "Are you or were you a Communist?" he asked. "No," I said. "Good. What can I do?" he asked. We joined forces.

I found of course that Harvard could not formally assert my innocence without investigating me as a basis for its opinion, and that it would not do. My case was directly between me as a citizen and the McCarran committee as my accuser, both of us having certain legal rights and limitations. A top State Street lawyer could be of great help. Meanwhile I had the help of my Harvard office secretary and plenty of moral support from faculty friends. I circularized everybody with news of our change of plans: "There is no denying I was in China before the Communist victory, but I do not go as far as some in causally connecting the two phenomena. I have met everyone I could who was Chinese or interested in China for twenty years past, so that my 'associations' must include a considerable number of dubious characters, quite aside from friends to whom this present greeting may come."

By October 1, I had compiled for distribution twenty-two pages of *Excerpts from Writings and Speeches, 1946–1950,* which included all my key statements about the nature of the CCP and what to do about it. I thought it quite impressive (though I now regret to note that in the *Harvard Summer Crimson* for July 20, 1950, I said, "To succeed fully in Korea, the United States cannot stop at the 38th parallel. We must continue into North Korea and develop a policy which seeks a United Korea." Only after we went to the Yalu and China intervened in October did I point out that no great power can afford to let an enemy sit on the frontier of its major industrial area. This kind of delayed wisdom is the privilege of historians, who receive their illumination only after the record is in.)

My excerpts concluded with an *Atlantic* article of November 1950. The CCP, I said, espoused "all the reforms and freedoms dear to the liberal heart and denounced all Nationalist evils. This made the liberals regard the Communists as almost liberal, and made the Nationalist right wing regard the liberals as almost Communist." I was still trying to get across the idea that Communists could seem good in China though bad in America. It was a fact of life but lacked much plausibility in the United States, where the newspaper interest was on accusations like those of Bentley and Budenz.

A Washington *Post* editorial of September 7 pointed out my predicament: the McCarran committee gave "no opportunity to make a public answer before the subcommittee which permitted the charges to be made publicly. No form of trial is available to him since he has not been charged with any crime and since the allegations about him were made under the protection of congressional immunity. Not even a Loyalty Board clearance procedure is open to him since he is not a Government employee."

The Army responded by setting up a Military Entry Permit Review Board which would follow the procedure used in loyalty-security hearings for civilian government employees. On December 5–6, 1951, I had a hearing before it and dealt with a dozen charges. On February 11, 1952, it sent me a list of ten further charges, to which I replied in writing. On March 11 I had a closed afternoon ("executive") session before the McCarran committee and on March 12 a day-long public session. Thus I sampled both types of investigation, the administrative loyalty-security procedure at the Pentagon, secret from the press, and the congressional committee hearing on Capitol Hill, open to the public. The contrast was fascinating.

On December 5, 1951, Dick Wait and I made our way through the appointed level, ring, and corridor in the Pentagon to an office where we found our board. It was presided over by an old Harvard man and municipal reformer from Cincinnati, Murray Seasongood. He was flanked by two members, a Mr. West and a General Phillips. My counsel presented my written answers to the charges plus various exhibits as well as twenty-five character references from three ambassadors, four generals, two senators, and other public figures. He then produced in succession three witnesses: Don McKay (my Harvard colleague), Bill Youngman (then head of American International Underwriters), and John Melby (my embassy liaison in Nanking), who all declared I did not seem communistic.

The bill of fare was not easy to get our teeth into because it consisted mainly of snippets evidently from FBI files with no sources given. Thus—

"4. You reportedly acted as an adviser to a group of Chinese Communists at Cambridge, Mass." I could not recall any such group, much less advising it; no one else knew anything about it.

"7. You were an active member on the board of trustees of the IPR in 1947, 1948, and 1950." Yes. So what?

"11. "The *Daily Worker* of 3 January 1949 contained an article which listed your name as a signer of an open letter to the members of the 81st Congress urging the abolition of the House Un-American Activities Committee." No doubt. The letter first appeared in the *New York Times*.

Such charges seemed piddling. The overall charge "1. You are reported to be or to have been a card carrying member of the Communist Party" I believe headed most such lists as a possible foundation for a perjury charge. No evidence was offered to back it up. Why "card carrying"? Isn't that the last thing one would do?

The hearing was really an occasion when I could be looked over in person. There we all were, a group of highly respectable WASPs gathered in a Pentagon office, deriving reassurance from my and others' reiterated asseverations that I was anti-Communist and would cause no trouble at large in Japan. My advocacy of recognizing the PRC before the Korean War was a little soft, no doubt, but could be accepted as a possible view; we recognized Moscow. Dick Wait along with the board's counsel conducted a skillful examination of me on all points and then at the end made a considerable summary of my case almost as for a jury. Avoiding damage to Harvard was his final point.

I came away impressed with the general courtesy and sincerity of the board but glad that my job did not depend on this quick look by outsiders at the often complex details of my function between hostile cultures. The board if in doubt had to protect the United States, not me.

The later ten charges were drawn from items in the IPR hearings. Again I answered in writing but I asked for no further hearing. I will not burden this account with all these charges, some of which are meaningless without bringing in complex details of circumstance. In general the later charges had a little more aroma of mystery. For example,

"d. In 1943 L. Rosinger indicated to W. L. Holland that he was 'looking forward to the comments of Fairbank and Hiss.' " (By 1952, of course, nine years later, Hiss had become a household word for Harvardian traitor.)

"f. I. Epstein has stated that you 'had come in from Kweilin' and that he had 'received something' from you." (The something was a report of the Chinese Industrial Cooperatives.)

"i. In 1943 your wife requested that payment for an article by Chien Tuan-sheng be sent to her for forwarding to him, in China." (Yes indeed. The fee of $100 had helped keep his family alive.)

Such activities could be suspect if the people mentioned were suspect. Once guilt by association began to operate, the stigma spread like a stain to form an endless world of possible conspiracy.

Since I spent most of the year 1951–52 researching my past associations, I retain copious files establishing the facts concerning each charge and indeed concerning other possible charges no one had yet leveled at me. The game was to fight uncertainty and suspicion with the facts. For example, Agnes Smedley, still suffering from stomach illness contracted among the guerrillas, came for tests to the Lahey Clinic in Boston in the winter of 1946–47 and stayed in my house for a week. I had had students in to meet her. As "pre-rebuttal," should the incident come up, I asked Conrad Brandt in 1951 to give me a statement recalling that she was outspokenly pro-CCP and made no attempt to hide it. This statement lies, still unused, in my files. (Agnes went to England and died there in 1950. The PRC embassy took charge of her manuscript on the career of General Chu Teh, the founder of the Red Army. It was later published as *The Great Road* but missing a chapter on the Long March period when Chu separated from Mao for a time.)

My public hearing before the McCarran committee on March 12, 1952, can only be understood as a small event in the ongoing game of politics. We met at 10:30 A.M. in Room 424, Senate Office Building, a large high-ceilinged room with a long green-covered committee table, another big table for the press, and space for a public audience of two hundred or so. I sat flanked by Dick Wait on the far side of the committee table so that I looked across it not only at the two or three senators but also beyond them to the press table, where I knew several of the correspondents who sat there: Phil Potter of the Baltimore *Sun* was an old friend from postwar China; Murray Marder of the Washington *Post* had just taken our survey course as a Nieman Fellow at Harvard. From watching their faces, directly behind my interrogators, Senators Ferguson and Watkins across from me, I could sense how the debate was going. Behind me sat Wilma with a file box of reference documents, the way Eleanor Lattimore had sat behind Owen during his sessions, and also my mother, whose histrionic instinct led her naturally to back me up with her presence.

I appeared at a propitious moment because Owen had been questioned morning and afternoon for almost two weeks, which suggested the totalitarian method of wearing down an accused person by continuous interrogation, and this became evident to the public. Owen had also used vigorous terms to describe the way he had been and was being treated. The senators by March 12 were definitely on the defensive. I was small fry, not needing to defend myself against charges of treason such as Owen faced. So we were comparatively conciliatory on both sides.

Dick Wait had found a relative and other things in common with Senator Willis Smith, who presided, and they had friendly conversations before and after the sessions. Wilma said to him indignantly, "Why do you butter up that man?" Dick replied like a good Yankee lawyer, "You catch more flies with honey than with vinegar."

Elmer Davis, who had resumed being the Walter Cronkite of the day (except that he presented *all* the nightly news himself), came in and called out to me in a loud voice across the room, "John, can you have dinner with us tonight?" I believe he came simply to make that gesture.

I also had gotten the jump on the committee with a headline in that morning's Washington *Post* based on my prepared statement. The committee in our executive sessions, very briefly on March 10 and at length on the afternoon of March 11, had decided it could not let witnesses take up its time by reading long statements into the record and so had not decided what to do with mine. When I emerged from the closed session March 11, Murray Marder and Phil Potter were waiting to ask me, "Will your statement be accepted for the record?"

"Not yet decided," I said.

"Then you can release it to us now, since they have not made it part of their record." So I gave them copies and got the next morning's headline. One of the chief points they quoted was the single insertion that Dick Wait had suggested—that I wanted my expert knowledge to be of help to my country, but how could it be if I was unjustly accused?

I was amazed in the hearing at the degree to which we argued about definitions and procedures. We were not bound by legal rules of evidence but the senators were extremely legalistic. Our colloquy discussed freedom of speech, freedom of contact, hearsay as evidence, was Mme. Sun a Communist?, what is a Communist?, fellow travelers, spy rings, front organizations, covers, infiltration, the party line, E. C. Carter as a promoter, around and around, on and on. I finally read all of my seventeen-page statement into the record.

Several things impressed me. Elizabeth Bentley had testified I carried a letter from Mme. Sun Yat-sen (characterized as "a top Chinese Communist") to the China Aid Council ("a spy ring"). Her characterizations were both wrong. But the point for me was that Bentley's knowing I had brought Mme. Sun's letter to Mrs. E. C. Carter at the China Aid Council proved some kind of CP apparatus had been active there. The CP effort was fact, not mere hearsay.

How far Tai Li and company, the Nationalist Chinese security apparatus, fed material to McCarthy-McCarran and company is an unexplored question. In testifying about Jack Service to the State Department Loyalty Board I had recorded my having known Chou En-lai's liaison officer Kung P'eng in wartime Chungking. But the only Chinese-based accusation in my hearing was in the pre-gallows "confession" dated April 10, 1950, of a certain Li P'eng, said by the Taipei *Central Daily News* of September 3, 1950, to have been executed as a Communist spy. This struck me as the flimsiest evidence imaginable.

At my "executive" session I was given a photostat of the Chinese text and an English synopsis to examine overnight. In the synopsis Li

P'eng was stated to have stated (not very direct evidence) that "Fairbank, Connors and Butterworth wittingly or unwittingly allowed diplomatic secrets to leak to the Soviet intelligence officers." (We agreed to leave Connors and Butterworth out of my hearing.) The Chinese text was a bit different, that we "wittingly or unwittingly disclosed diplomatic secrets, which then were transmitted by way of the embassies of third-party countries to the——intelligence officers' ears." In the blank where the character *su* for Soviet might be expected, there was no character printed.

Seeing no legal value whatever in this stuff, I put the above facts in the record (regarding third-party embassies and no character for Soviet) and let it go. I reckoned without the American news machine. The headline for my day's hearing in the Boston *Post* was "PROF. FAIRBANK LINKED TO SPIES. Senate bares gallows confession saying Harvard man leaked U.S. secrets to Reds in China." Even Elmer Davis, with whom we dined after hearing his news summary, put this spy charge in his reference to my hearing. Embarrassed, he explained it was the only hard news in the day's proceedings. I suppose he was right. McCarthyism is the best way to get your fellow citizens' attention. Thus the Chinese Nationalist secret police were able to hit a target in the United States.

On the other hand, in my hearing the senators were all trying hard to justify themselves in their interrogation, while of course I was trying to justify myself, all of us talking before the press and for the record. We shared a common belief in such concepts as fair play and the people's right to know, though we disagreed on how to apply them. Smith, Ferguson, and Watkins did not strike me as thoroughly cynical and innately evil like McCarthy. (Watkins later moved the vote of censure against him in 1954.) In other words, the situation was highly political but also, I felt, educable; prior public education could have affected it, given time. Since the McCarran committee hearings were congressional investigations, they led only to a published report, which in this case turned out to be a political document.

Real-life investigations in the press and on the tube are as fascinating as mystery stories, and more gripping; you can't turn to the last chapter to see how they come out. When oneself is the subject under investigation it is almost too fascinating, you can't stop thinking about it. You get sort of preoccupied. But after this March hearing we waited till July to get our military clearance for Japan. Significantly, it came through only *after* the nomination of Eisenhower. By that time the purely political aim of the McCarran committee had become evident in its insupportable final report of July 2, 1952, to the effect that the IPR was a conspiracy that through Communists in the State Department lost China, etc. I felt honored to be included in an "inner core" that also included John Carter Vincent and Philip Jessup.

This report is a formidable document for the newcomer—packed with names, dates, references to testimony, analyses, and conclusions. It is a fancy structure built on two principles—first, that anyone a man like Budenz under congressional immunity said he knew to be a Communist ("not by personally meeting him but by official reports" no longer available) *was* a communist. Second, that all contact was collusion. Very little of this farrago would survive in a court of law. It was a Big Lie to use in American politics. But it is still treasured on Taiwan to explain the KMT failure on the mainland.

As a Big Lie it of course contained some small truths. A CPUSA apparatus was indeed active in the United States. The CCP was supported by a lot of Chinese. An enormous social-military revolution had attacked our interests in China, defeated us in Korea, and opposed us in power politics. The Cold War induced warlike fear and hatred. The struggle was ideological, and the technology of subversion that so mesmerized the senators was a new danger in our youngish country.

In a circular to friends, August 20, 1952, I tried to sum up the year's experience. I felt Communist subversion, taking advantage of civil liberties in order to destroy them, was a real danger, but it must be met by appropriate procedures to protect both state and individual. My conclusion was a paradox, that the congressional committee that smeared me was less of a menace institutionally than the loyalty-security procedure that cleared me. The latter was based on a flaw; it set up a government of men, not of laws, because it operated outside the judicial process. "The McCarran committee can denounce, browbeat, vilify and generally excoriate its accused witnesses but it cannot fine, imprison or dismiss them from their jobs except by indirect influence. On the other hand a loyalty-security board has to decide about livelihood without the legal safeguards of due process, cross-examination of witnesses or the like. A board is expected to reach a decision even when it has no way of evaluating an accusation's source." I am able to reveal the fatuous accusations against me only because I was in the unique position of being an applicant for a permit, not a government employee, and so my case was not classified. My board was composed of fair-minded and conscientious persons but the task assigned them was to make a decision without regard for those safeguards of the individual which the law has worked out over the centuries. Judge Murray Seasongood, whom I met again a few years ago in Cincinnati, was a monument of probity but he was put in an unsound position.

How McCarthyism affected our Foreign Service and the quality of our policy making still needs concrete analysis. In general, the Foreign Service's China-trained members were either forced out of government work or shunted off to lie hidden in out-of-the-way places. Let me cite just three examples.

John S. Service, one-time captain of the Oberlin track team, showed the qualities of stamina, persistence, and clear-eyed lucidity that are most needed among diplomats in tight places. After being cleared six times by the State Department Loyalty Board, he was fired by the top man of the central Loyalty Review Board, Hiram Bingham, very possibly for personal reasons that had nothing to do with Service himself. He and his lawyer went to work, took his case to the Supreme Court, and eight years later won a victory—reinstatement with back pay. He left the Foreign Service only when it became apparent that it would use him only for moving furniture or as consul at Liverpool. Meanwhile, when thrown out, Jack Service had gone to work for a steam trap company. With an engineer he soon invented an improved and much smaller steam trap and became president of the international part of the steam trap company. Having thus risen in government and in business, after his final resignation from the State Department, he entered academia and soon had a political science M.A. from Berkeley, where he became an editor and assistant director of a China center. Jack Service was omnicompetent.

John Davies, who had served in Moscow and on the Planning Staff, when thrown out by Secretary John Foster Dulles (who then phoned him and said, in his typically two-faced fashion, "Let me know if I can help you") went into the furniture business in Peru, later became a writer, and gave his six daughters and a son the educational experience of living successively in all the major capitals of Europe.

Edmund Clubb quickly became a professor and wrote leading studies of twentieth-century China. All these men have written books dealing inter alia with their experience, and E. J. Kahn of *The New Yorker* has written a piece of prosopography *The China Hands*. If any one of these three had been assistant secretary of state for East Asia in place of officials without much Asian background at the time President Johnson was getting us mired in Vietnam, the fate of the American people might have been far happier. The point is that these men knew from their China experience the capacity of communism to use nationalism and of nationalism to modify communism, and Vietnam had some very similar features.

When I was invited to Washington for an informal session with the then East Asian assistant secretary in 1964 and later in 1967–68 when I served on a China advisory council under the Johnson administration (and was cleared to see secret documents), I was struck with the handicap we all faced: none of us civilian advisers had had field experience dealing with the CCP. The able assistant secretary (the bottom man on the team of half a dozen from LBJ and Dean Rusk on down who made policy) had had even less contact with peasant Asia. The background and perspective of a Davies, Service, or Clubb could have injected an essential note of realism into our Vietnam crusade. To quote the devil for a worthy purpose: After all, guns don't make wars. People make wars.

In the late 1960s graduate students who formed the Committee of Concerned Asian Scholars (CCAS) began to research how the preceding generation had led us all astray. Looking at the record, some of the more excitable announced that the McCarthy years had devastated China studies, broken our spirit, and silenced us. This I doubt. China specialists are not autonomous publicists but function on public demand. If China is not a popular subject, the talk shows will bypass it.

In my own case I was very talkative in 1950–51, appearing on sixteen radio shows. These included nine on WCOP Boston, two on WEEI, three on the NBC Round Table, and three on WGBH Boston, even after I had been accused. After that I was off the air until 1958, occupied as follows: early 1952 preparing for hearings, 1952–53 in Japan, and then publishing books in 1953, 1954, 1955, 1957, and

1958, with several articles, conference papers, and book reviews along the way. The only way to sound off on policy was through letters to editors.

My emotional experience was interesting. When publicly accused, one tends to feel guilty. This is the psychological trip wire by which thought-reform victims in a controlled accusatory environment are led to explode of themselves, confessing guilt to become cleansed. My guilt feelings, however, could not far exceed my actual conduct, which I did not consider particularly guilty.

Public accusation also rouses one to self-defense. The flow of adrenalin makes one nervous. Counter statements and arguments go round in one's head. Life is not tranquil.

However, surviving controversy, especially if self-expression is possible, soon leaves one hardened. My name in a headline raised a practical question, how to react. (The usual impulse is to overreact.) The basic aim was to keep the record straight, as by publishing denials, which can be quoted later, and rectifying misconceptions, for the record.

I found the news media were potential friends of the accused because of their belief in presenting both sides. Denials, however, seldom caught up with accusations. One was therefore prompted to do some accusing oneself.

The safe ground for accusation was that procedure had been violated. An appeal to the American faith in due process put one on the high ground.

These elementary tactical thoughts about public controversy made me quite prepared for more. But all this experience was really superficial. My livelihood and security were never at stake.

In the post-McCarthy years China was unappetizing. A dog may return to its vomit, but all the McCarthy era left behind was feces to warm over, either widespread treachery if you believed one side or widespread injustice if you believed the other. Meanwhile, the loquacity even of China hands is inhibited by ignorance. Once the country was closed to us, the realities in the PRC were a matter of guesswork and dispute. It was a fine time to study history and develop the academic field and this is what we did.

PART SIX

●

DEVELOPING
THE CHINA FIELD
1953–71

26

BUILDING A RESEARCH CENTER

THE ANSWER TO McCarthyism in the case of China had to be education. My being publicly denounced over the "loss of China" gave me
an abiding commitment to educate the American public. The alternatives of fighting the Chinese, as in Korea, and of blaming alleged
conspirators among us, as in the McCarthy era, had both been tried.
Both had failed to get the results they sought. Korea was not unified.
Communists were not found in the State Department. It was time to
use knowledge and reason instead of violence and fear.

The buildup of American research on China after 1954 was thus
an act of national policy even though it was carried on mainly by the
private sector of foundations and universities. As we went ahead with
our training and research at Harvard and other centers it became
plain that we were creating a body of knowledge and a corps of
teachers that the country needed. This idea was not invalidated but
rather reinforced by our subsequent experience in Vietnam, and the
need for knowledge and rationality is greater today than ever. More
and more of us recognize that our future will not take care of itself.
We note that more than 99 percent of all the species that ever lived
on earth are now extinct.

The East Asian Research Center at Harvard was not hard to
create. It simply accumulated. By 1955 the Regional Studies–East
Asia two-year M.A. program was turning out about fourteen students
a year. Several would begin Ph.D.s in history. The joint Ph.D. degree

in History and East Asian Languages had twenty-six candidates enrolled in 1956 (and would have seventy in 1975). These were all research workers whose dissertations might become books worth publishing. In 1947 we had begun to put out an annual volume, *Papers on China,* to distribute seminar work produced either in Regional Studies or in my Ch'ing documents seminar. Thus our training assembly line automatically led on toward publication.

Our more formal organization of a research center was inspired in 1955 by a Ford Foundation emissary who offered us support for research on the Chinese economy. Thus funded, we were happy to employ Dr. Alex Eckstein, who came originally from Hungary, a man of great warmth and determination to develop his subject. At the same time we were given some Carnegie Corporation funds for Chinese political studies. These research grants were administered by my assistant from 1956 to 1973, Mrs. Virginia Briggs, who also handled the M.A. (RS-EA) and joint Ph.D. (HEAL) budgets. In 1960 Ford gave us a million more for work on contemporary China, also Japan and Korea, and we faced a need for reorganization.

A funny thing had happened. The Regional Studies M.A. was drawing most of the beginners on East Asia in the graduate school. The joint Ph.D., which required both Chinese and Japanese but only three fields of history, instead of four, was enrolling most of the Ph.D. candidates. These new programs, adjusted to the needs of the day, had more students on East Asia than the departments of History or of East Asian languages but they were all being managed by me and Mrs. Briggs at 16 Dunster Street.

This building had been a posh 1910 dormitory with paneled suites rising five stories around a huge enclosed court. Fancy ironwork and a marble courtyard at the bottom gave the place a faded grandeur. Chinese Christmas carols could be sung from the balconies while people danced below. The old studies were the size of conference rooms and the old bedrooms the size of modern studies. Of course such waste of space could not last. Sixteen Dunster Street came down to make way for an up-to-date hutch called Holyoke Center, designed to protect its users from the fierce sun of an eternal Spanish summer which existed in the mind of the architect.

When we moved in 1960 to the old Ambassador residential hotel (later renovated as Archibald Cary Coolidge Hall to be a center for research centers), we benefitted for fifteen years from the plentiful supply of bathrooms, one to each one or two studies. The bathtubs gave us storage space and the other equipment a sense of personal freedom, not on an assembly line concatenated with others. With the Russian Research Center and the Middle East Center we subsidized a lunchroom, where the grandmotherly Mrs. Black set out home cooking for a line of thirty or forty people every day.

For our reorganization in 1960 we followed Ed Reischauer's suggestion that Regional Studies be moved under the care of the East Asian Languages people, who were already doing its language teaching in any case. We also got a half-time administrator solely for the joint Ph.D. program, who could help the students campaign, as Ph.D.s must, in the job market. This took the research center out of training. From 1960, it was solely in the research business, but still run by faculty members who were primarily teachers. In short, we erected on top of the Harvard Graduate School of Arts and Sciences, with its flow of advanced researchers for degrees, an institution that could help dissertations become books. While the center financed some research projects, the great part of its work that saw publication was started in the graduate school.

The figures for personnel at the East Asian Research Center make a very interesting picture. About 25 professors, first and last, served on the executive committee. In the twenty years 1955–75 the research fellows and others who received grants of $1,000 or more each totaled about 200 persons. Some 60 others came and used space without funding from us. More than half the fellows and grantees were born outside the United States: about 50 in China, 35 in Japan, half a dozen in Korea, a dozen from other parts of Asia, and a dozen from Europe—making a very international crowd. Advanced graduate students writing theses also used center space. Over 60 received Ph.D.s in History and East Asian Languages in this period. This compared with another total of 275 or so who earned doctorates on East Asia in various other departments or programs at Harvard. For this flux of people, the center each year had between 25 and 40 desks available in space supplied by the university.

The center's publication program started gradually in the late 1950s and then in the 1960s became a flood. Manuscripts, money, and management all came together for a couple of fortunate decades. I never believed Ph.D. thesis research should be for training only. In the new field of Modern China we needed a monographic foundation for historical thinking. Narratives of key events, solid biographies, studies of thought and of institutions were all urgently desired to give us a common fund of information readily available in English. Fortunately our state of learning was just at the point where key contributions could be achieved in a Ph.D. thesis.

The essential thing was editing, and one secret of our output was Elizabeth MacLeod Matheson, chief editor 1955–74, who trained able colleagues to assist her. Graduate students whose seminar papers and book manuscripts went into production through her often learned how to write as an unexpected by-product of publication.

Thomas J. Wilson, director of the Harvard University Press (1946–67) was a big, friendly aficionado of ideas. His imagination and enthusiasm could be quickly aroused by a readable manuscript on a new frontier. From the East Asian Research Center we offered the Harvard UP a bargain it could hardly refuse—a series of manuscripts whose time had come, as explanations of the Chinese Revolution, its background and development. These manuscripts had already been edited and their weird-language problems taken care of. Our editors could check the accuracy of romanizations and superintend the compiling of glossaries and bibliographies that used Chinese, Japanese, and other East Asian languages. The center supplied the calligraphy. HUP was spared the cost of crossing the transpacific literary gap. A book on the Ch'ien-lung Emperor could go through HUP like a book on Winesburg, Ohio; no sweat.

Tom Wilson and I valued our correspondence as an outlet and surcease from clichés. When he undertook to publish a small collection of my essays and book reviews (*China: the People's Middle Kingdom and the USA,* 1967), I sent along an "anonymous reader's" report "to save you trouble." Tom published it in his HUP newsletter.

> The miscellany of articles is arranged under four headings but the author's style is so discursive and repetitive that this division of subject matter does little to decrease the impression that we have here a real omelet. This material would be of great interest to the few people who have already read it.
>
> One cannot envy an editor who undertakes to make a nonrepetitive sequence out of this mish-mash. Mr. Fairbank has obviously been talking to students for years but never to the same ones and his capacity for the restatement of well-

worn themes would excite the envy even of a Richard Nixon. The exoticism of the subject matter may however be used to foist this product upon the public in a moment of national calamity.

Compared with 37 volumes in the first ten years, the center and/or Harvard UP published 103 volumes in the second ten years (of which 25 were on Japan or Korea). In the two banner years 1970 and 1971 the total was 43 volumes, almost two new books a month, enough to satisfy the most avid producer. We had hit a jackpot and got into big-time production a few years ahead of Stanford, Berkeley, and the others. We published manuscripts not produced at Harvard, sometimes without ever seeing the author. The word spread and for a time we had the pick of the country in China manuscripts.*

To my mind the Harvard East Asian series was a means to help a graduate student complete his training and land a good teaching job. Something published helped one to get started. A good book could lead to tenure. It was as important to add to the country's teaching staff as it was to add to the available fund of knowledge. I told seminar students to see themselves as book writers from the start. I showed them early issues of *Papers on China,* where seminar papers appeared that foreshadowed books published years later. The early papers and subsequent books made quite a list, proving incidentally that choice of a seminar topic was as crucial as choice of a spouse. It would probably occupy more of one's waking hours for a long time to come, and divorce from it after years of labor, files of notes, and piles of manuscript would be nearly impossible.

Here again we were lucky at Harvard to be in on the ground floor, producing teaching candidates who were also authors and became available just as jobs opened up around the country. At a rough estimate, East Asianist Ph.D.s from Harvard went out to teach at seventy-five or so institutions; and sometimes several Harvard graduates went to one place, like half a dozen at Ann Arbor.

---

*The scope of these publications appears in our twenty-year report in 1976 under these major headings in Chinese studies (total 124 volumes): government and administration (8 volumes), economic history (26), foreign relations (18), American-Chinese relations (16), military history (3), education (3), the modern revolution (23), thought and literature (17), history of religion (4), bibliographies and syllabi (6). In Japanese studies (23 volumes): early modern and modern political history (7), intellectual history (7), economic and social history (5), foreign relations (4). In Korean studies (4 vols.).

This explosion, as it seemed to us, in East Asian studies would hardly have made a blip on a radar screen compared with physics, biology, or chemistry, but it gave us an exhilarating sense of growth in academic work on China in the aftermath of the McCarthy era. The China field was not at all demoralized, as some have assumed, because it was expanding and therefore full of opportunity. This was due in turn to the Ford Foundation's investment of funds. In 1970 John Lindbeck's survey of Chinese studies worldwide estimated that Ford put $30 million into them in about fifteen years. Of this Harvard received about $5.5 million, of which $1 million was to help establish four professorships and the rest went for research. No matter how demandingly history may knock on the door, without funding not much happens. Let us give credit where it is due.

One question commonly put to research directors is, How do you decide what topics should be researched? The answer is, You don't decide. Each topic is selected, formulated, refined, and pursued by the researcher who works on it, as her/his choice and responsibility. If the appropriate committee of professors will not accept it, she/he has to improve it, seeking advice from all quarters. It is a system of individual enterprise. This of course seems chaotic to authoritarian planners in some countries. But it avoids loading a center with topics of A-level quality being worked on to no avail by B-level talent.

When a critical mass of talent has accumulated around the world on a certain undeveloped subject, a research center can make a breakthrough with a research conference and resulting symposium volume. We were able to do this on three major topics: *The Chinese World Order: Traditional China's Foreign Relations* (conference 1965, volume 1968), *The Missionary Enterprise in China and America* (conference 1972, volume 1974), and *Chinese Ways in Warfare* (conference 1968, volume 1974). On the other hand, in the 1950s we held two week-long conferences on the Chinese economy (1956) and the Chinese polity (1959) but in each case our focus was too broad and no book resulted.

Of course the books we turned out were less important than the people. Area studies in particular produce students who penetrate the local scene and find friends that illuminate the life of the area. For example, we found warm Russian friends in Leningrad through Mark Mancall, and met saintly Indian intellectuals in the awful human offal of Calcutta through Stephen Hay.

Of the many things one can do for a graduate student, the most important may be to help get a book finished. The bond between student and manuscript is sometimes stronger than between the sexes. There are other men or women in the world but a manuscript is uniquely one's own. To stop working on it is like giving up breathing or eating. It may be finished, accepted, revised, edited, and awaiting publication, yet the author can't let go of it even though his worldly advancement depends on it. The problem then is to get possession of the manuscript and break the umbilical cord by simply putting it into production. Once at Princeton, when a tenacious young instructor let me see his manuscript, I picked it up and got out the door with it. It made a good book and helped his career.

Involvement with students gave us almost more friends outside Cambridge than at Harvard, and younger ones too. From 1950 we were also kept young by a new family life, which cannot be left out of a personal memoir. Ambition may make one tick but family life supplies most of the clockwork. In our early forties we acquired two baby daughters, who have enriched our lives ever since. The social workers who venerated Wilma's aunt, Miss Ida Cannon, outdid themselves for us. I first met Laura King Fairbank as a six-month-old pink-and-white bundle of energy, annoyed at our bursting in on her. But when I picked up this solid chunk of irate personality and held her firmly, she calmed down and put an arm around my neck: we knew we were made for each other.

One of Wilma's gifts for motherhood was her joy in play. To my goal-oriented mind (*Finem respice* is on the Fairbank coat-of-arms) the Cannon family seemed to play around a lot in their spare time —card games, ball games, word games, or just the games of conversation or painting. Play involved novelty and the unexpected. So did travel. My straightest-line-between-two-points approach was constantly violated by Wilma's penchant for taking back roads, exploring the countryside en route anywhere, coming back a different way, and generally avoiding repetitive routines. "Where we going today, mommy?" was the girls' morning greeting.

Holly Cannon Fairbank joined us at three months, blonde and beautiful like Laura. Very early she began to put her life directly into motion. Both girls were accustomed to a constant flow of new faces and new places. In summer we rented horses and used the riding trails we had cut through the woods at Franklin. Laura and Holly made the transition from horses to boys without a hitch. Fortunately the sexual revolution had arrived. It all seemed very natural, as indeed it was. They occasionally moved out but then moved back in again. This early socialization, if I may try to be sociological, made them more ready, I think, to decide about careers.

They solved their problem of sinological parenthood very neatly, Laura by going in for nursing, Holly for dancing. Outsiders to both, we couldn't say a word except to ooh and aah at their adventures. Laura began assisting in a mental hospital, fascinated by the people. Eventually she took the three-year nurses training course at the Massachusetts General Hospital, which made her a scientist as well as a take-charge type. Later she earned her B.S., and later still took an M.S. in cardiac nursing. It is a noble profession, helping people into, through, and out of life and also keeping the doctors out of trouble.

Holly meanwhile went to Sarah Lawrence College in New York, to which she was ideally suited, and then stayed on in the city studying modern dance—surely one of the most hard-working and rewarding, though least remunerative, of professions. Soon she was herself choreographing while also taking an M.A. degree. Holly has an extra-beautiful figure, which producers like to put in the front row, but given such a resource, dancing seems to be an unremitting search for new forms of the poetry of motion.

Having baby daughters in our forties gave us a common bond with graduate students, some of whom were producing dissertations and children simultaneously. Dissertations take longer than babies although of course they don't change so much afterward.

In addition we were fortunate to find close friends among our colleagues, whose work was of great interest and help to me. Mary Clabaugh Wright was nominally almost my first student, but actually she was more like a junior colleague. She hardly had time to study with me or take my nascent seminar, once she decided to shift from Europe to China. She came to Radcliffe in 1938, not so much a southern belle born in Tuscaloosa as a *summa* from Vassar, beautiful but very, very sharp—not a rough diamond; a polished one already finely cut. After Mary Clabaugh met Arthur Wright at one of our teas, in 1940 they married and took off for Kyoto and, in 1941, Peking, where I visited them after they came out of internment, in 1945.

Since I was working on China's foreign relations in the 1850s,

Mary bit off the 1860s. She began Japanese in Kyoto, read Ch'ing documents with Peking teachers, and during internment studied Russian, while I was writing wartime memoranda. Once started, she was a plunger, not a fence straddler, and with her own private copy of the Ch'ing *Veritable Records* (1,200 volumes printed in 1936) she took on an across-the-board study of the whole post-rebellion restoration of the 1860s. *The Last Stand of Chinese Conservatism: the T'ung-chih Restoration 1862–74* is a primary study of the efforts of Confucian-trained leaders to quell rebellion and salvage the traditional state. They triumphed but "amid lengthening shadows," as she put it.

After Arthur and Mary went to the Yale History Department in 1959, we saw each other more easily *en famille*. Wilma and I and our two daughters could be absorbed into the guest wing of Landfall, the seaside estate that Arthur bought with his Portland, Oregon, inheritance. The Wright boys, Duncan and Jonathan, became first-rate sailors in the local yacht club races. Going to visit the Wrights' big house with its cook and butler was an event.

Mary Wright's brilliant career can be appreciated only in a double focus. She lived on a forefront of scholarship in Chinese studies and at the same time in a very real struggle for women's liberation. Her Alabama background cast her in the role of a beautiful woman of feminine charm devoted to wifedom, motherhood (she had two sons), household management, and social life. Her intellect and imagination pushed her ambitiously into historical scholarship as a library curator (at the Hoover Institution), lecturer at Stanford, researcher, professor at Yale, and research director. This was a double life, alternating in action on two stages with no rest room in between. Like Edna Millay's, her candle burned at both ends. It was a tense existence. Tobacco and at the end of the day alcohol might relieve the tension, as well as Arthur's skillful management of a happy domestic life. But Mary felt constantly in a minority, harassed by fate. Not without reason. The Stanford History Department would not make her a professor. The theory was that a husband and wife both acting in a professional group would have warped judgment, either always agreeing or always disagreeing, I forget which. At Yale she was more fully appreciated, but to be the first woman professor was not devoid of strain. Men can say one thing and do another.

At Yale Mary shifted her focus to the end of the dynasty and organized an international research conference in 1965 on the Revolution of 1911. Afterward she was hospitalized with nervous exhaustion for some months but emerged and got the symposium *China in Revolution: the First Phase 1900–1913* published in 1968. With her long introduction, it is the basic work in its field. By 1969 at age fifty-one she had seemingly won the battle and was back in action. Her intellectual commitment to the analysis of China's history, her passionate tenacity in pursuing and comprehending all aspects of a subject had made her already a star in our field. One day she went for a routine medical checkup and was told she had an inoperable cancer and about six months to live.

Mary responded with her usual realism, clarity, and activism. She gave her family and the president (Kingman Brewster) the news direct, calling in friends, setting things in order. She soon realized, I think, that in such downturns of fate all one can try to control is oneself, acting out one's tragic drama with whatever style one can muster. She did it superbly. When chemotherapy produced a remission, she and Arthur had an Italian spring fortnight in Florence. In June she attended a departmental reception, beautifully dressed as usual, seeing friends; and a few days later died in her sleep.

This was a shattering blow to many people. So was the death of another brilliant star, Joseph R. Levenson, who was accidentally drowned in California in 1969. Joe had been my tutee in Kirkland House. World War II gave him Japanese. His Ph.D. was on the great Chinese reformer Liang Ch'i-ch'ao. He became a Harvard instructor and we taught Modern China together. At Berkeley he pioneered China's intellectual-cultural history with a brilliantly arresting and provocative style. His trilogy, *Confucian China and Its Modern Fate*, made the Taoist point that every quality implies its opposite: heat implies cold; good, evil. He reveled in the resulting paradoxes: "the routinization of intuition," "academic anti-academicism." His virtuosity at word play, however, masked an underlying concern for larger issues, Chinese values in conflict with historical events. Above all Joe Levenson was irrepressibly creative—a joyous mimic, by turns witty and histrionic. His gaiety of person is what one remembers. A group of us were in his living room. As the conversation paused, a large cat walked in rather self-importantly. With a look at his wristwatch Joe said severely to the cat, "I can give you just two minutes." His tone and manner were unforgettably convincing.

We lost Mary Wright and Joe Levenson tragically before their time. Arthur Wright was fortunate to find a new life for himself but died too soon in 1976. He was an organizer like me and we worked together on many things.

Arthur Wright's taste in Peking furniture, rugs, and paintings carried over into his scholarship. A classicist studying Buddhism in the Sui and T'ang, he left modern China's politics to Mary but found a special interest to pursue in the field of Chinese thought through the centuries. He saw it must be brought into a confluence with the study of Western thought. China's absorption and use of Buddhism, for example, could be compared with Western movements like Christianity and even Marxism-Leninism.

At a strategic moment in 1954 I engineered a meeting of Professor Robert Redfield, the leader of social anthropology at Chicago, and Arthur Wright, out of which came the Committee on Chinese Thought of the Association for Asian Studies and a program of study conferences which Chicago for a time could help finance. The field of Chinese thought—biographies, textual studies, movements—had reached a critical mass such that Arthur and his chief co-worker, Denis Twitchett of Cambridge University, could invite contributions from scholars in many lands—Britain, France, Germany, Australia, Japan, Hong Kong, Malaya, Canada, the United States—who were at a common level of learning and theoretical sophistication. Half a dozen symposium volumes resulted.

In sum, what can a teacher say of his students and colleagues and their works? I participated in some fashion in the conception, gestation, growth, and publication of books by younger professors on their way up in the academic world. To name these authors and books in any meaningful fashion here would take a separate volume. They were of a generation that changed the contours and content of Modern China's history as known to the English-reading world. Like senior professors at other universities I presided over a part of this creative process. I was, in Dean Acheson's phrase, "present at the creation."

27

ORGANIZING THE FIELD

To RESPOND TO China's revolution with understanding, not with warfare or hysteria, was a national task. Producing teachers and books at Harvard could set an example—that was the least we could do, given Harvard's special resources. But the China and East Asian field urgently needed organization so that new money could flow to talented recipients on a nationwide basis. We needed new academic structures to bring this about. The organization of the research center at Harvard and of research conferences led me on very naturally into the national scene.

As president of the Association for Asian Studies in 1959, I found one major problem was to secure foundation support to help the growth of the association's services. A Michigan professor served without pay as treasurer and there was a salaried administrator, so that the money was properly handled and the meetings and committees were kept going. But policy-wise the AAS high command was made of eiderdown. The directors, three elected each year for three-year terms, had a three-year memory of business. Two years after receiving a grant, only a minority could recall its origin. After three years no one could. But most things worth doing needed five-year grants.

Since the Ford Foundation, especially the Board on Overseas Training and Research, was heavily engaged in an effort to spend $30 million wisely on East Asian studies, I tried first to compensate for the revolving-door nature of the AAS leadership. Coopting other stalwarts like Hugh Borton (Japan) and Norman Brown (India), I set up an AAS Advisory Committee on Research and Development (ACRD), whose membership would rotate on five-year terms and consist of experienced oldsters who had been around and might command foundation confidence. They were called "advisory" to forestall the directors' suspicions and avoid a constitutional amendment.

By this time China specialists all over the country were full of schemes and projects. Their Chinese might still be sketchy but as Americans they saw the need for bibliographies, library building, translation digests, language training, a Hong Kong research base, research conferences, and so on. A long shopping list of such needs had been accumulating since the 1930s. The most essential were a predoctoral fellowship program for training and a postdoctoral program for research projects, both on a national scale to open the door wide to talent. Ford and others were ready with funds. Only an administrative structure was needed.

Such a structure, however, had to consist of scholars who could cooperate in the national interest and with mutual confidence. As I wrote the Ford Foundation in April 1959, the last fifteen years' events in China and America had produced a high level of "emotional involvement" on the part of China specialists. I could see it in others; perhaps I even had some myself! Consequently, I felt, in the new field of Contemporary Chinese Studies (i.e., studies of the CCP and the PRC), "we face a serious problem at the level of personal cooperation." It was essential that we form "a minimal working relationship on an agreed basis which is as neutral and feasible as possible." In short, we had to get beyond the McCarthy-era split in the China field.

One of the simplistic clichés is that McCarthy-McCarran split the China field "down the middle." Not at all. It was more like a horse-rabbit stew, one horse and one rabbit. Aside from Professors Colegrove and McGovern at Northwestern and a few others like David Rowe and Dick Walker at Yale, the main scholarly proponents of a pro-KMT intervention were at the University of Washington at Seattle in the Far Eastern and Russian Institute that George Taylor had pulled together after 1946. This group included several sinologist refugees from Nazi Germany, including Karl August Wittfogel, as well as refugee scholars from mainland China. Getting them to focus on an in-depth, documented, and interdisciplinary study of the great Taiping Rebellion that convulsed China from 1850 to 1864 was a considerable administrative-intellectual achievement. Building a Chinese library almost from scratch was only part of it. George had to maintain the morale of a community of displaced persons while also fighting off local red-baiters who had him on their list of suspicionable professors.

His background and sympathies being pro-KMT to begin with, he had been a friendly witness before the McCarran committee, while his German-born colleagues were much concerned to warn of pro-Communist ideological deviations. Native-born American China hands were on the whole less sensitized to the ideological struggle. The McCarthy era left Seattle feeling like a beleaguered minority. But the group's deeply felt interest in the rise of communism in China put them in the main line of concern to which the Ford Foundation was responding. It was essential that we all pull together.

The Gould House conference was brought together on June 19–21, 1959, at a conference place belonging to New York University at Dobbs Ferry, New York. The practical aim was to suggest channels through which Ford could finance the development of the contemporary China field. Having just been president of the AAS, I was asked to head an organizing committee of three, along with Martin Wilbur of Columbia and Arthur Steiner of UCLA. I set up the agenda with the bland assumption that a development committee should naturally be created under AAS. Pro forma, the conference was called by the new AAS Advisory Committee on Research and Development headed by Bill Lockwood of Princeton, to whom we would report.

From a Seattle point of view this was the Eastern Establishment playing ball with itself—Harvard, Columbia, Princeton, with UCLA as West Coast ballast. More important was the whole issue of how to study communism in China. Some AAS China hands might view it as merely a phase of Chinese history, whereas it was also part of a worldwide movement given shape and direction in the USSR. George and his principal colleague, Franz Michael, also stressed the necessity of the multidisciplinary area-study approach, bringing all the social sciences to bear on the problem, as well as whatever could be learned from the field of Soviet studies. In retrospect it is plain that this was the way to go. It pointed in the direction of the Social Science Research Council as a sponsor of a developmental committee.

Nevertheless, I went ahead with AAS in mind from April to June, corresponding around the country to work out an invited conference membership of about twenty-five people, including some from government and the Ford Foundation, and working out also an acceptable agenda to include papers on our various kinds of needs. The Gould House conference in late June 1959 held five sessions in three days and canvassed numerous projects with a good deal of agreement. Only when presiding at the last session, to settle on the auspices for a developmental committee, did I find how much opposition there was to AAS auspices—not only from Seattle but from a political scientist like Lucian Pye of MIT. The idea began to get through to me that the real issue was the area approach *vs.* the disciplinary approach. Our aim should be to secure attention to China from the disciplines, but AAS had no way of judging who was a good economist or a good sociologist, whereas SSRC represented the major disciplinary associations and could find people to make such judgments. Another consideration was administrative. The fact that AAS was a democratic kaleidoscope, in which the leadership changed every year and no board of directors could remember anything beyond three years back, could hardly inspire a foundation's confidence as to continuity of aim, whereas SSRC was run by long-term professional administrators with long memories and proven reliability, at hand from day to day in New York.

An acrimonious discussion wound up with a split vote, nominally supporting my proposal of AAS but with many abstentions. I began to see there was quite a point to be made in favor of a developmental committee under SSRC, about which I didn't know very much. The split vote gave the Ford people a weak basis for action. I decided to reverse course and join the minority. I persuaded my colleagues on the organizing committee to go along and we asked Bill Lockwood to take soundings.

This eventuated in a session with Pendleton Herring, head of SSRC, who had known George Taylor in the Harvard graduate school. If SSRC would set up a development committee to use Ford funds, who would head it? I suggested George because I thought he would have the knack for doing it, and his appointment to such a central spot would reduce the "split" between Seattle and the East Coast. After some discussion, I phoned George, who had not been at Gould House, to proposition him. (I thought this quite dramatic!) He accepted, the Joint Committee on Contemporary China came into being, John Lindbeck at Harvard acted as secretary, and so we turned a corner. We were fortunate to have as SSRC staff member, assigned to keep his hand on the throttle and the committee on the rails, a Latin America specialist, Bryce Wood, who was a pleasure to work with. Much of the penetration of China into the disciplines has been under JCCC auspices.

By definition the Joint Committee on Contemporary China was developing studies of China's twentieth-century transformation. In the 1960s, however, most of the China field in the United States still consisted of historians, and their shopping list of needed facilities was as long as the twenty-four dynastic histories. We needed a counterpart committee to JCCC on China before 1911; otherwise the war between the humanities and social sciences would ravage the field. In 1962 I promoted a meeting at ACLS at which leaders in early history like Derk Bodde of Penn, Arthur Wright and Ted de Bary of Columbia were urged by me, George Taylor, and John Pope (my Exeter classmate then at the Freer Gallery) to form a Committee on Studies of Chinese Civilization. This was done, and Arthur Wright served as its chairman for the next ten years. He added European leaders of sinology to the membership, and imposed his critical sense on a wide-ranging growth of training, research, and projects in history, literature, philosophy, and even the arts. Arthur's combination of Stanford-Oxford-Harvard-Kyoto scholarly standards and Portland, Oregon, entrepreneurial capacity paid off to everyone's benefit.

In 1959 I had met again at Yale John Matthew Henry Lindbeck, whom we had first seen as a studious youth in his missionary parents' house in Loyang in 1933. He had his Yale Ph.D. in political science. I suggested he come to assist me at Harvard while publishing his thesis on the Boxers and the missionaries in 1900 and lecturing in the Government Department. He came and stayed for eight years, 1959–67, until he went to be director of the East Asian Institute at Columbia, so we had a two-man management at Harvard such as I felt was essential for running any real operation. John Lindbeck was a handsome and very amiable diplomat-promoter, the spark plug in creating several key institutions in the China field. He spent hours on long distance as the research center's veritable foreign secretary. He had the true diplomat's capacity to round up the personal interests involved in a problem and reconcile them amicably in a practical solution. For the Joint Committee he helped George set up disciplinary subcommittees to develop China studies in economics, sociology, and political science. John then branched out into meeting national needs, which included a research base to study the PRC in Hong Kong (the Universities Service Center), a Chinese Materials Center to supply hard-to-get publications in Washington, D.C., and looking to the future, a joint ACLS-SSRC-National Academy of Sciences (i.e., National Research Council) Committee on Scholarly Communication with the PRC. He was a prime mover in setting up all three. He died suddenly in 1970, a very great loss to us, but these institutions he fostered have continued to function.

John left us as his testament a report for the Ford Foundation published in 1971 as *Understanding China: an Assessment of American Scholarly Resources.* This small volume summarizes very neatly the growth of China studies all over the country, including the hundreds of fellowships given after 1958 by the National Defense Foreign Languages program, the allocation of funds for major centers, and so on. Indeed it provides just the data and the discussion of issues needed to correct the distortions inherent in a memoir by a single participant like myself.

The Lindbeck report estimated that some $40 million from outside the universities was put into China studies in the period 1958–70. In dollars this made a small tail to wag, compared with the massive bulk of expenditures for our Pentagon dog. I am told that the dinosaur, the biggest thing that ever lived, had only a pea-sized brain. I hesitate to draw the obvious conclusion. In my half-dozen appearances at the National War College in Washington I found a consistently high level of intelligence among the student officers. They were trapped into surveying all the world's power politics in just a few weeks' intensive reading and discussion. It was the proportions in the allocation of time and resources between hardware and brainware that were wrong.

John Lindbeck and I shared an ecumenical view, as I believe he would have called it. We believed the entrance of revolutionary China into the international world was a global problem, and Chinese studies in the United States should be of help to those elsewhere, including Europe. In the summer of 1955 I attended two conferences, in Leyden and Rome, and began to get an idea of European sinology.

At Leyden the Eighth Congress of Junior Sinologues met in a medieval castle inside a moat, converted to be a youth hostel and conference center, on the edge of town. The Junior Sinologues, who by this time were middle-aged, had taken the name to avoid inviting old Moule and old Giles and other worthies who might have done all the talking.* English was widely used. We all slept on cots in a garret dormitory, used a common washroom, and had a chance to get acquainted. Robert Ruhlmann from Paris led us in singing songs like "Alouette, gentille Alouette" and the universal penury of academic life gave us a common bond. My report on the training programs at Harvard, where the shelving of library books cost more than the books themselves, must have seemed typically American—equipment first, learning later.

Two historians came from the PRC—Chien Po-tsan, an oldster who had produced a Marxist-modified general history, and Chou I-liang, a Harvard-trained Sung specialist, now reconditioned and producing textbooks at Peita. When the European leader Balazs wagged his finger at old Mr. Chien in an argument on the floor, he felt insulted by Balazs's didactic manner and we had to restore his face by apologies for the aggressive Western style of disputation. Europeans, we explained, had argued in their universities for hundreds of years before Gutenberg while Chinese scholars had been using paper, brush, and printed books all the time.

I told Chien and Chou we heard good things about some of the revolutionary changes in China but no word of birth control. What was being done to avoid overpopulation?

"That," they replied, "is a Malthusian, imperialistic error. We know from Marxism that man's labor power creates everything, so the more people we have the better."

I have always remembered this exchange. There went the ball game! After a doubling of China's population in the thirty years 1950–1980, the standard of living under Mao's revolution was just

---

*The core organizers included Otto Berkelbach van der Sprenckel, a Ming specialist from England, Denis Twitchett and Piet van der Loon from Cambridge, Étienne Balazs from Paris, Herbert Franke from Munich, Jaroslav Prusek from Prague and Wolfgang Franke from Hamburg.

about where it had started. Marx's anti-Malthusianism led to one of history's greatest fiascos.

Moving on to the Tenth International Congress of Historians in Rome, I presented a paper on "The Influence of Modern Western Science and Technology on Japan and China," which derived from several discussions among Harvard colleagues for whom I was rapporteur. We saw the great contrast between Japan's dynamic response and China's lethargy in modern times as due to socio-cultural differences between the two countries, an anti-Leninist view. Dr. Joseph Needham from Cambridge attacked the paper as underplaying the evil influence of imperialism. I had had some exciting discussions with Joe Needham on his plans for study of Chinese science and technology in wartime Chungking when we were opposite numbers under our respective embassies (if a Jeep and a truck can be called opposite numbers). Later he had certified that Americans had used germ warfare in Korea. Now he was being doctrinaire about Japan. It seemed to me more egregiously ideological than his massive contributions on *Science and Civilization in China.* I wondered if an omnicompetent scientist, versed in the "laws" governing so many fields, was unable to confront the social scene without a similar recourse to "laws," in fact to the "science of society" which Marxism claimed to be. If so, it was a challenge to the rest of us to explain China's history in our multidisciplinary manner.

This raised still another question of organization—whether the flood of new ideas could be caught in a textbook that could help the East Asia survey courses now being widely given around the country. Ed Reischauer and I, reshaping and refining Rice Paddies from year to year, felt the need of an up-to-date summary as a necessary foundation for more advanced work. We began discussing it about 1951, felt uninspired by one publisher and shifted to another, and finally set to work in the late fifties. I was helped by the fact that Widener Library has an admirable system for work on Sundays. You arrive at an hour when the guard is seen to be changing, as you peer through the Massachusetts Avenue entrance door. You get the door unlocked so you can enter and sign a special register where your name is already listed. You are then free for the day—no people, no phones, a sandwich, and the quiet of a Trappist monastery.

The great textbook problem of course is what to choose, to know enough so you can suppress most of it, to put in your narrative the names and events that can represent the essential themes. General and particular keep interacting. Marco Polo is unavoidable for himself. He also represents a flow of Western contact to China, a Mongol use of foreigners in ruling China, a legend in Western folklore, and so on.

A History of East Asian Civilization, Volume 1, *East Asia: The Great Tradition,* came out in 1960; volume 2, *East Asia: The Modern Transformation,* in 1965. The combined condensation, *East Asia: Tradition and Transformation,* followed in 1973, and then *China: Tradition and Transformation* in 1978. In such a genealogy I suppose grandchildren will be conceived of in due time.

When Ed became John F. Kennedy's ambassador to Japan (1961–66), we got the help of our junior colleague Albert M. Craig to deal with Japan in the twentieth century. The latest on the Japan side is Reischauer and Craig, *Japan: Tradition and Transformation,* 1978. It will be noted that Ed Reischauer is a switch hitter who deals with both early China and early and modern Japan.

I deplored the bifurcation into China and Japan volumes because it shortchanged our basic concept of East Asian civilization as an entity, "the Chinese culture area." In our survey course this led at first to Japan's receiving only a third of our attention while Inner Asia, Korea, and Southeast Asia were also surveyed. But, as Japan loomed larger and larger on the American horizon, if not in the public imagination, it demanded more attention. A Chinese intellectual hegemony through the concept of the Chinese culture area (which includes Vietnam) had to be given up. It will make a comeback in due time.

Writing these textbook volumes was for me an awesome business. I felt my colleagues on Japan were standing firmly on large masses of scholarly publication, whereas on China we had many sinological facts but not so many social-science interpretations. Work of Maurice Freedman and G. William Skinner was just emerging. Few modern-trained Chinese historians had had a chance to put China's history together during the decades of invasion, civil war, and revolution. China's modern literature had as yet attracted few students. Statistics on China were hard to get; whereas in Japanese history one could begin with a volume of bibliography that contained nothing but bibliographies—a whole book listing lists of books—on every conceivable topic.

Our volumes showed their necessary primitivism in stressing institutions and the ruling power. By the time we had characterized the dynastic house, its conquests and revenue system, major rulers and achievements in art and literature, it was time to move on. How life had been for the common man we could hardly say. The common man and woman, in fact, are perversely hard to find. Anyone you do find is ipso facto uncommon. Social history is not so easy as you might think. You can generalize about conditions, invoke statistics, and condemn the rapscallions of the elite. But anyone who expressed himself and did something is likely to be disqualified as atypical.

In any case I felt we were about at the level of Stubbs's *Charters,* which used to be the starting point for English constitutional history. We had to set up the institutional framework for Chinese and Japanese history—events, periods, movements. We got Wilma to help us illustrate these books, and Houghton Mifflin made them into works of art. In the end we felt nothing was in them that didn't have to be there, just to begin to do justice to the subject. After all, we were cashing in on the greatest opportunity since Polo himself. The result of course was a concentrate. Any three pages of our text could be expanded into a lecture. One student said to me, "I can't read your book but I sure as hell can study it."

That was twenty years ago and we can see our survey now as a summary of the Chinese literati-ruling class's view of itself and its achievements. The revolution has added the life of the common people, mainly the peasantry, as a new focus with a multitude of problems to study. Meantime, translations of Chinese literature have blossomed forth and are being used by humanist historians like Mary Wright's student and successor, Jonathan Spence. Chinese modern history needs a new textbook.

Organization of training, research, and publication fostered a growth of scholarly opinion. Having seen how national communities can indoctrinate themselves with ideas that later seem specious or biased, I felt it essential that China specialists in America be in touch with their counterparts elsewhere. This seemed especially desirable when "imperialism" was so lively an issue worldwide, including the American role in it.

28

ITINERATING AROUND THE WORLD

ONE ADVANTAGE OF being a pioneer is that one can map the terrain, discover the gold mines, and work the most promising sites. Within the modern China field I had an inveterate impulse toward a comprehensive grasp, as though I wanted to put a tent over it to get it within manageable compass. First in books: with Wilma's help I filled several file drawers with bibliography cards, all the stuff in English as of 1936, even before I returned to Harvard. I wanted to know about every author who had ever written on China. As my language efforts went along, this became an awesome task, but I got Chinese and Japanese help in compiling the various descriptive bibliographies mentioned above.

Second, I wanted to know everyone in the field and what he was doing. This kept me very busy at conventions or association annual meetings. It expanded into a practice of traveling around the country to lecture, see centers, and meet people. I customarily worked out itineraries so that en route to one place I could stop at others and find out what was going on. "Have China, will travel"—I announced my availability at minimal cost, with the result that over the years I made hundreds of talks in scores of places across the country.

This urge to spread the word I can only attribute to a sort of missionary impulse (I notice Ed Reischauer has it too), more rife in America than elsewhere. I suspect many people in older societies find it slightly crazy, wondering how we can be so energetic about it except as greed or a power drive or fanaticism moves us. Perhaps it is best understood as academic entrepreneurship, a pale reflection of the concurrent expansion of corporate capitalism.

For my part I felt everyone in Chinese studies was a co-worker and a potential friend and possibly could be helped. I never hesitated to offer encouragement to people more advanced than I. I felt we all needed moral support. In this respect I could understand the motives of the drummers and promoters of Main Street who spoke at Rotary and Kiwanis Club meetings, exemplars of our American organizational impulse. We all believed in growth as the salvation of the world. The more hard-headed idea that growth is really our chief menace was not to our liking. More is better, at least in one's own field, even as things get worse generally.

Our real salvation no doubt lies in better organization and cooperation, putting a tent over the world. In my case travel abroad was a natural part of it.

Our ten months in Japan in 1952–53 had been pretty much at the graduate-student level, studying language and bibliography. We found good friends among the small group of non-Marxist Japanese specialists on China. The most international-minded among the Tōdai (Tokyo University) professors was Tatsurō Yamamoto, a patrician of great skill and aesthetic grace, impeccable in French, English, Chinese, and other tongues, a leader in Sino-Vietnamese studies and Japan's representative on international academic bodies. The Yamamotos had been at Harvard in 1951–52. Typically we ran into Tatsurō later in India directing a Japanese survey team that was measuring and photographing architectural monuments all across the country, as systematically as silkworms eating mulberry leaves. His wife Sumiko in 1953 had helped Banno and me complete our bibliography of Japanese works on modern China. She taught at International Christian University and published her doctorate on the anti-Christian movement in China in the 1920s. Such naturally graceful friends often left us feeling uncouth in comparison.

In the 1960s I went around the world twice and so did John Lindbeck. We both saw Chinese studies as a worldwide cause and were eager to find out what other countries were doing and how we could cooperate, especially in Taiwan, Japan, and the USSR.

In 1960 Wilma and I found that Laura, aged ten, and Holly, aged six, added greatly to the excitement of our trip and our ease of contact with local people. We began with the sights of Rome and Athens, followed by a week with the British ambassador to Bulgaria, my Balliol classmate Sir Anthony Lambert, in his spacious embassy in Sofia. The Lamberts' two daughters and ours enjoyed playing together while Wilma and I got our first feel of a Communist capital —the street crowds on foot, the suppressed intellectuals so eager to exchange even commonplaces with Americans. With Tony we exchanged political views in whispers while playing music. We assumed the embassy was bugged.

Other weeks in Israel and in New Delhi under Nehru and a side trip to Nepal showed us their national efforts at regeneration, and then we went for a fortnight in Burma. Arthur Hummel, Jr., head of USIS in Rangoon, gave us every support, and we visited Mandalay and then jeeped to Pagan to photograph most of the forty major temples still standing at that medieval Buddhist site. It was a dry, sunny outing in shorts, British style. The Burmese under Prime Minister U Nu, with whom I had a long philosophical interview, were already slipping gently into that abstention from industry, Cold War, and even tourism which has left them poor, antiforeign, and perhaps happily out of the news ever since. Bangkok, Kuala Lumpur, Singapore, Saigon, and Hong Kong by contrast seemed modern and disjointed by the speed of change.

The Hindu or Buddhist lands south of China seemed academically unresponsive to the Cold War. New Delhi was much concerned about the long-disputed border with revolutionary China, and by 1962 Indian troops would even attack the Chinese on the border and be decisively defeated. But except among the Foreign Office diplomats there was no trained linguistic talent, nor much serious study going on in universities. Burma had nightmares of a Chinese invasion but only one China-specialist faculty member, who had studied Chinese at Yale. Thailand was even more directly under the gun but did even less about it. A few days in each capital city revealed the near absence of sinological competence in these bordering states. Kuala Lumpur, Singapore, and Saigon of course were semi-Chinese cities, yet study of the PRC was barely getting started even there. Manila had a bare beginning, one of my Harvard students teaching under Jesuit auspices. In each capital city a few days sufficed to meet the key people, make a few speeches, and see old friends. The latter were usually either journalists or diplomats, the two main types in international service.

Hong Kong of course was the most advanced center, yet its business firms were not foundations, and research on the PRC, even here on its doorstep, depended mainly on the Ford Foundation in New York. Somehow the use of trained minds to deal with such abstractions as social science and history was beyond immediate calculations of profit, so no one could afford to invest in it. I was welcomed to pontificate on "Chinese Studies in the USA" at the Hong Kong branch of the Royal Asiatic Society, but few were moved by the suggestion that knowledge of history was the best protection against ideological fanaticism, while only a few in my audiences were inspired by that wondrously efficacious academic spur, degree candidacy. In just under a month I gave a dozen talks to various groups at half a dozen institutions, while we caught up with scores of friends.

One outstanding experience for all four of us had been to see our Washington friend Wolf Ladejinsky again in Saigon. His first-hand know-how and warm enthusiasm had made him a key figure in the land reform in Japan, as he was in Taiwan, the Philippines, and India subsequently. He and our daughters were friends immediately. The fact that he was about to move on, after working as adviser to President Ngo Dinh Diem on land reform in South Vietnam, was an omen of trouble ahead.

Our travel in 1960 also allowed me to catch up with Modern Chinese history in Taiwan. When we reached Taipei for a seven-week stay in a house of National Taiwan University, the reorganized KMT and its creature, the Republic of China (ROC), had had a good ten years to consolidate their position as a modern, reforming regime intent on land reform and industrialization. For this purpose nearly everything was in their favor. The half-century of Japanese colonial government 1895–1945 had left a solid infrastructure of railroads, roads, hydropower, literacy, public health, and farm extension services. The Japanese had done little in higher education, however. One of the more corrupt and infamous KMT generals (Ch'en I, governor of Fukien) had suppressed peaceable 1947 demonstrations in Taipei protesting the corruption of the KMT takeover, by slaughtering something like ten thousand urban Taiwan Chinese, and so there was not much local leadership for the Nationalist government to contend with. The mainland refugees who fled to Taiwan with CKS in 1949 included an invaluable pool of administrative talent. Under the uncorrupt General Ch'en Ch'eng as governor they put through a genuine land reform that abolished absentee landlordism and helped scientific farming.

The main agency for land reform was the Sino-American Joint Commission on Rural Reconstruction (JCRR) set up on the mainland in 1948 by act of our Congress and headed by Chiang Monlin, former chancellor of Peita in Peking and Kunming. The JCRR revived the old farmers' associations created by the Japanese and developed their capacity to provide credit and agronomic skills to the countryside. One of its strengths was its single-echelon structure—American and Chinese specialists worked on a single team, not as "opposite numbers" (something like Eisenhower's successful Anglo-American command structure at his headquarters in World War II).

When we saw Dr. Chiang he said at once, "If we had only known on the mainland what we know now, we could have defeated Mao Tse-tung." This gave me to reflect. Chiang Monlin (1886–1964), as he indicates in his autobiography, *Tides from the West,* had embarked from the first on a scholar-official's career, except that by 1904 he knew his scholarship must be from America. He studied education at Berkeley (LL.B., 1912) and at Columbia under John Dewey (Ph.D., 1917), and was head of Peita, with some gaps, from 1919 to 1945, an impressive record.

Chiang Monlin also had the merit of being from a gentry and banker background in CKS's home province of Chekiang. Despite his American modernity, he retained the old virtue of loyalty to his ruler. When I saw him during World War II in Kunming and Chungking, at a time when he was practically starving and his wife was secretly seeking a paying job, he said to me more than once, "I keep in touch with Chiang Kai-shek and offer my advice. When the time is right, you will see him suddenly institute reforms and save the situation." In 1960 in Taipei he did not repeat this pious thought, but in fact in the smaller and more manageable province of Taiwan, the JCRR reforms had indeed done much to save the situation.

I concluded that the ancient scholar-gentry ideal of loyal service to one's ruler was still alive and well in Chiang Monlin's generation. It was incapable of revolution or even rebellion. During all those wartime years when the CC clique let the Kunming professors starve, Dr. Chiang was their chief representative. What did he ever get out of CKS? This of course we cannot know. He was certainly a very humane and yet durable official. He gave us a warm welcome in 1960 and had JCRR take us on a tour across the island.

A similar persistence in old ways characterized the KMT political leadership. After a soul-searching review of why they lost the mainland, CKS and his faithful concluded it had been primarily a lack of discipline and dedication. (At that time they did not blame it on lack of U.S. aid due to "Communists in the State Dept.") They resolved on the reconquest of China by moral regeneration of the KMT and revival of Sun Yat-sen's ideology, if such it may be called. But pride and practical politics combined to make them preserve all the outward shows of a great sovereign power in a continuous game of make-believe. I was reminded of the Sherwin Williams Paint Company's "Save the surface and you save all."

The old Japanese governor-general's office, in the fanciest red brick style of 1900, became President Chiang's headquarters. Two legal fictions supported the power structure. First, the civil war went on, a front was maintained on offshore islands like Quemoy, a showcase of "the front" in Amoy harbor, and so martial law ruled Taiwan for the next thirty years after 1949. The military stayed in power, bugles blew, and you ran into pill boxes and barbed wire all around outside the city. Second, the government of ROC China at Taipei retained on paper and in numerous sinecure posts a dummy top administration for Nanking and all the provinces, ready to go back to power at a moment's notice, while the nominal local government of Taiwan province was set up at Taichung out of the way and not really in power on the island.

These fictions salved the humiliation of defeat. They also appealed to the pro-underdog liberalism of the Nationalists' American backers, for whom Chinese hospitality was warmer than ever and the opportunity for benevolent support of worthy ideals seemed all the greater. Taiwan became a truly ambivalent symbol, poised on the boundary between Chinese and American values, and meaning something different to either side.

To the Nationalist refugees it meant consistency, "never give up," an undefeated spirit of implacable hostility, still at war, bloody but unbowed, true forever to their original commitment as loyal followers of Dr. Sun and CKS—in short, a fine moral posture. Part of this stance was to act as if the ROC sojourn in Taiwan was temporary and it continued to be the government of all China though out of power for the time being. This could be done as long as the USA went along with the charade.

To its American supporters, quite the contrary, Formosa (the Portuguese and therefore "imperialist" name) was an island state still defying the Communist horde, still fighting our battle for us and struggling to maintain its independence of the mainland. Such front-line bravery deserved our aid. The constitution spoke of the democratic freedoms (martial law was temporary), the press showed some diversity (if you could read Chinese), and business began to boom Japanese-style, export-oriented. All the different China communities in America: business, Christian missions, Chinese studies, the military, *et al.* found Taiwan a congenial place to continue, usually on a smaller scale, the things they had been doing on the continent. The Seventh Day Adventist Hospital was the best in Taipei. The Foreign Service ran a language school at Taichung. Also at Taichung was the Christian college successor to Yenching, Tung-hai ("Eastern Sea") University on a fine new campus with many staff members from Peking. The U.S. MAG (Military Assistance Group), the U.S. Air Force, the CIA, each had installations and staffs at Taipei. National Taiwan University had faculty members from Lienta in Kunming and Peita in Peking. Academia Sinica erected new buildings at Nankang, six miles outside the sprawling city. There we found our old friend Li Chi, who was year by year completing the voluminous reports on the Anyang finds of the Shang dynasty which Liang Ssu-yung had led the work on, during the war, until he died of tuberculosis. Li Chi's total commitment to this task sustained him until it was completed, and he died, in 1979.

When JCRR took us on tour by train and Jeep and we negotiated the still incomplete cross-island highway to the rockbound east coast, we found the same quality of dedicated determination in the soldiers building the highway. Descending from the high mountain pass to the spectacular Taroko gorge, we crossed mountainsides of loose shale, where the truck traffic dislodged small avalanches of rock, sometimes wiping out sections of the route already bulldozed at lower levels. Many troops, we were told, had lost their lives but their persistent conquest of nature compensated for their defeat on the mainland. I accepted this story because it seemed to exemplify an indomitable quality I sensed in the whole community.

My own contact was mainly with the Academia Sinica Institute of Modern History (IMH), headed by a conscientious and careful scholar, Kuo T'ing-i. He was trusted by the KMT, but because he was a professor not at Taita (Taiwan National University) but at Taiwan Normal University, I was told he had less access to the top talent. Whatever the facts, Mr. Kuo turned this apparent weakness into a point of strength because the research fellows he recruited from the Normal University remained loyal to him and to the IMH, instead of using it as a stepping stone to careers in the United States. By checking the drift of talent abroad, the IMH developed a knowledgeable staff who produced a series of systematic and factual studies particularly of the era 1861–1927. Their principal and unique resource was the archives of China's first foreign office, from which they published a notable series of documentary collections.

Having just negotiated for Harvard with the Ford Foundation, I was able to help Mr. Kuo seek its support for a program of publication and travel that would bring his institute into closer contact with American centers. The IMH staff of a dozen or more productive scholars noted how American monographs sometimes erected studies that were more analytic on a smaller factual base, whereas the Chinese chronicler's tradition still inclined them to string their voluminous data into a chronological list. I arranged to meet Mr. Kuo's patron in the information and propaganda section of the KMT and suggested that archives on the CCP, which they kept under control like a contagious disease, could be a positive attraction for American researchers.

In government and academia were old friends of the thirties and forties. Hu Shih had come back to head Academia Sinica and we saw him several times. Looking back, in scholarly style he deplored his getting into public life as ambassador to Washington and hoped he would be remembered as a scholar who had shown up the fakery of Zen Buddhism in medieval China. His special charm for Americans was as a historic Chinese figure of personal warmth who remembered their personal names and could handle their small talk. He had lived almost half his life in America.

When Dr. Hu suddenly died later in the year, a fine memorial was erected at Academia Sinica on which his name was balanced in size by that of President Chiang Kai-shek, still trying to get a last bit of mileage out of the Peking intellectuals. In the adjoining museum the

May Fourth Movement of 1919, when Hu Shih electrified his whole generation, was perfunctorily relegated to a corner. The KMT never liked May 4, not having thought it up; the CCP had preempted it. If we had imagination, we Americans would offer a bust of John Dewey to stand by Hu Shih's grave.

Of the Nationalist ministers I had seen in wartime Chungking, the party organizer Ch'en Li-fu had retired to raise chickens in New Jersey, whereas the more liberal Wang Shih-chieh was still in the cabinet and responsive to my proposals for more academic contact and opening of archives.

For me Taipei in the 1960s in one respect echoed Chungking in the 1940s: in both eras the American connection was important in the local scene, I could be of use, and so I became again a bystander-participant in local situations. In 1960 the one-time KMT leader Lei Chen, editor of *Free China (Tzu-yu Chung-kuo),* had begun to organize an opposition party. His group sought my "advice," i.e., foreign support. When Lei Chen later in 1960 was ostentatiously railroaded into a ten-year jail term on flimsy grounds of CCP contact, his movement was quashed in classic style, by decapitation. I duly fired off a letter to the *New York Times* commenting on the KMT style of dictatorship. In 1964 I called on his wife, who said all their friends had fallen away, except Mr. Wang, and her life was sadly isolated. "What Mr. Wang?" I asked. "Our old friend Wang Shih-chieh," she said. Her protection by a central KMT stalwart left me feeling again that legal-official relationships were a mere overlay of the pervasive personal-and-kinship network that held Chinese society together.

As a sense of insecurity and even political hysteria mounted in the late 1960s, another case arose. Professor Yin Hai-kuang was a philosopher, a student of our friend Y. L. Chin, well versed in Western thought and an unrepentant free thinker of the H. L. Mencken or I. F. Stone type. He regarded Sun Yat-sen's Three Principles as flatulent, almost as pernicious as Marxism, and he doubted that Taipei was the capital of all China. He was victimized for his independence of mind, his university salary was cut off, and in his final illness he was supported by a handout research grant we arranged from the Harvard-Yenching Institute. It was a thoroughly disgraceful incident.

Political pressures were also rising in Japan. In Tokyo in the middle of June 1960 we watched the anti-security-treaty demonstrations that led to cancellation of President Eisenhower's visit. The modern "demo" with its weaving ranks of chanting students and phalanxes of shield- and stave-bearing police had a distinctly medieval, almost ritual, air. No one bothered American bystanders. It was quite decorous compared with the Korean students who in April 1960 had marched against Syngman Rhee's machine guns in Seoul. Many lost their lives to bring his reign to an end.

China studies in Japan and Korea were a similar contrast. Sinology in Japan was one of the oldest academic fields. The Tokyo and Kyoto schools of interpretation had a generation of disagreement behind them. During three weeks renewing old ties in each city, I visited and talked to a score of research or discussion groups, all of them sinologically proficient in one fashion or another. I came away each time loaded with more books, name cards, and institutional data.

A week in Seoul seemed more like home in being on a frontier of growth. South Korean sinology was just getting into contemporary studies of the PRC but lacked the Marxist assumptions that underlay so many Japanese studies of China. The research center at Korea University was eager for advice on how to approach the Ford Foundation. What was the golden phraseology to use? It determined to have an international conference on modernization in Asia, at a time when Japan's Marxists were still baying after imperialism as the key to modern disaster.

A Harvard professor was still ace-high in both countries, royally welcomed by enough people to make it seem sincere, but I found a differential in the terms used. I noted that "the Japanese could hardly care less about the American retailers of Oriental history," whereas in Korea "local introductions make me out as one hell of a sapient mastermind, probably a good index to the low level of history here. It continues to be disconcerting, having got about what a good graduate student should have in my field, to be billed as the all-time worldwide pundit on Modern China." This resulted from my having appeared in print on policy problems, always a portentous step for a scholar in East Asia, and done it in the United States, the center of power.

In 1964 we circumnavigated eastward again through much the same itinerary. We jumped from London to New Delhi, where modern China studies, though certainly loquacious, seemed to have made less progress than in Kuala Lumpur and Singapore.

Unlike our 1960 trip, when both children came with us, this time

Laura stayed home in school. But Holly, aged ten, accompanied us and learned about the world. When we spent a week in northwest Thailand with Lauri Sharp of Cornell among the hill tribes, Holly found a great interest in anthropology. We photographed hill-tribe women, for example, who wore low-slung skirts which showed a lower cleavage in back. When we stayed with Ambassador Philip Sprouse in Pnom Penh, Cambodia, Holly had no trouble being guest of honor at formal dinners. She told the guests about the hill tribes.

Returning to Saigon in 1964 we found the ao-dai national costume had been motorized. "The silk-pantalooned and varihued-skirted" young women on their motorbikes with wide straw hats and flowing black hair seemed "more like live apsaras [Buddhist angels] than ever, floating calmly along the tree-lined avenues." Holly had some ao-dais made in green and pink, very fetching. Her silk pajamas were covered by a long gown with colorful front and back panels high-split at the sides. Being the right size and shape, she passed for sixteen and bewitched young journalists at cocktail parties.

Korea expanded Holly's experience even more. When we reached Seoul, an International Junior Chamber of Commerce meeting had flooded the downtown hotels. We found lodging in a first-class marble caravansary, Keum Soo Chang, on top of a hill. "Will this be all right?" asked our troubled hosts. "It is the only space left in the city." Since it had the sort of grandeur we ran into only when calling upon friends, we reassured them and settled in.

The hotel was quite luxurious. The beds were enormous. Many shoes were parked, Japanese style, in the lobby entrance to the bedroom corridors. Holly made friends with some of the maids and reported that dozens of limousines were parked around the inner entrance to a bosky back area built in old Korean style, where the evenings were especially busy with food, music, and song. We were in fact in the best house in the city and found it quiet and decorous all the week we stayed there.

Retracing our steps after four years impressed us with the explosive growth of high-rise construction in cities like Hong Kong, Manila, Taipei, and Seoul. The view from the vice-chancellor's lodge above Hong Kong University, where we stayed happily for a third time with Sir Lindsay and Lady Ride, showed Kowloon across the harbor had become as big a city as Victoria on the island. Universities had grown accordingly. The Jesuit Ateneo de Manila had expanded.

Outside Taipei the Academia Sinica had a new faculty village, where we occupied a house for a month.

One satisfaction in Taipei in 1964 was to see T. F. Tsiang again. After a very substantial career on the Security Council, where his superior intelligence somewhat compensated for his representing a fictitious great power, T. F. had become ambassador in Washington. On his visit to Taiwan he raised the idea of doing a Chinese history of China on modern lines, to make the story more fully available to the world. He had been out to CKS's think tank, a college of Chinese culture put together by KMT acolytes as a rival to Academia Sinica. T. F. said he had looked through the many historical works produced there—"They made me want to cry." If he had lived, Dr. Tsiang might have brought a Chinese history of China into being.

In Taiwan, however, the stultifying personality of CKS still held sway. Our old friend from Peking George Yeh (Yeh Kung-ch'ao), one-time professor of English literature at Tsing Hua, had risen by sheer talent to be the Republic of China's foreign minister for a decade and then ambassador in Washington. But now, having refused to follow the Old Man's diplomatic ideas, George was tethered in Taipei as a cabinet minister without portfolio. He was a Chinese renaissance man who embraced both cultures. A grandfather and an uncle had been prime ministers at Peking. George was a calligrapher of note and an expert on Chinese painting. Yet he had got a Western education too at Urbana, Bates, Amherst, and Cambridge University. He had been through the London blitz and the fall of Singapore and knew many power holders around the world. Now he took us by car to see the imperial art collection at Taichung, which Larry Sickman was photographing. We stayed at the First Bank of Taiwan guest house and met businessmen in whose future George saw some promise for the island. It was a happy interlude with a valued friend.

In all our stops as well as during three months in Japan and a week in Korea, I was mainly showing the Harvard flag, visiting institutions to meet researchers and give talks. A worldwide network of Chinese studies was rapidly taking shape. In Tokyo our friend Professor C. Ichiko was building up the formidable resources of his Seminar on Modern China at the Tōyō Bunko library. Modern China research was now beginning to get results with Ford Foundation and other support in Hong Kong, Taipei, and Tokyo.

Marxists in both China and Japan inveighed against this as cultural imperialism. A concerted propaganda effort imposed an effective boycott of the use of Ichiko's invaluable materials. The argument was that the source of one's support inevitably influences one's work, and Ford grants even with no strings attached would still warp the judgment of researchers so they would condone evil. This view is sound if you think it is, and not if you don't. Given the Confucian-Japanese need for reciprocity in human relations and the overwhelming sense of obligation that can bedevil the life of a Japanese scholar who is merely late with his manuscript, I could understand the point. For myself, however, "imperialism" was a gaseous term of ideology so widely applied that by now it included all international contact and was essentially meaningless. Ford funds would energize studies that could not be made by any amount of moral posturing, however correct it might be. In this sense I was obviously delighted to be an imperialist.

Confucian-tinged Marxist polemics, however, do not allow one to be an honest devotee of evil. The CCP newspaper *Ta Kung Pao* in Hong Kong denounced me as "a spy in a professor's overcoat" and the faithful were warned. My persona or legend as Fei Cheng-ch'ing meanwhile went on growing of its own accord. In 1977 in Hong Kong I was given a restricted *(nei-pu)* CCP volume on *American Researchers on China* containing a summary of Fei Cheng-ch'ing's career. The Americologists poring over our publications in Peking and applying (Chinese) common sense to their evidence had not been idle. Sharp eyes had noted that Fei Cheng-ch'ing had been vice-president of the Far Eastern Association in 1950 but had not advanced to the presidency, a setback to his career presumably attributable to a decision of Wall Street's central executive committee (who else calls the tune in our capitalist circles?).

One may hope, but probably in vain, that our deductions in the exercise of Pekinology are more accurate. What really led to my dead-end vice-presidency was an unplanned, American-type happening that would strain Peking's credulity. When we met in 1948 to make the Far Eastern Association (which had been publishing its *F.E. Quarterly* since 1941) into a professional membership association, Ed Reischauer headed an organizing committee that nominated Knight Biggerstaff to preside. When Knight asked for any amendments to the draft constitution, my scholarly but highly impractical colleague Charles Sidney Gardner arose and said, "Instead of reading that 'the vice-president shall succeed to the presidency,' I move to insert the word 'not' before 'succeed.' Thus we can honor double the number of people, some as president and others as vice-president." This was true in theory but nonsense in fact. Instead of killing it, Knight felt pressed for time, called for a vote, and the audience, egalitarian-minded like sheep, voted for the change. When I became the lame-duck vice-president in 1950, I moved to amend the constitution back to where it should have been, claiming I was best qualified, as the incumbent, to urge the change. It passed, and so when I was elected vice-president for real in 1958, I was the only two-time holder of the office and became president in 1959.

Other Chinese journalists' accounts of Fei Cheng-ch'ing take on a Paul Bunyan quality. For example, they tell how Fei was imprisoned during the McCarthy era but after he got out of jail he eventually became adviser to Nixon. When it was learned in 1971 that Nixon was being guided by *The United States and China,* a Chinese translation of the first edition was quickly resurrected for Mao and Chou to read. Here we confront the kind of gossip, including "reasonable" deductions from "facts," that help create folklore.

In our two circumnavigations of 1960 and 1964 we had visited two dozen countries, in each of which I appraised the present state or absence of Chinese studies. I saw fifteen or twenty research centers, depending on how you define the term, and made something like a hundred presentations, talks, or speeches. My conclusion was that research on China is easier discussed than carried out, that few were adequately trained to do it, that our books did not reach many far places; but that we were gaining ground and had a great opportunity at Harvard for contact with like-minded researchers abroad.

29

VIETNAM AND AMERICAN–EAST
ASIAN RELATIONS

DURING THE 1960s boom in research on Modern Chinese History, the American image of East Asia suddenly expanded to include Vietnam. It was Pearl Harbor all over again. Events hit us where we were least prepared.

In 1960 when we flew in high over the multiple streams of the Mekong Delta, to Saigon, I had a sudden comeuppance. Vietnam was so obviously part of the Chinese culture area, why had we spent those weeks in Burma instead? Here was a land with a heritage of the Chinese classical teaching and the Confucian family system, with a recently defunct imperial government modeled on the Ch'ing dynasty in China. We saw in the old capital at Hué the palace with its ground plan like Peking's Forbidden City. Less than a century of French colonialism overlay this ancient Sinocentric culture. Vestiges of Chinese acculturation were on every side, as in Korea and Japan.

Why had I not realized this? Protestant missionaries, like American traders, had been excluded by the ardent French desire to emulate Britain's empire. Vietnamese books were nonexistent in the great Harvard-Yenching collection. Colonialism, in short, had called the tune for American East Asian scholarship.

My emotional incomprehension of the specific existence of the Vietnamese culture and polity, even though I had lectured and written about the area for years, was a profound shock. Harvard had been as unprepared on Vietnam as the American people generally. I could think of no more outstanding failure of intellectual leadership than my own in this case. It was more than just an attitude of "win some, lose some; you can't do everything." This was a failure by a big-picture specialist to see the big picture in East Asia. It suggested we China-wallahs were as culture bound as anyone, unable to see what was before our noses because we had not been introduced to it by Vietnamese books, personal travel, or American residents returning from there. For thirty years we had preached the necessity of intellectual preparedness about East Asia. Now a crisis came and we were caught flat-footed. As the Vietnam War developed I began to preach the necessity of Harvard's adding Vietnamese studies to its East Asian program. We had to build a library, begin language instruction, and find a professor of Vietnamese history and culture. The professor would have to be the spark plug.

At Harvard in the early sixties I recruited a brilliant young Canadian graduate student, Alexander Barton Woodside (whose father, provost at Toronto, I had met as a Rhodes scholar at Corpus in Oxford) to pursue modern Vietnamese history. He proved a whiz at languages and comparative institutional studies. His path-breaking book *Vietnam and the Chinese Model* (1971) showed how Vietnam's new line of rulers in the early nineteenth century had modeled their state upon the Ch'ing at Peking with interesting adjustments. He began to teach a history course on Vietnam.

I visited Saigon a second time in 1964 just as American military intervention was about to get under way. On March 3, after talks in Saigon, it was apparent that

> the South Viet Army doesn't really want to fight their country cousins. The officers prefer to stay in cities; the troops are country boys considered lower class, with little motivation. No amount of fancy equipment and exhortation can erase the class lines of the local society or provide a common aim, even though Vietnamese nationalism might in the end be most aroused by the traditional dislike of Chinese domination. Peking is still smart enough to let the American simple psychology of action get us into the focus of anti-foreignism. Hilsman's replacement by W. Bundy is generally taken to mean U.S. activism will try some kind of firepower solution, the kind of thing we can understand and logistically support, letting the

real battle of motivation be turned against us. Having a power potential, materially, we see a clear duty to use it, but will find the cultural-psychological power factors, beyond our control or full comprehension, will defeat us. No doubt we have an historic mission here, to get shoved out as nationalism matures.

In Hué we visited the new university but ate at the U.S. Army "Hué Advisors Mess," where we talked with American officers. One told me, "Buddha is the main problem with the South Viet army. They favor not taking life. Live and let live." The commonest remark to U.S. advisers was "Don't go there. Vietcong are there, very dangerous."

> So they march through a valley with VC on the hills, don't climb the hills because "dangerous," and everyone survives. The war goes on and so does U.S. aid. But he says losses here are no greater than from combat practice at home, and this here is more practical, free training.

Within a few months, of course, the American leadership, never having marched through a valley with VC in the hills, much less studied the history of Sino-Vietnamese animosity, saw their duty to stop the march of "monolithic communism" from China through Vietnam. This was, quite simply, a failure of intellect to control wishful thinking and debunk false assumptions. But I thought it had an institutional basis in that American education offered no perspective on the Vietnam scene. It was not the Little Big Horn in Wyoming, but General Custer's brave and overconfident spirit still survived among us.

At Harvard in the three decades of building up China and East Asian studies from 1936 to 1965 we had failed to get Vietnam in our sights, and this failure could not quickly be caught up with. In the literature in English, Vietnam was an underdeveloped subject. It would take many years to pursue the studies necessary to guide national policy toward the area. I could, and of course did, join in the vocal opposition to the American intervention in Vietnam, but I could claim no special knowledge of the area or offer the insights of historical study.

We began in 1966 to seek funds for a chair in Vietnamese history.

We also collected Vietnamese books in a room at the center though the Harvard libraries still did not handle Vietnamese materials. The country was still under "French Indo-China" in the Widener stack. By 1975, with the help of the East Asian Visiting Committee, especially its two members of the Board of Overseers, Osborn Elliott and Teddy White, and only a decade after our national plunge into Vietnam, we had secured funds at Harvard for a professorship on Vietnamese history. We named it for one of our earliest graduates, the late Kenneth T. Young, who had been Kennedy's ambassador to Thailand. With some pulling and hauling, Woodside was appointed. It was the only such post in the country. But he remained a Canadian patriot at heart and was properly disenchanted with America's Vietnam War. He soon left Harvard to teach at the University of British Columbia. The Harvard post is still open.

My belief that an enormous foreign-policy problem like Vietnam needed attention at Harvard was not simply a knee-jerk reaction to a crisis in public understanding. Vietnam has intrinsic interest in itself and also as part of the Chinese culture area. It holds out an opportunity for comparative studies with China, Korea, and even Japan. Harvard's capacities for study of these adjoining regions create an obligation to study Vietnam too. Eight years of warfare, finally, have now made it a necessary focus of attention in the field of American–East Asian relations.

This success-and-failure in Vietnamese studies, really a defeat in the effort to see Harvard lead the way, came partly from a failure in institutional growth. The faculty was not organized to accommodate an increase of tenured professors in East Asian history. The History Department had already suffered a downturn in its own cohesion and this was part of the institutional problem. The sense of community in the History Department was fragmented from many angles. As survey courses penetrated the schools, they lost their appeal in college. Specialization absorbed teachers and then students. Everybody went more fully in his own direction intellectually. As my colleague Bernard Bailyn (president of the AHA in 1981) put it, "Individuals seem content to be virtuosos, leaving their work as technical studies."

Another dispersive factor was administrative diversification. Many took on tasks outside or appended to the department. Those that went off to World War II came back addicted to secretaries and

Dictaphones, projects and separate budgets. Soon a number of department members were involved in something separate, outside the department.

Another factor of decay, I think, was Harvarditis—becoming so impressed with Harvard's magnificence that one could not avoid a certain arrogance, otherwise known as a collective swelled head. In people of personal humility this might take the form of they-shall-not-pass intransigence about new appointments. Feeling oneself barely worthy of the honor, one must hold the pass, maintain standards, and keep out mediocrity, even if it meant instruction stopped. It became increasingly difficult to find scholars considered good enough to add to the charmed circle.

I realize the rise and decline of academic groups is a most complex social phenomenon. My attempt to explain what happened to us historians is woefully incomplete. But I am quite aware of my own contribution to the process of fragmentation. I kept calling attention to it even as I kept on doing it.

The special language requirements (both Chinese and Japanese) for East Asian history and the special funding of this new field combined to create an *imperium in imperio*. In the end we met the needs and opportunities of the situation by setting up standing committees of the faculty to administer the undergraduate concentration for the A.B. in East Asian studies, the Regional Studies–East Asia A.M., and the Joint History and East Asian Languages Ph.D. In order to tie in the Harvard-Yenching Library committee and the federally supported East Asian Language and Area Center (an annual fund) as well as the East Asian Research Center, we ended by establishing within the faculty a Council on East Asian Studies as a coordinating and fund-raising committee that included all faculty members active in the East Asian field. The council had its own East Asian Visiting Committee deputed by the Board of Overseers to join in an annual powwow with the faculty on the state of the field, its problems and needs.

The result of all this ad hoc development, put through by a little band of willful men, chiefly myself and Ed Reischauer, was to give the East Asian historian special treatment from beginning to end of his time at Harvard. He could become a finished product without ever being under the jurisdiction of the History Department. His funds after 1958 might come from the federal government under the

National Defense Education Act or from the Ford Foundation, sometimes indirectly via SSRC. The East Asian history community so administered and funded had its own meeting places, seminar meetings, speakers, and social events, even its own library collections and reading rooms.

Similar tendencies were visible in the Russian and Middle Eastern areas and in International Affairs. The History Department could not be the center of all this new growth. But all faculty members on permanent tenure appointments had to be on the budget of a department, not a committee. This meant that the new area historians had to be evaluated and recommended by the History Department, whose tendency was to steer by a candidate's capacity to write a good book, rather than by his comprehension of weird languages. The outstanding quality we all sought in new appointees had to be shown in written English. Moreover, the department already had a big teaching job to do within the bounds of the received tradition. While struggling to keep Greece and Rome alive in the curriculum, why stock up on Vietnam?

This academic constipation was part of our larger national problem, how to bring reason and learning to bear on so mysterious and separate a region as East Asia. Our ejection from China after a century of friendship under the protection of British gunboats had been followed by a bitter war in Korea, and this inspired us even more righteously to a China policy of containment, which by 1965 meant containing North Vietnam's civil insurrection to conquer South Vietnam.

The Chinese and American performances in the late 1960s, if we compare them, may give us the wry satisfaction of beginning to see how we respectively knocked ourselves out. How many of America's current ills trace back to the Vietnam War! And how many of China's trace back to the Cultural Revolution! From Vietnam we first got our inflation and our sense of insecurity and uncertainty in foreign policy. From the Cultural Revolution China got a ten-year setback in education and technology, with resulting poverty and backwardness. Note that the Vietnam War and the Cultural Revolution went on *simultaneously* in the periods 1965–73 and 1966–76 respectively. The two disasters were not unconnected in origin.

The American Cold War refusal to accept what we sentimentally termed the "loss of China" to communism led us rather casually to provoke Chinese intervention in the Korean civil war of 1950. The resulting Chinese-American war in Korea led us into alliance with Taiwan and a policy of I-hope-you-croak "containment" of the People's Republic, including nonrecognition and embargo for twenty years.

Inside China, once the reliance on technology transfer from the Soviet Union came to an end in 1960, there was no chance to substitute American technology. Mao's peasant-minded reinvent-the-wheel enthusiasm for a do-it-yourself development by muscle power and sheer patriotism won the day. It shut down the universities, harassed the modern-educated Chinese, and left the billion people of the PRC far behind in trained leadership.

Things didn't have to go to these extremes. Like most disasters in history, they could have been handled better. For one thing, we didn't need to oppose the Chinese Revolution as righteously, wholeheartedly and violently as we did. We could have adjusted to it better if we had known more about it and been more objective about our own fearful feelings. The same is true of Vietnam.

LBJ's State Department tried to catch up with this situation and restore contact between Washington and the universities concerning East Asia. At the end of World War II some of the early Research and Analysis Branch (of COI and OSS) academics like myself had returned to university work; others like Burton Fahs had stayed on in government. Burton was head of the East Asia division of the Office of Intelligence Research (OIR) in State until in the 1950s he became head of the Humanities Division of the Rockefeller Foundation. This illustrated the rather close tie-in between academia, government, and the foundations, among which Americans could shift back and forth more easily than the British or the Japanese. So great was the need for experienced research direction in Washington that in 1947 I was still a consultant to OIR and some there even contemplated my being an officer part time while still teaching at Harvard.

All such relations were disrupted by the McCarthy era. But as we went into Vietnam under LBJ in 1965 the idea of mobilizing academic wisdom gained favor again. In 1966 an effort at public enlightenment was made by Senator Fulbright in China-policy hearings before the Senate Foreign Relations Committee. A long list of China specialists testified, most of us giving the PRC credit for meeting some of its vast problems and being no great menace to the United

States. As chairman, the senator led me along toward saying that Vietnam was much like China, and our policy equally ill advised. I shied away from this opportunity, not wanting to be used by the Congress against the Executive or change the focus from China to Vietnam. And as he drove us to the airport, Senator Fulbright chided me in his gentle way for not making an obvious point. He was right. I should have done so.

These Senate hearings on China in 1966 were a nine-day news wonder in Taipei, where Doak Barnett and I especially were denounced for our treacherous advocacy of contact with Peking. On the list of several hundred academic and other Taiwan leaders who published a denunciation of us, almost the first name was that of our old friend Li Chi. Later when visiting us in Franklin he remarked that he had first seen this denunciation when it was published with his name on it, but on the other hand he didn't disagree with it.

In the State Department a China Advisory Panel was set up in 1967 under the assistant secretary for East Asia. Between February 1967 and November 1968 it had five two-day meetings, each one well prepared with agenda and documentation. The panel of ten persons included two former ambassadors (Philip Sprouse and Julius Holmes) plus a selection of professors.* We were all cleared to see documents classified as high as secret. (I was told my clearance came through last, but they waited for it.) We were briefed by the assistant secretary, Bill Bundy, and others and eagerly delivered our judgments in wide-ranging discussions. Everyone agreed, for example, on the need to forestall PRC intervention in Vietnam by giving assurance that American troops would not invade North Vietnam on the ground.

The China advisory panel, I found, was protected from being a sole and possibly harmful influence by a filtration system. Its recommendations were funneled into a larger East Asian and Pacific panel, which included stalwarts of the right like Dr. Walter Judd, whose support of the Nationalists would be as absolute in 1977 as in 1947. In this way all voices could be heard, but in turn. I suspect LBJ

---

*The economist Alex Eckstein of Michigan, A. Doak Barnett, then at Columbia, George Taylor, and the two outstanding political scientists in the China field, Lucian Pye of MIT and Robert Scalapino of Berkeley, among others.

thought up this gerrymander. It showed how strongly the China *vs.* Taiwan issue survived in U.S. politics.

What do you say to advise an administration that has sent 500,000 troops abroad on a false assumption? In the China advisory panel we were not asked to decide about Vietnam, but we put forward as individuals a considerable argument for unilateral American moves toward more normal relations with China *especially at this time in 1967–68* when China was weak from domestic turmoil. I had argued in 1967 (*New York Times,* Op-Ed, May 20) that the Cultural Revolution within China and our military escalation in Vietnam created a great opportunity and need for diplomatic initiatives to reduce China's isolation. "What use is our anti-China trade embargo when third parties sell China our products? Why not abolish it, as a useful gesture? Why hold out against Peking's entry into the United Nations?"

While we were impressed with the open-mindedness of Assistant Secretary Bundy and the staff in FE, we saw Secretary Rusk only once. When I first met Dean Rusk at an ACLS China committee meeting about 1939, he was dean at Mills College in California, a Rhodes-scholar educator slightly junior to me. By August 1941, however, he was in war planning at the Pentagon, in on the ground floor of what became the China-Burma-India (CBI) Theater, where he rose to be deputy commander. I think Ken Galbraith is correct that Rusk's role as assistant secretary of state for the Far East during the Korean War gave him "a lasting commitment to the unity and comprehensiveness of the communist design for world rule and the role of military force as the answer."* He became the quintessential cold warrior, ready for another Alamo or to stand back to back with George Custer on that grassy knoll above the Little Big Horn. In other words, Dean Rusk as Secstate seemed to me intellectually inflexible as though morally committed to an anti-Communist stance and unwilling to think—in short, an ideologist. FE had many constructive ideas but apparently he blocked them. Alex Eckstein, fearlessly outspoken as usual, wrote Dean Rusk objecting to his image of "a billion Chinese armed with nuclear weapons." It built them up unjustifiably as a menace and was counterproductive as propaganda for us.

A Life in Our Times.

In the winter of 1967–68 I shared a widespread feeling that the strong sense of disillusion and dissent among our graduate students needed an outlet in organization and discussion. I encouraged Philip West and others among our Ph.D. candidates to create an inter-university group. They were in touch with like-minded young people already active at other centers across the country, and out of this came a founding meeting of the Committee of Concerned Asian Scholars (CCAS) at the time of the annual Association for Asian Studies (AAS) meeting in Philadelphia in the spring of 1968. The AAS had long followed a rule that its meetings should not get into controversy over current political issues, beyond the professional defense of freedom of scholarship. CCAS was therefore founded in an auditorium at the University of Pennsylvania, separate from AAS. I was asked to preside over the meeting and see the agenda carried through. I was delighted to be asked. I love to create organizations and this one seemed to me much needed.

In the packed auditorium the atmosphere was tense. Disruption of meetings, with battles over microphones, had occurred in many places. I arranged with the janitor to have two mikes, one at the podium for speakers and one at a separate stand for me as presiding officer. Mine was on a neck ring, defensible, and turned up so high that if I shouted I could shake the rafters and drown out the other mike. Just before the meeting began an old friend came up from the audience. A refugee thirty years before from the Nazis, he feared a fascist takeover in the United States. "John, don't do this," he said with tears in his eyes. "Don't involve us scholars in politics."

The meeting went off well enough. Only one prima donna Vietnam specialist blasted us all and stalked out. The agenda worked out by young East Asia specialists from a score of institutions went through and CCAS was in business.

In the pages of the CCAS quarterly *Bulletin*, Harvard, and I in particular, were soon on the receiving end of half a dozen polemical articles: "The Roots of Rhetoric: the Professional Ideology of America's China Watchers," "Harvard on China: the Apologetics of Imperialism," and the like. I replied, others joined in, and we had some lively exchanges.

The American failure in Vietnam had bankrupted our China containment policy. Indeed, the Cold War had reached a dead end, though our nuclear stockpiling mindlessly continued. I agreed with the student protest. To be denounced by my students for having gone along with stupid policies was refreshing. But then what? How were we to break out of national-cultural loyalties that might require us to fight? For mankind's basic dilemma, how to get beyond warfare, I had no solution. To be sure, there was little doubt that China studies had become part of America's educational establishment. Yet the evil of imperialism, if one saw it at work in Vietnam, was far from simple. Certainly in origin it was less materialistic than spiritual, less economic than strategic. It seemed to me high time that we scrutinized the great American expansiveness. Since East Asian studies were part of it, we should look at ourselves in particular.

I tried to do this in my presidential address to the American Historical Association in December 1968. The student rebellion of the late sixties was about to change the nature of the organization, making it much more service-oriented, for helping teachers to teach and the young Ph.D.s to get jobs. I came into the presidency, as far as I can figure out, through the operation of the system of management that had evolved along rather elitist, in-group lines since 1884. Inviting me to present a paper in 1956 on "East Asian Views of Modern European History" had been a kind of post-McCarthy rehabilitation. My early sponsor at Harvard, Jim Baxter, came and sat in the front row to hear me. And in 1964 I had been nominated and elected for a three-year term on the Council, an obvious kind of preparation.

As president, aside from presiding vigorously to speed up the Council meetings, I ran into only one command decision I had to make. The televised police action against student anti-war demonstrators in Chicago during the Democratic convention of 1968 aroused widespread resentment. Mary Wright, for one, phoned me from Yale, very determined, to say she had two hundred signatures of historians old and young who would boycott the AHA if it met in Chicago as scheduled after Christmas. I realized she could gather a lot more support than that. Conferring with Paul Ward, as the executive secretary, I found the same hotel company could let us have the Statler Hilton in New York. I took responsibility in August for switching the location for December. It seemed to me that for us administrators it was entirely a matter of expediency, how to get the annual meeting to meet, with no great principle involved. I was used to being pushed around by Mary if she really got set on something.

The only catch, it turned out, was that the Statler Hilton in New York beneath those famous names was really the old Hotel Pennsylvania, long past its prime and about ready for dismantling. We found that only three elevators worked for six thousand people. The Hotel New Yorker was used too, but the general result was a sort of *fin de siècle* service. Nevertheless, we had a presidential reception to mix East Asianists with the mainstream. No one rioted, or tried to take over the business meeting and change the constitution.

In the following year my successor C. Vann Woodward of Yale bore the main brunt of the student rebellion in an AHA business meeting in Washington that went on well past midnight. I had unwisely recommended to Vann a parliamentarian, sight unseen, and had failed to get him to an earlier Council meeting to be checked over. As the meeting got under way with complex parliamentary maneuvers, Vann found that my parliamentarian was not only quite deaf but slow-witted and sometimes just wrong. It was like bringing a cross-eyed umpire to a baseball championship. I felt crestfallen indeed.

From the floor those of us who tried to fight off policy resolutions on Vietnam, which we felt would prostitute the AHA for nonprofessional ends, got into shouting matches. At one point I found myself wrestling with my friend Howard Zinn over a floor mike, claiming I had a priority motion to make. All in all, a raucous occasion.

My presidential address in 1968 bore the title "Assignment for the '70s," by which I meant the study of American–East Asian relations (AEAR). The American Oriental Society went back to 1842, the American Historical Association to 1884. Sinology and history had grown up parallel. Area study had brought them more fully together, but there was a long way still to go. Take Vietnam as an example, I suggested.

> Suppose that our leaders in the Congress and the executive branch had all been aware that North Vietnam is a country older than France with a thousand-year history of southward expansion and militant independence maintained by using guerrilla warfare to expel invaders from China, for example, three times in the thirteenth century, again in the fifteenth century, and again in the late eighteenth century, to say nothing of the French in the 1950s. With this perspective, would we have sent our troops into Vietnam so casually in 1965?

Raising this flag was a tactic in a larger strategy. No sane pedagogue would expect a student to master East Asian culture, using the languages, and also master American history, using the documentation, and then go on to study East-West relations for his Ph.D. AEAR was really three fields in one, something for geniuses more gifted than their teachers (who fortunately keep turning up). Why set so impossible a task? The answer was, to confront the facts and the issues. Left to themselves, East Asianists would live in their languages and cultures and Americanists would live in their documentation without ever meeting. We saw it happen every day. We had to break down the parochialism on both sides. Our strategy was to put the international-relations organizer types on the defensive. Their theories must be made to confront the discrepancies in American and East Asian philosophies and conduct.

A group of us at Harvard had been pursuing this hybrid subject through a History Department committee on American Far Eastern Policy Studies. Having secured some funds, the department chairman, Oscar Handlin, had written to forty history departments seeking their recommendations of students of promise in American history who would like to study Chinese and/or Japanese and so become versed in both sides of the history of American–East Asian relations. Oscar's appeal turned up some eight people over two years to whom we gave fellowship support for a new mixture of training.

Most notable in this group was a brilliant young Japanese, Akira Iriye, who had graduated from high school in Tokyo and then pursued English history at Haverford. I had met his father (Iriye Keishirō), who was a pioneer in international history in Japan. Akira is now at Chicago, the leader in the field. His preeminence reflects his truly bicultural background.

For several years we had occasional meetings on American-East Asian relations, usually at John Carter Vincent's house on Garden Terrace across from Radcliffe. After the McCarran committee in 1952 tried by their usual foul means to dump the "loss of China" on John Carter, and after Dean Acheson was replaced by John Foster Dulles, that Jesuit in Presbyterian clothing, John Carter was forced to retire from the Foreign Service. He made a new life for himself as a citizen of Cambridge, Mass. He and Betty, professional diplomats, soon had charmed a wide circle of friends. He wrote his book on the late phase of extraterritoriality in China as an associate of the

East Asian Research Center. Also living in Cambridge was Dr. Dorothy Borg, who published her second volume on American Far Eastern policy in the Harvard East Asian series in 1964. With such experienced colleagues on hand and China still cut off by the Cold War, we were able to focus on problems of policy formation, particularly the assumptions in the minds of opinion makers and journalists.

During my AHA presidency I was able to secure the setting up of a national committee on American–East Asian relations. Like other developmental committees, it sponsored a session at the annual AHA meeting, recruited Americanists as well as East Asianists, and soon issued a newsletter to give the AEAR field substance and locate its clientele. At the Harvard University Press we began to publish a series of studies, beginning with a bibliographical survey volume from a Cuernavaca conference that summarized the main work accomplished and the opportunities for a new growth of ideas.

One of the conclusions of my AHA address in 1968 had been that the overseas missionary was the "invisible man" in American history. Almost no one had studied him except other missionaries. Amazingly, it appeared that American historians of the westward movement had paid little or no attention to the China trade, yet it helped finance our western railroads. American historians of religion had paid no attention to missionaries. But Methodist missionaries reached Foochow at the same time they reached California. It seemed as though the East Asian dimension of American growth had been woefully neglected.

By 1976 the Luce Foundation became interested and set up a program of grants for research seminars and conferences in this new field. Henry Luce had put me about on a level with Judas Iscariot, as I could sense when we both spoke at a China Institute memorial service for Hu Shih in 1961. But I feel sure, were he still alive, that he would applaud the entrepreneurial imagination with which his foundation has pursued our China connections.

PART SEVEN

●

TURNING SOME CORNERS

1972–81

30

NEW AND OLD
IN THE PEOPLE'S REPUBLIC

UNTIL 1941 AND EVEN 1949 China specialists were accustomed to China's accessibility as they were to Europe's. The *New York Times* plus a few other media kept us up to date. Travelers kept coming back.

After 1949 and especially after the outbreak of Sino-American hostilities in Korea in late 1950, China became enemy territory and we were cut off. Chinese official pronouncements nourished us like a diet of popcorn floated through a tube. After twenty-five years of studying China from the outside, we were left with two images—our recollections of the 1930s and '40s and an overlay of the current scene viewed through the eyes of others. Tillman Durdin's *New York Times* type of reporting of incidents in the round was supplanted by look-see travelogues, what the guide said on the way to the hog farm. One of the few old-timers to get inside the PRC was Edgar Snow, who was allowed to travel about extensively in 1960 and gave us an informative account of the transformation *(The Other Side of the River: Red China Today).* But for the most part it was a new cast of characters on a new stage, dimly lit and not too intelligible.

For Wilma and me returning to Peking in 1972 was like a fortieth class reunion, as we tried to identify the remnants of the past while understanding and appreciating the new generation's overlay. Our trip was made possible by the New Nixon's surprising, if sensible, flip-flop.

Having got his start on anti-communism, Richard Nixon had abetted our Cold War with China and the alliance with Taiwan through which we maintained it. But after 1960 he could begin to see the Sino-Soviet split as a fact, and by 1968 when he became President he could imagine a Sino-American rapprochement as a power-politics move to influence Moscow.

Once committed to opening relations with Peking, Nixon and Kissinger orchestrated a succession of signals, mainly changes in Cold War terminology and in the regulations aimed at containment of the PRC. I had run into Henry Kissinger on the Eastern shuttle from New York to Boston sometime in 1967–68. We got onto the question how PRC-USA relations could be resumed. I offered the precedent of the tribute system in which foreign rulers might well appear at Peking as honored (sort of) guests of the Emperor. (I could still remember Dr. J. C. Ferguson's telling me apodictically in Peking, anent my getting in touch with a senior professor, *"You* must go to *him!"* The rules were strict.) Mao, I suggested, could receive any chief of state but hardly go abroad himself, whereas American Presidents could go anywhere in the world with little difficulty. I sent Henry a reprint of my article "China's World Order: the Tradition of Chinese Foreign Relations" published in *Encounter* 27 of December 1966. When our symposium volume *The Chinese World Order* came out in 1968, I sent him that too. Henry later reminded me of the talk we had had, with the unstated implication that it changed history; I have always admired his capacity for the personal touch. The idea, of course, is a rather obvious one.

The secret Kissinger visit to Chou En-lai of July 1971 and Nixon's startling announcement that he would go to Peking before May 1972 reinvigorated the whole China question. Our policy had finally turned a corner. Senator Fulbright signalized the triumph of the liberal view by holding a closed hearing of the Senate Foreign Relations Committee with John Davies, Jack Service, and me to testify. I felt honored to be included with these two old friends, whose careers had been so disrupted by their China reporting while mine, if anything, had been enhanced. What a curious differential in our professional roles! They had been targeted by McCarthyism as Foreign Service officers while as a professor I had only been denounced and meanwhile a journalist like Teddy White had remained comparatively unassailed.

The future security of Taiwan was now at the heart of our China problem. In a *New York Times* Op-Ed piece of August 12, 1971, I argued for the historical feasibility of "Taipei's autonomy under Peking's sovereignty." It was headlined "Taipei Can Coexist with Peking."

"The Chinese civil war can die away," I said, "if the United States will stop backing one side. Taiwan need not be a rival of Peking, nor need it be governed from the mainland. . . . We should maintain our Taiwan defense commitment but otherwise not try to unscrew the inscrutable." (Later on, this same article, slightly enlarged and with a different ending, was published under the same headline on the Op-Ed page of the *New York Times* for February 19, 1972, a few days before the Shanghai communiqué was issued by Chou and Nixon on February 28.)

In *The New Republic* of May 13, 1971, I doubted the strength of. any Taiwan independence movement and doubted also the validity in Chinese political thinking of self-determination by plebiscite. Voting by the ignorant masses' show of hands had never fit with the duty of the scholar to advise the ruler.

The TV from Peking airport gave us instant history when President Nixon arrived on February 21, 1972, but no historian was there to put the event in focus. You may remember how solid the ranks of the Chinese fur-capped honor guard looked, waiting on the cold tarmac. Then the majestic nose of Air Force One slid into the top of the picture, far sleeker and taller than a gunboat. The door opened and the lone figure of the ruler of the American empire came down the steps, a bit tentatively, possibly wondering if a Seventh Crisis lay in wait at the bottom. But of course it was Chou En-lai, who then received the handshake Mr. Dulles had refused him at Geneva in 1954.

Then, China's turn—the visitor's inspection of the honor guard. Such inspections can be small events or big events. As the cameras shifted, Mr. Nixon, still alone, started down the long line of troops. He looked back briefly. Chou En-lai following behind on his right flank motioned him on. During several thousand years, hundreds of foreign rulers had trudged past miles of Chinese guards, armed and at attention, on their way to see the Emperor of China. For a moment this inspection on February 21 was the tribute procession of the king of America, come to pay his respects at the Chinese court.

After the Shanghai communiqué of February 1972 that ended Nixon's visit to Peking, we began to receive invitations from Chou En-lai to visit the New China. Everything was indirect. Talking to Scotty Reston of the *New York Times,* who sutured a bit of Sino-American friendship by having his appendix removed in the Capital Hospital (formerly PUMC), the prime minister mentioned us among others who were old friends and should come to visit. Similar remarks were reported to us from Chou's vice minister of foreign affairs, Ch'iao Kuan-hua, and others. After four invitations had been thus voiced, I tried some indirection in return. I asked the PRC's new UN ambassador, Huang Hua, if he could find out whether, if Wilma and I turned up in Hong Kong, we could enter China. A week or so later, at the memorial service in New York for Ed Snow, Huang Hua said to me, "You will be welcome. Just see the China Travel Service in Kowloon." It was like the mutual trust in the Old China Trade at Canton—an oral agreement, no document needed.

This informality also reflected, I think, the tentative and experimental nature of the opening toward America. In pursuing it Chou En-lai had to be on guard against the Gang of Four, who had some degree of control over Mao. In the end this major shift of PRC policy would be their undoing. A growing American connection would encourage the new policies of modernization that Chou would enunciate as one of his last official contributions in 1975. As of 1972, however, the Cultural Revolution slogan of class struggle was still in vogue.

On this informal basis we took off on May 13 for Honolulu. Travelers to the People's Republic had already established a cliché image of the place, so I sent back a pre-summary of our trip as a circular letter. My secretary at the time, a practical young woman who loved horses, by a rapid mental calculation figured that in a few days I could not have spent three months in China, so to be on the safe side she introduced my remarks with a "Secretarial Note: A J. K. Fairbank attempt at fiction or novel writing!" (By the time I returned she had rejoined the horses, which I am sure pleased them as much as it did me.)

Number One, May 14, 1972. No one who has just spent three months traveling the length and breadth of China will be content with the old clichés about this remarkable country.

The Chinese are a great people, incredibly industrious, inured to patient suffering, and the largest country on earth! Their history goes far back (into the past), but as we go forward (into the future) one cannot help feeling that their future will be bound up with that of another once great people, the Americans.

Our first impression after crossing the border at Shumchun was of a people hard at work (in fact, incredibly industrious), building a new country under the leadership of Chairman Mao (Tse-tung), and little concerned with the outside world. Indeed the first thing that our guide Miss Wang Li said to us in Canton was, "We are little concerned with the outside world" (*Wo-men pu kuan ni-men yang-kuei-tzu,* literally, "We take no account of you foreign devils"). No one ever asked us about America, although the grizzled secretary of the Revolutionary Committee at the Airport Commune seemed to be approaching the subject when he began his speech to us by saying, "The Chinese people are a great people and the Albanian people are a great people," but Miss Wang Li stopped him.

Another thing that immediately impressed us was the fastidious honesty of the Chinese. Our Canton hotel guide (room-boy) Comrade Li Wang caught up with us at the airport, breathing hard, and said, "Masta, hab got one piecee paper Missy done leave behind, no belong this fella pidgin, chin-chin you makee-takee." Miss Wang Li took a quick look at the piece of typewriter paper and motioned us aside, where an unostentatious security guard who had stayed in our bathroom discussed it with her. "We think you owe the Chinese people an explanation," she said, "you know Chairman Mao will not tolerate American aid, and as for the party, he is quite capable of dealing with it himself. We shall brook no interference!" I looked at the paper, which read "Now is the time for all good men to come to the aid of the party." We took the plane the next day.

Undoubtedly the high point of our trip to the People's Republic was our eleven-hour discussion with Prime Minister Chou En-lai, which took place in one of the small halls of the Great Hall of the People. Mr. Chou looked older than when he was a student in Paris—to be continued. JKF.

After arriving from Honolulu we spent several days in Hong Kong —the "island between" as Chris Rand called it—the last treaty port, a showplace of how modernity could come to China under foreign-commercial auspices.

David Osborn, who had been a brilliant student at Harvard and was now consul general, invited us to stay at his residence,

a James Bond kind of place on the crest of the Peak. From the balcony you look down on one side to the myriad lights of the harbor and the thousand high-rise structures on both sides of it, but if you walk across the terrace, about the size of a Bond landing pad, you look down on the back of the island and out over Repulse Bay and the islands in the mist toward the Pacific. The driveway up to the house has a stop-and-go light so guests won't meet on the way. The whole peak is laced with such driveways, leading up off hairpin-turn roads that were not here before, and the glass houses look down on high-rise apartments even up here in the clouds. Take a rock and throw spaghetti on it and you have a model of the Hong Kong road system. The whole foreshore of the city is now overlaid with a throughway. The automobile has conquered here too.

At the Universities Service Center across the harbor in Kowloon we found researchers, mainly American, using some of the Union Research Institute press files on PRC developments.

Forty or fifty people crowded into a drab lunchroom that made me feel immediately at home. We discussed mainly the American academic setup, including research councils and funding, and the general problem of relating scholarship to politics. Several of those present had been on trips into China.

When we went to the China Travel Service, the man in charge said, "We have been expecting you," and gave us train tickets for Canton. We found that our Cambridge colleagues Jerry and Joan Cohen of the Harvard Law School were also going in with a group of concerned scientists.

They were already battling with their delegation as to how it could add law and art to science as its field of investigation.

Delegation life has many of the features of shipwreck. It produces conflicts of basic interest. Wilma and I are lucky to have only each other to contend with.

The last thing we did was to visit the vice-chancellor of the new Chinese University of Hong Kong, Choh-min Li. As a bridge partner in wartime Chungking and later as an economist at Berkeley, C. M. had seemed to me a rather quiet observer of events. But now here he was creating a great new institution, using his Cantonese background in a most dynamic way, raising funds and getting a whole community behind him. He had

a plan for building two further college complexes (for United College and New Asia College) on the hill overlooking the Ch'ung Ch'i College campus and putting the general university headquarters, library, and research center in the middle. From a loose grouping of three rather different institutions, he is creating a genuine university on a magnificent site of buildings, all of which is overlooked from the vice-chancellor's lodge on the highest peak. My Oxford classmate Harold Lee is chairman of the Chinese University Board in addition to the Mandarin Hotel and other Hong Kong real-estate operations. Apparently as one gets older the world becomes smaller, one-time students become consuls general, classmates become magnates, and old acquaintances vice chancellors. C. M. Li's administrative girl turns out to have been my Chungking librarian in 1943, etc.

All this renewal of contact in Hong Kong gave us no hint of our future in the PRC.

The whole venture seems slightly peculiar and on a remarkably personal basis. An aged couple turn up at the border with an intangible aura of past contacts and some kind of prestige. What next befalls them, you will have to get from a succeeding chapter.

Once across the border, I had two impressions: one, that the pace of life was more tranquil. If revolution meant frenetic activity, then it was going on in Hong Kong, not Canton. Second, the afforestation of the formerly bare eroded hills of Kwangtung province was astounding. Whole mountainsides were sprouting young trees. There had been a great collective effort.

At the Canton station we were met by a representative of the Chinese People's Institute for Foreign Affairs, our host organization, who lodged us in the Kwangtung provincial guest house. In its small park with its magnificent trees and miscellaneous buildings, this had once been the residence of high Ch'ing dynasty officials who governed Canton, then after 1858 of the British consul general, who dealt with the Ch'ing officials, and after 1938 of the Japanese generals who had ousted the British. Now it was the turn of American guests.

When we visited the British-made island of Shameen, where we had stayed with L. K. Little as Customs commissioner in 1934, we found the greensward supplanted by useful cabbage patches and every building crowded with people. From the bund on the Pearl River side we could see the new People's Bridge that now spans the broad stream. "Two big cannon cast for Commissioner Lin in 1841 and excavated in 1963 now face the waters where the gunboats used to lie at anchor. Commissioner Lin would be gratified."

Next day we flew to Peking, were met by a group at the airport, and lodged in the old central section of the Peking Hotel, on whose roof we used to dance as imperialists in the 1930s.

Unlike the China tourism of today, where you pay your money and thereafter have only to make it to the bus on time, in 1972 we paid nothing and were given VIP treatment. Four people looked after the two of us—an ex-ambassador (K'o Po-nien) my age, a young political officer who later came to the UN, a logistics arranger, who kept phoning ahead, and a young interpreter just back from two years' training in London English. When our entourage of six reached a site, we picked up liaison officers and the local responsible person so that we swarmed or flocked into the installation being visited in a very face-making manner indeed. We soon realized we were on well-trod paths, where Indonesians, Tanganyikans, Albanians, and others from many countries had set the norms and turn-around times to follow every day. Communist China's public relations had had twenty years' warm-up before the Americans came again.

At our first powwow with our escorts we asked to see North China countryside where we had traveled in the thirties, avoiding all textile plants and industries. In the absence of any capacity to compare before and after or foreign and Chinese, seeing factories would simply impress our ignorance and leave us goggle-eyed. This was accepted. We were obviously not the industrial type.

Another peculiarity of our visit was its Rip Van Winkle aspect. We had known Peking best just forty years before, and kept looking nostalgically for old landmarks, while our handlers wanted us to see the new subway. Wilma was woefully distressed to find the Peking city wall and all but two gates demolished. The city lost its shape thereby. Though the palace compound (the Forbidden City of the Ming and Ch'ing) was more magnificent than ever, the laborious destruction of the massive outer city wall and of nine of its eleven double-towered gates during the Cultural Revolution suggested either that the situation had been out of control or that those in charge were stupid, or both. We found big Ming dynasty bricks from the wall used in new structures outside the city. The architectural heritage had been cannibalized.

The saddest before-and-after was our old house in the east city. Our five servants had occupied the front or service court while our own courtyard had focused on a big blue wisteria vine over the entrance to the main hall. Now the two courtyards were merged into one tawdry slum with thirty inhabitants, no flowers, a few vegetables, quite unrecognizable. The son and daughter-in-law of our old landlord, Mr. and Mrs. Chin (Gold), now lived in two of the three *chien* or beam-sections that I had used as a study. Most of the residents were office workers. Peking had grown several times over in population. Here was the result.

In our former courtyard we also saw the cover to the entrance to the underground tunnel that traversed the area, each house's tunnel section dug out by its inhabitants. Later in the business district outside the Front Gate (Ch'ien Men) we were surprised when part of a shop floor rolled aside to disclose a stairway leading down twenty feet to a tunnel network complete with electric lights, toilets, and whole rooms available as first-aid stations, and, when we were there, music and incense! All this tunneling explained why we saw so often along the streets large piles of bricks, sand, and U-shaped cement arches that, inverted, formed a ceiling above the brick side walls of tunnels. Peking's whole population had been tunneling as protection against Soviet attack. Possibly it was a morale builder. Certainly it was an enormous boondoggle of no practical use and considerable danger.

Tunnels wide enough for two to march abreast could evacuate people from a firestorm area but also asphyxiate and entomb them. The great earthquake of August 1976 just before Mao's death (surely a devastating omen) presumably ended the tunneling vogue.

Other achievements seemed fraught with a similar ambivalence. Health care, for example, had reached the populace. We saw the availability of the semi-trained "barefoot doctors" in the countryside. Gone were the goiters, scalp sores, and skin eruptions formerly visible in a poorly nourished street crowd. But with public health had come population increase that ate up the gains of the revolution.

Wilma and I, an artist and a historian, were not easy for our guides to deal with. We knew too much about things that interested us, yet were woefully ignorant about Mao's thought and the great ideological campaigns of the revolution. Our conversations were generally superficial. Food, language, and geography were our common ground. Our manager, Mr. Wu, learned to throw a Frisbee with me for daily exercise on tour. The ex-ambassador gave us occasional monologues on the iniquities of the ex-chief of state, Liu Shao-ch'i, setting forth Mao's current line. We replied with skepticism, "If Liu was so evil, how come he rose so high?" That always led to a change of subject or a luncheon break.

As we began to get our bearings in Peking, we found ourselves still straddling the two worlds of the regime and the intellectuals. In 1972 the Cultural Revolution and its harassment of the educated and professional classes, as we now know, was far from over. Maoist egalitarianism was still the excuse for cutting specialized leadership elements down to size. Our patron was Ch'iao Kuan-hua, vice-minister of foreign affairs and a risen star in Prime Minister Chou En-lai's entourage, though not a power in the party. A few months before, in October 1971, Ch'iao had come to New York as China's first ambassador to the UN. He came out of the plane with a wide grin on his face like a Chinese Jimmy Carter and never ceased grinning for the American press, no matter how fierce his remarks. I invited him to visit Harvard, but he was accredited to the UN only, not the United States, and could not leave New York. Since we had been friends in Chungking thirty years before, he now played host to us in Peking and dropped in to greet us at the first evening's dinner hosted by Chou P'ei-yuan, head of the Peita faculty.

Also at the dinner was our old friend the sociologist Fei Hsiao-t'ung, just back from a cadre school (May 7th School) where he had learned to grow cotton. He showed us his muscles developed by tossing bricks up to masons on a wall. But Fei was rather subdued, having been told not to speak English with us. Later, when we visited his Minorities Institute, he also kept silent while the man in charge, a soldier with no ethnological background, gave us a pretentious briefing. We sensed that all our professor friends were still on a short leash, allowed to greet us but little more.

Going out to the new Peita (Peking University) we found a heroic-size white statue of Mao greeting us as we entered the old Yenching campus, which Peita had taken over and quadrupled in size. Chou P'ei-yuan welcomed us to the president's house, where Leighton Stuart had presided forty years before. There we found survivors of the Lienta faculty I had lived with in Kunming in World War II— Deison Ch'en, still teaching economics; Shao Hsun-cheng, the historian of Sino-French relations; also Bob Winter, the one American permanently on the faculty, still cutting tapes for teaching English. It said much for academic cohesion that these people were still functioning together. Bob Winter remarked that he was hardened to meeting students who had not long ago been harassing him and now seemed a bit embarrassed.

The Kunming liberal who had been most resolutely individualist and Anglo-Saxon during World War II was Chang Hsi-jo. Yet, curiously, he had survived most effectively as a collectivist bureaucrat, at one time even in charge of higher education. He came to see us with his sweet wife and a nurse who was constantly prepared to take his blood pressure. (As long as he could tolerate her presence, presumably he was all right.) We were glad to meet again but Hsi-jo did most of the talking and said little. We got no hint of the secret of his survival as a high official. A few months later his blood pressure finished him.

The cohort of our friends had of course been depleted. Our closest friends, Liang Ssu-ch'eng, the historian of Chinese architecture, and his wife Lin Hui-yin (Phyllis Liang) had died, she in 1956 and he only in January 1972, a few months before our reappearance. She had helped design the great seal of the People's Republic and had received plaudits from Mao himself at the National People's Congress. Ssu-ch'eng, like so many scholars, had received support from Prime Minister Chou.

My friend from Chungking Yang Kang, the literary editor, who had come to Radcliffe in 1945–47, had risen to be an assistant editor of the *People's Daily.* No communication had passed between us. In 1957 Yang Kang was badly injured in a traffic accident. In fact, she found her brain had been so badly damaged that she could no longer do useful work. She killed herself.

Kung P'eng, Ch'iao's wife, who had been Chou En-lai's information officer for almost thirty years, had died of a stroke in 1970. For weeks as she lay in a coma Chou had come to hold her hand and talk, but she never came to, and died when they operated on her. Her husband, Ch'iao Kuan-hua, could still not bear to speak of it.

When Ch'iao gave a dinner for us, both his teacher Y. L. Chin, the logician, and Ch'ien Tuan-sheng attended, old friends indeed, wearing new uniforms and brought by car. Both had been in seclusion, Ch'ien since 1957 as a "rightist" barred from public life. In fact he was seated at the very foot of the table, as far away as possible from the host. I almost expected to see him served dog bones for dinner. Ch'iao, in a loud voice all could hear, suggested Ch'ien and Chin come to see us at the hotel. This obviously authorized the security men to arrange it. When they came to our room, we had a warm emotional reunion but they offered nothing about their personal experiences. I described my brush with McCarthyism, when I was accused of associating with Ch'ien. He said nothing of his equivalent experience, when he was accused of writing to me. His one emphatic remark, that China would be following Marxism five thousand years from now, neatly gave us the message—like hell it will!

One of T. F. Tsiang's early students, whom he had put to study Sino-French relations, was Professor Shao Hsun-cheng. As we were saying goodnight after a dinner party, he suddenly said to me *sotto voce,* "Keep on writing!" The very innocuousness of this remark made it all the more poignant as a veiled plea for help. Shao died a few years later.

Vice-Minister Ch'iao also asked me to a discussion session just between the two of us at the Foreign Office's new People's Institute for Foreign Affairs, which turned out to be in the building of the old Chinese Social and Political Science Association. In 1933 I had given my first academic lecture there, on the opium trade of the 1850s, under the sponsorship of T. F. Tsiang. Almost forty years later we now sat in the usual white-covered overstuffed chairs with all four of my team plus an interpreter, a shorthand reporter, and Wilma all taking notes—a real conclave of chieftains.

Ch'iao's main policy message to me was that the "autonomous regions" for minority peoples as in Tibet were not feasible models for Taiwan's future status, as I seemed to suggest. I countered by explaining that by "Taiwan's autonomy" I meant a quite different situation of actual local self-government within an acknowledged framework of being a Chinese province under PRC sovereignty. (This was rather like the arrangement that was to be worked out in 1979.) The two-way interpretation on this official occasion slowed things down and I didn't feel we had said much, except to agree that the American-returned generation of Chinese scholars trained in the United States had not been well suited to lead the necessary revolution among the people.

In a big room of the Peking Hotel I gave three presentations to a Foreign Office group of fifty to ninety men and women. The first was on Chinese studies in the United States, featuring a chart I had had mimeographed. In order to understand it, one had to make the distinction between public and private. For example, disciplinary associations like the American Economics Association and research councils like the Social Science Research Council were private; government funds (federal or state) were public; but foundations were private. Such legal distinctions could only begin to describe what really complex structures we have of alumni, endowments, and government contracts. But I tried to set things forth systematically and felt *en rapport* with the audience.

My first lecture was obviously dissected in a study session and no doubt shown to be veiled cultural imperialism (perhaps I so intended it). At any rate my second lecture, on the Chinese and American foreign policy traditions of respective self-sufficiency and expansiveness, was received less warmly. Questions were prearranged. So with the third. Nevertheless it was exciting to be talking across the gap of terminology and experience between us. To be even half understood would be an achievement. The concept of individualism alone was enough to shunt us off on different tracks. "In conversations I have to try to describe what is a corporation and how a public hospital can be a private institution."

On the list of people we wanted to see in Peking I had not included the top leftist intellectual of the Chungking era, Kuo Mo-jo.

As head of the PRC Academy of Sciences, the highest-ranking schol-ar-writer in the establishment, he had become a political weather-cock, denouncing himself, renouncing his earlier work, with each shift of the ideological wind. My Harvard colleague Professor George Wald reached Peking on a peace mission and had written me from the Peking Hotel on January 24, 1972, that "Kuo Mo-jo said you are welcome to bring a delegation of scholars; the best time might be May or August." But I had not pursued this possibility. I had an innate aversion to taking any all-out ideological stand or even seeming to underwrite one. My own line didn't go with a party line.

One institution of prime importance in Mao's new order was the cadre school. On May 30 we all drove out in our Zim limousine north of Peking on the formerly bare and windswept plain encircled by the mountains and the Great Wall on the north. New tree-lined roads brought us to an irrigated area and buildings with a row of students holding up a banner, "Welcome to American Friends." It was the May 7th School (or cadre school) for the Western District of Peking. It took teachers for six months, administrators for three months, and taught them all the aspects of farm work, including the importance of pig manure. We saw students working in the fields and after lunch in a small-group study session for self-criticism. We were told every-one had spent a first month living with a peasant family. The lunch-eon for us, a culinary triumph, was avidly enjoyed by the three stout school managers. At day's end, seated in a bare hall, we watched the sudden eruption of a song-and-dance troupe, brightly costumed, who put on eight acts to music—bringing in the harvest, curing a sick pig, and so on. The expansive smile, wide-eyed stare of defiance, and raised fist of determination were all faithful to the new operatic style.

If you had tried in the 1930s to devise some way to break down the class barriers between long-gowned bureaucrats and woebegone peasants, you could hardly have devised a more effective procedure. Like boot camps in the U.S. Marines that teach military discipline, cadre schools aimed to lay bare and reduce class differences. This was Mao's egalitarian social revolution at work. But we foreign observers with our limousine and welcoming banquet represented still the ruling-class privileges of the past. It gave us feelings of great ambiva-lence.

Our safari from Peking—all six of us—into the North China coun-tryside was made by rail and auto. There could be no doubt of the enormous transformation that had occurred: small family-held strips combined into enormous fields farmed by production teams the size of half a village. Trees planted everywhere along new roads traversed by trucks and tractor pullers as well as by rubber-tired carts pulled by mules or people. As many as eight lines of wires for power or communication paralleling the railways. Electric pumps supplying water for irrigation and reclamation of sandy soils. Chimneys of new plants scattered over the countryside to bring small-scale industries to the people and hold down the proliferation of cities.

Yet behind this immense panorama of progress lurked a troubling question: What was the people's productivity compared with that of other countries? Following the famous Red Flag Canal at Lin Hsien along the arid base of the rocky T'ai-hang Mountains, our Tientsin-made touring bus took us past mile after mile of walls built of hand-hewn stone. The Honan plain was double-cropped and interplanted —cotton and cabbage, and corn and beans—so that both planting and harvesting of enormous fields had to be by hand. Eroded canyons in Shansi had ten-foot-high stone-lined tunnels running miles down the canyon floor to carry off the excess rain water a few times a year while the fields above remained uneroded. All this use of muscle power was heroic if back-breaking but it did not bring China far into the twentieth century.

The slogan "In agriculture learn from Tachai" had shouted at us from a hundred walls in four provinces by the time we made a special trip to see the model Tachai Brigade in Shansi province. Others had been there before us—several hundred Chinese a day in busloads of delegations from all over the country. The barrackslike housing and heroic tales of production all tried to convey the message of do-it-yourself and work-only-for-the-group. Tachai was a Chinese-type model to emulate, a brigade of heroes, few of whom one could ever talk to, however. Its national role as a shrine to visit for inspiration has now been tarnished by ugly revelations of fakery in production figures and only pretended self-sufficiency.

Flying into Yenan I was struck by the impenetrability of the deeply eroded loess tableland north of Sian. Even Jeeps would slow to donkey pace negotiating the intersecting canyons. Tanks and trucks could be given a very hard time. Thus protected, Yenan was shown us as another shrine, centered on the cave houses where Mao had lived. Here again was ambivalence. This cradle of a great revolution was redecorated to show only Mao in its museum and exhibits, plus his security chief (K'ang Sheng) and a few others. Those Mao had later victimized—Liu Shao-ch'i, Lin Piao, and others—were all cut out of the picture. The eighteen-year-old young women in pigtails, bright and smiling information officers from Peking, seemed to know only what they had memorized. My query about the coalition government line hatched in the central committee meeting of the summer of 1945 left them speechless. History to the CCP seemed still to be a picture of the past that would serve the politics of the present day, changeable on demand.

Chou En-lai has recently been downgraded because he was, after all, Prime Minister during Mao's imperial tyranny in his final, Cultural Revolution decade. But we can't take the overblown Mao out of modern China and still retain the revolution. So with Chou. He served on the CCP politburo for forty-eight years. Once he accepted Mao's leadership in 1935, Chou devoted himself to making it work. He was the classical prime minister, always picking up the pieces, while Mao was very much the imperial dragon, appearing and disappearing among storm clouds. Amid everything else Chou took care of foreign relations and the Americans.

The buildup before we dined with him lasted forty-eight hours. We suddenly changed plans and returned direct from Yenan to Peking. Jerry and Joan Cohen, the Harrison Salisburys of the *New York Times,* the Dick Dudmans of the St. Louis *Post-Dispatch,* and others broke off their travels and reappeared at the Peking Hotel. We were told a big event was impending, not to stray beyond call. At 4:45 P.M., a phone call: please come back to your hotel room. Met at the hotel entrance: please stay in your room. Mobilized at 6: we are to see the Prime Minister.

On the south steps of the Great Hall we found our colleagues formed in a column of twos. We were put at the head of the column, leading by seniority, and all marched up the steps, motioned on by stationary attendants. I envisioned the old tribute procedure—the kowtow would have come next.

But as we came in past a big column, there was the slight gray-suited figure of Chou himself, hand extended, "Ni hao. Ch'ing chin," with his New York–born interpreter, Nancy T'ang, just behind him in a simultaneous cadence, "Hello, please come in." We first had a picture taken, then sat in a big circle in the reception room, then dined around a table for twenty in the Anhwei Room, and after 10 P.M. (four hours) broke up for taking more pictures and departed. Harrison Salisbury spent the whole time taking notes in his lap and wrote it all up in one of his many books, *To Peking and Beyond* (1973).

When I sat down by Chou, he said in Chinese, "You knew Kung P'eng." "Yes," I said. What more could one say? Close to, I found Chou En-lai had catlike eyes that darted about. I felt his pleasant exterior covered burnished steel.

Jerry Cohen of the Harvard Law School was on his other side, the only promoter of Chinese studies I know more persistent than myself. Between us we were soon reiterating how Harvard would welcome Chinese scholars under a variety of schemes, taking turns with our bright ideas, until the Prime Minister looked at his watch and opened up the more general discussion of Vietnam that he wanted to convey to the journalists. At the Geneva conference on Vietnam in 1954, Chou said, Dulles had hoodwinked him. He still regretted it. This, we assumed, was for Henry Kissinger, who was due in two days.

Later that week, at lunch with the French ambassador, we received a phoned request from Henry to come and see him at the state guest house (Tiao Yü T'ai, where I would later stay with Vice-President Mondale's party in 1979). Fortunately the luncheon was over and we could leave the French embassy without being insufferably officious. In that period Henry was a major focus of world diplomatic news.

The guest house on the west of Peking is actually a park with half a dozen or more thirty-person hostels separated by lakes but connected by bridges, a beautiful place well under control.

Henry began by taking the two of us out for a stroll by the lake and then took me into a conference room. We sat on a couch. "Why do you suppose Chou En-lai asked me to see you?" he said. I thought hard. "Probably because we have toured the countryside we knew before and are much impressed by the transformation." I gave examples. We then broke up so Henry could go to see the Prime Minister again.

Our fortieth wedding anniversary was June 29, 1972, and we asked to extend our stay by two weeks to celebrate it in Peking. Our guides worked this out and gave us a banquet with old friends when the time came. We left very much indebted and reached Hong Kong in time for Consul General David Osborn's July 4 reception for the American community. I had meanwhile written an article for *Foreign Affairs* to report my impressions and it was published in the October 1972 issue as "The New China and the American Connection." It reported on the material achievements, appraised the Washington-Peking conflict of the past, and concluded that on the whole the Chinese "have the better of the argument."

This more-than-tourist immersion in seeing the new China in 1972 was an enormous intellectual challenge to comprehend the changes of forty years. It put a premium on our sophistication in appraising situations partly invisible to us, and also put me in a position where I might be expected to know more than I actually did— not a new experience by any means but now more unavoidable. When Senator Fulbright asked me to his office, where most of his Foreign Relations Committee colleagues dropped in, I tried to supply a before-and-after long-term perspective on China's revolution.

The whole PRC procedure of inviting foreign guests at state expense was a public-relations program comparable in detail to those of American corporations. For example, in 1960 we had enjoyed staying in the sumptuous guest houses of Bill Youngman's American International Underwriters in Hong Kong and Singapore. But that was personal generosity on Bill's part, still at a private level. In 1972 we enjoyed a six-week investment in us by a political animal, the PRC. No strings were overtly attached. Rather than take it as a debt to repay, I put it in the category of a government grant awarded by competent authority to be used as best I could.

31

FAILURE WITH THE SOVIETS

DURING MY HALF century of activity in the Chinese modern history field, from 1929 to 1979, world politics shifted about rather disconcertingly. For the first sixteen years from 1929 to 1945, Japan's increasing aggression on China dominated East Asia and American concerns there. But, from the beginning of the nuclear age in 1945, Soviet-American rivalry has for thirty-five years magnetized world politics. The Cold War against the Chinese Revolution might wax and wane, Americans might fight Koreans and Chinese in Korea, and Vietnamese in Vietnam. But behind all this warfare loomed the arms race between the USA and the USSR, probably the most wasteful enterprise in all history.

This was a rivalry between peoples who had enough in common to know why they feared each other. From Athens *vs.* Sparta down the ages to France *vs.* Germany, the most enduring rivalries seem to have been within cultures where intelligible differences could stand forth prominently for all to see on both sides. On all three of my sojourns in the USSR, in 1960, 1972, and 1977, I was conscious that my Russian friends and contacts had their eyes set on catching up with America. (It was a bit like my first visit to Yale, where they talked so much about Harvard. This has died down recently.)

My Soviet connection had begun in early 1960, when Harvard hosted a Leningrad University delegation that included my opposite number in the chair of Chinese history. Professor G. V. Efimov was a rather round gentleman, who wrote textbooks. On both sides we found this meeting exhilarating. Harvard staged a banquet in the 17 Quincy Street ballroom that contains our best chandelier. In our house at 41 Winthrop Street, Professor Efimov noted how rickety our windows would be against the Russian winter. In my study at Widener I snowed him with printed matter—personnel directories, pamphlets, publications, revealing everything of the sort I figured he might regard as secret. When we visited Leningrad later in 1960, we dined in the Efimovs' flat.

The payoff from my bibliographic largesse came in 1968, when Efimov's staff member L. A. Bereznii published in Russian a 261-page volume with 1,000 footnote references—*A Critique of American Bourgeois Historiography on China: Problems of Social Development in the Nineteenth and Early Twentieth Centuries.* It dealt in large part with Harvard publications, especially my own, on the stated assumption that so-called liberal scholarship in America was by intent devoted to supporting our capitalist imperialism in East Asia and therefore "wants to disprove the Marxist-Leninist scientific understanding of the historical process." (I quote from a summary I had made and circulated widely as a pamphlet.) "Marxist-Leninist historians," says Bereznii, "can proceed from their general social laws concerning world history and, after distilling the results of empirical research, arrive at formulations concerning the specific working out of the historical process in a given country." Here was the primacy of ideology again! All you had to do was pin the right labels on things, and history was understood and could even be foretold.

Bereznii's main point was that we American historians were all apologists for capitalist imperialism and for Mao's catastrophic nationalist deviation from Marxism-Leninism. Some of his critique was worth thinking about. At least it did us the honor of reasoned discourse that saw our errors as due to wrong ideas, not purely to a sordid conspiracy. By the time I met him in Leningrad in 1972, Bereznii had produced a further volume of his critique. He was inoffensive in person, rather a philosopher, though the hard-boiled realists at the Far East Institute in Moscow laughed at him as overly theoretical.

Wilma and I went to Moscow first for the International Congress of Orientalists in 1960. We stayed in the Stalinoid high-rise Hotel Ukraina (twenty-nine stories) and began to get some sense of how bureaucratization can spoil life. Far from free supply in the dining hall, our meals were held up for hours, first getting a waiter's attention, second while he lined up to put in the order, third while he lined up to pay his own cash for it, fourth while he lined up to show his receipt, get the food, and deliver it to us. We felt no society capable of such inbuilt inefficiency could offer America much of a threat. We heard our fellow Bostonian Mr. Mugar, builder of the Star Market chain, describe what he had told the Soviet food purveyors about their lack of zip.

The Congress of Orientalists, a massive show with a cast of two thousand, opened in the main hall of Moscow University under eight big six-level chandeliers, which were surrounded by twenty-one smaller three-level chandeliers. We each carried a small receiver with earphones to pick up a simultaneous English translation of the speeches. In contrast with this material magnificence, the speakers extolled Marxist scientific thinking as the way to pursue the history, literature, etc. of the peoples of Asia and Africa. The injection of politics into every subject seemed to me essentially anti-intellectual and self-defeating. In bookstores, however, Russian books on China were cheap and plentiful, and we shipped dozens of volumes home.

The event that colored the whole conference was the surfacing of the Sino-Soviet split, a process under way since 1958 but now dramatized by the nonappearance of Chinese scholars from the PRC. The Soviet Union had withdrawn its technicians and their blueprints from scores of projects in China just a few weeks before. World politics had turned a sharp corner and Sino-American rapprochement was on the cards from here on. But for reasons as yet unexplained except by Cold War stupidity, this historic split seems to have had little impact on American minds unprepared to receive its obvious message. Once one decides that all events are staged by hidden conspiracy, it becomes difficult to recognize a genuine event when it happens.

The chief excitement at the Congress, at least for the American organizing committee, was the Soviet effort to censor our book exhibit. We found 25 books had been removed from the American display of 155 volumes. The missing items included my *United States and China,* as well as books by Albert Feuerwerker and Richard L. Walker and K. A. Wittfogel's *Oriental Despotism.* We of course raised hell about it in a polite but insistent way. The excuse offered was that the books in question were "too political" in content. The trail led to Professor S. Tikhvinskii, historian-diplomat-apparatchik. Irate negotiations secured the return of the absent volumes on the last day of the conference, too late to be widely viewed.

When a Columbia sociologist presented in one China session a report on field-work methods and prospects in Taiwan, Tikhvinskii arose in the crowded hall and scathingly denounced it in English as nonacademic, undocumented opinion, not worth taking the time of a learned body. I followed and sharply disagreed: social scientists need to communicate on work in progress; American scholarship has benefited from such reports; documented history is not the whole story. In fact, learned gatherings might do better to stress such reports.

I had met Professor Tikhvinskii first in Peking and then at the Junior Sinologues congress in Europe—an astute scholar and supervisor of scholars, with a self-confident air of busy authority, reputed to be *very* well connected (I mean with the state police). In Moscow he entertained us cordially at a grand Chinese restaurant that had fired its Chinese cooks and substituted Russians. As Pekingites we were outraged when our host busily doused the half-dozen Chinese dishes indiscriminately with a bottle of soy sauce. I explained to him that his one-time friend in Peking student days, Mary Wright, had hit the ceiling when he reviewed her book as a "falsification of history" because in English the term implies a conscious intent to lie, rather than merely being unsound in interpretation. Tikhvinskii's style has always seemed to me heavy-handed.

When we visited Moscow again in 1972, after our trip to China, we stayed at the National Hotel, still in the Stalinesque tower style, and visited Leningrad again. I gave half a dozen presentations to audiences mainly of researchers in institutes, reporting on trends in American publication on China, answering well-informed questions on conditions in China.

I found my audiences quite ready to accept the idea that the USSR and USA were on converging courses—technology was bringing us both into a new world where we would have more and more in common, beginning with the desire to survive. My belief was that they would have to be more like us and let the individual express himself more freely. Perhaps some Soviet scholars tacitly agreed with this but others certainly retained a belief that America would have to come to socialism, which was presumed to exist in the USSR. The concept of convergence thus papered over the basic issues rather sleazily. It was only rhetoric but permitted us to converse on what seemed like common ground.

In 1960 Tikhvinskii had introduced me to his studious colleague V. N. Nikiforov, and the two of us took a walk, exchanging broad platitudes. Finally he asked in some embarrassment if I believed in God. My negative answer seemed to relieve his mind. I suspected it enhanced his own faith. We agreed on the necessity of comparing our world views, but no correspondence ever developed. I saw Nikiforov again briefly in 1972. In 1977 we lunched at the Harvard faculty club (he had finally come to visit America). I suggested that after seventeen years our relationship had been a complete nonstarter, and he glumly agreed.

By 1976 the trend toward a Peking-Washington normalization seemed to me well set. We therefore had a last chance to establish contact with Soviet scholars on China before being caught up in new Sino-American relationships. Believing in learning as a solvent for fear and hatred, I wanted to see contact and indeed common projects among historians of China all around the world. In holding this view I was of course a naïf idealist. (What other kind is there?)

I therefore accepted membership on the ACLS or American part of the Joint ACLS–Soviet Academy of Sciences Commission on the Humanities and Social Sciences. The issue was whether American China specialists should try to have Soviet contact as well as Chinese. I polled more than a score of colleagues across the country. They were equally divided between claiming Soviet contact as a professional academic right and avoiding it as an inexpedient gesture likely to yield little and offend the Chinese. I stayed away from the Joint Commission's first meeting in the United States in March 1975 but decided to attend the second meeting in Moscow in June 1977.

In Moscow I found the Institute of Oriental Culture more crowded than ever in its shabby quarters. But the Joint Commission met in a long room in the new Ministry of Information, the opposing teams strung out on opposite sides of a narrow table covered, you guessed it, with green cloth.

With my opposite number in Chinese studies, Lev Deliusin, head of the China section of the Oriental Institute, and with the help of S. Tikhvinskii as a senior figure, I was able to get agreement on a section of the protocol for East Asian studies as a subject separate from law, economics, literature, and the like. To accomplish this, however, I had to beat back an effort by the Soviet chairman to classify East Asian studies as an aspect of history. I was invited up into a sort of witness box at the head of the room and asserted the independence of AAS from AHA both organizationally and intellectually, which required keeping the fields separate at the American end. This was accepted. Deliusin and I worked out a program for a Soviet China specialist to visit American China centers, testing out what interest and cooperation could be obtained among Americans in Chinese studies.

On the final day, however, signing the protocol was held up by a "breakdown" of the mimeographing capacity in this enormous new ministry that covered a city block. After an hour it was explained that collating the Soviet and American versions of the protocol would take several days' work. Very evidently, the security or other powers behind the scenes were holding us up. The impressive heads of institutes and departments, for all their scholarly qualifications, were powerless. We broke up, agreeing informally to act as though the agreed-upon protocol had been accepted and was operative. For the China section of it, a trip by Deliusin to the United States was arranged, his arrival plane was cabled us, but he was not on the plane when it arrived. Later his trip was postponed indefinitely.

I had begun studying Russian too late to get anywhere. My approach by way of a descriptive bibliography of Russian work on China had been frustrated. Now the idea of personal contact and conferences had aborted. I gave up and resigned from the Joint Commission.

It is hard to avoid emotional distaste for the Soviet style. Scholars seemed to work at the sufferance of the authorities, to whom foreigners had no access. If in Peking one's project might be slain with a perfumed stiletto, in Moscow it would be with a meat axe. Always in the background was the nagging question, How can the Russians be such warm human beings on the personal level and yet treat each other so badly in public life?

Our Soviet problem in Chinese studies continues to baffle me. The China field in American academia has simply failed to get the history of Sino-Soviet relations into its sights—a good example of scholarship evidently being hamstrung by the political climate of the time. This makes a good case study because the causes are quite complex.

For a sinologist committed to reading Chinese and Japanese, the adding on of Russian requires either the linguistic flare of a polyglot language wizard, who may not be much of an analyst, or the drudgery capacity of the long-distance-runner type of scholar, who has to postpone thought until he can translate. It is hard to be quickly productive.

Another difficulty is that Soviet libraries and facilities seldom smooth one's path with an eager welcome. Soviet historians themselves are kept within rather strict limits on what they can see and say. Between the marginal importance of the Russian aspect of Chinese history and the unappetizing difficulties in the Russian world of scholarship, Americans have not been much attracted to study Russian activities in China. The Chinese of course have offered no encouragement to Americans to do so.

The result is that the Russian experience in China has been neglected, including the opportunities for comparison—for example, of Soviet aid and mediation in the mid-1920s united-front period and American aid and mediation in the late-forties coalition-government period. This is a distinct loss. Russians appeared on the Ch'ing dynasty's horizon from its inception in the early seventeenth century, 150 years before Americans reached Canton in 1784. In Peking's strategic concerns, Russia bulked larger than America throughout the nineteenth century and still does so today. The Russians have a mystique of eastward expansion, as we do of western expansion. In our history in Asia we have more in common than we realize. The Chinese will go on playing us off against each other. But since we share one uniquely overwhelming concern—survival—we must keep on dealing with each other as best we can.

I reflected on my sporadic contact with S. Tikhvinskii at academic meetings over the years—a quick, intelligent man, a diplomat high in Foreign Office circles, very much in the establishment, at the same time author of a book on Manchu rule in China, another on Sun Yat-sen, most recently editor of a leading historical journal. My harshest critics on the left might even call Tikhvinskii a Soviet Fairbank.

I recall a conversation in which he denounced the Chinese for ambushing Soviet troops on the disputed border and delaying negotiations about it. He slapped the table. "They know very well we could be in Peking in forty-eight hours!" He sounded like an American I knew who admired MacArthur.

Naturally, I never contemplated setting up any kind of common project with Tikhvinskii. He would have tried to impose his own ideas whereas I would have wanted to follow the dictates of reason (as I saw them). So there is the problem.

32

UPS AND DOWNS AS A FRIEND
OF CHINA

AN AREA SPECIALIST functions by profession as a teacher but he may easily slop over into being a pundit. By punditry I mean giving a judgment on a distant and obscure situation which is essentially unknowable but in which the public media are interested, at least for the moment. Descended from shamanism, this public function will always be performed, even if only by dopes and dupes, so why not by oneself? Better a little wisdom than none at all.

Peoples abroad are therefore confronted by American sages who pontificate on their affairs. Chinese have long been accustomed to the foreign *Chung-kuo t'ung* (Japanese *Shina-tsu*), Chinakenner or sinologue, people who when in China are students of China and when at home teach all about China. It is a venerable profession.

In my case the fascination of Sino-American contact and interaction gave me a lively interest in American China policy, a game in which any number can play. Given the strategic importance of American policy in Chinese life after 1941, I was helicoptered into public policy discussions from 1946 on, and after thirty more years of this activity began to be referred to as a "dean" of China scholars, which in my book is a very dubious thing to be. Deans are usually ex-professors. (It has been said that old deans never die. They just lose their faculties.)

When you pare it down to the bone, what I had to offer was generally a segment or a whole capsulized history of China at the rather broad history survey level, or else a suggestion that our policy should be viewed in a historical context from both sides. From 1949 to 1979 both these gambits were applicable to our Taiwan problem. In fact this problem didn't go away with the Washington-Peking normalization of 1979. We still have it and many cherish it. It will continue to be with us.

The Taiwan problem is many things: the symbol of a civil war that was lost except as Taiwan can blow hard on the embers, the irredentism about a province kept detached from the motherland, a product of imperialist aggression by Japan and then America, an island base of 18 million for reconquest of 1,000 million, an economic miracle, our sixth-largest trading partner, an unsinkable language school and research center, an accessible repository of art and archives swiped from Peking, the last treaty port writ large, our inoffensive, deserving, and demanding ex-ally, and much much more. Something for everybody. Let us not underrate its positive values just because of its nuisance value.

In 1977 I was excluded from the PRC with stony silence and greeted in Taiwan by a vociferous press attack. Obviously both Chinas were trying to tell me something.

Chou En-lai's parting remark in 1972 was in English: "See you next year or later." It sounded like an open door but I did not try at once to follow up on it. Once back in Cambridge, we developed some four hundred slides and I put on a slide show for the China community in the ballroom of the American Academy of Arts and Sciences. It was then at Brandegee House in Jamaica Plain, where we usually staged a research-center summer symposium. The slides recapitulated our tour, ending with a shot of Wilma in the bathing pool of that all-time T'ang beauty, Yang Kuei Fei.

Other projects then supervened to postpone for several years any effort to visit the PRC again. In the latter part of 1972 we went around the globe via London, Paris, Munich, Moscow, Tokyo, and Taipei from mid-September to mid-December. I then found 1973 was full of editorial work to bring out our one-volume text *East Asia: Tradition and Transformation* and edit a symposium volume, *The Missionary Enterprise in China and America,* derived from a January 1972 conference at Cuernavaca (published by Harvard in 1974). I also began pulling together volume 10 of the *Cambridge History of China,* which was completed in 1976.

Meanwhile I became more involved in contact with Harvard alumni and eventually in fund raising. Harvard Alumni Clubs are especially good audiences because they have a sense of community as a social group in themselves and also as part of the alumni organization. Their constant search for talent to nominate for admission and sometimes to back financially is a concrete boon to Harvard. A professor's donation of his time is appreciated. If he brings news of men and women getting their educations more efficiently in the same dormitories it may rouse discussion. In the 1960s the decline and fall of the parietal rules also evoked interest. The master of Lowell House lost the obligation to inquire why an amateur photographer always needed a Radcliffe assistant in his darkroom. Radcliffe rules were reduced to checking in by 8 A.M. to prove a student still lived and was ambulatory.

When I agreed to lecture in a community forum or lecture series, I often arranged to talk to the local Harvard Club too. Altogether I suppose I got on the program of forty different clubs, some more than once. It always seemed worth doing.

With this background Wilma and I enjoyed helping to inaugurate the summer Alumni College as a new institution. Most of the hundred or so students could remember Pearl Harbor. You didn't need to explain who Joe McCarthy was. Their week or ten days of living in Kirkland House and surveying Chinese history and art intensively was a kind of college reunion. Wilma's half of the lectures made good use of the Fogg and the Boston Museum of Fine Arts. Usually we found ex-ambassadors and China hands in the group who could join in a symposium on policy. We did this in the summer schools of 1973, '74, and '76.

As part of Harvard's fund raising for East Asian studies we made a summer 1976 trip to Honolulu, Hong Kong, Singapore, Taipei, and Tokyo, talking to Harvard Clubs to lay a basis for soliciting funds from the rising business community of Maritime China.

Mao Tse-tung's death in September 1976 ended our long though tenuous association, in which he, by making revolution from 1927, had enhanced the rationale for my studying China since 1929. Mao's death was the top news, the media needed their message, and I was still on everybody's short list of China pundits. But I persisted in driving to North Hatley, P.Q., to visit our dear Canadian friends, Frank and Marian Scott. A resourceful CBS producer in New York met the problem by having a seaplane lift us from Lake Massawippi to Montreal, where I could appear on a panel split with Washington and Pasadena. We agreed on Mao's death being a turning point both for him and for the world, and I took the occasion to claim that we still had a Taiwan problem. Thus it was 1977 before we sought visas again for the PRC.

The Chinese care and feeding of "friends of China" is a delicate operation. The category is a valid one in Chinese thinking but does not have similar moral potency in the outside world. It goes back to the Confucian ideal of moral integrity manifested in loyalty to one's patron and ruler. Officials willing to serve a conqueror's new dynasty, after having eaten the rice of its defunct predecessor, forfeited their honor. Since Chinese international relations are in the same moral continuum as interpersonal relations, friendship between peoples is like that between families and individuals, a bond to be honored as a duty, embodying mutual claims and obligations. A friend of China is a foreigner who has been taken into the Chinese network of inter-personal relations and dutifully holds his end up. He can be counted on.

Westerners are notoriously likely to backslide in this relationship because they may put other considerations before consistency of friendship. Journalists in particular have a code of calling things as they see them. Over Agnes Smedley's ashes in the cemetery for revolutionaries out at Babaoshan on the western edge of Peking is a stone inscribed:

> In memory of Agnes Smedley,
> American revolutionary writer
> and
> Friend of the Chinese people

One can imagine how A. Smedley would have reacted to the depredations of Chiang Ch'ing (Jiang Qing), recently revealed, during the Cultural Revolution decade. My guess is that her anti-establishment propensity would have made the air blue, supposing she had not already decided that Mao was a tyrant back in 1957. Perhaps the only way to be a friend of China for keeps is to die at the right moment.

In practice the foreign journalist is worked upon, as in most lands, to keep him on the government's side. Threat of exclusion from

China is used as a material incentive affecting his livelihood. Foreign professors can be influenced in the same way but not quite so easily. On their part, both American journalists and professors are likely to remain critically disposed toward the established authority, so that people they befriended when out of power become targets of criticism when in power. This is unfriendly.

PRC disenchantment with me after their investment in our six-week tour in 1972 must have started in fairly soon. Our tour through Europe in the fall of 1972 included three weeks in Moscow-Leningrad and half a dozen presentations, none of them public or anti-Chinese in my view. But, given the high sensitivity of Chinese-Soviet relations, my merely going to the USSR could seem dubious in Peking. Presumably it was reported in Soviet media to China. This supposition comes from my trying to imagine what I would have done if I had been S. Tikhvinskii. While this admittedly strains my faculty of imagination, it suggests to me that a China specialist who visited Peking and then Moscow and Taipei in 1972 must have seemed to be a crass opportunist even though I regarded myself more favorably as a professor seeking all sides of his subject.

In any case one overt act as a nonfriend seems to have been my review of *Prisoner of Mao* by Jean Pascalini (Bao Ruo-wang), who had been born in Peking of a Chinese mother and French father. He had worked for the U.S. Marines, been arrested in 1957, spent seven years in labor camps, and been released in 1964 as a French citizen when De Gaulle recognized Peking. Pascalini was a genuine Peking-ite, young and adaptable, who mastered the lingo of thought reform, was able to survive his heavy work quota, and survived the general malnutrition of 1960–61. His story, written down and organized by an American journalist, rang true and gave us a sudden insight into the PRC equivalent of the Soviet *gulag.* When these two authors visited Cambridge, their veracity and objectivity became quite apparent.

My review in the *New York Review of Books* (November 1, 1973) brought out how Chinese work camps differed in the early sixties from the Soviet: the guards and administrators were uncorrupt and sincere, there was no underworld of tyranny by older prisoners, the only sodomist discovered was summarily shot, the wardens showed that their own fare was just as bad in the starving time. The comparison was to China's credit even though the whole system was highly repugnant to American readers and had not before been so concretely exposed.

On my next visit to the PRC Liaison Office in Washington Ambassador Han Hsu (Han Xu), a charismatic diplomat in the image of Chou En-lai, said my reviewing *Prisoner of Mao* had been an "unfriendly" act. I should not have done it. I countered that in American terms a professor cannot put friendship before professional duty. The book was significant and I could not duck the responsibility to appraise it. It was my business to do so. What use would I be if I refused to review it in fear of giving offense? Han Hsu was not impressed by my argument that the book put the PRC in a better light than the USSR. We parted stiffly.

In 1977 our visa applications went in and were never turned down. There was simply no reply from Peking. By that date any number of factors may have operated. I listed Ch'iao Kuan-hua as someone I wanted to see, though I knew he was in the doghouse for having demonstrated against Deng in April 1976. Huang Hua had succeeded Ch'iao as foreign minister.

I had been writing and lecturing on what to do about Taiwan with increasing frequency as it grew more evident that the PRC would finally make it into the UN and the Washington-Peking relationship would have to develop. That no Sino-American rapprochement had got under way in 1960 when the Sino-Soviet split became so evident was only one sign of the righteous passivity, if not rigidity, which engulfed the Chinese and American (Mao-Chou and Kennedy-Rusk) leaderships on their respective sides.

My trip to Moscow on the ACLS-USSR commission in June 1977, though I informed the PRC Liaison Office of it, may have been enough in itself to seem unfriendly. As time ran out, I retrieved our passports from the Liaison Office in order to get Japanese and Korean visas. The young Chinese secretary who handed them to me at the door averted his eyes in embarrassment. He was more conscious of my loss of face than I was. The loss of face was considerable because we had been invited to stay in Peking (everyone has to have a place to stay) with the Canadian ambassador, Arthur Menzies, once a student at Harvard. Inviting guests was a diplomatic privilege. No visas for us affronted Canada, especially when the ambassador had gone to bat for us at the FO.

We stopped in Tokyo to see friends and I gave a talk at International House, the peerless home for foreign scholars that had sheltered us half a dozen times. Then we went on to lecture in Seoul for the leading paper *Tong-A Ilbo,* who had paid our way. Peking being beyond reach, we decided to spend ten days in Taipei. I phoned a former student, Bill Ayers, currently public-affairs officer in the Taipei embassy, to test the waters. He found no Foreign Office objection, we got ROC visas, and Bill booked us into the Grand Hotel.

My concern about our reception in Taipei stemmed from the books that had been published there about Fei Cheng-ch'ing (me). About 1966 a group of anti-Communist patriots in the Legislative Yuan, possibly inspired by Senator Fulbright's 1966 hearings on China policy, had discovered the fourteen volumes of the 1951–52 McCarran committee hearings on the IPR. As they read how Free China had been sold out to the Reds by the IPR conspiracy, their hair stood on end and they came into print like time bombs detonating after fifteen years' quiescence. Half a dozen sizable books appeared in Chinese in 1968–69 under titles such as *The Institute of Pacific Relations and the John K. Fairbank Clique, The Great Conspiracy of the John K. Fairbank Clique in Taiwan* (792 pages!), *John K. Fairbank and Communist Mao,* and the like. Our visit in 1972 had been brief and in 1976 had been in a group to seek support from the Harvard Club of Taipei. But now as disaster to Taiwan loomed, the insidious survivor of that small hard core who had engineered the Loss of China twenty years ago suddenly reappeared, evidently intent on the Loss of Taiwan too!

In the large lobby of the Grand Hotel, with its massive red columns like Karnak-on-the-Pacific, there suddenly emerged an intrepid Taiwanese journalist named Flora Fu, who had once phoned me in Cambridge to get a story. She told me that nine concerned gentlemen including three members of the Legislative Yuan and authors of books on me had issued a statement in the *Central Daily News* warning against Fei Cheng-ch'ing's pro-Communist sympathies and his efforts to lead China astray. They called a public meeting for two days later and invited some sixty intellectuals and journalists to join in a forum. Once this news was out, Kuo T'ing-i's conservative successor as director of the Modern History Institute sent a message that he could not see me. A more liberal scholar who wanted to set up appointments for me in another institute across the street phoned the vice-minister of Foreign Affairs, got no support, and had to cancel out. The organizers of the public forum could influence the research institute's budget allocations and had a legislator's power of investigation.

I therefore looked forward with some anticipation to lunching with the vice-minister, Fred Ch'ien (Ch'ien Fu). His father had been head of Taiwan National University and Academia Sinica. He had been to Yale, had a very good-looking, up-to-the-minute wife, and expressed himself vigorously in American terms. He was incensed at my urging acceptance of Peking's demand that the U.S.-ROC security treaty of 1954 be dropped. I argued that Taiwan's security would be better assured if Washington and Peking achieved a workable normalization. The idea that the ROC in Taiwan was China had lost any validity after twenty-eight years' make-believe. Its security could now be assured informally or unilaterally as an autonomous province of China. I urged "working out some equilibrium now rather than letting things slide along, but he of course remained unconvinced."

I was under pressure because Fred Ch'ien had invited to lunch the secretary of the Taipei Harvard Club, who said he had just sent $185,000 to Harvard to meet the club's pledge of $200,000. This was obviously real friendship of the kind that counted and Chinese reciprocity demanded I lay off opposing the security treaty. But my hosts also recognized the American distinction between public and private, as well as between politics and education. An editorial on me the next day was a bit less condemnatory, suggesting I might realize my errors.

The public meeting to denounce me was held at Liberty House and was attended by some two hundred people. An adventurous Harvard language student attended and took a recording. My chief critic (Hu Ch'iu-yuan) challenged me to a debate for $100,000, he to speak English and I Chinese. If I won, the money would go to my research center. If he won, it would support a program against normalization. The accusations against me, aside from the IPR "conspiracy," were ill-informed and fanciful—for example, that I spread Wittfogel's idea of Chinese stagnation in an "Asiatic mode of production" (not his point, nor mine). The critics had largely invented their version of Fei Cheng-ch'ing. What came through was mainly righteous indignation. Some fifty letters denouncing me appeared in the press.

Flora Fu intrepidly surfaced again with a message that Dr. T'ao

Hsi-sheng would like to see me. He had been a principal ideologue for CKS, the chief writer of *China's Destiny*. He had come to see me at Harvard unexpectedly in 1968 and we had had a brief noncommunication because his English was too much like my Chinese. To see him now would be like a meeting between Walter Lippmann and Rasputin or vice versa according to one's view. I asked that he bring an interpreter, he did so, and I accepted his invitation to a session at his Mainland China Study Center.

We met at the new Sun Yat-sen Memorial. The score of people present included four or five who had had the KMT brand of political reeducation *(lao-yü)*, one in particular announcing that he had done ten years in jail to remold his thinking, after which, however, he showed us no samples of it. Dr. T'ao and I were rather mild and professorial. The tone was academic and a bit tired.

Wang Shih-chieh and his articulate son also had us to dinner and a lively discussion. Of all the KMT leaders Dr. Wang seemed to me the most statesmanlike, ready to hear all sides. I persisted in seeing a bright Taiwan-American future on an informal basis without the security treaty. Both these meetings in 1977 with leaders of CKS's old guard were aimed, I think, at appraising my animus. Was I an enemy of Taiwan? Or was it true as I claimed that I thought Taiwan would find itself in a better status as part of a Washington-Peking normalization deal?

Our chief pleasure in Taipei was to see ex-Foreign Minister George Yeh again, still the same strong individual, still frozen in position as a minister without portfolio, island-bound yet asked to handle the budget. Secret police trailed him when he was out but Chiang Ching-kuo came to see him when he was hospitalized—a curious stultification of top-level talent.

George was interested in a modern-dance troupe and took us to their performance before two thousand people in the Sun Yat-sen Memorial. The show was a good try and the crowd seemed thoroughly Western-international in spirit. Literature and the arts were developing in Taipei. It was part of the great world.

On the whole my anti-reception in Taipei in the tense late summer of 1977 seemed to me a logical extension of the McCarthy hysteria of so many years ago. Just as a Chinese written character may acquire several layers of meaning as it comes down the ages, so my public persona had taken on several guises. The public scene, I realized, is full of misunderstood, mislabeled personalities. When badly needed they sometimes even have to be invented.

To be condemned by both Chinas at once I considered to be some kind of record. At the least it represented exasperation with an outsider who obviously didn't know very much but nevertheless kept sounding off about the necessity of saying, "There is only one China, one China," while the Americans kept on dealing with both.

My egress from the PRC's doghouse came about from the American end after normalization was achieved as of January 1, 1979, by the Carter administration. When the doughty Vice-premier Deng Xiaoping came to Washington in January, we and the Teddy Whites were invited to President Carter's dinner for him, so we arrived for this historic event in the same taxi at the East Wing entrance to the White House. The rather low-key and businesslike entrance room was full of keen-eyed young men, and as we went through the corridor, up the stairs, and past the U.S. Marine band, we found handsome young men and women in gold braid uniforms standing at attention every ten feet or so on either side. Unlike British horse guards, however, they were not looking off into space but at us, politely but penetratingly. I realized security consisted of the home team outnumbering the guests. I was sure that at a moment's notice they could have had us all face down on the floor. I commented on this to the cordial and handsome officer who escorted us into the East Room. "Yes," he said, "and there are some things you can't see, too."

The room soon filled up with a lot of celebrities we knew by sight and others in person. As at any East Asian conclave, I started introducing people, like Doak Barnett to Bill Seawall, head of Pan Am, but I realized this Winthrop Street proclivity had better stop short of law partners and senators. They were not graduate students.

When the Klieg lights came on and the media, massed at the end of the room, began to put us before the people, I went through the receiving line early. Prompted by his interpreter (Harvard '52), Deng recognized my name and I went into the banquet hall reassured I existed. I found my table by number and my place card. On my right the card read "Shirley MacLaine." On my left, "Rosalynn Carter." I was at the head table.

What an honor! I suppose I was an appropriate symbol of the China tribe, having advocated for thirty years the normalization that was now occurring. But I was not programmed for this, caught with my self-image down. Between the actress and the First Lady I felt like a donkey between haystacks.

It was a curious dinner without a host. We were at a true turning point in history but no informal toasts were drunk at our table. I suddenly saw the systemic disaster of the Carter administration. The President sat there absorbed in his own thoughts. He did not take charge of us as a group. Rosalynn Carter on the other hand was superb—very good looking, percipient, forthcoming. If only she could have handled her husband's small-group situations, he might be in a second term today.

Shirley MacLaine was there because she had helped put together the entertainment to follow. She had acquired China by leading a menagerie of American women, one of every known kind, on a culture-shock trip to the PRC that simply beat the pants off any other culture shock she had ever had. She baited Deng about an artist who had raised tomatoes in the Cultural Revolution. "Maybe he liked tomatoes," said Deng.

My colloquy with China's leader was as follows:

D. "How old are you?"

F. "Seventy-two."

D. "I am seventy-four."

F. "But you still have your hair and I don't."

D. "You have obviously used your brain too much."

What a missed opportunity! We should have toasted the memory of Chou En-lai and gone on from there to have a Chinese-type party. I felt like an utter failure.

The entertainment that followed at the Kennedy Center was a mixture of corn and brass plus Rudolph Serkin. At the end Deng and Carter went up on the stage to thank the variegated cast. Deng looked up at a Harlem Globetrotter who was double his height. He also sort of kissed a schoolgirl singer on the top of her head. Later in Texas he wore a ten-gallon hat in a stagecoach. Barbarian taming obviously grows more strenuous with time.

Our return to Peking in April 1979 was made auspicious because we traveled with the Pan American World Airways board of directors, I having served two years as a member of their International Advisory Board. Wilma and I secured visas to let us stay another two weeks with the Canadian ambassador, as planned in 1977, and the handsome Han Hsu (Han Xu), now in the FO, came to dine with us there, thus burying my sins of the past, whatever they had been.

My failure to perform properly at President Carter's dinner bothered me but I had a chance to catch up with it in August 1979. Vice-President Mondale invited me to go with him on a ten-day trip to Peking, Sian, and Canton to signalize the completion of the normalization of Washington-Peking relations. At our second dinner in the Great Hall of the People, the vice-president, escorting the vice-premier, suddenly appeared behind me. Deng Xiaoping congratulated me on having helped Sino-American relations. Instead of being simply flabbergasted, I had the wit to propose that we also drink a toast in memory of Chou En-lai, which we did.

By 1979 under Deng's leadership the CCP had largely caught up with the excesses of the Cultural Revolution decade, insofar as injustice can be righted by retrospective pronouncements. This "reversal of verdicts," removing stigma of ideological error from many many thousands of names, had traditional overtones. It echoed the Confucian chronicler's practice of labeling historic persons with terms of praise or blame in the record for posterity. Thus Mao's number two, the chief of state Liu Shao-ch'i, top target of the Cultural Revolution, who died disgraced, was a decade later "rehabilitated." This was a necessary gesture if the CCP was to continue as the ruling power, successor to the Sons of Heaven who as part of their cosmic act gave forth moral judgments. The CCP, in short, had a papal function to perform as well as that of a Supreme Court. It affected many of our friends and acquaintances who had been hit by the revolution.

For example, our old friend the political scientist Ch'ien Tuan-sheng, our house guest in 1947–48, had represented the PRC in the early 1950s on several missions abroad. In 1954 he telephoned us from a conference he was attending at Pugwash, Nova Scotia. But in the anti-rightist campaign of 1957 Ch'ien was "capped" as a rightist, barred from public life. For twenty-two years he lived in his Peking house, or part of it, on a small stipend, his talents unused. In January 1979 he was rehabilitated, but the PRC today lacks the men he might have trained in law and government. In August 1979 I was delighted that I could escort Joan Mondale to call on the Ch'iens as a gesture among liberals.

The leftist writers Wilma and I had seen at Kalgan in 1946 had been similarly stultified. At that time we met Chou Yang, the literary commissar; Ting Ling, the woman novelist; and the poet Ai Ch'ing.

In 1957 Chou Yang led the attack on Ting Ling as a rightist. She was forced to confess to individualism and was consigned for twelve years to chicken farming in the remote Northeast and then spent five years in prison. When rehabilitated in 1979 she said the root cause of this harassment had been the coming into power of "sectarianism" in literary circles. Ai Ch'ing was exiled to the far West for sixteen years. The commissar Chou Yang had the good fortune, as it turned out, to be attacked and disgraced himself in the late 1960s and so he could join his earlier victims in being rehabilitated in 1979, once again to pontificate on literature and art.

Others fared worse. Hsia Yen, the playwright, whom I saw in Chungking and Shanghai in the 1940s, was beaten by Red Guards, who broke both his legs. The distinguished novelist Lao She, who stayed with us in Cambridge in 1948 when he had one of the State Department exchange fellowships that Wilma administered, was beaten and his house trashed in Peking in 1966. Next day he was beaten again and killed. Chien Po-tsan, the older CCP historian I met at the Junior Sinologues congress at Leyden in 1955, was tortured and killed in 1969.

The extensive record of such savagery in the Cultural Revolution brings us to the rim of an abyss of incomprehension. Beating to death is not as simple as trigger pulling. One's muscles must take part. For Chinese youths to beat to death innocent people simply because they were educated poses a problem like that of the holocaust. When the Nazis lit their gas ovens for the Final Solution, where was the influence of Christianity? In the country best known for its esteem and pursuit of education, when Chinese levelers vented their fury upon the educated, where was the influence of Confucianism? There was some explaining to do. Understanding China did not seem to become easier as history unfolded.

33

EPILOGUE

THE YEAR 1979 ended thirty years' estrangement between the United States and China and also concluded fifty years of my effort to be a China specialist. Obviously, my efforts to inform my countrymen had mainly coincided with the thirty years' estrangement although they had been made possible by my first twenty years of contact with China. By 1979 history was turning a corner and so was I. Rites of passage had already begun to mark my progress into the wings.

In May 1967 my sixtieth birthday was celebrated by more than a hundred China academics who gathered secretly in the Signet Society on the opposite corner of our block. I was told Arthur and Mary Wright were taking us out to dinner but part way around the block we met James C. Thomson, Jr., also formally dressed. When we stopped at the Signet I found former students from all over, a real surprise! Jim Thomson was a superb toastmaster and there were many skits, poems, and other offerings. Al Feuerwerker, Rhoads Murphey, and Mary Wright had organized, edited, and actually got published at Berkeley a twelve-article Festschrift volume, *Approaches to Modern Chinese History*, a feat which was both amazing and deeply gratifying to me. The articles were of high quality and broad range, while the introduction, I thought, showed Mary's specially penetrating capacity to build up a subject (in this case, me).

This assemblage of talent was a product of World War II, a generation of specialists called forth by the need of the times. I could serve as their mentor and leader insofar as I sensed what they needed and what contributions they could make. It was a case where the leader would do well to march backward so he could see where the troops were going and stay in front of them.

INSIDE MY SIXTIETH BIRTHDAY— A PERSONAL CIRCULAR

. . . Reflecting on all this heart-warming event, I have the honoree's usual problem—how to square the inside view of one's shortfall with the tributes of friends from outside. The encomiums seem ahistorical. My "achievements" in the development of this field convince me more than ever that the times make the man. I am moved to reply, "Shucks, fellahs, it was easy! Just get in on the ground floor between the world's greatest revolution and the world's greatest university—it's a pianola!"

The point of this celebration has been to acknowledge the human element that makes institutions tick, the friendship of teachers and students being scholars together. Here the point is that the teacher-student relationship is a bit one-sided, which makes it more fun for the teacher, who is on the giving end, and sets up a sense of debt on the part of the student, which can sometimes be a burden. But all our debts are really to our society, and for all students who feel indebted to their teachers the rule is, "Don't feel you should try to pay it back. Instead, pass it on."

Without a common interest in the substance of Chinese history, we should never have faced its problems together, and so for lack of time and contact, we should never have been friends. Look at all those students who got away, or all the faculty colleagues one would like to know. If only they were China specialists!

A teacher's function in a big university is partly to set an example, but an example of effort more than of perfection. If the elder-born can read a Chinese text, it shows the way; but if he cannot read Russian, for example, this failing can be a source of ego support to the student who can. In this high-challenge, high-effort field, the student's ego is the principal motor to keep greased and fueled. One means available in the pioneer era has been to publish a student's contribution and establish his scholarly identity before his self-confidence is damaged in the exploding universe of scholarship.

Professors also need moral support, as the new talent emerges and whizzes past them, and as they realize that distinction merely precedes extinction, and so this is a thank-you letter in more ways than one. (May '67)

On the chance, I had prepared some doggerel on the Confucian "at-fifty-I-knew-the-decrees-of-Heaven" model. It concluded:

> Now at sixty this highly trained poobah
> Puts the League of Women Voters in a perfect stupah!
> Dispensing wisdom-on-the-East, during crises-in-Cathay,
> Seems just what is needed in the U.S.A.
> Since history only exists in the mind
> Historians always follow behind.
> They pick up the spoor of History,
> The droppings it leaves, as a mystery,
> Examining each with consummate care
> And then pronouncing what used to be there.
> The files, when examined, will demonstrate
> That this "Fairbank" so-called was a syndicate
> Who were busy writing memos and in other ways
> During Benjamin Schwartz's earlier phase.

After forty years of going uniquely about my business at Harvard University, it had occurred to me that the other high achievers who were my faculty colleagues were unique too. As we pursued our unique goals we found ourselves, each of us, dealing mainly with students, junior colleagues, and women helpers. This superior role in day-by-day activities helped us to function in our faculty peer group, though I still felt shy about joining the long table at the Faculty Club where deans often sat. The curious ambivalence to be found in an establishment largely composed of loners should be a separate study. In my case it was highlighted in 1970 when I received an honorary LL.D. at the Harvard commencement. President Pusey's citation read: "Our nation's capability in East Asian studies is indebted to the creative efforts of this percipient and persistent man."

I had enjoyed other honorary degrees, partly because I liked to dress up and be looked at. Though lacking the Lincolnesque grandeur of a John Kenneth Galbraith, I was able in my Oxford gown to add color to any commencement procession. I also recognized that by transporting myself to the site I provided part of each commencement program gratis. It was a fair exchange. To be singled out of my own faculty, however, was an event of an entirely different magnitude. In my motivational world it was the *summum bonum ne plus ultra.* Granted that any system of honors is set up to provide targets *pour encourager les autres,* it is very satisfying to be the one honored. Scotty Reston was one of my classmates at Harvard in 1970.

Another great satisfaction was the publication in 1975 of *The I.G. in Peking: Letters of Robert Hart, Chinese Maritime Customs, 1868–1907,* with an introduction by L. K. Little, who was of course Hart's successor, the last foreign Inspector General. These two volumes annotate 1,437 weekly or fortnightly reports on himself and the Customs that Hart wrote to his confidential agent in London, one of the great inside stories. My gifted co-editors were Elizabeth MacLeod Matheson, who before she died gave the book its style, and Katherine Frost Bruner, who tracked down every person, book, or event that Hart referred to. The result is not only a fascinating monument of scholarship like editions of Pepys or Boswell or the Adams papers. It is also a foundation for the Hart industry that will get under way as the Customs is further studied. Luckily this uncosted project was taken on by the Harvard University Press in a moment of euphoria during a change of management. The cost overruns came later. Dr. H. B. Morse, '74, would rejoice to see his alma mater serving scholarship so well.

Unlike dictators who lack terminal facilities, professors are programmed. In my case I escaped by a few months a new rule for teaching half time after age sixty-eight and so taught full time till age seventy, retiring in 1977. Final lectures of retiring professors are of two kinds. In the on-with-the-show, firm-upper-lip style, the aged pedagogue concludes his course as though nothing were happening to bring in those friends and colleagues who may be hearing him lecture (perhaps luckily) for the first as well as the last time. When the lecture is finished he simply marches off the platform into history. I thought this too simple. Rites of passage require costume, so I contrived to justify putting on my Oxford D. Phil. gown, a small tent of red flannel faced with bright blue. Oxford had invented it rather late to go with a new degree demanded by Americans and colonials. It was the sort of colorful gewgaw the Hudson's Bay Company might have run up to dazzle the Northwest Indians. Since its acquisition had marked my licensing to teach in 1936 and it had not been worn out in commencement processions and when receiving honorary degrees, I put it on as part of the show along with some one-liners like "Women's emancipation requires a male sartorial comeback" and "If you have to ride off into the sunset, you might as well look like a sunset."

At a Visiting Committee dinner in 1977 Teddy White unveiled a placard reading "John King Fairbank Center for East Asian Research." My colleagues had decided to name the center for me as a retirement gift. (It is now directed by my omnicompetent successor, Philip A. Kuhn.) By this renaming they were giving me immortality, if only we could keep the center financed, and I realized my public persona was beginning to supersede me, preparatory to remaining behind after I should disappear. This was a new project, quite fascinating. The theme of "me and my shadow" was simple compared with "me and my public persona." Having willy nilly constructed a public image, perhaps I could usefully add to it. The American Historical Association had had since 1968 a "John King Fairbank Prize" to be awarded every other year. Now here was a Fairbank Center. How far could this trend continue? Having come to see how much a writer is part of his writing, I was moving on from Chinese studies by Fairbank to Fairbank studies *tout simple,* as in this present volume. Retirement had its opportunities.

Actually, of course, I did not feel particularly retired. Having had the Boy Scout spirit since childhood, I had forged a protective regimen of diet, rest, and exercise designed to keep me, as the British like to say, fit. In college I ran cross-country and rowed a single in a gentlemanly way. In China I cultivated a postluncheon nap habit and in the United States kept it up, not always unostentatiously, by leaving luncheon committee meetings early. My study and office always had a couch for rest periods. I cultivated fast walking. For years I threw Frisbees with anyone willing to play.

The result was that at age seventy-two I was in good shape, and was already doing everything good for my health. I could not give up smoking, drinking, late hours, prolonged strain, being overweight, or hypertension and worry because I didn't do or have any of them. The result was that I was defenseless and had no fall-back position. I offer this as a sort of warning to the overvirtuous.

In addition, my heredity was auspicious. My father had died at sixty-three of leukemia. But my mother lived to be 105 with all her faculties, in fact keeping house till she was 100. She died quietly in her own bed in her own home on October 15, 1979, not of any particular ailment.

Psychologists, at least of some sorts, will be interested that five weeks later on Thanksgiving Day I had a massive coronary heart attack.

Finding that I had survived, I naturally distributed a circular about it, still trying to accumulate the record.

A CIRCULAR TO FRIENDS
FROM J. K. FAIRBANK

December 11, 1979

A nonfatal heart attack is, I am sure, much more interesting than the other kind. In addition to a closer involvement with one's physiology and what can be done about it, it also calls forth expressions of love and friendship which are really heart-warming. Since I do not reach Personal Letter Writing until Stage 17 in Rehabilitation, I send you this as a preliminary thank-you note (or in some cases an announcement).

Preliminary Arrangements. On Thanksgiving Day, hoping to salvage a little office time before we began giving thanks, I walked over to my office at 1737 Cambridge Street about 8:30 and was soon safely inside the locked doors of the empty building and of my suite on the third floor, near where the Alfred North Whiteheads used to have an apartment. I noticed an ache between my shoulder blades and phoned Wilma, who was, however, in the basement at 41 Winthrop Street salvaging some laundry. So then I phoned Laura Fairbank, R.N., in Arlington, Massachusetts, about five miles away, and she said, "Daddy boy, just lie down, take it easy, and we'll be there."

Since my memory fails at this point, I have pieced the following together from oral sources. While Laura dressed in one minute, her husband, Bill Haynes, phoned Wilma, and

Wilma phoned the Harvard Police, who are extremely adept and active in keeping the students out of trouble and the professors alive. On their way two hundred yards to 1737 they activated the equally able Rescue Squad at the Cambridge Fire Station which is only one hundred yards away. So by the time the family arrived at 1737 in about twelve minutes, the police and the squad were bringing me in a chair out to the ambulance.

Where to go? Laura said Mt. Auburn Hospital, where she has spent five years, the last two years as head nurse of the eighth floor (surgery). Mt. Auburn is at the bend of the Charles River opposite the Harvard playing fields, and has one of the best cardiac units east or west. So they got me to the clinic on time.

Sure enough, when we got there the entire staff were out on the steps smiling and clapping under a banner that read "Huan-ying Mei-kuo p'eng-yu Fei Cheng-ch'ing" (Welcome to our American friend, John King Fairbank)—although it is possible that I confuse this occasion with a visit to the May 7th School of the Western District of Peking in 1972.

As I was slid out of the ambulance still holding Laura's hand, I told her I was going to pass out, which I did. The Squad had had me on oxygen all the way, but my heart muscle now went into an every-which-way sort of dither known as fibrillation. It happened that the top specialists of the Cardiac Clinic were at Mt. Auburn that morning also salvaging a bit of time, no doubt, and within seconds they had zapped the fibrillation with a milli-second shock of 100 volts, followed by three more, that altogether had a very edifying effect. They simultaneously put an oxygen tube into my trachea for my lungs, attached monitors, injected various chemicals in veins that opened capillaries, prevented blood clotting, reestablished rhythm, etc., and generally caught up with the situation. As my physician, Dr. Voukydis, has remarked, I did indeed arrive with a bang.

When I came to a few hours later in Intensive Care, I was checked for brain damage by being asked, "Where do you think you are?" Laura, who was present, was a bit mortified to hear my reply, "I'm in a second-rate nursing home in New

Haven." ("How did *you* get here?" I said to her.) However, this was taken to represent confusion and poor judgment permissible for retired professors, rather than cerebral disaster.

My next slice of remembered life was in a four-bed monitoring ward focused on a big black TV screen, across which marched in vivid green the four lines of our respective 100,000-times-a-day heartbeats. Each recorded little bang was of course a minor reverberation of the BIG BANG of some billions of years ago. What a variety! Depending on the hookup, no doubt, there were marching rows of halberds and pikes, miles of barbed wire and bicycle chains, and some Mozartian scores that showed variations on a theme more admired in music than in cardiology.

Our survival training consisted first in testing whether we could open the integuments of plastic that now cover and preserve the biscuits, jellies, drinks, and other condiments offered for our gastronomic preservation. I soon found that if I could liberate a fork I could generally liberate the rest.

The other training was equally realistic, to see if we could reenter the American climate of TV, that fibrillating monster that now surrounds us. Without looking I heard all the confused mayhem of the sack of Tehran—the cries of Muezzins, the shouts of the Ayatollahs, the curses of the Imams, the ringing of gongs, the moans of Mullahs, and the screams of Kurds in ecstatic agony—in short, all the cacophony of an ancient civilization self-destructing. It gradually became clear, however, that I was listening not to the natural violence of a social revolution but to the better organized and more lucrative progress of a welterweight championship boxing match staged in freedom's land.

Do not ask whence the coronaries come. They come from the tube's long-term inducement of inexpressible impulses toward pain, hunger, fear, and rage. (I remember how my heart pounded double when I watched Roger Bannister break the four-minute mile.) So I got transferred to a less-exciting room.

Wilma, with the help of my able secretary, Joan Hill, meanwhile was acting as a mobile command post and information center, cutting the future down to size. After three weeks of mellifluous attention from nurses and therapists whose comeliness is exceeded only by their competence, I am about to remove to our rebuilt house at 41 Winthrop Street. The skill of the Mt. Auburn Hospital doctors has not only kept me from moving on to the adjacent and beautiful but rather less active Mt. Auburn Cemetery (Cambridge has everything you need); their advice has also greatly simplified the future and made it more attractive. I am now committed to no articles, no reviews, no lectures, no letters, no consultantships, no conferences, no meetings, and only six books to write or edit. What could be more pleasant?

With Christmas and New Year greetings from us both,

jfk

The preceding account suggests that I was lucky in my time and place. I found the opportunity to pioneer in a field that grew in significance as I worked in it. I was enabled to work at Harvard, the most strategic spot for the purpose.

The historical context of the preceding success story, however, puts it in a rather different light. The half century 1929–79 has seen its full share of warfare around the world and also of the explosive growth in people, consumption, and armament that makes for further conflict. Technological progress has led to a proliferation of worldwide problems too sadly familiar to us to need listing here. Our intellectual resources are stretched thin trying to cope with difficulties that grow more ominous as we work upon them. China studies have been a small part of our general effort at world crisis management. One can hardly claim much success for them. The Korean War against China in Korea (1950–53) and the Vietnam War (1965–73) confer little glory on our mental processes, either official or popular.

Throughout this somber world scene the race between rational management and ideological fervor is not necessarily being won by the forces of reason. Witness the egregiously impractical oppositions to birth control and to handgun control, oppositions which invoke faith but make for social disaster. Thus the unreasoning American tradition of growth at home and expansion abroad still leads us to figure mightily in the life of East Asia, an area rich in the potentialities for Western crusading overseas.

We can rejoice then in the skill with which we have, for the moment at least, liquidated our participation in the Chinese civil war of the 1940s. To accept the shibboleth of One China, which has such political value in the Chinese people's image of themselves, has been our first necessity. To deal with the People's Republic officially and with Taiwan province only unofficially, as we arranged to do in 1979, has been statesmanship, not least because we had sense enough to follow the Japanese example in this arrangement. Japan preceded us in recognizing Peking and reducing its Taipei embassy to an unofficial agency staffed by former diplomats. If we do not maintain this posture we shall regret it.

For the first time in thirty years we have adjusted our diplomacy to the Chinese realities. Our commercial and cultural relations with Taiwan province continue under our unilateral Taiwan Relations Act passed by the Congress April 10, 1979. Our relations with the People's Republic meanwhile develop on the basis of our recognition as of January 1, 1979, that the One China so necessary to Chinese political thinking heads up in Peking. We no longer recognize the existence of our 1954–79 ally the Republic of China, although we continue to sell defensive arms to it. It is a delicate official/unofficial balance, difficult for legalistic American minds to understand. To alter this hard-won balance could bring us a disaster we don't need.

In the future we shall face great perils in the Chinese area because we are a party to its modernization. We should not assume that we, as early modernizers, can be China's model. In some lines our example is what *not* to do, and in some lines our circumstances are too different for us to be a relevant example. This is true especially of the problems of modernization in the countryside among China's peasant masses, a bloc of at least 800 million persons whose rural way of life may change materially more quickly than their ways of thought and social conduct. This uniquely large and perhaps unassimilable lump of humanity, still relatively inaccessible to outside influence, may hold unhappy surprises for us. China's peasant tradition as thus far understood seems to contain rather little concern for civil liberties under law but a good deal of capacity for righteous indignation, secret organization, and destructive fanaticism. If common problems bring us and China's elite and urban strata closer together in joint efforts, we may find ourselves again involved in China's domestic politics without much understanding of what we are dealing with. We may have still another chance to tie ourselves to a repressive regime as its people turn against it.

In the face of these ominous prospects, I retain some faith in the efficacy of historical perspective. Help is on the way in the form of written history, in fact a super-symposium in sixteen volumes. In 1966 I accepted the invitation to be one of the two general editors of a *Cambridge History of China*. As librarians know, the Cambridge histories published by the Cambridge University Press are multivolumed collections of specialists' articles designed to give nonspecialists a readable historical account of a large subject. I joined Denis Twitchett (then at Cambridge, now at Princeton) in planning this addition to the dozen or so Cambridge histories already in being or under way. We first planned six volumes but soon realized we had a bear by the tail. China's history is a protean subject undergoing a delayed response to China's revolution. The series on China is now projected at sixteen volumes—in fact, probably eighteen.

My experience of the *Cambridge History of China* thus far leads me to think such monuments of scholarship may have an inner reality different from their public image. For example, there is an almost uncontrollable tendency to grow in size. An article commissioned to be 75 manuscript pages long may come in at two hundred pages but so full of new evidence and insights that it is impossible to reduce without sabotaging the much-desired growth of the subject. This is because an able researcher, having summarized the current knowledge of it, finds more worth saying from fresh evidence and new studies. Happily, the Cambridge University Press is often able to accommodate this growth. Yet to do so it must raise the volume's price. And so, the more massive our history becomes, the fewer its readers may be. One has to believe in the trickle-down theory. This I do. Major historical subjects require treatment in many forms. The references and bibliographies in the *Cambridge History of China* can assist further work. The specialists' articles can be read simply for the story they tell.

More than a hundred scholars from a dozen countries are contributing to this Cambridge history. Volumes 10 and 11 on the nineteenth century appeared in 1978 and 1980. My co-editors of volume 11 (Kwang-Ching Liu), volume 13 (Albert Feuerwerker), and volumes 14 and 15 (Roderick MacFarquhar) are already above my level in mastery of their areas. Volume 13 has the particular opportunity to summarize the life works of a whole generation of modern-minded Chinese patriots who acquired an education in the Atlantic community and tried to make it useful in the modernization of the western Pacific. Meanwhile, I am in the happy position of the teacher who has started something he can't finish but knows that many others will carry it forward.

After fifty years of trying to get things done in Chinese studies, what is my message for those citizens so intelligent as to ask?

The bad news is that human social behavior persists in established ways with greater inertia than we Americans like to think. Our virgin continent has given us expectations of perpetual economic growth and legislated reform that now face limits. Yet neither we nor the Chinese are going to change our inveterate ways, values, and national styles easily, least of all to accommodate the other. However, similarities may grow between us because of harsh necessity. We share global problems. Unfortunately, as we see how the growth of technology clashes with that of civil liberties, America and China may meet crises of misunderstanding.

Already China's late-blooming nationalism has brought forth a nation of 1,000 million people. If China's modernization follows Japan's example, by and large, we may find ourselves living by an exchange of American food for Chinese manufactures. The news will be worse if China's nationalism leads her into the kind of competitive chauvinism that modern nations have so generally enjoyed since the Sung period, i.e., when China was the top of civilization and Europe was emerging from its Dark Ages. Our present organization of the world economy and polity by armed sovereign nations augurs pretty obvious disaster. Cool logic suggests that homo sapiens may survive better than our current civilization.

The good news is that China's billion people are the world's largest talent pool. Their high achievers already throng our universities. They are becoming available to staff the new world structures. If the world economy and polity were ill-advisedly leveled by nuclear blasts, the Chinese with their low material living standard would be prime candidates to lead in rebuilding it.

If we face down the gloom and doom that cool logic suggests, China can offer many examples of social management. For instance, maintenance of social order was an ancient Chinese specialty. The Chinese citizen, being unprotected by law, could be the more edified by example. On the busy thoroughfare where one man had killed another, the assailant's head could be mounted on a pike, in the position where we might place an advertisement, widely visible. For a more odious crime the perpetrator could be caged and allowed to starve more ostentatiously, where you might thoughtfully pass him for many days on your way to and from work. The old Chinese empire had its means of law and order.

Yet the final message, I think, is positive. The Chinese revolution is much more our friend than our enemy. It is peculiarly self-absorbed and nonaggressive abroad. As we grow closer, we can help each other.

The main necessity is for us to correct the hardware/brainware imbalance in our survival effort. China's great commanders, who were usually civilians, held to the ideal of getting their way in warfare with the least possible fighting. Curiously, the nuclear age has forced this concept upon us too. Yet we still prepare our soldiers to use their weapons and do not prepare them primarily to be able to avoid using their weapons. Our mental effort is a speck of dust compared with our arms building. Until as a people we study our problems more wholeheartedly, taking religious faith as a motive but not a principal means of salvation, our survival will remain more doubtful. When we find, as we may a few years from now, that more people read English in China than in America, Chinese studies, heretofore in the wings, may come to center stage in American education. It will not be too soon or at all illogical. Thus my message after half a century is to keep on trying, but try harder, to study China. (What else did you expect it to be?)

Let me put it this way: China and America are now major centers of the coming world struggle, which will be less between nations than within them, between mechanists and humanists. Mechanists believe in both technological gadgetry and in ideology, the potent combination of material might with intellectual righteousness. The mechanists' only problem is that this combination of might and right is precisely what the national enemies always believe in, too, but in opposing terms. This is a prescription for unremitting conflict and mutual annihilation.

Humanists, on the other hand, are good guys, intellectually more flexible, who have more faith in the individual human personality than in any set of great principles. For example, humanists favor the welfare of women, who are already persons, over the welfare of fetuses, who don't yet function as persons. Humanists put their faith in human rationality rather than in any particular teaching or form of words. On this humanist front the Chinese intellectuals (necessarily an elite) stand with the readers of this book, who are of course humanists even if (or especially if) they are also into things like computers. In the late 1960s and early 1970s, during the Vietnam War and the Cultural Revolution, humanists in both America and China took a beating. Now we have more chance to work together. Let us seize the opportunity.

LIST OF ABBREVIATIONS

Note: The academic bureaucracy is almost as acronym-prone as the government. But abbreviations help. For most of a lifetime I have said simply "ACLS." If I had had to say "American Council of Learned Societies" each time I might have avoided mentioning it. I have tried to use abbreviations only where the context makes them pretty plain.

AAS	Association for Asian Studies
ACLS	American Council of Learned Societies
ADA	Americans for Democratic Action
AEAR	American-East Asian Relations
AHA	American Historical Association
ATC	Air Transport Command
AVG	American Volunteer Group
BAAG	British Army Aid Group
CBI	China-Burma-India Theater
CC	Ch'en brothers clique, Organization clique of the KMT
CCH	Ch'eng-chih hui, Association for the Realization of Life's Ideals
CCAS	Committee of Concerned Asian Scholars
CCP	Chinese Communist Party
CP	Communist Party
CI	Communist International

CIA	Central Intelligence Agency
CKS	Chiang Kai-shek
CNC	Chinese national currency
CNAC	Chinese National Aviation Corporation (Pan Am affiliate)
COI	Coordinator of Information
CPUSA	American Communist Party
CU	Cultural Relations Division, Department of State
FDR	Franklin Delano Roosevelt
FE	Far Eastern division, Department of State
FO	Foreign Office
Gimo	Generalissimo Chiang Kai-shek
GOP	Republican Party
HUP	Harvard University Press
IDC	Interdepartmental Committee for the Acquisition of Foreign Publications
IMH	Institute of Modern History
IPR	Institute of Pacific Relations
JCCC	Joint Committee on Contemporary China
JCRR	Joint Commission on Rural Reconstruction
KGB	Soviet state police
KMT	Kuomintang (National People's Party)
LBJ	Lyndon Baines Johnson
LC	Library of Congress
Lienta	National Southwest Associated University
LSE	London School of Economics
MIT	Massachusetts Institute of Technology
OIR	Office of Intelligence Research, Department of State
ONAF	Overseas News and Features, OWI
ONI	Office of Naval Intelligence
OSS	Office of Strategic Services
OWI	Office of War Information
PA/H	Political Advisor/Hornbeck
Peita	Peking University
POW	Prisoner of war
PPC	People's Political Council
PRC	People's Republic of China
PRO	Public Record Office, London
PUMC	Peking Union Medical College
PW	Psychological warfare

R and A   Research and Analysis branch (COI, OSS)
RC   Cultural Relations Division, Department of State
ROC   Republic of China
SACO   Sino-American Cooperative Organization
SI   Secret intelligence
SO   Secret operations
SSRC   Social Science Research Council
SX   San Francisco
UCR   United China Relief
UNRRA   United Nations Relief and Rehabilitation Administration
USIS   United States Information Service
VC   Viet Cong

INDEX

Abortive Revolution, The (Eastman), 248n
Above Suspicion (MacInnes), 141
Academia Sinica, 59, 74, 194; wartime visit to, 223; outside Kweilin, 259; on Taiwan, 382; Institute of Modern History at, 383; expansion of, 387
Acheson, Dean, 302–303, 304, 338, 365, 402
Acton, Harold, 120
Adler, Nord Deutscher Lloyd, 31, 36
Adler, Sol, 209
Adventures in Retrieval (W.C. Fairbank), 107
Aglen, Sir Francis, 63
Agriculture, 421
Ai Ch'ing, 311, 444–445
Aid to China (COI study), 176
Air Transport Command (ATC), 299
Allahabad, 190
Alsop, Joseph, 273
Alumni College, Harvard, 435
Amerasia, 320
American Academy of Arts and Sciences, 434
American Committee for Non-participation in Japanese Aggression, 163–165; backers of Nationalists in, 334
American Council of Learned Societies (ACLS), 98, 100, 166, 167, 370; wartime aid by, 231
American Defense: Harvard Group, 165
American-East Asian Relations (AEAR), field of, 402–403
American Historical Association (AHA), 98, 143, 430; presidency of, 368; during the Vietnam War, 401;

presidential address to, 400, 401; Fairbank Prize, 450
American Publications Service, 210–219
American researchers on China (CCP list); Fei Cheng-ch'ing in, 388
American Volunteer Group (AVG), 176
Americans for Democratic Action (ADA), 317; study group on Asia, 339
America's Cultural Experiment in China 1942–1949 (W.C.Fairbank), 295n
America's share in Japan's war guilt, 164
Annotated Bibliography of Selected Chinese Reference Works (Teng and Biggerstaff), 147
Antiforeignism: fostered by CKS, 253, 282; roots of wartime, 281
Anyang: tomb excavations in, 59, 134; removal of artifacts, 224; reports on finds from, 382
Approaches to Modern Chinese History, Festschrift volume, 446
Area study; *see* Regional Studies
Arima, Tatsuo, 149
Arnold, Fortas and Porter, 335
"Assignment for the '70s," 401
Association for Asian Studies (AAS), 399, 430; Committee on Chinese Thought, 365; presidency of, 366; Advisory Committee on Research and Development, 366–367; and contemporary Chinese studies, 367–368; and Gould House conference, 368–369
Atkinson, Brooks, 270, 273, 279

[463]

Atom bomb: Soviet, 332; threat of, factor in McCarthyism, 332
Atlantic, articles in, 315, 342
Augustana Synod Mission, 60
Augustine Heard & Co. (Lockwood), 121n
Austen, Jane, translation of, 274
Authoritarianism, Chinese, 258
Autobiography at Forty (Ssu-shih tzu-shu) (Hu Shih), 47
Ayers, William, 439

Backhouse, Sir Edmund, 96
Bailey, Cyril, 140
Bailyn, Bernard, 393
Balazs, Étienne, 372n
Baldwin, Hanson, 253
Balliol College, Oxford, 19, 20; friends at, 24-25
Bangkok, 378
Banno, Masataka, 149
Barnard, T. L., 289
Barnett, A. Doak, 397, 442
Barnum, Rollie, 12
Barrett, Edward, 289, 292, 297
Baxter, Glen, 107
Baxter, James Phinney III, 18, 101, 144, 154, 400; in R & A Branch of COI, 174, 175, 208
Beale, T. C., 139
Begeotis, 12
Belém, 187-188
Bell, David Allen Erskine, 119
Benedict, Ruth, 290
Bentley, Elizabeth, 341, 346
Bereznii, L. A., 426
Bergère, M. C., 318
Berkeley, Edmund Callis, 10, 14
Berlin, blockade and airlift, 331
Bertram, James, 30
Bibliography, work on, 149-50, 376, 776; suggested reading in *U.S. and China,* 327; *Modern China: A bibliographical guide,* 328; *China's Response to the West,* 329; *Documentary History of Chinese Communism,* 329; attempts at Russian, 430
Biggar, James, 158
Biggerstaff, Knight, 135, 147, 294, 388-389
Bingham, Hiram, 349
Bingham, Woodbridge, 135
Birth of China, The (Creel), 134
Bishop, Carl Whiting, 101
Bisson, Thomas Arthur, 253
Black, Mrs. 357
Blofeld, J., 238
Blum, John Morton, 147
Boatner, Haydon, 95, 179
Bodde, Derk, 135, 167, 370; in OWI, 290
Bodde, Galia Speshneff, 135
Bodily Changes in Pain, Hunger, Fear and Rage (Cannon), 45

Borg, Dorothy, 167, 403
Borton, Hugh, 133
Boston Post, 347
Boxer indemnity, used for Tsing Hua, 86, 88
Boyce, Etta Estey, 7, 98
Boyce, Jesse, 7
Boynton, Grace, 274, 276
Brandt, Conrad, 117, 329, 344
Bridgman, Percy, 144
Briggs, Virginia, 356
Brinton, Crane, 143
British Army Aid Group (BAAG), 259
Brooks, Van Wyck, 159
Bruner, Katherine Frost, 449
Buck, Paul, 144, 155, 337; letter to, 301-302; on JKF loyalty case, 341
Buck, Pearl: article on wartime China by, 253
Budenz, Louis, 336, 341
Bukharin, Nikolai, 77
Bullock, T. L., 22, 23, 30
Bundy, William, 391, 397, 398
Burke, Gordon, 118
Burlington House, London, Chinese art at, 138
Burma: threatened by Japan, 179, 184; travel in, 378; lack of Chinese study in, 578
Burma Road, 176, 191-192, 305
Butterworth, W., 347
Byrnes, James F., 296

Cadre schools, 417, 420
Cairo, 189
Caldwell, John C., 304
California College in China, 39
Cambridge History of China, 434, 456; subjects and authors, 456-457
Canard, Père, 81
Cannon, Cornelia James, 25, 118; in China, 125
Cannon, Helen, 125
Cannon, Ida M., 48, 160, 361
Cannon, Walter B., 25, 45, 160; in China, 125; and Spain, 168
Cannon, Wilma Denio, 26, 31; trip to China, 49; *see also* Fairbank, Wilma Cannon
Canton, 444; trip to, 122; OWI office in, 300; 1972 impressions, 413-414
Capitalism, and the KMT, 318
Carnegie Foundation, 356
Carroll, Wallace, 290, 291, 292
Carter, Edward C., 322-323, 336, 346
Carter, Mrs. E. C., 285, 346
Carter, Jimmy, dinner for Deng Xiaoping, 442-443
Carter, Rosalynn, 442, 443
Caute, David, 322
CC organization clique, 286; leadership of, 249; role of, 251; and Lienta faculty, 259; tactics of, 281

Central Political Institute, 92, 248, 249
Chamberlain, Neville, 168
Chambers, Whittaker, 331–332
Chung Chih-tung, 235
Chang Ch'un, 233
Chang Hsi-jo (Shiro), 129n; in Kunming, 193–194, 198, 231; in 1972, 417
Chang Po-ling, 87, 206, 239
Chao Chia-pi, 310
Cheang, Ken, 25; in Shanghai, 64–65
Cheeloo University, 232
Ch'en Ch'eng, 380
Ch'en Ch'i-mei, 249
Ch'en Chia-k'ang, 270, 278, 279, 285
Ch'en I, General, 379
Ch'en Kuo-fu, 248, 249, 263
Ch'en Li-fu, 198, 248; career of, 249; conversations with, 249–250; as Minister of Education, 250–251, 263; retirement of, 384
Ch'en, Pearl, 245, 253
Ch'en Sung-chiao, 210; "Day in the life of," 211–213
Ch'en Tai-sun (Deison Ch'en), 129n; at Kunming, 192, 231; in Peking, 309; at Peita, 417
Ch'en Tu-hsiu, 75, 275
Cheng, Anna Mae, 310
Cheng, Chen-to, 310
Cheng Te-k'un, 119, 232
Ch'eng-chih hui (CCH), 87
Ch'eng Fang-wu, 311
Ch'eng-te, 1934 trip to, 81–84
Chengchow, 57
Chengtu: Christian colleges at, 232; trip to Chungking from, 241–242; OWI branch at, 300
Chennault, Col. Claire, 176, 202, 207
Ch'i River, 227
Chia-hsiang, shrine at, 107
Chialing River, 202, 269–270
Chiang Ch'ing, 227, 436
Chiang Ching-kuo, 441
Chiang Kai-shek (CKS), 18, 76, 109, 175, 183, 224–225, 249, 258, 263, 294, 319; opium imported by, 82; and T. F. Tsiang, 89; policy toward Japan, 126, 128; and Amer. Comm. for Non-Participation, 164, 334; in Chungking, 203, 207; and Sun Yat-sen's family, 207; and Tai Li, 216; as leader, 244; and New Life Movement, 248; effect of *China's Destiny*, 252–253; gradual loss of mandate, 264, 277, 281, 288, 316, 320; anti-foreignism of, 281, 283; after Japanese surrender, 298, 299; writing by, 320; in Taiwan, 381, 387
Chiang, Mme, 206, 207; in Washington, 245, 253–254; interview with, 245–247
Chiang, M. H., 250

Chiang Monlin, 129n, 230–231; and JCRR, 380
Ch'iao Kuan-hua, 102, 307, 410, 438; host in Peking, 416, 418
Ch'iao Mu (Ch'iao Kuan-hua), 271, 272, 276, 277, 306, 307; in Peking 418
Chicago, University of, Chinese studies at, 133–134, 140
Chien Po-tsan, 372, 445
Ch'ien C. C. (Ch'ien Ch'ang-chao), 221, 306
Ch'ien, Fred (Ch'ien Fu), 440
Ch'ien Tuan-sheng (T.S. Chien), 129n, 239, 344; in Kunming, 194, 198, 231; in Cambridge, 321–322; in 1972 Peking, 418; rehabilitated, 444
Chin Chung-hua, 308
Chin dynasty, 52
Chin-ts'un tombs, 58–59
Chin, Y. L. (Chin Yueh-lin), 104, 105, 108, 384; in Kunming, 192; in Peking, 418
Ch'in Shih Huang-ti, 61
China: Webster on, 17–18; study of at Oxford, 19; H.B.Morse on, 21–22; first trip to, 35; maritime vs. interior, 114, 124; lack of U.S. knowledge of, 136; documents of, 146–147; as issue vs. Japan, 162–165, 166; Washington personnel working on, 173–180; return to in wartime, 187; failure of U.S. political science to grasp, 237; analysis of political situation in, 255–258; summary of 1943 impressions, 280–281; 1945 trip to, 299; reoccupied, 300; basis for "loss of," 334–335; lack of material for study of, 373–375; neglect of Russian experience in, 431; role of loyalty in, 436–437; dangers of modernization for, 455; prospect of relations with, 457–459
China Advisory Panel, State Dept., 397
China Awake (Payne), 328
China Childhood, A, (Pruitt), 48
China Daily, 309
China Defense Supplies, 175
China Forum, 79
China Foundation, 203
China Hands, The (Kahn), 350
China in Revolution: The First Phase (Wright), 364
China Inland Mission, 30, 110, 112–113
China: The Land and the People (Winfield), 328
China League for Civil Rights, 69–70; and Yang Chien, 71–72
"China Lobby," 334
China Old and New, filmstrips, 155
China: The People's Middle Kingdom and the USA (JKF), 358–359
China Perceived (JKF), 317

China policy: letters to Hiss on, 195–197, 237–239, 281–284; memos on, 198–199, 233, 250; consequences of identifying with Nationalists, 244–245, 256–257; 1946 articles on, 316–317; confusions of, 318–319; in reviews of books, 319; summarized for FPA *Bulletin*, 320–321; history of in *U.S. and China*, 327; and Taiwan, 396; role of sinologues in, 433

China Press, 78

China section, OWI, USIS, 290; ONAF, 291–292; post-war work of, 294; circular letters on work of, 292–293, 303; Shanghai headquarters, 301, 309–310; personnel in, 302; purpose of, in China, 303–304; dinner by CCP for, 306–307; translations, 310; departure from, 312

China Today—Political (Hornbeck), 177

China: Tradition and Transformation (Fairbank and Reischauer), 374

China Weekly Review, 79

China's Destiny (Chiang Kai-shek), 441; reception of, 252; English version, 320

China's Destiny and Chinese Economic Theory (Chiang Kai-shek), 320

China's Red Army Marches (Smedley), 77

China's Response to the West 1839–1923, 328–329

"China's world order" (JKF), 408

Chinese, The: Their History and Culture (Latourette), 134

Chinese Communist Party (CCP), 253; and Agnes Smedley, 67; and KMT, 74–76, 79–80; Long March, 93; supposed weakness of, 233; at Yenan, 265; representatives in Chungking, 266–272; headquarters in Chungking, 268–270; group around Chou En-lai, 271; attitudes of Americans in Chungking toward, 271–272; contacts with, 276–277; tactics of, 280; chances of success, 283; after Japanese surrender, 298; U.S. efforts to mediate, 298, 306; entertainment by in Chungking, 306; strength of organization, 308; at Kalgan, 310–312; JKF writings on, 341–342; Taiwan archives on, 383; reversal of verdicts by, 444

Chinese-English Dictionary: (Giles), 95; (Mathews), 95

Chinese language: beginning study of, 22–23; characters, 23; continued in Peking, 39–40, 42–43; unknown in U.S., 136

"Chinese outlook, The" (H. G. Wells) 275

Chinese Renaissance, The (Hu Shih), 46

Chinese Social and Political Science Review, 101, 138n

Chinese 10 on the Far East, 166

Chinese University of Hong Kong, 413

Chinese Ways in Warfare, 360

Chinese World Order, The, 360, 408

Ching, F. T. (Ch'en Fu-t'ien): in Kunming, 192, 198; at Tsing Hua in Peking, 309

Ch'ing Documents, 95, 146–147

Ch'ing government: language of, 95; documents of, 146–147

Chiu-lung-p'o ("Nine Dragon Slope"), 201

Ch'iu, Alfred K'ai-ming, 98

Ch'iu-ching Middle School, 202

Choate, Hall and Stewart, 341

Chou En-lai, 417, 418, 422, 434, 443, 444; in Chungking, 266–267, 271; headquarters of, 268–270; at USIS dinner, 306; use of personnel by, 307; Kissinger's visit to, 408; and Nixon's visit to Peking, 409; on renewed American contact, 410; host at dinner, 422–423

Chou, Mrs. (Teng Ying-ch'ao), 306

Chou I-liang, 372

Chou P'ei-yuan, 129, 259, 416

Chou Yang, 311, 444–445

Christian China, 87

Christian colleges, in wartime, 232

Christian Occupation of China, 87

Christianity, in China, 62, 87, 113

Chrysanthemum and the Sword, The (Benedict), 290

Chu Teh, General, 265; Smedley's book on, 344

Chung-kuo t'ung, 433

Chungking: air defense of, 180; COI representative in, 185, 201; trip from Miami to, 187–191, 201; air fields of, 201–202; arrival in, 202; information services in, 203–204; leadership in, 207; seen from an invalid's bed, 242–243; leftist community in, 366; Russian embassy in, 277–278; departure from, 285; 1945 arrival in, 299; OWI branch at, 300, 305

Churchill, Winston, 331

Civil war, prospects for, 232–233

Clabaugh, Mary, 158; *see also* Wright, Mary Clabaugh

Clark, Sir George N., 139

Classic of Filial Piety (Hsiao Ching), 134

Clubb, Edmund, 206, 208, 350

Coble, Parks, 318

Cohen, Jerome, 412, 422–423

Cohen, Joan, 412, 422–423

Cold War, 316, 322, 348; results of, 395–396

Colegrove, K., 367

College of Chinese Studies, Peking, 38–39, 94
Collins, Ralph, 153
Committee on Asiatic Studies in American Education, 167
Committee of Concerned Asian Scholars (CCAS), 350, 399
Committee of Eight, Harvard, 151–152
Committee on Scholarly Communication with PRC, 371
Communications and Imperial Control in China (Wu), 147
Communism, as basis for China policy, 316–317
Communism in China and the Rise of Mao (Schwartz), 329
Communist Party USA, 317, 331, 333, 348
Complete account of the management of barbarian affairs (Ch'ou-pan i-wu shih-mo), 86
Conant, James B., 151–152
Confucian China and Its Modern Fate (Levenson), 364
Confucianism, 436; and "reversal of verdicts," 444
Connors, Bradley, 302–303, 347
Contemporary Politics in the Far East (Hornbeck), 177
Coolidge, A. C., 153
Coolidge Hall, Harvard, 356
Coordinator of Information (COI), 173; reorganization, 186–187
Corcoran, Tom, 175
Coronary heart attack, 451–454
Costin, W. C., 139
Cotton mills, 65
Council on East Asian Studies, 394
Council on Foreign Relations, 322–323
Craig, Albert M., 374
Creel, Herrlee Glessner, 134
Crimson (Harvard), 168
Critique of American bourgeois historiography on China . . . (Bereznii), 426
Cross, Samuel, 165
Cultural Relations Division, U.S. State Dept., 182, 203; memo on policy of, 233
Cultural Revolution (Great Proletarian Cultural Revolution): and the class struggle, 319; effects of, 395, 398; changes in Peking during, 415; reversal of verdicts from, 444
"Cultural Treasures unearthed during the Cultural Revolution," 58
Cultural Work Committee, 261
Currie, Dorothy Bacon, 175
Currie, Lauchlin, 175–176, 179, 183, 196, 203, 213, 233, 281; reports to, 195; post-war plans, 220; on aid to academics, 231; letters to, 259–260; in economic warfare, 289

Customs College, teaching at, 100, 101
Customs Service, Chinese (Chinese Maritime Customs Service), 21, 47, 63, 123; Morse's service in, 22; Groff-Smith of, 47; lectures on history of, 103; in wartime, 208; *see also* Little, L. K.
Czechoslovakia, 162, 331

Daily Express (London), 82
Danger from the East (Lauterbach), 328
Daughter of Earth (Smedley), 66
Daughter of Han, A (Pruitt), 48n, 54–55
Davies, John Paton, 179, 260, 408; and SACO, 220; in Chungking, 208, 277; reports on Yenan, 293; later career, 349–350
Davis, Elmer, 289, 292, 345, 347
Dean, Arthur, 333
De Bary, W. Theodore, 370
Dehn, Sheila, 158
Deliusin, Lev, 429–430
Democracy, and individualism, 257
Democratic Party, 333
Demos, Raphael, 144
Deng Xiaoping, 438, 444; in Washington, 442–443
Desert Road to Turkestan, The (Lattimore), 44
Dewey, John, 47, 89, 262, 380, 384
Dewey, Thomas, 331, 334
Different Kind of War, A (Miles), 216, 220
Dixie mission, 260, 293
Documentary History of Chinese Communism, A, 329
Dodd, E. Merrick, 152n
Donham, Wallace B., 96
Donovan, Col. William J., 173, 175, 179–180, 181, 215; on COI representative, 186, 203; and Miles, 218, 219, 285
Dorn, Gen. Frank, 231
Dow, Sterling, 144
Drew, E. B., 21
Dudman, Richard, 422
Dulles, Allen, 70
Dulles, John Foster, 349, 402, 423
Durdin, Tillman, 407
Dye, Daniel, 248

East Asia: Tradition and Transformation (Fairbank, Reischauer, Craig), 374, 434
East Asian History survey course, 167
East Asian Language and Area Center, 394
East Asian and Pacific panel, 397
East Asian Research Center, Harvard, 490; inception, 355; grants, 356; settings for, 356–357; 1960

East Asian Research Center *(cont.)*
  reorganization, 357; personnel, 357;
  publication program, 357; editing,
  358; subjects for research, 360;
  conferences and symposia volumes,
  360
Eastman, Lloyd, 248n, 318
Eckstein, Alex, 356, 397n, 398
Education, Ministry of: lack of control,
  247–248; Ch'en Li-fu as Minister,
  250–251; politicizing of, 251–252; lack
  of plans for, 282
Efimov, G. V., 425
Eisenhower, Dwight D., 348, 380,
  384
Eisenhower, Milton, 338
Elisseeff, Serge, 97, 100, 145, 148, 153,
  337
Elliott, Osborn, 393
Elliott, William Yandell, 20, 324n
Emerson, Rupert, 324n
Eminent Chinese of the Ch'ing Period
  (Hummel), 99
Emperor, Japanese: status of, 294; and
  terms of surrender, 297
Empress Dowager (Tz'u-hsi), 96, 155
Encounter, 408
Engels, Friedrich, 319
England; *see* Great Britain
English-Speaking Union, 28
Ennin's Travels in T'ang China
  (Reischauer), 145
Epstein, I., 344
*Excerpts from writings and speeches
  1946–1950* (JKF), 341
Exeter Academy: *see* Phillips Exeter
  Academy
Extraterritoriality, 67, 84

Fahs, Charles Burton, 133, 166; in Far
  Eastern Institute, 167; in Washington,
  180, 185, 204; in OIR, 396
Fairbank, Arthur Boyce, 5, 107, 141–142,
  451
Fairbank, Holly Cannon, 361–362,
  377–378, 386
Fairbank, John Barnard, 4–5
Fairbank, Laura King, 340, 361–362,
  377–378, 386, 451
Fairbank, Lorena King, 608, 295; in
  England, 11, 30; move to Washington,
  142; liberal orientation of, 285; hostess
  to E. Lattimore, 335; at McCarran
  committee hearing, 345; death of, 451
Fairbank, Wilma Cannon, 58, 157, 160,
  208, 288, 361, 376, 434, 453; in
  Peking, 49, 51–52; in Shanghai, 63; on
  A. Smedley, 68–69; and the League
  for Civil Rights, 72; trip to Ch'eng-te,
  81–84; earning a living in Peking, 101;
  stone rubbings by, 106–107; in
  Washington, 175, 181, 182, 213, 231,
  239, 260; in Chungking for embassy,

294, 300; professional travels in
  China, 305; mission to Kalgan,
  310–311; in Nanking, 312; at McCarran
  committee hearing, 345; on
  illustrations for textbook, 375; in
  Japan, 377; 1960 trip around the
  world, 377; in China 1972, 407; in
  Russia, 426; and Alumni College, 435;
  in China 1979, 443–445
Fairbank Center for East Asian
  Research, 450
Fan Pang-k'o (Douglas Fairbanks), 224
Fang Chao-ying, 99, 329
Far Eastern Association, 100, 388
Far Eastern Institute, 167
Far Eastern International Relations
  (Morse and MacNair), 36
Far Eastern Quarterly, 388
Far Eastern and Russian Institute,
  Seattle, 367
Far Eastern Survey, 253
Fay, Sidney B., 143
Fei Cheng-ch'ing (John King Fairbank),
  224; career listed by CCP, 388;
  Chinese accounts of, 389; books on in
  Taiwan, 439
Fei Hsiao-t'ung, 324n, 416–417
Feng, Yeate (Feng I-tai), 310
Fenn, William, 92, 232, 241–242
Ferguson, Senator, at McCarran
  Committee hearings, 345, 347
Ferguson, John C., 56–57, 106, 408
Ferguson, Mary, 57
Ferguson, William Scott, 143, 145, 152n,
  154
Fetté, Russell, 101
Fetté, Ruth, 101
Feuerwerker, Albert, 427, 446, 456
Field, Frederick Vanderbilt, 323
Finletter, Thomas K., 181
Fir Flower Tablets (Lowell and
  Ayscough), 134
Fisher, Francis McCracken, 203, 205,
  208, 224, 289, 308; relieved at
  Chungking, 295
Flight of an Empress, The (trans.
  Pruitt), 48n
Flowering of New England, The
  (Brooks), 159
Flying Tigers (14th Air Force), 192
Fontein, Jan, 58
Foochow, trip to, 117–118
Foochow Missionaries, The (Carlson),
  117n
Footbinding, 54–55
Ford, Alice, 302
Ford, John, 202
Ford Foundation: funding for Chinese
  studies, 356; for East Asian studies,
  360, 366–367, 368–369; for IMH, 383;
  funding in East Asia, 387–388
Foreign Affairs, 424
Foreign Policy Association, 166

Foreign Policy Association Bulletin,
  320–321
Formosa, 382
Forty-one Winthrop Street, 356
Foster, John Burt, 309
Foster, William Trufant, 14
Four Modernizations, 89
Franco, General Francisco, 168
Frank, Glenn, 14
Franke, Herbert, 372n
Franke, Wolfgang, 372n
Frankfurter, Felix, 146, 152n
Franklin, N.H., 159–160
Free China (Tzu-yu Chung-kuo), 76,
  384
Freedman, Maurice, 374
Freer Gallery, 167
Friedrich, Carl J., 324n, 326
"Friends of China," Confucian concept
  of loyalty, 436; misunderstood by
  Westerners, 436–437
Fu, Flora, 439, 440–441
Fu Ssu-nien, 129n, 130, 229
Fulbright, Senator J. William, 396–397,
  408, 424
Furth, Charlotte, 46

Gailey, Dr. Robert, 43, 56; on China, 62
Galbraith, John Kenneth, 398, 449
Gale, Esson McDowell, 186, 187, 202,
  204
Gang of Four, 410
Gardner, Charles Sidney, 135, 389
Gauss, Clarence, 203, 204–205, 207, 280;
  embassy quarters of, 242–244
General Education Board, 115
Giles, H. A., 32, 95, 372
Gilmore, Myron, 158, 337
Glass, Frank, 78
Glimcher, Sumner, 155
Goldman, Emma, 285
Good Earth, The (Buck), 253
Goodrich, L. Carrington, 135
Gould, Randall, 66
Gould House conference, 368–369
Government Operations Committee,
  334
Graves, Jane, 181
Graves, Mortimer, 98, 135, 166, 167; in
  Washington, 181, 215
Great Britain: in wartime China, 195;
  sentiment against, 233
Great Britain and China (Costin), 139
Great Fear, The (Caute), 322
Great Fear, and McCarthyism, 332
Great Road, The (Smedley), 344
Green Gang, 79
Greene, Jerome, 164
Greene, Roger S., 164
Griswold, Erwin, 144, 341
Groff-Smith, Everitt, 47, 49, 208
Groff-Smith, Helen, 47
Guam, 163

Hall, Charles, 97
Hall, Martel, 265–266
Hamilton, Max, 178, 233, 236, 295
Hammond, Edmund, 195
Hammond, Mason, 144, 165
Han Hsu (Han Xu), 141, 438, 443
Handlin, Oscar, 402
Hankow, OWI branch at, 300
Haring, C. H., 144
Harris, Seymour, 144
Hart and the Chinese Customs
  (Wright), 37
Hart, Sir Robert, 21, 47, 63; at Ningpo,
  116; and the Open Door, 162; circulars
  in the style of, 303; letters of, 449
Hart, Lady, 21
Harvard Alumni Bulletin, 168–169
Harvard Alumni Clubs, 435
Harvard Guardian, 169
Harvard Journal of Asiatic Studies, 107,
  147
Harvard Summer Crimson, 342
Harvard University, 8; student at, 13;
  debates at, 15; History Dept. (1936),
  136, 143; study of Ch'ing documents
  at, 146–147; work on Japanese studies
  of China, 149–150; teaching East
  Asian history at, 152; tutoring at,
  155–157; house at, 157–159; on leave,
  173; return to, 391, 392;
  fragmentation of History Dept., 393,
  394–395; East Asian studies at, 394;
  and East-West relations, 402
Harvard University Press, 327, 449;
  T.J.Wilson at, 358; Harvard East
  Asian Series of, 359
Harvard-Yenching Institute, 96–97, 149;
  wartime aid from, 231
Harvard-Yenching Library,
  bibliography of books in, 328
Hatem, George (Ma Hai-teh), 309
Hawaii, 163
Haushofer, 44
Hay, John, 162
Hay, Stephen, 360
Hayden, Joseph Ralston, 174, 180, 186,
  187, 192, 194, 203
Hayes, Carleton J.H., 87
Hayes, John D., 40, 43, 49
Hayes, Mrs. J. D., 83
Haynes, William, 451
Hermit of Peking (Trevor-Roper), 96
Herring, Pendleton, 369
Highet, Gilbert, 24, 30, 141
Highet, Helen, 141
Hill, Joan, 453
Hill, Richard Hirst, 286
Hilsman, Roger, 391
Himalayas, wartime flights over, 191
Hippisley, Alfred E., 162
Hiss, Alger, 178, 344; letters to, on
  Kunming, 195; memo to on Tsing
  Hua faculty, 195–199; memo on China

Hiss, Alger *(cont.)*
  policy to, 233; further letters to, 237–239, 281–284; case of, 331
Historical Materialism (Bukharin) 77
History of East Asian Civilization (Fairbank and Reischauer), 155, 374–375
History 83, Harvard, 166
Hitler, Adolf, 18, 133, 139, 162; and Spain, 168
Ho-chiang, 227
Ho Lien (Franklin Ho), 208
Ho Ying-ch'in, 207, 278
Hofer, Philip, 165
Holcombe, Arthur N., 321
Holland, William L., 295, 298, 300, 344; departure from China, 302; and the IPR, 323; on McCarran committee methods, 336
Holmes, Julius, 397
Honorary degrees, 448–449
Hong Kong, 27; trips to, 120–122, 435; Chinese research in, 379, 387; growth of, 386; in 1972, 412–413, 424
Honolulu, 296, 435
Hoover Library, collection on revolutionary China at, 309
Hopper, Bruce, 135
Hornbeck, Stanley Kuhl, 153, 176–177, 195, 295; memo on China policy to, 233–235; comment from, 235–236; further memos for, 281–284
Hoyt, Dr. and Mrs. 112–113
Hsia Yen, 276, 316, 445
Hsiao Hsin-ju, Major, 216–217
Hsu Ch'ih, 310
Hu Ch'iu-yuan, 440
Hu Feng, 261
Hu Lin, 276
Hu Shih, 45–46; and the China League for Civil Rights, 69; inspection of prisons by, 71–73; Ambassador to Washington, 179; on Taiwan, 383
Huan Hsiang, 308
Huang Hua, 309, 410, 438
Huang, Gen. J. L., 207–208
Hudson, Geoffrey, 139, 299
Hué, 390, 392
Hughes, E. R., 193
Hull, Cordell, 178
Hummel, Arthur W., 96, 99, 181, 203
Hummel, Arthur, Jr. 378
"Hump," The, 191, 192, 288
Hung, Professor William, 97
Hurley, Patrick, 256, 294; post-war policy of, 299

I.G. in Peking, The (Fairbank, Bruner, Matheson, Little), 449
I-pin, 224, 227, 229
Ichiko Chūzō, 150, 387, 388
Idols of the Tribe (Isaacs), 81

Imperialism: as scapegoat, 253; foreign aid as, 281; Needham on, 373; cultural, 375, 388, 419; so-called, of American historians, 400, 426
In Search of History (White), 156, 319
Independent Critic, The (Tu-li p'ing-lun) (ed. Hu Shih), 46
India, 190; contrasted with China, 192
Indo-China, 291
Industrialization, planning for post-war, 282
Inflation, Chinese, 298; wartime, in Kunming, 194; attempts to control, 251–252; and CKS, 280
"Influence of Modern Western Science and Technology on Japan and China, The" (JKF), 373
Inner Asia, 374
Inner Asian Frontiers of China (Lattimore), 45
Institute of Pacific Relations (IPR), 295, 322; and E.C.Carter, 322–323; hearings on, 332, 336–337; part of hearings on JKF, 343; final report on, 348
Intelligentsia: wartime plight of, 228–230; disaffection of, 252–253, 280–281; impotence of, 283
Interdepartmental Committee for the Acquisition of Foreign Publications (Indec; IDC), 203; materials for, 213–214; growth of, 288
Internal Security Subcommittee, 333; seizure of IPR files by, 336; and JKF, 340
International Congresses of Orientalists: Ann Arbor, 340; Moscow, 426–428; censorship at, 427–428
International Cultural Service of China, 210
International Institute of Pacific Relations, 323
International Relations of the Chinese Empire (Morse), 20, 36
International Settlement, Shanghai, 36, 37
Introduction to Mahayana Buddhism, An (McGovern), 165
Iriye, Akira, 402
Iriye, Keishirō, 402
Isaacs, Harold, 74n, 327, 339; reporter on KMT terror, 78–80; trip to Ch'eng-te, 81–84; on India, 190
Isaacs, Viola Robinson, 79, 81–84
Isolationism, 162, 164
Israel, 378

Jacoby, Annalee, 319, 327
Jaffe, Philip, 320
Jameson, R. D., 42, 65
Jansen, Marius, 326
Japan: in 1930s, 18; in undeclared war, 35–36; expansionism of, 62;

Japan *(cont.)*
  occupation of Jehol, 81–82, 90; seizure
    of Manchuria, 90; first visit to, 125,
    377; aggression in Peking, 127; work
    on, 153; invasion of China as moral
    issue, 162–165, 166; U.S. policy toward,
    168–169; status of Emperor, 293, 296;
    terms of surrender, 296–297; material
    on, 374; sinology in, 385; 1964 visit
    to, 384, 387; recognition of PRC by,
    455
Japan: Tradition and Transformation
  (Reischauer and Craig), 374
Japanese Studies of Modern China
  (Fairbank and Banno), 149
*Japanese Studies of Modern China
  since 1953* (Kamachi and Fairbank),
  150
Japan's emergence as a modern state
  (Norman), 337
Jardine Matheson & Co., 37, 120;
  archives of, 120–121
Jehol: 1934 trip to, 81–84; Japanese
  occupation of, 81–82, 90
Jensen, Dr. J. C., 229
Jessup, Philip, 348
Johnson, Lyndon B., 350; and Vietnam,
  396
Joint ACLS-Soviet Academy of Sciences
  Commission on the Humanities and
  Social Sciences, 429–430, 438
Joint Committee on Contemporary
  China (JCCC), 370, 380, 382
Jordan, Wilbur Kitchell, 144
Journey to the Beginning (Snow), 127
Jowett, Benjamin, 20
Judd, Walter, 164, 328, 397

Kahn, E. J., 350
Kaifeng, 58, 60
Kaji Wataru, 293, 310
Kalgan, 310; CCP capital, 311;
  experiences in, 311
Kamachi, Noriko. 150
K'ang Sheng, 422
K'ang Yu-wei, 104
Karpovich, Michael, 144
Kates, George N., 266
Katō Shigeshi, 150
Kennedy, John F., 384, 393
Keswick, John, 121–122
Keswick, W. J., 120, 121
Khubilai Khan, 53
Kilgour, Frederick G., 203–204, 213, 214,
  288
King, Admiral Ernest J., 215, 217, 219
King, John H., 6
Kirkland House, 155, 435
Kirstein, Lincoln, 285
Kissinger, Henry, 408; in Peking, 423
Klauber, Ed, 289
Kluckhohn, Clyde, 12–13, 290
Kluckhohn, Florence, 290

Knettel, Harry W., Jr., 169
Knox, Lucy, 62
Kohlberg, Alfred, 334
Koji Ariyoshi, 307
Korea, 47, 153, 355, 374; sinology in
  (1960), 385; 1964 trip to, 386,
  387
Korean War, 302; effect on
  McCarthyism, 336; JKF on, 342;
  Chinese intervention in, 396
Kowloon, 386, 412
Ku Chieh-kang, 274
Ku, Dr. Joseph, 306
Kuala Lumpur, 378
Kuang-hsu Emperor, 53
Kuhn, Ferdinand, 290
Kuhn, Philip A., 450
Kung, H. H., 203, 207, 234; personal
  contact with, 210; and Lienta, 258
Kung P'eng (Kung Wei-hang), 267, 271,
  276, 277, 278, 306, 346, 423; career
  of, 267–268; fiancé of, 271, 272;
  increasing surveillance of, 271, 277;
  illness of, 272; with truce team in N.
  China, 307; death of, 418
Kung P'u-sheng, 278–279
Kunming, 191–192, 287, 296; refugee
  universities in, 192; report on
  academics in, 195–199; plight of
  academics, 258–259; in Army base
  hospital at, 244; bitterness against
  CKS in, 252; OWI branch at, 300
Kuo Mo-jo, 260, 262, 308, 419–420;
  interview with, 261; birthday party,
  261–262; at CCP cocktail party, 306;
  at farewell dinner, 312
Kuo Te-tsung, 75
Kuo T'ing-i, 383, 439
Kuo Yu-hsiu, 96
Kuo-yü (Peking dialect), 40
Kuomintang (KMT), 64, 220; and A.
  Smedley, 67; and CCP, 74–76; terror
  reported by Isaacs, 79–80; policy
  toward Tsing Hua, 198–199; gradual
  decline of, 241, 244, 251, 259, 316;
  American observers' disillusionment,
  253, 283; US propaganda of, 284, 288;
  backed by Hurley, 294; in reoccupied
  areas, 312; and capitalism, 318;
  demoralization of, 320; on Taiwan,
  379, 381
Kwangsi clique, 207
Kweilin, visit to, 259
Kyoto, language school in, 148–149

Lach, Donald, 328
Ladejinsky, Wolf, 379
LaFollette, Belle Case, 285
LaFollette, Senator Robert M., 11–12,
  285
La Follette, Isabel Bacon, 175
Lambert, Anthony, 24, 25, 137, 378
Lanchow, OWI branch at, 300

Land and Labour in China (Tawney), 88
Land reform: urged by T.F. Tsiang, 89; on Taiwan, 380
Landis, James, 165
Langer, William L., 17, 143, 146; in R and A Branch, 174, 204, 285
Languages: Latin, 15; French, 15; German, 15; Greek, 15; Chinese, 22–23, 40, 96; Japanese, 148; Russian, 150, 430
Lao Chin, 194; *see* Y. L. Chin
Lao She, 28, 445
Laski, Harold, 146
Lasswell, Harold, 185
Last Chance in China (Utley), 328
Last Stand of Chinese Conservatism (Wright), 363
Latourette, Kenneth Scott, 134
Lattimore, Eleanor Holgate, 45, 335–336, 338, 345
Lattimore, Owen, 44–45, 323; as target of McCarthy, 335–336; and McCarran committee, 337–338, 345; and Wittfogel, 339, 340
Lauch; *see* Currie
Lauterbach, Richard, 328
Le Carré, John, 70
League of Nations, 18, 62, 133
Lecturing: styles of, 153–154; slides for, 155
Lee, Harold, 25, 413
Lee, Willis A., 217
"Legalization of the Opium Trade before the Treaties of 1858" (JKF), 101
Lei Chen, 76, 384
Leighton, Alexander, 290
Leland, Waldo G., 98, 181
Leningrad, 426, 428
Leninism, 276, 319, 373
Leopold, Richard, 144
Levenson, Joseph R., 364
Lewis, Ruth, 302
Leyden, 8th Congress of Junior Sinologues in, 372
Li Chi, 69, 129n, 252, 397; in Taiwan, 382
Li Choh-min, 413
Li-chuang, 224; journey to, 225–227; visit in, 227–229
Li Hung-chang, 47
Li P'eng, supposed "confession" of, 346–347
Li Ssu-kuang (J. S. Lee), 259
Liang Ch'i-ch'ao, 104–105, 364
Liang dynasty, 92
Liang, Phyllis (Lin Whei-yin), 104, 105, 113, 138, 194; and the Japanese, 128; in Li-chuang, 224, 229; death of, 417
Liang Ssu-ch'eng, 104, 113, 128, 138; background of, 105; summer at Yü Tao Ho, 108; work of, 108–109; trips

with, 109–113; in wartime, 194, 323; visit to, 228; death of, 417, 382
Liang Ssu-i, 128
Liang Ssu-chuang, 229
Liang Ssu-yung, 129n, 224
Liao dynasty, 52
Liberal Club, Harvard, 285–286
Liberals, Chinese: on civil rights, 73; and KMT-CCP split, 74–75; academic, 88–89; lack of contact with reality, 88–89; scattering of, 128–129; threatened by Nationalists, 315–316
Liberals, US, 317; plight of in 1951, 333; caution of, 338
Library of Congress; Dr. Hummel at, 99; Far East section of COI at, 174, 175, 180; collection of Chinese sources by, 202, 219
Lienta (Southwest Associated University), 192; and the KMT, 198; and UCR, 230–231; proposals to Chungking, 258; assassination at, 315–316; faculty from, on Taiwan, 382; at Peita, 417
Life, 253
Lim, Robert K.S. (Lin K'o-sheng), 130; Major General, 232
Lin Ch'ang-min, 105
Lin Piao, 422
Lin Whei-yin, 104; background of, 105; *see also* Liang, Phyllis
Lin Yutang (Lin Yu-t'ang), 74n, 75, 275
Lindbeck, John Matthew Henry, 60, 360; on JCCC, 370; at Harvard, 370–371; report by, 371; travels of, 377
Lindbergh, Anne Morrow, 78
Lindbergh, Charles, 78
Lindsay, A. D., 20, 139, 140
Lindsay, Michael, 266
Linen, Jim, 289
Lingle, Mrs. Jean, 86
Literary Inquisition of Ch'ien-lung (Goodrich), 135
Little, L. K., 449; at Canton, 122–123, 414; at Chungking, 208
Liu Kwang-Ching, 328, 456
Liu Shao-ch'i, 53, 319, 416, 422, 444
Liu Tsun-ch'i, 302, 308
Lockwood, Stephen, 121n
Lockwood, William, 369
London, 11; exhibit of Chinese art (1936), 138
Long March, the, 93, 128
Loon, Piet van der, 372n
Lorenzen, Fred, 15
Lowell, A. Lawrence, 14, 16, 152, 154, 155
Lowell, Amy, 134
Loyalty-security case of JKF, 340–351; hearing before Military Review Board, 343–344; charges, 344; hearing before McCarran committee,

Loyalty-security case of JKF *(cont.)*
  346–348; summary of lessons from,
  348–349; by-products of, 351
Loyang, 56, 57; missionary
  establishments in, 60
Lu Hsun, 67, 275
Lu Hsun, Mme, 307
Luan River, 82–83
Luce, Henry, 403
Ludden, Ray, 266
Lung-men caves, 56, 57

Macao, 187, 188
Macartney, Lord, 153
MacArthur, Douglas, 157, 215, 292; in
  Korean War, 332
MacDonald, Dwight, 10
MacDonald, Malcolm, 15
MacFarquhar, Roderick, 456
MacInnes, Helen, 30, 70, 141
MacLaine, Shirley, 442, 443
MacLeish, Archibald, 203, 296
MacNair, Florence Ayscough, 134
MacNair, Harley F., 36–37, 133
Maiduguri, 188–189
Majestic, the, 137
Mancall, Mark, 360
Manchukuo, 127
Manchuria, Japanese seizure of, 18, 36,
  62, 125; Lattimore on, 44–45
Manchuria, Cradle of Conflict
  (Lattimore), 44
Mandarin *(kuan hua;* official speech) 40
Manila, 296, 378, 386
Mao Tse-tung, 53, 319, 332, 380, 396,
  408, 417; on rural reconstruction, 126;
  and cadre schools 420; Yenan as
  museum of, 421–422; death of, 435
Mao Tun (Shen Yen-ping), 261;
  interview with, 262
Maps: for courses, 153; for COI, 183
Marco Polo, 54, 374
Marder, Murray, 345, 346
Marshall, General George Catlett, 207,
  208; mediation of, 298, 300, 304, 306,
  316; news conference of, 305;
  exchange arrangements, 310; return
  of, 321
Marshall Plan, 331
Martin, A. J., 119
Marx, Karl, 319; and Malthus, 372
Marxism, 283, 317, 373; and Soviet
  study of China, 339
Mason, Edward S., 324n, 326
Mass Education Movement, in
  Tinghsien, 126
Masses (Ch'un-chung), 271
Matheson, Elizabeth MacLeod, 358,
  449
Matthews, Herbert, 190
Mathews dictionary, 95
Maugham, Somerset, 117
Mauretania, the, 137

May Fourth Movement, 128, 275;
  legacy of, 286; and the KMT, 384
Maze, Sir Frederick, 47, 63, 208
McCarran, Senator Pat, 336; hearings
  before committee of, 336–337,
  345–347; methods of, 336; report of
  committee, 336, 348; report used in
  Taiwan, 348, 439
McCarthy, Joseph, 322, 334; committee
  hearings of, 335–336; censure of, 338,
  347
McCarthyism, 322, 441; factors
  contributing to, 332–334; and the
  news, 347; effect on government
  policy, 348–351, 396
McGovern, William Montgomery, 165,
  367
McHugh, James, 217
McIlwain, C. H., 143, 337
McKay, Donald Cope, 144, 165; in R.
  and A. Branch, 174; in Regional
  Studies, 324, 327; witness for JKF,
  343
McKinley, William, 163
Meadows, J.A.T., 116
Mei Yi-ch'i, 230; in Kunming, 192, 194,
  198
Melby, John, 303; witness for JKF, 343
Menzies, Arthur, 153, 438, 443
Menzies, James, 100, 106
Merk, Frederick, 154, 337
Merrill, Henry F., 47
Merrill Hall, 159
Merriman, Roger Bigelow, 153–154
Michael, Franz, 368
Microfilm: use of for scholarly
  publications, 210; projectors for, 213;
  difficulties with, 213–214; Ch'en Li-fu
  on, 250–251
Miles, Milton, 215; career of, 216–217;
  connection with Tai Li, 217–218;
  coordinator of OSS, 219–220, 285
Miles, Wilma, 216
Military Entry Permit Review Board,
  342–344
Missionaries: students of Chinese
  language, 40; hospitality of, 111–112; in
  wartime, 232; lack of US study of,
  403
*Missionary Enterprise in China and
  America, The,* 360, 434
*Modern China: A bibliographical guide
  to Chinese works 1898–1937* (K.C. Liu
  and Fairbank), 328
Modernization *(chin-tai hua),* Tawney
  on, 89
Mondale, Vice-President, 4, 423, 444
Mondale, Mrs. Joan, 444
Mongolia, Lattimore on, 44
Moral Endeavor Association, 92, 207
Moral Man and Immoral Society
  (Niebuhr), 274
Morgan, Edmund M., 152n

Morison, Samuel Eliot, 144–145
Morse, H. B., 20, 21, 36, 47, 162, 449; visit to, 21–22; death of, 139
Moscow, 426, 428, 429, 438
Moseley, Philip, 174
Mukden, OWI branch at, 300
Murdock, K. B., 152n
Murphey, Rhoads, 326, 446
Murphy, Henry Killam, 85
Mussolini, Benito, 18, 133; in Spain, 168
My Country and My People (Lin Yutang), 275
My Several Worlds (Pearl Buck), 47

Naganuma, 148, 149
Nankai School of Economics, 323
Nankai Social and Economic Quarterly, 138n
Nankai University: T.F. Tsiang at, 87–88; in Kunming, 192, 199
Nanking: OWI branch at, 300; US embassy in, 306
Nanking government: T.F. Tsiang in, 90, 221; efforts in rural China, 91
Nanking University, 203; at Cheng-tu, 232
Nanyang Brothers Tobacco Co., 64–65
Napier, Lord, 224
National Central University, 223
National Library of Peiping, 209
National Research Council, 371
National Resources Commission (Nationalist), 221
National Taiwan University, 379, 382
Nationalism, Chinese, 235, 257
Nationalist Government, 221, 256, 298, 312; and the China hands, 164; renewed hostilities with CCP, 315; U.S. relations with, 316, 321 334
Nationalist Revolution (1925–1927), 74, 122
Naval Group China, 218
Needham, Joseph, 273
Negrín, Juan, 168
Nehru, 378
Nelson Gallery, Kansas City, 41
Nelson, William, 326
Nepal, 378
"New China and the American Connection" *(Foreign Affairs),* 424
New Delhi, 378, 385; lack of study of China in, 385
New Life Movement, 92, 207, 248–249, 255
New Republic article on Taiwan, 409
New World of Negro Americans (Isaacs), 81
New York Times, 343, 384, 398, 409; articles in, 169; reports of PRC in, 407
New York Times Book Review: review of *Thunder Out of China* in, 319;

review of CKS in, 320; review of *U.S. and China* in, 327
New York Review of Books, review of Pascalini in, 437
New Yorker, 350
News Materials (Hsin-wen tzu-liao) 303
Ngo Dinh Diem, 379
Niebuhr, Reinhold, 274, 339
Nieh Jung-chen, Gen., 311
Nikiforov, V.N., 429
Nimitz, Admiral, 292
Ningpo: archives of, 115–116; trip to, 116–117
Nixon, Richard M., 332, 389; reversal on China, 407; arrival in Peking, 409
No Peace for Asia (Isaacs), 327
Nock, Arthur Darby, 144
Norman, E. Herbert, 153, 337
North Atlantic Treaty Organization (NATO), 332
North China: Japanese encroachments in, 90, 127; 1972 visit to, 420–421
North China Associated University (Chang-chia-k'ou), 310–311
North China Herald, 66
North China Union Language School (Hua-yü hsueh-hsiao), 39
North Korea, 332
Notes on Far Eastern Studies in America, 166
Nozaka Sanzō, 293

"Offering Shrine of Wu Liang" (Wu Liang Tz'u), 106
Office of Intelligence Research (OIR), 396
Office of Naval Intelligence (ONI), 174, 215, 291
Office of Strategic Services (OSS), 186, 202, 215, 218, 285; and SACO, 219
Office of War Information (OWI), 186, 295; in Chungking, 203, 215; growth of, 289–290; China section, 290; Japan section, 291; Voice of America, 291; Overseas News and Features, 291–292; stockpiling for after war, 294; departure of staff from China, 298, 300; post-war changes, 300–301
Officers Moral Endeavor Society, 92, 207
Open Door, the, 162–163
Opium, 230; poppy-growing, 82
"Oracle Bones from the Waste of Yin" (Menzies), 106
Ordeal by Slander (Lattimore), 335, 336
Oriental Despotism (Wittfogel), 339, 427
Osborn, David, 412, 424
Oswald, Lee Harvey, 75
Otake Fumio, 150
Other Side of the River: Red China Today, The (Snow), 407

"Our Chances in China" *(Atlantic)*,
315; dilemma treated by, 316–317
"Our Choice in the Far East" *(Harvard
Alumni Bulletin)*, 168–169
Overseas News and Features (ONAF),
291–292, 302
Owen, David, 121n, 144
Oxford University, 19–31; thesis at, 21,
22; study of Chinese at, 22–23, 30;
health at, 24; social life in London,
27–30; completing thesis, 125, 133,
138; examination 139

Pacific Affairs, 323
Pagan, Burma, 378
Pai Ch'ung-hsi, 207
pai-hua (vernacular), 43
Pan American Airways: wartime
transport by, 187; in 1979, 443
Papers on China (EARC), 28, 356, 359
Paris, 7, 27, 30
Parsons, Talcott, 324n, 326
Pascalini, Jean (Bao Jo-wang), 437
Paton, Gus, 214, 218
Payne, Robert, 327–328
Peake, Cyrus, 106, 135
Peake, Marie, 106
Pearl Harbor, attack on, 182
Peasants: dangers of industrialization
for, 282, 455; poor vs. rich, 319;
included in modern history, 375
Peck, Graham, 226, 259, 266, 309
Peck, Willys R., 182, 236
Peiping, OWI branch at, 300
Peiping Chronicle, 139
Peitaiho, 83
Peking: arrival in, 38; Wilma's arrival,
49; keeping house in, 52; history of,
52; explorations of, 52–54; excursions
from, 56–61; earning a living in,
101–103; and the Liangs, 104–109;
Japanese aggression in, 127; student
demonstrations in, 127–128; departure
from, 129–130; in 1946, 305, 309; USIS
office in, 310; Nixon's arrival in, 409;
1972 return to, 407, 414–424; old
friends in, 416–418; talks to groups in,
419
Peking and Beyond (Salisbury), 423
Peking National University (Peita), 45,
86, 380; in Kunming, 192; library of,
209–210; revisited, 417
Peking Union Medical College (PUMC),
45, 48, 101
Pelliot, Paul, 97
Pendar, Kenneth, 9
Pendar, Oliver, 9
Penfield, James K., 277
P'eng Te-huai, General, 268
People's Daily, 308, 418
People's Knowledge, 274
People's Political Council (PPC),
239–240, 279

People's Republic of China (PRC), 372;
proclamation of, 332; arguments for
US recognition of, 343, 398; Nixon's
change toward, 407; Nixon's visit to,
409; concepts of loyalty in, 436–437;
lack of visa for, 434; US recognition
of, 455
Perkins, Elliott, 144
Perkins, Elsie (Mrs. W. Youngman), 158;
in Washington, 175
Perkins, Maxwell, 158–159
Perry, Ralph Barton, 152n, 165
Pettus, W. B., 39, 40
Philippines, 163
Philippines, The (Hayden), 174
Phillips Exeter Academy, 9–11; debating
at, 14–15
Phillips, Captain, U.S.N., 291
Pleasants, Helene, 302
Political Action Committee (PAC), 317
Political parties, U.S., imbalance
between, 333–334
Pope, John, 370
Postan, Michael, 140
Postwar planning, 220–221
Potter, Philip, 307, 345, 346
Powell, J. B., 126
Power, Eileen, 27–28, 42, 140
"Present situation in China, The"
(T.F.Tsiang), 89n
Price, Frank, 91–92, 164, 232; on
provincial government, 256
Price, Harry, 164
Pride and Prejudice (Austen), 274
Prisoner of Mao (Pascalini), 437–438
Pritchard, Earl, 135
Proletariat, confusion in term applied
to China, 319
Pruitt, Ida, 48, 84
Prusek, Jaroslav, 372n
Psychological warfare (PW), 203
Public Record Office, London, 27, 140
Pusey, Nathan, 448
Pye, Lucian, 369, 397n

*Quarterly Bulletin of Chinese
Bibliography,* 209
Quemoy, 381

Radcliffe College, 435; lecturing at,
154–155
Radio: OWI communication by,
300–301; discussion shows, 328, 350
Raisz, Erwin, 153
Rand, Christopher, 307, 412
Reader's Digest, 253
Red Star over China (Snow), 77, 127,
266
Redfield, Robert, 365
Regional Studies—China, 324; meetings
of, 325–326; graduate students in,
326; results in writing, 326–327; and
EARC, 355

Reinsch, Paul, 177
Reischauer, Edwin O., 376, 388; in History Dept., 144–145; language textbook by, 148; on history of EA civilization, 155; in EA survey course, 166; and EARC, 357; work on textbooks, 373–374; ambassador, 374; and Council on EA Studies, 394
Religion and the Rise of Capitalism (Tawney), 88
Remer, Carl (Charles F.), 180, 185
Republic of China (ROC), 379, 381; as symbol, 381–382
Republican Party, 333–334; use of China issue by, 337–338
Research and Analysis Branch, COI, 173–184; representative in China, 185; in merger of OSS, 186–187
Reston, James, 410, 449
Retirement, 449
Retrogression, Law of, 22
Revolution in China: prospects for postwar, 316; need for, 286; in-evitability of, 295; character of, 319
Rhee, Syngman, 385
Rhodes Scholarship, 15–16; in Peking, 30
"Rice Paddies," 325; textbook for, 373–375
Richards, I. A., 193
Rickshaws, 110–111
Ride, Col. (Sir) Lindsay, 259, 386
Ringwalt, Arthur, 259
Roberts, Major Frank, 179
Robertson, Walter, 304, 305
Rockefeller Foundation, 167, 396
Rockhill, W. W., 162
Roe, Gilbert E., 11, 66, 285
Roe, Jack, 11, 15
Rome, 378; 10th Int. Congress of Historians in, 373
Roosevelt, Eleanor, 278
Roosevelt, Franklin Delano, 175, 183, 204, 253, 299, 334; and SACO, 219
Roots, Logan, 40
Rosinger, L., 344
Rowe, David Nelson, 185, 186, 208, 367
Roy, Andrew Tod, 40, 91–92, 232, 248
Roy, Margaret, 91
Royal Asiatic Society, 379
Royal Institute of International Affairs, 323
Royal Ontario Museum, Toronto, 58
Ruhlmann, Robert, 372
Rural reconstruction, 126
Rusk, Dean, 179, 350, 398
Russian Research Center, Harvard, 395
Russia, *see* USSR

Saigon, 378, 379; 1964 visit to, 386, 391
Sailer, Randolph, 290
Saipan, 296
Salisbury, Harrison, 422–423
Samoa, 163

San Francisco: broadcasts of VOA from, 291, 292; U.N. meeting in, 295; broadcast of surrender terms from, 296
Scalapino, Robert, 397n
Schaeffer, Amy, 302
Schaller, Michael, 183n, 220
Schlesinger, Arthur, Sr., 143, 152n, 165, 166, 337
Schlesinger, Arthur, Jr., 155, 299; and ADA, 317, 339
Schlesinger, Marian Cannon, 26; in China, 115, 117, 119, 120, 122; in IPR, 323
Schumpeter, Elizabeth Boody, 166
Schwartz, Benjamin, 326, 329, 448
Science and Civilization in China (Needham), 373
Scott, Austin, 144
Scratches on Our Minds (Isaacs), 81, 190
Seasongood, Murray, 343, 349
Seawall, William, 442
Seoul, 385, 386, 439
Senate Foreign Relations Committee, China policy hearings, 396–397
Senate Judiciary Committee, 336
Service Center for Academic Materials (Hsueh-shu tzu-liao fu-wu ch'u), 210
Service, John S., 279, 280, 346, 408; reports from Yenan, 293; later career of, 349
Sevareid, Eric, 273, 277
Shameen, 122, 414
Shanghai: arrival (1932), 36; under Japanese fire, 36; trips to, 63–65; industrialization in, 65; study of archives in, 115; OWI office in, 300, 302, 309–310; postwar, 301; departure from, 312
Shanghai Conspiracy (Willoughby), 67
Shanghai Evening Post, 78
Shao Hsun-cheng, 417, 418
Shapley, Harlow, 152n
Sharp, Lauriston, 12, 27, 386
Sherwood, R. E., 180n
Shaw, George Bernard, 73–74
Shen Chih-yuan, 261
Shu, C. C. (Shu She-yu; Lao She), 28
Sian, 38, 444
Sickman, Laurence C. S., 41–42, 56, 57, 138, 387
Sinclair, Charles A., 116
Singapore, 378, 435; fall of, 169, 184
Sinism (Creel), 134
Sino-American Cooperative Organization (SACO), 219; activities of, 220
Sino-American Cultural Institute, 234, 310
Sino-Soviet split, 408, 427
Sinology, as global concern, 371–372
Sioux Falls, 8, 9, 12–13, 15–16, 25, 29, 31, 141–2

Sixteen Dunster Street, 356
Sixtieth birthday dinner, 446–448
Skinner, G. William, 374
Sloane, William, 261, 319
Smedley, Agnes, 66–70, 79, 115, 277, 436; and the China League for Civil Rights, 72–74, 75; in Russia, 76–77; death of, 77; at Harvard, 344
Smith, Preserved, 103
Smith, Senator Willis, 345, 347
Snatched from Oblivion (M. Schlesinger), 26
Snow, Edgar, 77, 126–127, 218; in New Delhi, 190; reports on CCP, 266; in China after 1949, 407; memorial service for, 410
Snow, Helen Foster (Nym Wales), 126–127
"Social and Economic Background of the Taiping Rebellion" (Taylor), 290
Social Science Research Council, 369–371
Society for Research in Chinese Architecture, 107
Sofia, 378
Solzhenitzin, Aleksandr, 70
Soochow, 36
Soong Ch'ing-ling, 73, 75; *see also* Mme Sun Yat-sen
Soong, T. V., 179–180; China Defense Supplies, Inc., 175; role of, 318–319
Soothill, W. E., 21, 22, 30
South Korea, 332
Soviet Union; *see* USSR
Spanish Civil War, 162, 168
Spence, Jonathan, 375
Speshneff, Galia, 135
Sprenckel, Otto Berkelbach van der, 372n
Sprouse, Philip, 273, 276, 277, 279, 316; in Cambodia, 386; on China Advisory Panel, 397
Stalin, Josef, 77, 80, 319, 332
Stalin's Failure in China 1924–1927 (Brandt), 329
State Department, US, 220; Hornbeck's role in, 176–178; Cultural Relations, 182, 219, 294–295; Far Eastern office, 295; and "loss of China," 335; OIR in, 396
Steele, Arch, 190
Steffens, Lincoln, 285
Steiner, Arthur, 368
Stettinius, 299
Stevens, David, 115, 135, 167
Stewart, James, 203, 293, 295
Stilwell, General Joseph, 184, 203, 207, 213, 280, 292, 294; and SACO, 219, 220
Straw Sandals (Isaacs), 79n
Stuart, J. Leighton, 86; and Harvard-Yenching, 96

Studies in Ch'ing Administration (Fairbank and Teng), 147
Stylus Club, 158
Sullivan, Michael, 232
Sumner, B. Humphrey, 25, 140
Sun, E-tu Zen, 329
Sun Fo, 207, 278
Sun Yat-sen, 62, 63, 74, 262; communism and, 319, 381
Sun Yat-sen, Mme (Soong Ch'ing-ling), 127, 346; in Chungking, 207, 276, 285
Sung Chiao-jen, 76
Sweezy, Alan R., 11; at Harvard, 14, 16; question of appointment procedure, 151–152
Swing, Raymond Gram, 292
Szechwan: Yangtze in, 226; social structure of, 347

Ta Kung Pao, Tientsin, 128, 273, 274; on anti-foreignism, 281; Hong Kong, 388
Ta-t'ung, 56
Tachai Brigade, 421
Taft, Robert, 337
Tai Li, General, 216; recruitment of Miles, 217–218; work of Miles with 218–220, 285; training of police by, 220; assassination by, 316; incriminating material to US from, 346
T'ai Shan, 60–61
Taianfu, 60
Taichung, 381, 382, 387
Taipei, 434, 435; OWI branch in, 300; 1960 visit to, 379; growth of, 386; meeting on Fei Cheng-ch'ing, 439–440
"Taipei can coexist with Peking" (*N.Y.Times* op-ed), 409
Taiwan, 64; scholar refugees in, 129n; 1960 trip to, 377, 379; KMT in, 379, 381; foreign activities in, 382; and Nixon's visit to Peking, 408; conversations with Ch'iao Kuan-hua on, 419; as "problem," 434; 1977 trip to, 434, 439–442; present U.S. relations with, 455
T'ang Chi-yao, 192
T'ang, Nancy, 422
T'ao Hsi-sheng, 440–441
T'ao H. C. (T'ao Hsing-chih), 262–263
T'ao, L. K. (T'ao Meng-ho), 45, 129n, 252; trip to Li–chuang with, 225
T'ao, Mme, 221, 230
Tawney, R. II., 28, 88–89, 140
Taylor, Charles, 144
Taylor, George, 92; on Far East, OWI, 290, 294; in Washington, 304; in Seattle, 367; head of SSRC development committee, 369–371; on China Advisory Panel, 397n
Taylor, Hudson, 112

Temple of the Sleeping Buddha (Wo Fo Ssu), 56
Teng Ssu-yü (S. Y. Teng), 147; work on *China's Response*, 328–329
Thailand, 291, 393; lack of Chinese studies in, 378
Thelin, Guy, 40, 118
Thomson, James C., Jr., 446
Three Principles of the People, 319
Thunder Out of China (White and Jacoby), 319–320
Tides from the West (Chiang Monlin), 380
Tientsin, 37; visit to Groff-Smiths, 47, 49; Nankai University at, 87; OWI branch at, 300
Tikhvinskii, Sergei, 309, 428, 429, 431–432
Ting, V. K., 45–46
Ting-hsien, 127
Ting Ling, 75, 311, 445
Tokyo, 125, 133, 434, 435, 439; demonstrations in, 384–385
To Lhasa in Disguise (McGovern), 165
Tombs of Old Loyang (White), 58–59
Tong, Holly, 254, 278
Tōyō Bunko Library, 150, 387
Trade and Diplomacy on the China Coast (JKF), 161
Tragedy of the Chinese Revolution, The (Isaacs), 80
Translation, 274; under USIS, 310
Traveling: basis for, 376–377; Japan (1952–53), 377, (1960), 384; around the world, 377, 434; Taiwan (1960), 379–384, (1964) 386; Korea (1960), 385; around the world (1964), 385; to PRC (1972), 413–424; to Moscow (1960), 426, (1972) 428, (1977) 429; fund-raising (1976), 435; to Taiwan, Korea, Japan (1977), 439–442; to Peking (1979), 443
Treaty ports, 114; study of archives at, 115; Ningpo, 116–117; Foochow, 117–118; anti-Chinese atmosphere of, 118; Amoy, 119–120; Hong Kong, 120–122; Canton, 122
Trevor-Roper, Hugh, 96
Trickey, E. G., 30, 112
Trotsky, Leon, 80, 329
Truman, Harry S., 304, 331, 334, 338
Truth Is Our Weapon (Barrett), 297n
Ts'ai Yuan-p'ei, 73; and Yang Chien, 74; surveillance of, 75, 76
Tsen, Lindel, 58
Tsiang, T. F. (Chiang T'ing-fu), 85, 198, 418; career of, 86–88; at Tsing Hua, 88, 101; influence of Tawney on, 88–89; in government 90–91, 126, 128; in wartime, 208–209, 254; as propagandist in US, 288; in Taiwan, 387
Tsinan, archaeology in, 106

Tsining, 107
Tsing Hua, 42; history of, 85, 88; T.F.Tsiang at, 88; teaching at, 91, 102; in Kunming, 192; memo on faculty of, 195–199; rehabilitation of, 309
Tu Lien-che, 99
Tung-hai University, 382
Tung Hsing Lou restaurant ("Pavilion Rising in the East"), 45
Tung Pi-wu, 279, 295
T'ung-meng hui (Revolutionary Alliance), 74
Twitchett, Denis, 365, 372n, 456
Two Kinds of Time (Peck), 309
Tydings subcommittee of Senate Foreign Relations Committee, 335, 336

U Nu, Prime Minister, 378
Un-American Activities Committee, 333
Understanding China: An Assessment of American Scholarly Resources (Lindbeck), 371
Unequal treaties, 36, 63–64, 217; and the Open Door, 163
USSR: Smedley on, 76–77; on help against Japan, 89; and Spain, 168; embassy in Chungking, 277–278; and the CCP, 319–321; and IPR, 323; works on China, 329; and China studies, 425, 427–431
United Asia Herald, 128
United China Relief (UCR), 165, 195, 334; attempt at academic relief, 230
United Nations, 295
United Nations Relief and Rehabilitation Administration (UNRRA), 301
United Press, 169
United States: Chinese students in, 86; lack of policy toward China, 196, 237, 298; embassy in Chungking, 201; lack of knowledge of Yenan, 272; attempts to mediate in China, 298; USSR relations, 425; prospects for future Chinese relations, 456–458; *see also* China policy
United States and China (JKF), 326, 339; suggested reading in, 327; later editions, 327; read by? Nixon, Mao, Chou, 389; censored in Moscow, 427
U.S. Crusade in China, The (Schaller), 183n, 220
U.S. Information Service (USIS), 300, 303; circulars as director, 303–304; office in Shanghai, 309–310; Peking office, 310
Universities, student unrest in, 127–128
Universities Service Center, Hong Kong, 371; Kowloon, 412
Urquhart, Dean, 25
Utley, Freda, 328

Veritable Records, Ch'ing, 363
Viet-cong, 392
Vietnam, 374, 379; ignorance about, 350, 355, 390, 392, 305, 423
Vietnam and the Chinese Model (Woodside), 391
Vincent, John Carter, 304, 348; at Chungking, 203, 205; aid from, 242; head of FE, 295; in Cambridge, 402
Voice of America (VOA), 291

Wada Sei, 150
Wade-Giles romanization, 40
Wait, Richard, 341, 342–343, 345, 346
Wald, George, 420
Walker, Richard L., 367, 427
Wallace, Henry, 317
Walsh, Ray, 151–152
Wang, Anna von Kleist, 276
Wang Ch'ung-hui, 207
Wang Hao, 105
Wang Ju-mei (Huang Hua), 127
Wang P'eng-sheng, Gen., 218
Wang Ping-nan, 276, 279
Wang Shih-chieh, 278, 288; in Taiwan, 384, 441
War Area Service Corps, 207–208
War in China, The (weekly, COI), 183
Ward, Paul, 400
Ware, James R., 146–147, 156
Warner, Langdon, 41
Washington: work for COI, 173; return to, 287–288; OWI in, 289
Washington *Post*, 342, 345–346
"Washington Weekly Intelligencer," circular letter, 292–293
Watkins, Senator, 345, 347
Weber, Max, 339
Webster, Sir Charles Kingsley, 16, 85, 88, 101, 115, 140, 154; on T. F. Tsiang, 89; on WWII, 139; after the war, 299
Webster, Nora, 299
Wei Jing-sheng, 76
Welles, Sumner, 178
Wells, H. G., 275
Wen Hui Pao, 308
Wen I-to, assassination of, 315–316
Wen Yuan-ning, 129n
Weng Wen-hao, 90, 209; *see also* Wong Wen-hao
Wenley, Archibald, 167
Wertheim, Barbara (Tuchman), 323
West, Philip, 399
West China Union University, 232
Western Hills, 56
Wexler, Irwin, 292
Whampoa, 123, 249
What I Know about China (Keswick), 121–122
White, Theodore H., 158, 393, 408, 450; as tutee, 155–156; in New Delhi, 190; in Chungking, 266, 279; review of

book by, 319–320; at dinner for Deng, 442
White, William Charles, 58–59
Wilbur, C. Martin, 39; at Gould House conference, 368
Williams, Frederick Wells, 134
Williams, Myron, 10
Williams, Samuel Wells, 134
Willkie, Wendell, in Chungking, 205–207
Wilson, Howard E., 167
Wilson, Thomas J., 358
Wilson, Woodrow, 177
Winfield, Gerald, 328
Winter, Robert, 193, 194, 417
Wisconsin, University of, 11–13, 15
Wisdom of the Body, The (Cannon), 160
Wittfogel, Karl August, 338–340, 367, 427, 440
Wolfe, Thomas, 159
Wong Wen-hao, 90, 221
Wood, Bryce, 370
Woodside, Alexander Barton, 391, 393
Woodward, C. Vann, 401
Woosung, 36
Wright, Arthur, 158, 309, 341, 362, 446; work of, 365; and Committee on Studies of Chinese Civilization, 370
Wright, Duncan, 363
Wright, Jonathan, 363
Wright, Mary Clabaugh, 141, 158, 341, 400, 428, 446; in Peking, 309; career of, 362–363
Wright, Stanley F., 37, 64
Writers League, 310
Wu I-fang, 233
Wu Liang Tz'u, rubbings from, 106
Wu, Silas H. L., 147

Yamamoto, Sumiko, 150, 377
Yamamoto, Tatsurō, 377
Yang Ch'ao, 307–308
Yang Chien (Yang Ch'üan; Yang Hsing-fo), 71–73; photo by, 74n; career of, 74–76
Yang Kang (Yang Ping), 308; career of, 273–275; insights of, 275–276; death of, 418
Yangtze River, 35; 1931 flood, 78; at Chungking, 201–202; boat trip on, 225–227
Yarnell, Admiral Harry E., 292
Yeh Chien-ying, 306, 307
Yeh, George (Yeh Kung-ch'ao), 129n; in Taipei, 387, 441
Yen Hsi-shan, 109
Yen, Jimmy (Yen Yang-ch'u), 126
Yen Wen-yuan, 193
Yenan, 126; reports of CCP at, 265–266; American ignorance of, 272; reporting of, 293; in 1972, 421–422

Yenching University, 85; and
    Harvard-Yenching Inst., 96–97; at
    Chengtu, 232
Yetts, Percival, 138
Yin Hai-kuang, 384
Yorke, Gerald, 120
Young, Courtenay, 28; to Shanghai, 31;
    in Peking, 68, 95
Young, Sir George and Lady, 28
Young, Kenneth T., 393
Youngman, William, 158, 424; in China
    Defense Supplies, Inc., 175; witness
    for JKF, 343

Youth Corps (KMT), 232, 255
Yuan dynasty, 52
Yuan Ming Yuan, 85
Yuan Shih-k'ai, 76
Yuan, T. L., 209–210
Yun-kang, cave temples at, 56
Yung-an, OWI branch at, 300, 307
Yunnan, 201
Yunnan University, 199

Zacharias, Admiral Ellis, 294
Zinn, Howard, 401

About the Author

John King Fairbank, a specialist on China and member of the Harvard faculty since 1936, became Francis Lee Higginson Professor of History at Harvard University in 1959 and for eighteen years (1955–73) was Director of Harvard's East Asian Research Center (now renamed the John King Fairbank Center for East Asian Research). He retired from teaching in 1977.

Professor Fairbank went to Peiping in 1932 as a Rhodes Scholar and later was Lecturer at Tsing Hua University. He spent 1952–53 in Japan. In 1960 and 1964 he traveled through Southeast and East Asia, and in 1972 he and his wife spent six weeks in the People's Republic of China. In 1979 they returned for another visit in April, and he accompanied Vice-president Mondale in August.

During 1941–46, Professor Fairbank served with the Coordinator of Information and Office of Strategic Services in Washington; was Special Assistant to the American Ambassador in Chungking; and in the Office of War Information, Washington, D.C. He was Director of the United States Information Service in China, 1945–46.

Born in Huron, South Dakota on May 24, 1907, he attended the public schools of Sioux Falls, South Dakota and Phillips Exeter Academy, the University of Wisconsin, Harvard and Oxford (Balliol College). He is a member of Beta Theta Pi (Wisconsin) and Phi Beta Kappa (Harvard) and has twice received a Guggenheim Fellowship.

Professor Fairbank is the author of *The United States and China*, first published in 1948, with a fourth revision in 1979; and a long list of other publications (see front of book).

In 1959 he was president of the Association for Asian Studies and in 1968 president of the American Historical Association. He is honorary chairman of the China Council of the Asia Society and has served on a number of committees of the American Council of Learned Societies and Social Science Research Council. He is a fellow of the American Philosophical Society, the American Academy of Arts and Sciences, and the Massachusetts Historical Society.

As a young instructor at Harvard in 1939, Professor Fairbank joined his colleague Edwin O. Reischauer in inaugurating their joint survey course on East Asian Civilization. He became the first head of the Regional Studies program on China in 1946 and was chairman of the Faculty Committee on the Ph.D. in History and Far Eastern Languages from 1956–73. He has received a dozen honorary degrees, including one from Harvard in 1970.

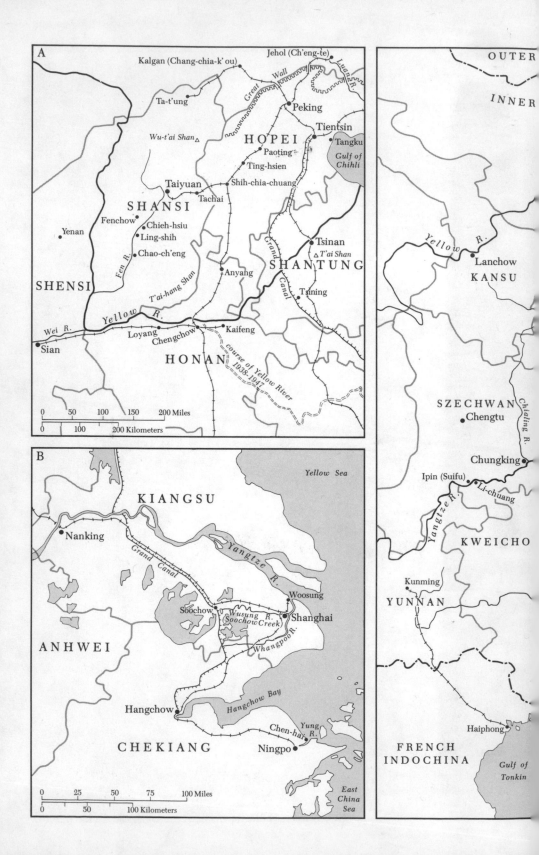

A

OUTER

INNER

Kalgan (Chang-chia-k'ou)

Jehol (Ch'eng-te)

Great Wall

Luan R.

Ta-t'ung

Peking

Tientsin

Wu-t'ai Shan △

HOPEI

Paoting

Tangku

Gulf of Chihli

Ting-hsien

Taiyuan

Tachai

Shih-chia-chuang

SHANSI

Fenchow

Chieh-hsiu

Ling-shih

Fen R.

Chao-ch'eng

Yenan

Tsinan

△ *T'ai Shan*

Grand Canal

SHANTUNG

Anyang

T'ai-hang Shan

Tsining

SHENSI

Yellow R.

Wei R.

Loyang

Chengchow

Kaifeng

Sian

course of Yellow River 1938-1947

HONAN

0   50   100   150   200 Miles

0   100   200 Kilometers

Yellow R.

Lanchow

KANSU

SZECHWAN

Chengtu

Chialing R.

Chungking

Ipin (Suifu)

Li-chuang

B

KIANGSU

Yellow Sea

Nanking

Grand Canal

Yangtze R.

Woosung

Soochow

Wusung R.

Soochow Creek

Shanghai

Whangpoo R.

YUNNAN

Kunming

Yangtze R.

KWEICHO

ANHWEI

Hangchow

Hangchow Bay

Chen-hai

Yung R.

CHEKIANG

Ningpo

FRENCH
INDOCHINA

Haiphong

East China Sea

Gulf of Tonkin

0   25   50   75   100 Miles

0   50   100 Kilometers